LEFT OUT

LEFT OUT

The Inside Story of Labour Under Corbyn

GABRIEL POGRUND &
PATRICK MAGUIRE

THE BODLEY HEAD
LONDON

7 9 10 8 6

The Bodley Head, an imprint of Vintage,
20 Vauxhall Bridge Road,
London SW1V 2SA

The Bodley Head is part of the Penguin Random House group of companies
whose addresses can be found at global.penguinrandomhouse.com

Penguin
Random House
UK

First published in the UK by The Bodley Head in 2020

www.vintage-books.co.uk

A CIP catalogue record for this book is available from the British Library

Hardback ISBN 9781847926456

Typeset in 11.5/14 pt Dante MT Std
by Integra Software Services Pvt. Ltd, Pondicherry

Printed and bound in Great Britain by Clays Ltd, Elcograf S.p.A.

Penguin Random House is committed to a sustainable future for
our business, our readers and our planet. This book is made from
Forest Stewardship Council® certified paper.

'Heavy is the head that wears the crown'
Stormzy

'We won the argument'
Jeremy Corbyn

'I own this disaster'
John McDonnell

Contents

Prologue

The Few

Just after 10 p.m. on 12 December 2019, Jeremy Corbyn emerged, ashen-faced and bleary-eyed, from an anteroom in the offices of Freedom from Torture, a charity for refugees with post-traumatic stress disorder in his Islington North constituency. The premises had been requisitioned as a venue for what many of Corbyn's aides hoped against hope would be a victory party. Labour MPs had not wanted an election. But those closest to Corbyn believed he could recapture the energy and optimism of the heady summer of 2017. At that election, he had gathered his close circle in the tiny living room of his terraced home in Finsbury Park to learn of what they were certain would be a defeat, if a valiant one. Only his two closest aides, Karie Murphy and Seumas Milne, and his wife, Laura Alvarez, had been there to witness the miracle, along with a handful of intimates.

No expense had been spared for 2019. Over the past six weeks, the Project had faced its final test. Corbyn, a private man unwilling and unable to accept the press intrusion all party leaders must endure, wanted to receive the results in peace, untroubled by the pack that camped every morning on his doorstep. No more than two dozen people, the Project's most loyal servants and Corbyn's family and closest friends, had been invited. His protection officers had vetoed his first choice of an Ethiopian restaurant next to Arsenal's Emirates Stadium. Earlier in the day, Corbyn's staff had been dispatched down the Holloway Road, returning with a Waitrose Victoria sponge decorated with a number 10 candle – a hopeful reference to his new address. Milne cast a jaundiced eye at the cake and laughed drily. 'We won't be needing that,' he confided to a colleague. 'We aren't going to win.' At best Corbyn might hope to form a coalition. A few miles away at Southside – the party's glass-and-steel head office in Victoria – tables groaned under the weight of bottles of Corbynista Victory Ale, brewed specially for the occasion.

Milne knew they would have no cause to open them. He had seen the internal polling that showed they were on course for an apocalyptic defeat. The figures had been kept secret. The Project lived in fear of leaks and at times did not even trust the numbers themselves. The final prediction of Labour's secret model, which drew on data from 25,000 voters, was just shy of 180 seats. On those numbers they would not be forming any kind of government. They would barely be able to function as an opposition party.

Still, many in the room believed they might be on the brink of power – or acted in that spirit. A week before the election, Nicolette Petersen, Corbyn's personal secretary, circulated an itinerary for election day among his inner circle. There was no doubt as to how the night would end: 'Day after: busy day!!! Number 10,' the document read. That same week, his office had circulated plans for the first days of a Labour government, listing its plans to reform some Whitehall departments, abolish others and appoint a Cabinet of true socialists. John McDonnell, Corbyn's Shadow Chancellor and oldest friend in politics, would go to Bloomberg and deliver a speech to calm the markets. He would then broker a confidence-and-supply agreement with the Scottish National Party. The question of a second Scottish referendum would be deferred to the next election. Diane Abbott, another intimate, would be promoted to Foreign Secretary and declare a new role for Britain in the world every bit as ambitious as Boris Johnson's plan to cut loose from Brussels.

As 10 p.m. and the exit poll drew closer, Corbyn's disciples filed into the party. With half an hour to go, the leader, his family and his close team were shown to a side room with a window looking out into the main area. His wife, Laura, did not leave his side. His three boys were joined by Milne and Helene Reardon-Bond, Corbyn's chief of staff. Andrew Fisher, his director of policy, followed, as did Anjula Singh, Labour's head of press. This was Corbyn's inner sanctum: those who he wanted by his side on the night. One aide pulled the blinds closed. This would be their result to savour alone, if only for a few moments.

The crowd gathered around the two televisions rigged up in each room. The chimes of Big Ben rang out from Sky News and the BBC. Every public and private poll indicated that Corbyn was heading for a historic defeat. But the convention and candour that had defined previous campaigns was absent. In 2015, Labour staff had been told at the outset that their mission was to deny David Cameron a majority, not to win. At the outset of the 2019 campaign, Corbyn's inner circle had aimed to win. Three months previously, Milne had written to colleagues: 'Our objective must be to win a majority, and that must underlie everything we do in the campaign.' Nor were they in the business of candour when the polls had refused to budge, given the need to maintain morale – and the seditious officials at party HQ who simply never went away. At the outset of the campaign, Corbyn himself had responded to the leak of the party's grid – the spreadsheet outlining the timing and responsibility of policy announcements – by emailing colleagues to say that 'It is disgusting the degree of self-absorbed disloyalty that some person or persons have. Our members do not sweat night and day to see their party damaged by this behaviour.' Polling would be circulated among only a handful of people. So it was that in 2019, in spite of all the evidence, many in the room and many of those members believed they would win – or, at worst, emerge as contenders in a hung parliament.

As the BBC revealed that Boris Johnson was on course for a majority of eighty seats – and that Corbyn was set to lead Labour to just 191 – the room fell silent. Those in Corbyn's antechamber were dumb-struck too. The party atmosphere turned funereal. Corbyn roamed a room overcome by silence. 'I'm sorry,' he said in turn to shell-shocked groups. 'This is on me.' His wife wept. Frances Leach, Corbyn's millennial head of events, cried as though 'someone had died'. For several generations of the left, something had.

It was immediately clear from the scale of the defeat that Corbyn was beyond saving. The job now was to save Corbynism. Milne imme-diately dispatched a pre-written briefing note for allies and Shadow ministers. 'This defeat is overwhelmingly down to one issue – the divisions in the country over Brexit, and the Tory campaign, echoed by most of the media, to persuade people that only Boris Johnson can "get Brexit done" ... Labour will have to learn lessons from this defeat, above all by listening to those lifelong Labour voters who we lost in working-class communities.'

For Corbyn, a long night was only just beginning. There would be no escaping the media at his constituency count. Corbyn and his wife sat side by side as Milne and Fisher fine-tuned the speech that he would deliver. At 2.20 a.m., having watched dozens of Labour MPs lose their seats, Corbyn, his son Ben at his side, made the short journey to a nearby leisure centre. In 2017, he had been a picture of unconfined joy at his count, joshing with cameramen and activists as he basked in his own glory. Now he walked alone.

Just after 3 a.m., Corbyn took to the stage. Yosef David, the Orthodox Jewish candidate of the Brexit Party, grinned over his shoulder. As they endured a long wait for the results, the odd couple had enjoyed an amiable conversation. Corbyn had even impersonated Johnson, to David's delight. In his concession, Corbyn said he would not lead Labour into another election but did not resign. He had told aides he believed Ed Miliband was wrong to quit immediately after Labour's humbling in the 2015 election. The left had a succession to navigate. As Corbyn was whisked from Islington to Southside, Labour redoubts across the country crumbled. In North West Durham, Laura Pidcock, Corbyn's putative successor, had been so confident of success that she had not prepared a concession speech.

Arriving at Southside, Corbyn found a party in shock. He headed straight to the booze-free eighth floor, to find Karie Murphy. Party workers sat motionless, with their heads in their hands. Seb, Corbyn's son, sat with a colleague who had produced a bottle of Pinot Noir from her desk, reserved for Labour's victory. She drank from the bottle in silence. Corbyn then emerged to deliver an impromptu speech to those who remained. 'Dust yourselves down,' he said. 'We've got a lot of work to do.'

*

Corbyn had assumed office in 2015 carrying the hopes of several generations on his shoulders. He had pledged to transform a party that, after winning power in three consecutive elections from 1997, seemed to have lost its principles. His Labour Party would be different. There would be no more compromise with business or the Conservatives, no more foreign wars. He had also promised to change the nature of politics itself, to rewrite Westminster's rules of engagement, to ignore the demands and conventions of the mainstream media, and replace the status quo with something kinder and gentler.

His many critics saw it differently. In the person who had stood alongside Tony Benn, for so long ignored as an irrelevance or derided as a crank, they saw a man who could not lead and did not want to. They saw an ideologue, surrounded by a court of advisers whose politics bore little resemblance to their own, who had changed their party into something they no longer recognised. They saw a man who had at best tolerated anti-Semitism and at worst indulged it. They saw an idealist whose utopianism did not endear him to the country he sought to govern. They saw a loser. But even those critics do not deny that Corbyn did indeed change the Labour Party – and British politics, too.

This book does not tell the full story of Corbyn's life in politics, or, indeed, his four and a half years as leader of the Labour Party. The story of his remarkable rise to the leadership, a job he had never coveted, has been extensively told. His reign began in an era whose politics and politicians are all but unrecognisable in 2020. David Cameron was prime minister, Barack Obama was president of the United States, and Brexit had not happened. It was only after the EU referendum and the 2017 general election, at which point our story begins, that Brexit and its culture wars came to dominate British politics, and Corbyn's own stances on anti-Semitism and foreign affairs came to wreak such damage on the Project.

At the time the result appeared to be the end of the beginning of Corbynism. After two years of bitter resistance from its internal opponents, the Project had finally assumed the authority it needed to run the Labour Party on its own terms. The grass roots were overwhelmingly loyal, empowered by a leadership in which it had invested so much, and energised by Momentum, a movement whose like British politics had not seen before. The hostility of MPs and party officials did not abate, as attested to by the vitriolic and abusive WhatsApp messages and internal emails among senior staff compiled by Corbyn's office in an internal report into Labour's handling of anti-Semitism over the course of a year and leaked to the press in April 2020, two weeks into Keir Starmer's leadership. For reasons of space and due to active legal proceedings the report's contents are not always directly attributed to individuals here, but the toxic, distrustful and openly mutinous culture of Southside is described and analysed at length. It was one of many obstacles imposed by hostile forces that the Project ultimately could not assail. The stories it contained were told privately by those intimately involved in the Project long before the report became public. Many are detailed here, from both perspectives.

Now it is clear that the 2017 election was also the beginning of the end. Corbyn's chance to remake his party and with it British politics was squandered. There are competing schools of thought as to why, and they still divide his inner circle. Some circumstances, like Brexit, were forced upon them. Every establishment force in British politics was arrayed against them. But many of Corbyn's intimates have since concluded that other factors, like the anti-Semitism scandal, the Project forced upon itself. In Corbyn they had a leader who did not deviate from principle, no matter how insignificant. He was led by events, rather than a leader of them. The 2017 parliament began with Labour on the precipice of power, and its left-most fringe – for so long alienated within its own party – closer to government than it had ever been, or perhaps ever will be. It ended with them even further away than they started. In those two years, Corbyn went from Glastonbury to catastrophe. In his wake lies a party that is bigger but more divided and further from power than at any point since 1983, when Corbyn was first elected as an MP. The story of his leadership did not begin in 2015, and nor did it end with his replacement by Keir Starmer. To understand the party Starmer has inherited, and now seeks to change, one must understand the story of the Project.

This account is the product of more than a hundred interviews with Corbyn's closest aides, members of the Shadow Cabinet, Labour MPs, party officials, and those who did all they could to obstruct and frustrate the Project, as well as their emails, text messages and other written records from the time. It is the first to tell the Project's second act, which was as extraordinary as it was disastrous. It does not claim to be an exhaustive history. Other books will tell the full story of the parliamentary drama over Brexit. Readers looking for blow-by-blow accounts of this amendment or that will be disappointed. Nor does it seek to apportion blame or settle factional scores. Instead, it recounts the remarkable journey those at the heart of the Project – and those who sought to destroy it – undertook together as comprehensively as memories and records of the period allow. In shaping the narrative we have been guided by those who worked most closely with Corbyn – and those who took to the barricades against them. It is a history of the losers, as well as the winners. Memories are fallible and the significance of events is not always immediately obvious. But those that appear in this account are those deemed most important by those who were there. The cast are more than occasionally profane. Expletives have been retained where they illustrate the sheer strength of animosity, passion and frustration that coursed through the Project and party.

Its action, for the most part, unfolds in Westminster and Islington, in the court of Corbyn. At its heart it is no different from any account of a political mission. It is a tale of egos bruised, friends betrayed, and opportunities missed – on all sides. But above all it is the story of a man whose like had never been seen at the top of British politics – and is unlikely to ever be seen again. The loyalty and hatred he inspired changed not only a party, but a nation.

This book is the story of how Jeremy Corbyn's sweetest victory became his decline and fall. But it is also the first inside account of the greatest experiment seen in British politics for a generation.

I

The Project

'Fuck.' Nobody remembers whether Jeremy Corbyn swore at 10 p.m. on 8 June 2017. Karie Murphy did. For it was at that moment that the leader of the Labour Party's closest allies, piled into his living room, discovered they had defied political gravity.

'What we're saying is the Conservatives are the largest party. Note they don't have an overall majority,' David Dimbleby, the veteran BBC News anchor, said as Big Ben chimed the hour. Theresa May's gamble had backfired. The Project's had paid off.

Eight weeks previously, on 18 April, Corbyn and his aides had discovered that they would be going to the country in the same way as the rest of the country: via the television news. Theresa May's Downing Street had not bothered to do them the courtesy of giving advance warning. And why would it have done? The point of the campaign to come was for the Conservative Party to flush Corbyn – and Corbynism – from Britain's body politic. Every available piece of evidence suggested it would be easy. On the day she called the election, May's poll lead stretched into the 20s. Labour's final internal poll chalked it up at 13 points. Nobody in Westminster, or even in Corbyn's living room, had any reason to believe otherwise.

Murphy, the flame-haired former nurse who served as his chief of staff, was perhaps the only woman who did. Earlier that evening, together with Corbyn and Milne, she had scribbled her prediction of Labour's vote share on a scrap of paper. At 39 per cent it was far higher than anyone else's estimate – even that of Laura Alvarez, Corbyn's wife. For such numbers to feel even remotely plausible was an achievement in itself. Earlier that day, Andrew Murray, the well-heeled communist airlifted into the campaign by Unite, Corbyn's biggest union supporter and piggy bank, had walked the leader through several scenarios. The best they might hope for would be a hung parliament, Murray warned. And even that was unlikely. Now it looked like a racing certainty.

Milne reacted as Tony Blair had to the landslide exit poll of 1997: with restraint laced with disbelief. 'It's too soon, it's too soon,' he said. 'Cassandra the prophetess of doom,' is how one colleague recalls his tetchy disposition. The reality would more than match Murphy's high expectations. Corbyn was on course to win 40 per cent of the vote, and May was on course to lose her majority.

To say the outcome was unscripted would be to understate the sheer implausibility of the journey those in Corbyn's living room had been on together since 2015, when the MP for Islington North was elected to the leadership of the Labour Party for the first time. He had been the very last of his close circle of comrades to acknowledge that he could win. His politics had only ever been a minority pursuit, even within Britain's party of the left.

For thirty-two years before his election to the leadership he had sat, diligent and inconspicuous to the mainstream of British politics, for his North London constituency. Corbyn had not been born there – he was a son of the Wiltshire and Shropshire countryside – but he had made it his home. He loved his constituents and by and large they loved him. It was his oasis. Politics to Corbyn was about caring for peoples otherwise ignored. He campaigned for the causes that the self-styled modernisers of the party's right – Neil Kinnock and then Tony Blair – refused to speak of in a loud enough voice, if at all. He pounded pavements to protest apartheid and the presence of British troops in Northern Ireland. Palestinian statehood and the plight of the Chagos Islanders were as important to him as anything that happened in his corner of North London. He had never abandoned that past, and nor did he want to. His real interest was in activism, not politics. The Christmas before the election, Gerry Adams, the Sinn Fein president, had sent him an Irish-language cookbook. Three months earlier he had boarded a plane at London City Airport in near-secrecy to attend the funeral of Martin McGuinness, only to be grounded by fog. They would always be his comrades.

Yet to the rest of the Labour Party, Corbyn had never been a comrade. Peter Mandelson promised that the Campaign Group, the motley crew of Bennite backbenchers who just about kept the flame of unapologetic old leftism alive, had been encased in a 'sealed tomb' upon the ascendancy of New Labour. Corbyn took his exile peaceably. He disdained Westminster's gamesmanship. 'You don't have to worry about Jeremy Corbyn suddenly taking over,' Tony Blair once said of his mission to remake Labour in 1996. The truth was that of all the members of the Labour left, Jeremy Corbyn was the man who did not want to lead the party. In 2015 he had run only because his old friends Diane Abbott and John McDonnell had done so before. It was his turn to field the hospital pass of running from the left. Colleagues nominated him out of pity, to 'broaden the debate'. But in beating the favoured sons and daughters of New Labour, Andy Burnham, Yvette Cooper and Liz Kendall, he did take over. The victory belonged both to himself and to a constellation of other interests. He had done what Benn himself had never done, and won control of the party's levers of power for its grass-roots members. But in doing so he owed his success to a younger generation, the children of the 2008 crash, battered and denied life chances by a Tory programme of austerity which the mainstream of the Labour Party did not see fit to challenge. Corbyn did. The two strains of idealism, one fluid and youthful and one old and dogmatic, made up Corbynism, a movement bigger than the snaggle-toothed 68-year-old who had that summer become an unlikely teen idol, feted by spontaneous chants wherever he went, but unmistakably bound together by him and him alone.

Blair says now: 'Once they actually managed to try and get control of the Labour Party in 2015, that's the first time in the history of the Labour Party these people have ever been in charge.' Once May called time on the 2015 parliament, the expectation was that the electorate would see that it never happened again. Corbyn was not made for leadership. Some believed him too decent for it. In the early 1980s, Ken Livingstone had introduced his wife to Corbyn at a St Patrick's Day dinner. 'That's the nicest man I have ever met,' she told Livingstone afterwards. Corbyn was congenitally incapable of letting people down. In practice, that meant an aversion to the decisions – some of them difficult, others painful – that constitute leadership. Nor was he one for its sartorial conventions. At home he preferred tracksuits, in Parliament – never his scene – suits of olive green or beige, with a vest always visible beneath his shirts.

At the time of his election he did not even own a red tie, de rigueur for any Labour leader, or cufflinks. The mainstays of the Westminster wardrobe were begged and borrowed from obliging aides, in one case just before a state banquet with the Chinese president Xi Jinping. Nor did he relish the prospect of moving to 10 Downing Street. If given a choice, friends say he would happily never have gone to Westminster again.

While there his approach to discharging his duties was idiosyncratic and rebellious. He would sneak out of the leader of the opposition's office suite in Norman Shaw South – a labyrinthine redbrick complex at the very edge of the crumbling parliamentary estate – for furtive lunches with Diane Abbott at Bellamy's, the strip-lit Commons salad bar on Whitehall. The Shadow Home Secretary, once a lover of Corbyn's, had been the first black woman elected to Parliament. Her political sense of self had been shaped by the abuse that she had been forced to endure along the way. Racists would call her office and scream the N-word down the phone. To an overwhelmingly white establishment she owed nothing. She retained that radicalism and never apologised for it. In their shared journeys home in Corbyn's government car to North London, where Abbott sat for Hackney North and Stoke Newington, she pressed him to stay true to the beliefs he had held dear when they had first met in the 1970s, no matter what the advisers installed around him said.

Corbyn was happiest at home, in Islington, with Laura, his third wife and the one to whom he was closest. An importer of fair-trade coffee from her native Mexico, she was his fiercest defender and his most steadfast friend. To her it was incomprehensible that anyone – in the Labour Party or the media – could dislike Jeremy Corbyn, as so many did. Laura seldom left his side willingly. To private meetings she would come to defend him against whatever spurious charge his advisers wanted to level. In a hostile world, Corbyn could always rely on her. It would take a lot to convince the couple to leave Islington for Westminster permanently, even if Corbyn became prime minister. In preliminary meetings on preparing for government, aides had offered them the chance to plant a vegetable patch – a substitute for Corbyn's Finchley allotment – in the Downing Street rose garden as inducement. The exit poll suggested that they might – just might – have to start digging.

After Dimbleby's announcement the camera panned to John McDonnell, the Shadow Chancellor. Beside him sat Michael Fallon, the Defence Secretary, a man renowned for his unflappability. As news of the lost majority dropped he gripped McDonnell tight by the arm, ashen-faced. 'Calm down, Michael, it's only a poll,' said McDonnell. For McDonnell it was so much more. It was vindication. To the former seminarian from Liverpool, socialism was religion. For two decades he had toiled thanklessly and largely alone on the outermost fringe of the Parliamentary Labour Party. Where others in the Campaign Group posed and protested, he set his heart and mind to preparing the left for government. Of that ambition he never lost sight, even at its most implausible. He had tasted power before, as Ken Livingstone's right-hand man on the Greater London Council. 'One of the most talented people I've ever met in politics,' is the verdict from Livingstone himself. Where Corbyn had been indulged by colleagues as an avuncular eccentric or benign crank, McDonnell was feared and loathed. On two occasions he had sought to pull off Corbyn's trick of reaching the leadership ballot, and both times he had failed. Nobody would even lend their nominations to the hard man of the hard left. Yet still he persisted. After every budget, Labour or Conservative, McDonnell would rise on the back benches to read an alternative of his own. He corralled left activists at the grass roots and assembled an advisory panel of economists to support him in his work. He never gave up, despite his isolation from colleagues. His wife, Cynthia, was known to joke of his pariah status. 'Jeremy's my best friend in Parliament,' McDonnell would say. 'No,' she would reply, 'he's your only friend in Parliament.'

The men were political soulmates. When it fell to Corbyn to appoint a Shadow Chancellor in 2015 there was in his mind only one candidate. He rejected entreaties from Unite to appoint Angela Eagle, a veteran of Blair's and Brown's governments, or Owen Smith, a rising star of the soft left. It could only be John. The first months of his tenure had been rocky. For years he had traipsed from hall to hall, speaking in the uncompromising language of the extra-parliamentary left, safe in the knowledge that only comrades were listening to his digs about assassinating Margaret Thatcher, lynching Esther McVey, the Conservative minister, or eulogising the violence of the IRA. Aides joked during the difficult opening months of his tenure that their job had been to respond to 'The Best of John McDonnell on YouTube'. In public he replaced the clenched fist with the fluttering eyelash. He apologised for and disavowed beliefs held for a lifetime with the fluency and media literacy of a Blairite. Electoralism, that thorny concept with which leftists always had an uneasy relationship, became his defining mission. In 1992 he had failed to win election to Parliament by only 53 votes, always blamed on Conservative attacks on Labour's 'tax bombshell'. McDonnell understood that to win power the left must appropriate a language of everyday pragmatism that Labour's self-styled modernisers had claimed as their own. In that respect his priorities diverged from those of Corbyn, who in his heart longed to be the left's Foreign Secretary. The liberation struggle that really animated McDonnell was the liberation of the British working class.

In that battle he sought unlikely allies. No sooner had he been appointed than he was deep behind enemy lines. The City was his first port of call. 'You'll have been told I'm a communist,' McDonnell told one suspicious interlocutor, before he quoted the capitalist's public pronouncements and writings at length. He worked at his brief with the zeal of the autodidact he was. In private he worked to make the Project a success with sometimes aggressive dedication. Unlike Corbyn, McDonnell had an explosive temper and a frail body, weakened by two heart attacks after years of chain-smoking. Where their politics overlapped their temperaments did not. On one occasion McDonnell had stormed out of a strategy meeting having banged his fists on the table and turned puce with rage. Corbyn strolled in whistling in his wake. To McDonnell the Project was treated with a seriousness that even to close comrades and colleagues seemed to border on fanaticism. To Corbyn, it often seemed like a pleasant surprise. It was in the latter spirit that McDonnell had received the exit poll. Though he urged caution in texts to his exuberant colleagues, the hard man of the left could not stop smiling.

Later, at 12.30 a.m., Milne received a call on his mobile. It was Patrick Heneghan, the lead elections official at Labour's HQ. Like the rest of the staff at Southside, the bespectacled Mancunian was an irreconcilable opponent of Corbyn's leadership. Together with his colleagues, most of them servants of the Labour right, he had spent the campaign coordinating a parallel campaign, out of sight and knowledge of Team Corbyn, to shore up MPs thought most at risk of being submerged by the Tory tsunami. The news he imparted to Milne and Corbyn gave neither him nor most of his Southside colleagues cause for celebration. He told the man whose demise he had so been looking forward to that it was now mathematically impossible for Theresa May and the Conservatives to win a parliamentary majority. Corbyn overflowed with almost childish glee: 'This is fantastic news, Patrick!' Through gritted teeth, Heneghan forced out the words: 'There's a small chance you could form a government, Jeremy.'

What Heneghan told the two men was as much a vindication for Milne as it was for Corbyn, who trusted Milne more than any other of his aides. Recruited from the *Guardian* to run his old friend's communications operation in 2015, Milne too had spent a lifetime on the fringes of the mainstream left. It had been almost as long as Corbyn's, despite his preternaturally youthful looks. His were a politics forged not on the streets, but on the comment pages of broadsheet newspapers. To Fleet Street he was an unreconstructed and unrepentant Stalinist, an ideology with which he had briefly flirted in his youth at Winchester College and Oxford. To Corbyn, he was a hero and seer, known only as The Great Milne ('Jemery' was the affectionate nickname accorded in return). The men shared an anti-imperialism that infused their politics, and a deep bond. Alvarez would make him vegetarian sandwiches that often remained untouched. Instead Milne did not so much menace, as commentators would have their readers believe, but waft about Westminster, apricot Danish and double espresso in hand. Colleagues in the leader of the opposition's office – known as LOTO – did not always venerate him as Corbyn did. They grumbled at his refusal to commit anything to text or email, a hangover from hostile leaks during the EU referendum campaign. Class warriors in Corbyn's circle occasionally saw it not as prudence but patrician obliviousness. One aide liked to tell colleagues that his first job had been washing the dishes of boys like Milne in Winchester's refectory. Those with long memories drew a straight line between his simultaneous flair and disorganisation as the *Guardian*'s comment editor, which saw pages dispatched to print later and later into the evening, and his stewardship of Corbyn's communications operation.

To some LOTO aides, Milne was a visionary and loveable rogue. To others 'a lighthouse in the Brecon Beacons': very bright, but useless. 'A good guy,' said another LOTO adviser, 'but it would be great if he'd spent more time on Planet Earth.' Most Labour MPs took the same view. To them his politics were of another planet entirely. They had anticipated that Corbyn and Milne together would lead them to destruction. Yet there the Corbynites stood, on the brink of government.

Of the small group drinking Peroni in Corbyn's living room that muggy summer night, only Karie Murphy had believed. She had come to Labour not through the quadrangles of Winchester and Oxford, as Milne had, but via the wards of inner Glasgow's hospitals and the trade unions. Now, sitting in his living room, she expected to be leading the Labour left to 10 Downing Street within days, if not hours.

Murphy's background, like her politics, lacked the refinement of Milne and Corbyn. She had been reared by an Irish republican in the upstairs rooms of a Glasgow pub. She did not meet a single Protestant until she was 12 years old. It was only on her entry into nursing that she realised that it was class, not the oppressive sectarianism of 1970s Glasgow, that defined and constrained her material condition. It was for her class that she fought with total commitment and self-belief. Opponents and disgruntled staff alike describe her style as one of brute force: 'Karie doesn't do politics. In fact, I'm not sure she has politics. Twenty-five years ago, she could have done exactly the same thing for Blair. Brutality is her thing.'

Murphy had been appointed to rule, not advise. By January 2016, it had appeared to John McDonnell that the left were squandering their once-in-a-generation opportunity. At the outset of Corbyn's reign in September 2015, some in his team had feared its downfall might be advanced by the security services. Aides recall an early conversation in his new post: should they sweep his office for MI5 bugs? Four months in, it looked as if it would be destroyed by its own incompetence. An anxious McDonnell moved to professionalise LOTO. He turned to Bob Kerslake, the former head of the Home Civil Service, with a job offer: would he become chief executive of the Labour Party? Kerslake, who sat in the Lords as a crossbench peer, had never been a Labour member, but had worked with McDonnell in McDonnell's days as a junior official under the Livingstone regime at City Hall. He turned down the invitation on grounds of age, but offered instead to carry out a 'short, sharp review' of LOTO's management structures. It laid bare the deep dysfunctionality of Corbyn's office. Executive decisions were so rare and the chain of command so unclear that 'people didn't know, when things didn't happen, whether it was cock-up or conspiracy'. Kerslake concluded that Corbyn's office bore closer resemblance to a start-up than a conventional political operation. A source familiar with their work recalls: 'It had sort of been set up as a collective. Half of the staff turned up when it suited them. It just wasn't working.' The bottom line was bleak. 'What came out of that review was, truthfully, chaos.' The manner of its delivery rather proved Kerslake's point: he delivered his findings orally, rather than on paper, for fear that they would immediately leak. Kerslake told Corbyn to recruit a chief of staff, who would wield the executive power Corbyn was either unwilling or unable to wield himself. 'You're not a huge fan of being in Westminster a lot,' he told him. 'But you need someone to be you when you're not here, basically. If you want to be out and about talking to people, then fine. But you have to have somebody who can organise and do things when you're not here.' Corbyn resisted at first. Though he did not dispute Kerslake's analysis, he bristled at the headline recommendation. He felt that the title 'chief of staff' was too militaristic. Eventually, he settled on a virtually identical role – an executive director of the leader's office. At the recommendation of trade unions and with McDonnell's blessing, Murphy got the job, and claimed the seat next to the door to Corbyn's private office. From that moment on, she was his gatekeeper – and the undisputed ruler of his office.

Murphy bore the Project on her shoulders like Atlas, sustaining the effort through sheer force of will. Without her, the Project would never have had its chance. Of the cast of characters whom Corbyn had to thank for his ascent to the leadership some two years earlier, it was to Murphy he owed the greatest debt – albeit accidentally. In 2013, she sought selection as Labour's general election candidate in Falkirk, in the central belt of Scotland. The then safe seat had become available after a brawl in a Westminster bar in which the incumbent MP, Eric Joyce, had headbutted and punched several MPs, triggering a police investigation and his suspension and resignation from the Labour Party. The candidacy in Falkirk thus became vacant. Unite, led by Murphy's close friend, Len McCluskey, proceeded to sign up union members en masse to swing the selection process in her favour. Ed Miliband, then Labour's leader, decried them as vote-riggers and reported them to the police, who ultimately said there was not enough evidence to bring a criminal prosecution. Murphy never got her seat in Parliament. Instead, she was suspended from the party.

Miliband then turned his fire on the unions. Men like McCluskey had put Miliband in office over his elder brother, David, in 2010 because of his promise to break with the New Labour politics, which, McCluskey believed, saw trade unions as a relic of Labour's past – and a problem to be managed. Ed Miliband promised to bring unions back into the tent. Under the electoral college system then in place for electing leadership candidates – introduced in the 1980s as a means to increase the influence of the Labour left – MPs, party members and trade unionists had one-third of the vote each. The support of union barons was enough to get the younger brother over the line. Yet Miliband came to feel they were a drag anchor, chaining him to an Old Labour machine and system built on patronage and factional fixing. He set about reducing their influence. In February 2014, in an attempt to kill McCluskey's influence for good, Miliband redrew the rules that handed the unions outsized power over the election of Labour's leader. He introduced a one-member, one-vote system. Firstly, MPs would nominate leadership candidates: anyone with the support of 15 per cent of them would get onto the ballot paper. Then, the contest would go to a vote of party members and one-off supporters, able to buy the franchise with a small fee. Now McCluskey's support would be worth no more than an ordinary party activist's. At the time, it looked like a catastrophe for trade unions. Far from securing a safe seat, Murphy appeared to have ensured that no union would ever install its favoured candidate as a Labour leader again. And in 2015, it seemed inconceivable that a sufficient number of MPs would nominate a candidate for the leadership with anti-austerity politics: the preserve of a handful of backbenchers on the fringe of the Parliamentary Labour Party, and the left-wing leadership of Unite. Yet they did. And not only that, he had won. Murphy had won.

The small band of comrades flanking Corbyn that June night were merely the leadership of a much bigger group, all of whom were regarded as and treated as his equals. Circumstance had thrown them together, and shared adversity over the last two years had been their adhesive. In May 2016, Corbyn had received a birthday present from his office: a collage of pictures from his first nine months as Labour leader. On the back were scrawled congratulatory messages from his fellow travellers, all still bowled over by the abiding shock of the privilege they enjoyed. 'Dad, keep up the fight and I look forward to celebrating in No. 10,' wrote Tommy, his youngest son. 'Love, T. PS. You'll always be an old slag.' Said Laura Parker, his private secretary: 'Am very much looking forward to being part of this dream.' Janet Chapman, who had made the unlikely journey from his Islington North constituency office to the leader's suite at his side, said: 'So much has changed in one year!'

More profound change was to come. Exactly twenty-eight days after Corbyn's birthday, the United Kingdom voted to leave the European Union. Though a Eurosceptic by conviction, Corbyn had voted to Remain, but from his travels across the country had intuited that Brexit would win the day. 'His ability to read politics is much more astute than many other people's, and when I say politics I mean public opinion, the mood, and so on. He's presented as some sort of woolly-minded ideologue who hasn't developed since the 1970s. It's all complete rubbish,' said a senior LOTO aide. If it was rubbish, it had near-universal purchase in the PLP. In the days after the referendum they launched a coup against the Project. The Shadow Cabinet, corralled by Hilary Benn – apostate son of Tony – resigned en masse, blaming Corbyn's supposedly lacklustre campaigning for the referendum result. Thirty-seven out of forty political advisers quit with them. In the following days, 172 Labour MPs, including the majority of the soft left, voted no confidence in Corbyn's leadership. Even the doggedly faithful *Daily Mirror* joined their cause, urging the leader to 'GO NOW' on its front page. The Project and its few allies – a handful of young MPs first elected in 2015, McDonnell, Abbott and Unite – would have to go it alone. The time had come to succeed or fail on their own terms. The decision to do so was taken at a strategy meeting at Unite's HQ in Holborn in the days after the coup. Only seven people were present. It was the Project against the political world.

Two men had stood between them and their plans to take Corbynism to the country. The first was Tom Watson, Corbyn's notional deputy and the de facto leader of the internal resistance to the Project at Westminster. Like the leader, he derived his legitimacy from a popular mandate from the Labour membership, who had elected him alongside Corbyn in 2015. At that point he had been Unite's man on the inside: a former flatmate of McCluskey, and a former employer of Murphy, who once worked in his parliamentary office. He was a man whose considerable weight implied an insatiable appetite, but it was power Watson had always wanted and hoarded: over the Blairites as Gordon Brown's fixer, over Ed Miliband, over Rupert Murdoch, against whose newspapers he had campaigned with relentless vigour, and now Corbyn. Months before the 2015 election, he had told aides of his intention to run for the deputy leadership. They were confused as to why, with his media profile and union pedigree, he did not instead covet the top job. 'Why don't you wait and see what happens to Ed?' one asked.

'Fat people don't get elected prime minister,' he said, matter-of-factly.

Though he told himself he could not be leader of the Labour Party, he always believed he could control who was. In the summer of 2016 he was wrong about that too. In the aftermath of the coup, Corbyn appointed a new Shadow Cabinet of veteran leftists and young conscripts. One day in July, Watson – in an act of charity to an old friend – warned Murphy that five of its members would resign, a walkout intended to inflict the *coup de grâce* on Corbyn. She then instructed Corbyn to turn off his phone, so that he could not receive news of resignations or requests to meet, let alone surrender to them. One by one she picked off those who had wavered, ensuring they did not resign. Watson was the inadvertent midwife of the Project's survival.

The second person standing in the way of the Project was Owen Smith, who challenged Corbyn for the leadership that summer. He hoovered up endorsements from the PLP, unlike his rival, who – as in 2015 – seemingly had no chance of meeting the 15 per cent threshold of MP nominations for inclusion on the leadership ballot. When Labour's ruling National Executive Committee (NEC) met to consider the question, the unions voted to allow Corbyn to stand without seeking the nominations – and thus guaranteed his re-election by the membership that so loved him. So disgusted were the party establishment that Iain McNicol, the party's general secretary, remarked at the time: 'That's the first time in the history of the Labour Party that the unions have voted to destroy it.'

The divide between Southside in Victoria, and Corbyn's office based in Parliament, had dogged his unhappy leadership. The former saw itself as the party's Civil Service, but seldom acted with the impartiality that Whitehall demanded. To many of them, anyone to the left of the centrists of New Labour was an unreconstructed Trotskyite, as bilious WhatsApp messages from the time attest. Almost all of its staff were aggressively and openly opposed to the leadership. It did, however, control the Labour machine: its money, its campaigns, and its staff.

Yet it could not control events. By the evening of 9 June 2017, when Tory Kensington finally turned red after a day of recount after recount, Corbyn's vindication was confirmed. He had delivered a net gain of thirty seats and with it the biggest increase in the Labour vote since Clement Attlee's 1945 landslide. From the second floor of Southside, where the customary party for staff had been convened on the night of the election itself, came screams and cheers. Andrew Fisher, Corbyn's bearded head of policy and the intellectual architect of the 2017 manifesto, and Niall Sookoo, a Corbynite elections official, embraced in disbelief. Beside them the sallow face of Simon Jackson, Southside's head of policy, wore a horrified expression. Murphy had arrived from Corbyn's house and was already celebrating. Around 11 p.m., she had invited two twentysomething staffers to pose for a photograph with a Jeremy Corbyn banner. As she grinned for the camera, she was heard saying: 'This all started in Falkirk. This all started in Falkirk!'

Earlier that evening, Southside's election team, led by Heneghan, had gathered on the eighth floor of HQ in the so-called war room – a meeting space kitted out with laptops, Diet Coke and television screens playing the election coverage on low volume. The smell of stale deodorant hung in the air. Their hatred of Corbyn's team was such that only his most senior aides had been permitted to join them: Milne, Murphy, Fisher and Sookoo. In fact, most of the Corbynites had had their security passes for the building cancelled by Jackie Storey, a veteran staffer. It was Storey who had ushered Tony Blair into Downing Street on the morning after his landslide victory, and she intended to be the one to banish the Corbynites after their landslide defeat. As one official recalls: 'The eighth floor was only to be for proper Southside staff, who are running a proper results service, and would essentially be around after Jeremy Corbyn was ritually humiliated by the electorate.'

It was not to be. As the cheers of young activists and staff filled the air downstairs, depression set in among those in the war room. Corbyn might not have won, but he had confounded their expectations. As Theresa May confronted the reality that she would not be able to govern without the support of the DUP, the hardline loyalists from Northern Ireland, it was not out of the question that Corbyn could become prime minister. Worse still for his opponents, Corbyn had earned the right to recast the party in his own image. They feared McNicol would be ousted, and with him, his team of executive directors – each of whom controlled a chunk of the party's budget. 'This isn't going to work out,' one of them told McNicol. 'They're gonna come for me. You're not gonna have my back any more.' Impassive, McNicol replied in his low Scottish burr: 'I know. I know.' Murphy, meanwhile, had taken a quick nap in McNicol's office, having spent most of the evening drinking red wine.

McNicol would not remain so placid. As dawn broke, a triumphant Corbyn travelled from Islington to Southside in a Chrysler people carrier to address his staff. The Labour leader was positively tiggerish. Crowds had gathered outside of his home, chanting: 'Oh, Jeremy Corbyn!' It made a welcome change from the press pack that greeted him early each morning. Unusually, Corbyn was joined not by his wife on his victory lap but by Murphy, who was photographed beaming at his side as she collected him from the car. Together, she and McNicol ushered him inside. As Corbyn strode to the general secretary's office, he rapped on staffers' desks. 'Get ready for another one!' he said. 'There's another general election coming, you know.' One exhausted official broke character and shot back: 'Please don't joke, Jeremy.'

Despite his grin, Corbyn was deadly serious. May's position was so weak that another election could come at any time. 'The one thing I didn't want to hear that morning was Jeremy Corbyn being prime minister,' a Southside official recalls. 'But the second thing I didn't want to hear is that I had to do it all over again to make that happen.' McNicol's response to the new reality was altogether less restrained. As was customary after elections, he and his party leader had shared a private moment together. 'Now is the time to reach out,' McNicol told Corbyn, urging him to invite his internal opponents in from the cold and unite the party behind him. 'That's a good idea,' replied a non-committal Corbyn. He would not take the advice. Instead,

Murphy strode into the office to address staff. Those present remember her speech not as a plea for unity, but as the moment Corbyn's internal opponents were put on notice: it was time for them to get on board, or get out of the way.

After Corbyn departed, aides seated outside of McNicol's office heard an almighty crash. Two rushed in to find the general secretary stood mutely staring out of his office window, surrounded by water and broken glass. A karate black belt who regularly used his training to turn light switches on and off with his feet, he appeared to have roundhouse kicked a full jug of water off his coffee table. After allowing his juniors to tidy the mess, McNicol approached a young official seated outside. 'I'm going to have to resign,' he sighed. The most senior survivor of New Labour had admitted defeat. He grasped a truth that few others could bring themselves to acknowledge that morning: the old certainties were dead, and a new era in Labour history had begun.

2

Jeremy Corbyn is the Prime Minister

Six days after the giddy joy of the general election, the nation awoke to news that Grenfell Tower, a twenty-four-storey tower block in West London, had been incinerated overnight. Some seventy-two people would die, with the death toll in the immediate aftermath assumed to be much higher. The conflagration became a horrifying parable for all that was wrong with twenty-first-century Britain: tenants, concerned by the refurbishment of the block with flammable cladding, had been ignored by their estate's privatised management company. The Conservative-run local council in Kensington and Chelsea offered a haphazard and maladroit response, which the prime minister would soon make look like a masterclass in disaster response. May, never given to spontaneity or public displays of emotion, was barracked and booed when she belatedly visited the scene, avoiding distraught survivors. Peter Brookes, the veteran *Times* cartoonist, caught the zeitgeist, depicting May as the last figure in a line-up of emergency service personnel before the Queen. 'And what do *you* do?' she asked the prime minister. In that week, Her Majesty spoke for a horrified nation.

Corbyn, by contrast, appeared to be the leader Grenfell, if not Britain, needed. Here was a situation that demanded the qualities that defined his politics: compassion and understanding of ordinary people. Unlike May, he comforted the afflicted, embracing sobbing locals in the street. The prime minister, still without a parliamentary majority, appeared to be living on borrowed time. Internally, Corbyn's team had already set their sights on government – and soon. 'We developed a new script pretty quickly,' recalls one senior aide. 'Keep up the momentum over the summer. Keep doing lots of rallies. And keep on saying we're ready for government. It was possible that the government would fall: that was the point.' Two days after Grenfell, John

McDonnell took to the stage at the conference of the radical Bakers' Union and called for a 'million-person protest' to force May from office. Once McDonnell, the pariah of the parliamentary left, had made such calls for extra-parliamentary action from the back benches. Now he could no longer be ignored. His most vocal supporters on social media coined a triumphant meme that spoke to the vacuum of leadership left by May: 'Jeremy Corbyn is the prime minister'.

As a long summer stretched invitingly before them, the Project felt closer to power than even the optimists within its ranks had ever imagined possible. Yet if they were to make good on their lofty ambitions to unite and transform a divided nation, they would first need control over the Labour Party. It was a prize that had eluded them from the moment Corbyn had taken office.

Corbyn well knew the scale of the task immediately. His life's mission had been not only to change Labour but democratise it. That doctrine had underpinned the thinking of the Bennite left for decades, yet it had found neither audience nor opportunity at the top of the party. Now, imbued with a new authority by the election, Corbyn had his opportunity. At Southside the morning after the night before, he produced a handwritten wish list of internal reforms. His mind was already focused on the next general election, and how the Project might guarantee itself a PLP willing to effect its will in government. To his mind, to take over Labour was to prepare for power. He declared that he wanted to radically reform the process by which candidates were selected – the left's generational struggle. 'I want you to make sure no candidate is ever just anointed again,' he said. Where previous leaders had used and abused the party's processes to ensure its candidates for high office were cast in their own ideological image, Corbyn demanded a fully open and democratic process. In those moments he was ruthless. Aides who received his instructions were in no doubt that he wanted to finish the job.

Since 2015 he had come to enjoy the leadership role he had never wanted. Yet proximity to power had not yet changed him. After all, he owed his success on the campaign trail to what aides dubbed his 'rebel mode'. In meetings with the staff ahead of the election he had been politely defiant: he would not move from Islington to Number 10, no matter the cost to the public purse. The thought of living in state-sponsored opulence, as prime ministers before him had, sat uneasily with Corbyn. He did not want to uphold the traditions of an office that had repeatedly failed Britain and the world; instead, he told those closest to him, he wanted to emulate José Mujica, the Uruguayan partisan who in old age had served as his nation's president from a ramshackle farm on the outskirts of Montevideo, driving a 1978 Volkswagen Beetle and eschewing a salary and the pomp and privilege of his exalted office. '[Corbyn] told me in 2017 that he wasn't moving out of that house,' said one senior LOTO aide. Armed with floor plans of the building, advisers told Corbyn and Alvarez that they could redecorate the living quarters above Number 10, and use their old home to house a refugee family. He would be like no prime minister who had come before. Though increasingly at home with the idea of wielding power, Corbyn had not yet come to terms with having to change to do so. Even if he did make it to government, the electors of Islington North would still come first. He would have never given up a full day in his constituency, no matter what his office demanded of him.

The police officers charged with protecting the leader of the opposition during the election and its aftermath found a politician quite undaunted by high office. On 9 June, in the hours after the election, officers had called their LOTO contact in a state of panic. 'The principal is missing,' they said of the absent Corbyn. 'The principal is missing!' Their man had slipped his noose and left Southside of his own accord. It was a small show of defiance but a significant one. Here was a man unwilling and unable to compromise for the sake of convention. Corbyn did not want a security detail, and so acted as if he did not have one. On this he had form. It was a habit that he had displayed during his first leadership campaign, when he happily wandered free from aides at London's Pride parade, and could not be located for the rest of the afternoon. In 2017, ahead of an election rally in Birmingham, he had jumped out of his car at a set of traffic lights so that he might make his way to the stage in his own time – the unbearable alternative being an interview with ITV's Robert Peston. The police, too, were wary, thanks to an incident in which Corbyn had slipped clear of David Prescott, a LOTO aide, and jumped onto a Tube train alone.

But he would not be changed. Corbyn's instinct was not to adapt to the world as it changed dramatically around him but to plough on.

Days in LOTO were punctuated by his small but meaningful defiances. He eschewed mainstream news. Even his daily copies of the *i*, far straighter in its coverage of his leadership than most other papers, and the *Morning Star*, went unread. His first request upon clambering into his government car would often be for the driver to turn off the *Today* programme. Instead he would flick through WhatsApp, drawing emotional sustenance from daily poems and inspirational quotes sent by a friend known to aides only as 'Raj'. Corbyn had enjoyed success without playing by the rules of the Westminster bubble or prostrating himself before the media. If he was to become the prime minister, he told himself that he could and would do it differently.

The new proximity to power seemed to weigh more heavily on those closest to him. The Project was faced with the prospect of taking control of the institutions that to them had seemed to symbolise the injustices against which they had spent a lifetime campaigning. In the last weeks of the campaign, after terrorists struck at the Manchester Arena and London Bridge, Diane Abbott had been invited into the Home Office. For a woman who had started her career as a Home Office civil servant and spent decades in Parliament campaigning against its policies, she found herself welcomed as if she were already in charge.

Nor could Westminster afford to shun the left any longer. As one aide to Corbyn recalls: 'We returned to Parliament acting like victors, wearing our "For The Many" lanyards and thinking we were cool. People took more notice of us. The pitiful and embarrassed looks we got from people in 2016 were now looks that said "we underestimated you" to "oh hell, you'll be around for a while longer now". Suddenly MPs wanted to acknowledge us again.'

Even the most outspoken opponents of the Corbyn project began to brief sympathetic journalists that they would be now willing to return to the Shadow Cabinet. Four days after polling day, the leader returned to the bear pit of the Monday-night meeting of the Parliamentary Labour Party, at which he appeared once a month. For the past two years, his appearances in front of almost every Labour MP and peer in Committee Room 14 had been little more than shouting matches, in which Corbyn, according to one close aide, felt 'bullied' by the moderate MPs. Throughout his leadership, packs of back-benchers would line up to barrack him in the hope of being overheard by the throngs of journalists waiting on the Commons committee corridor. The mutual enmity between Corbyn and his MPs occasionally became physical. Seumas Milne had filed an official complaint of physical assault to Southside in March after Wayne David, the cantankerous MP for Caerphilly, 'jabbed' Corbyn with a rolled-up order paper. While absurd, the clash – and Milne's reaction – served to illuminate the sheer scale of hatred and distrust between the leadership and a parliamentary party over which it had no hold. Another PLP irreconcilable, the combative Bermondsey and Old Southwark MP Neil Coyle, had been dressed down earlier that year by Nick Brown, the chief whip, over a barrage of dozens of abusive texts to Corbyn. LOTO had printed off page after page of ranting sent by Coyle to his leader, often late at night, occasionally alternating with businesslike exchanges. Having nominated Corbyn for the leadership in 2015 in an act of misguided charity, Coyle was among those MPs who could not live with the consequences. One LOTO aide recalled that their first and only conversation with the MP was when he uttered the unforgettable greeting: 'Why don't you just fuck off?'

The election had given the PLP their answer. At that first PLP meeting after the election they greeted their leader, whom a year earlier in the very same room they had sought to oust, with a forty-five-second standing ovation. Flanked by Milne and Murphy, Corbyn spoke with a new self-assurance as he made clear the Project would not be relenting: 'So now the election is over, the next phase of our campaign to win power for the majority has already begun. We must remain in permanent campaign mode on a general election footing.' It was a reaction born of relief as much as reflection. 'People had bought the narrative that the election wasn't as bad as we thought,' recalls Anna Turley, then MP for Redcar, who unlike other moderates refused to applaud Corbyn. 'If someone's dangling you off a cliff, and then they haul you back over, you're almost so relieved that you embrace them for having hauled you back over the cliff. It was almost a wave of relief. I was concerned, we'd still lost and potentially at that point we were going to have another five years of Tory government.' Even Chuka Umunna, the smooth centrist who, like Yvette Cooper, had anticipated launching his own leadership campaign in the days after Corbyn's expected humiliation by the electorate, joined in the chorus of praise with a glutinous show of compliance. 'Unity is the watchword,' he proclaimed to waiting reporters after Corbyn's speech. 'Government is the aim!' Umunna's conversion did not convince LOTO, and nor did the applause of his colleagues. Though he and other Corbynsceptics had made clear that they would serve in the Shadow Cabinet, there would be no return to service. Many in the leader's office viewed their grovelling with amused contempt. Corbyn became fond of telling inquirers from left and right: 'There are no vacancies.'

In truth, in the days after the election there had been private discussions of a unity reshuffle. There was, some of Corbyn's inner circle believed, an argument for bringing opponents of the leadership back into the tent on the Project's terms. That he resolved not to do so spoke to the two unshakeable traits that would shape his leadership: loyalty, and a pathological hatred of confrontation. 'Who would you take out?' he asked aides ahead of the mooted reshuffle. Aides responded that it was not for them to 'take out a comrade': Corbyn had to decide himself. The reluctant leader demurred. 'I don't want to take anyone out,' he said. Such was the scale of his achievement in the country that he did not have to.

Instead the stopgap top team appointed in the wake of the coup became permanent. In 2015, Corbyn had agreed to appoint a Shadow Cabinet that was, in the circumstances, as non-factional as possible. Though many high-profile members of Ed Miliband's Shadow Cabinet had pre-emptively ruled themselves out of serving, others had not. Over the subsequent year, however, those who had remained repaid Corbyn with insubordination. That November, Hilary Benn had risen in the Commons to publicly defy Corbyn and call for airstrikes against the Islamic State in Syria.

Then had come the coup and a new Shadow Cabinet composed of true believers, reluctant loyalists, and *Dad's Army*-style veterans. The gnome-like Paul Flynn, summoned to the front bench for the first time in his long parliamentary career, was 81 when he became Shadow Leader of the Commons. He was not alone. Others, like Angela Rayner, Rebecca Long-Bailey and Richard Burgon, had only been elected in 2015. On her appointment as Shadow Education Secretary, Rayner, a former UNISON official from Stockport and a mother at 16, rang a friend who could not tell whether she was laughing or crying about her new brief.

The experience had hardened left-wing MPs to the more seditious elements in the PLP. Those who questioned the Project were ritually derided. Shortly after the coup, Conor McGinn, the MP for St Helens North and a Labour whip, had accused Corbyn of 'bullying' him by threatening to ring McGinn's father, a former Sinn Fein councillor, so that he might stop criticising the leader. As he resigned later that summer, Ian Means, the Gateshead MP, sent a message to a WhatsApp group of left-wing colleagues and Corbyn aides, laying into McGinn: 'One of the nastier ones I've come across in the Commons and that's saying a lot!' Rayner opined: 'He's a real scumbag. I doubt his parents even like him he's that nasty. I too have never met anyone as vile as him and I was born in the trade union movement.'

The enmity was often mutual. When MPs returned to Parliament after the coup, Long-Bailey wrote: 'I was still deliberately blanked by a number of people.' Such sentiments contributed towards what one aide dubbed the 'siege mentality' sown in the Project's collective consciousness after the coup. Distrust took root like Japanese knotweed.

Thus three small tweaks to the Shadow Cabinet were made in lieu of a full reshuffle. Tom Watson was the first target. The weeks after the election were a period of acute political vulnerability for the man who had been living proof for Corbynsceptics that things would get better. Those who knew him within LOTO sensed a personal vulnerability too. They saw him as a quitter whose first instinct was to fold when the going got too tough. He had quit as a minister under Blair. He had quit Ed Miliband's Shadow Cabinet when the heat of the Falkirk scandal became too much to bear. On one occasion his former partner had prevailed upon his parliamentary staffer to drive him overnight from London to a political fundraiser in North Wales and then to Brighton for a wedding, such was his reputation for failing to produce the goods at moments of high pressure. Those at the heart of the Project believed that, in time, Watson would quit his resistance to Corbynism too.

The reality was less straightforward. For all his weaknesses, Watson was a singular and exceptional politician. Through sheer force of personality he had done remarkable things in politics. He had never been averse to wading through the dirt when he deemed it necessary. To be in politics was to plot and fix. As a Brownite foot soldier, he had precipitated the downfall of Tony Blair with a tactical ministerial resignation in 2006. Since then, when he wasn't playing computer games at all hours in the flat he had once shared with Len McCluskey, he had campaigned obsessively: against the Murdochs, against an alleged – and imagined – ring of paedophiles at the heart of Westminster, and to become deputy leader. The Corbynites could not sack him without a fight, such was the nature of his elected position. It fell to Watson to decide whether to stick or twist.

He took the decision to lay down arms – at least temporarily. 'Tom took the view, as did many people, that this is it now,' said an aide. 'We've just got to get on with it. There was an acceptance that Jeremy is the leader of the Labour Party now, and for as long as he should want to do it.'

While Watson remained deputy leader, he was stripped of his chairmanship of the party and replaced by Ian Lavery, the former president of the National Union of Mineworkers. Lavery's background and politics bore little resemblance to Corbyn's, and nor did his burly physique. Yet there had been few more enthusiastic defenders of the leadership in the 2015 Parliament. Tattooed and forthright, the MP for the pit constituency of Wansbeck was Old Labour made flesh. Often he would ask Milne, the author of an acclaimed history of MI5 collusion in the 1984 strike in which Lavery had picketed as a young apprentice, to visit Arthur Scargill with him. He also shared Milne's admiration for socialist struggles abroad, messaging colleagues upon the death of Fidel Castro to say: 'Are we sending anyone to Cuba to recognise Fidel?' Lavery had run the general election campaign in the manner of a flying picketer – shooting from media studio to media studio, at times bellowing the case for Corbyn. Alongside him had been Andrew Gwynne, a mild-mannered Greater Manchester MP who had never been of the left but happily served them, who was promoted to Shadow Communities Secretary. The retirement of another union bruiser in Dave Anderson had also created a vacancy at Shadow Northern Ireland. Unexpectedly, Corbyn extended an olive branch to the man who just ten months earlier had challenged him for the leadership: Owen Smith. 'It had to be somebody,' a senior aide recalls now. 'And Smith had been special adviser to a Northern Ireland Secretary. He was on the left half of the PLP. His adviser was someone we had appointed. So it seemed all right.'

But in extending only one desultory olive branch to his tormentors, Corbyn confirmed the perception that his leadership would remain a factional enterprise, even as it preached tolerance, diversity and inclusion in the country. The attempted coup had guaranteed that much. Bob Kerslake liked to joke that the resultant siege mentality had led to the Project practising not socialism in one country, but socialism in one corridor. LOTO feared that repaying MPs for their sedition with power would be to jeopardise the Project anew. The Project demanded the support of MPs and gave them nothing in return. As the applause faded, the seeds of distrust and resentment had been sown.

Twelve days after his unlikely ovation at the PLP, Corbyn received another when he took to Glastonbury's Pyramid Stage. There revellers feted him with a reception that rivalled any of the festival's headliners. He had rocked up to Somerset like a star surrounded with a retinue of fixers and fans. His sons had followed him from Paddington on the train and turned up without tickets. Michael Eavis, the festival's octogenarian founder, obligingly provided them as a favour to the man of the hour. They were declared as a gift under Parliament's stringent anti-sleaze rules, as corporate favours must be. But in those weeks Corbyn was not so much a politician bound by rules and convention as a countercultural icon. His appearance before the crowds on the day was an event without precedent in British political history. His speech distilled the essence of the man and his politics: 'If I may, I'd like to quote one of my favourite poets, Percy Bysshe Shelley, who wrote in the early nineteenth century many, many poems and travelled extensively around Europe. But the line I like the best is this one: "Rise like lions after slumber, in unvanquishable number, shake your chains to earth like dew, which in sleep had fallen on you – ye are many, they are few."' Corbyn was not used to speaking the language of power, but he went on: 'Let us be together and recognise another world is possible if we come together to understand that. Understand the power we've got and achieve that decent, better society where everyone matters and those poverty-stricken people are enriched in their lives and the rest of us are made secure by their enrichment.' The crowds burst into song: 'Oh, Jeremy Corbyn!' It was a performance New Labour could not have paid for even at the height of Cool Britannia. In the days after the election, John McDonnell had told friends: 'If we had had another week, we would have won the election and we would be in government.' One of Corbyn's supporters in the media recalls living in a state of reverie: 'For the three weeks after polling day, I can honestly only say that it felt like being on Ecstasy. I would wake up and think: "Who put this mandy on my cornflakes?"'

Some look back on those days of reverie with a tinge of regret. Theresa May was vulnerable. Discussions had already turned among Conservative MPs as to who might depose her in a leadership contest. She was still yet to sign off on a confidence and supply deal with the DUP, whose intransigence had forced the prime minister to lay out her Queen's Speech without a guaranteed parliamentary majority – a move almost entirely without precedent. The hardline Northern Irish unionists would only put pen to paper – at a cost of £1 billion to the Exchequer – the Monday after Corbyn's weekend at Glastonbury. Keir Starmer was among those who believed that Theresa May would have to seek Labour's help on Brexit. Instead, LOTO stood by as she found a majority via the DUP. 'There was a deal to be done,' one senior Shadow Cabinet adviser recalls now. 'We were busy congratulating ourselves while the DUP were publicly rebuking Number 10 for saying they'd signed a confidence and supply agreement. We could [have] come through the middle and asked for a soft Brexit. We could have blown the whole thing up. But nobody had a clue what they were doing.'

'Their approach,' another senior Shadow Cabinet aide recalls, 'was that blowing softly would blow the government apart. There was no strategy.' Even after May's deal with the DUP was done, some close to Corbyn thought it was vital to push forward and do a deal with the government over Brexit. If the DUP had given them a majority, Labour could provide a supermajority and resolve once and for all the question that would bedevil British politics for the coming months. Later converts to the plan included Andrew Murray, who felt it could be Corbyn's '1945' – a moment to unite the nation behind the left, and own the future. In that he had allies in the Shadow Cabinet. While Labour's vote had increased in nearly all of its constituencies, Labour MPs whose seats had voted to Leave in 2016 saw the Tory vote increase dramatically – even if they were still safe. Six fell to the Conservatives, most emotively the Nottinghamshire coalfield town of Mansfield. The likes of Jon Trickett, the cerebral Shadow Minister for the Cabinet Office, were as alarmed as they were exuberant at the results. Trickett, whose Hemsworth seat – a collection of deprived Yorkshire pit villages – had voted to Leave, believed 2017 was a canary in the coal mine. If

Labour attempted to obstruct or dilute Brexit, it risked annihilation by the very voters it claimed to represent. As one of the left's in-house intellectuals, he committed his thoughts to a strategy paper, in which he warned Corbyn that the only electoral strategy at Labour's disposal was to deliver Brexit.

Yet Corbyn was instinctively uncomfortable about dealing with the Tories. So too was Diane Abbott, who witheringly dismissed Murray's proposal as the 'Ramsay McCorbyn plan'. The inconvenient truth was that Labour did not yet know what it wanted from Brexit and its electoral coalition was split – between constituencies in London and the great cities that had voted overwhelmingly to Remain, and those in the north and Midlands that had plumped for Leave. The most vocal Corbynsceptics in the PLP had taken Labour's surge as evidence that Remainers wanted an outlet for opposition to May and her hard Brexit, and began to organise in kind. Chuka Umunna was the first to fire a warning shot to the leadership, tabling an amendment to the Queen's Speech demanding the UK remain in full alignment with the EU single market. Though it was ignored by Corbyn and easily defeated, fifty Labour MPs joined Umunna in defying the whip to vote for it. At the time, commentators chalked up the result as evidence of Corbyn's new-found strength – but it was also an illustration of the deep unease felt by a hard core of Labour MPs at any form of Brexit.

LOTO had no real desire to expend political energy and capital on answering the question either, especially if it shored up May's position. After all, they could be in Number 10 within weeks. Nor was there much sign that May was likely to abandon her rigid red lines on severing ties with the customs union and single market. At 4 a.m. on election night, Keir Starmer had been at the count in his Holborn and St Pancras constituency when he felt his phone buzz. It was a text from the Brexit Secretary David Davis, his Conservative opposite number. With the scale of the government's predicament already clear from the results, Starmer and his aides momentarily suspected – as others in the Shadow Cabinet later would – that May would be amenable to a deal on Brexit. He replied to Davis expecting to discuss just that. Later that morning, Davis replied – but only to confirm, as a courtesy, that the government was still committed to a hard Brexit. If compromise was to come, it would not start with the government.

In any case, the Corbynites had a more pressing battle on their hands than Brexit. Glorious though the night of 8 June had been for LOTO, why, with the wind in their sails and the country seemingly united behind Corbyn and against May, had they not won the general election? They had come within 4,000 votes of a parliamentary majority. What might have made the difference? To the Corbynites in LOTO and the Shadow Cabinet, the answer was obvious: a party headquarters that worked with, rather than against them.

The inquest began in earnest at a fractious meeting of the NEC on 13 July. By then the comedown had set in for the Corbynites; the adulation having faded, they wanted answers. Iain McNicol began proceedings with a homily to Corbyn that belied his deep personal animosity to the Project. 'Jeremy deserves a huge amount of credit for leading from the front of this election, with an energetic, positive and principled election campaign. We deprived the Tories of their majority and increased Labour's share of the vote. Something we can all be proud of.' If the use of the first-person plural implied solidarity between Southside and LOTO, it was not to last. McNicol's pre-prepared remarks quickly shifted to offering a defence of Southside's conduct in the preceding weeks. 'There is some suggesting that the Labour campaign was a purely defensive campaign. It wasn't,' he said. Perhaps, he wondered aloud, it wasn't defensive enough. 'This strategy was largely successful, returning the vast majority of our MPs. However, we were not completely successful in this and lost six seats that we had in 2015. If we hadn't, we would have deprived the Conservatives of forming a government with the DUP.'

To LOTO, McNicol's justification was a provocation, and confirmation that Southside's old guard simply did not understand the new politics of the Labour Party. Rather than accept responsibility for misreading the public mood – as the rest of the establishment had – the Corbynites saw McNicol as a man offering petulant apologies for his own mistakes, or, worse still, a defence of a deliberate strategy to deny them the majority they believed they could have won. The deep hostility and distrust between the two sides was borne out by a report by two other NEC members, Glenis Willmott and Andy Kerr. 'Work was hampered by the fact that planning was done separately,' they noted. 'There were also side meetings.' Of LOTO's own secrecy, which manifested itself in their refusal to share with officials their timetable of campaign engagements and announcements, they added: 'Access to the grid/information sharing was very limited.'

The language was coded with courtesy but the subtext was clear: Southside's parallel strategy in 2017, as it had been throughout Corbyn's leadership, operated in opposition to LOTO's. It was the last bastion of New Labour within the party's structures and had proven impervious to reform: its staff, almost wholly servants of the Labour right, were on permanent contracts and had no intention of relinquishing their hold on the party machine. It had always been their belief that Corbyn was on borrowed time, and the assumption that he would fail had informed their behaviour during the campaign – though only a handful of those sat around the NEC table that July afternoon knew the full extent of it.

Over the course of the campaign, Sam Matthews, a Southside official with a painstakingly blow-dried quiff, and Harry Gregson, an organiser who later became the de facto general secretary of the breakaway Independent Group, worked in secret from Ergon House, the Westminster headquarters of the London Labour Party, at the behest of Patrick Heneghan, whose contractual obligation was to oversee the campaign for Corbyn. The Corbynites believed staff at Southside were working slowly and without enthusiasm on the official campaign. In private, however, Matthews and Gregson were busying themselves funnelling hundreds of thousands of pounds of resources into the seats of devout opponents of the leadership – MPs like Watson and Yvette Cooper, whom the Corbynsceptics believed would rebuild the Labour Party in the wake of Corbyn's defeat. The primary weapon in their arsenal were leaflets sent directly to the homes of voters in Corbynsceptic MPs' seats. The template they followed was an election address written by Margaret McDonagh, the veteran Blairite, for her friend Joan Ryan, the irreconcilable MP for Enfield North. The message, according to one source who worked on its wording, was: 'Look, I know you hate Corbyn, but you don't hate him nearly as much as I do.'

For all the Corbynsceptic calls for party unity in the wake of the election, their bureaucracy at Southside had been acting as if they were a law – and organisation – unto themselves.

Matthews and Gregson, with the blessing of McNicol and Heneghan, worked in total secrecy. Business was conducted via an elaborate argot of code words in a WhatsApp group called the Deck Chair Realignment Society, a gallows joke about what appeared to be Labour's likeliest fate. The MPs it sponsored were referred to in internal communication as the deckchairs, while McNicol was The Captain. Said one official who worked at Ergon House: 'You'd have these messages going back and forth being like, "What's going on with Rachel Reeves's deckchair?"' Matthews and Gregson worked in full glare of other officials, yet knowledge of their work was confined only to a small circle at Southside. If others wandered into their corner of the office, they would slam their laptops closed, as they were once forced to when Polly Toynbee, the *Guardian* columnist, came to say hello during a phone banking session. Their plan would not trouble the public domain until 2020, but was nearly recorded in *Betting the House*, a book by journalists Tim Ross and Tom McTague on the 2017 campaign. Heneghan, urging the hacks not to tell a story that would cost officials their jobs, threw them off the scent. But soon the Corbynites would see to his exit.

Half-hearted attempts at reconciliation between the two camps were made. In the wake of the election LOTO and the Southside politburo met at Westminster's St Ermin's Hotel, where the Cambridge Five spies had met their Soviet handlers. There they drank and ate Mars bars together until late. Yet LOTO had already reached the conclusion that they had spent the first two years of Corbyn's leadership 'fighting with one arm tied behind our backs'. They could never allow that to happen again.

In mid-July, Corbyn's most senior allies, chief among them McDonnell, Murphy and Andrew Fisher, met with Iain McNicol and his deputy, Emilie Oldknow, in Corbyn's suite of offices in Parliament. Proudly lining an entire shelf on his bookshelf was a full bound copy of the Chilcot Report into the Iraq War. Above his desk hovered pictures of his 2016 leadership victory – which McNicol, of course, had sought to frustrate with Watson. With May on the brink of collapse, the official purpose of their gathering was to discuss strategy for the general election that all in Westminster believed to be imminent. Top of the agenda was agreeing which seats to target to secure a majority, and planning for a summer-long campaign to sustain the momentum of the election campaign just gone. Fisher channelled the hubris of the moment. 'The world is watching us,' he said.

The European-style social democracy of the hastily drafted 2017 manifesto would be replaced by a more ambitious, almost utopian vision
to fundamentally reshape the economy and society. Fisher explained:
'We need to go from transactional politics to transformational.'

Friction was soon apparent. McNicol, in a vain attempt to be
constructive, said it would be a nice idea to establish a slicker media
strategy for the coming months. Fisher responded by shooting him
down. 'It's important to be more organised,' he said. 'But let's not
get hung up on the negative media bubble.' John McDonnell agreed,
saying the party should instead rely on 'independent outriders between
now and conference'. Both men had in mind energetic, irreverent new
media outlets such as Novara Media, as well as hyper-partisan blogs
like SKWAWKBOX and The Canary. They would not need the spin
doctors or slick media strategies of the New Labour playbook any
more.

But just as pressing as questions of high principle were those of
power. For decades, Labour's left had longed to give the party membership the power to oust their MPs at will – and transform the ideological complexion of its parliamentary party. While hundreds of
thousands of members appeared to agree with Corbyn's agenda, no
more than two dozen Labour MPs did. Their ongoing resistance to
the Project would make governing difficult, if not impossible. Now
Corbyn's team took the first, tentative steps to bring them to heel.
On the pretext of responding to imminent changes to constituency
boundaries, the meeting set in motion a plan to allow the party leadership and local parties to call a vote of their local members at any
time on whether to retain their MPs as Labour candidates. Katy Clark,
then Corbyn's political secretary, was tasked with carrying out a wholesale review of Labour's internal democracy, again with the aim of
shifting power away from MPs to the grass roots.

Next they turned their fire on McNicol and his elections team.
Before the election, Corbyn had written repeatedly to McNicol to
accelerate plans to introduce a community organising unit – a new
army of paid officials to turn Labour into a national social movement.
It was his brainchild as much as Murphy's, whom Corbyn entrusted
with enacting it. Not only would it connect Labour to the communities it purported to represent, but it would lock the left's influence
into every constituency party in the country. Southside had stymied

and frustrated the plans at every step. Now Heneghan was given a week to produce what was euphemistically referred to as a 'spreadsheet of general election results by constituency'. What they really wanted was an explanation of why Southside had allowed Labour to settle for only thirty gains.

A narrative was forming. As one Corbynsceptic describes it: 'Jeremy and Momentum and the leaders had run this brilliant campaign. Absolutely awesome. And they were thwarted by the evil Blairites at Labour HQ, who, you know, if it wasn't for them, Jeremy would be [in] Number 10 now.' Southside sources believe the criticism was misguided. But the claim that HQ – led by Heneghan – had sabotaged Corbyn became a mantra for the left, even before they knew of Ergon House. As a creature of Westminster with a liberal appetite for profanity and little time for the pieties of the Corbynite left, Heneghan was the embodiment of the old politics they sought to exorcise from the party. Within weeks, they would get their wish. In September he took a generous redundancy payout and left. The internal resistance to Corbynism was losing its grip not only on key levers of power but on the most valuable commodity of all: the data.

That Heneghan was widely suspected within LOTO of leaking to the media made his resignation even more satisfying. During the first two years of Corbyn's leadership, much of the mainstream media had arrayed itself against him. Left-wing Shadow Cabinet ministers in turn held newspapers in unique contempt. When *Times* sketchwriter Patrick Kidd ribbed Diane Abbott and Angela Rayner at length in one of his pieces, Lavery wrote on WhatsApp: 'Scum, that's what they are, scum!!!!!' To Lavery, the *Sunday Times* was also a 'scum paper'. To Angela Rayner, the *Sun* was the 'scumbag *Sun*' while other newspapers were 'vile vipers'. With Heneghan gone, the vipers had lost one of their most dependable sources.

In September 2017, Labour gathered for its annual conference in Brighton. Southside officials had poked LOTO in the eye by running with a shortened version of their slogan 'For the Many, Not the Few' which omitted the last three words, neutralising its revolutionary bite. But LOTO caught wind of the decision and reversed it before it was too late, save for the banners outside the conference hall. Little could have punctured their mood, though. In his leader's speech, Corbyn received a reaction more rapturous than any leader since Tony Blair's valedictory appearance in Manchester, eleven years earlier. Though it was Corbyn's third conference as leader, it was the first year that he and his allies carried themselves with authority and an entitlement to lead. They were cheered by thousands of activists from Momentum, who had blossomed out of Corbyn's first leadership campaign. Its chairman, the Bennite sage Jon Lansman, had cut his political teeth agitating for Labour members to be given more power over their party – and attempting to oust right-wingers from the PLP. Momentum aimed to build a bridge out of Labour's new mass membership between the country and Westminster. Even Corbynsceptics conceded that the armies of young, energetic activists it had provided during the election campaign had been crucial to Labour's unexpected success in June 2017. In Brighton, Momentum ran its own parallel conference, The World Transformed, which hosted raucous, booze-fuelled game shows, radical policy discussions and 'Acid Corbynism' raves rather than the stuffy, tedious procedural debates that abounded in the main hall – and which had been the training for generations of leftists past.

The moderates, meanwhile, were enfeebled. Three months earlier, even David Sainsbury, the multimillionaire donor who had funded Progress, the internal pressure group that had formed the last bastion of organised Blairism within the Labour movement, had announced he was to quit politics and pull the plug on donations. Given the crowds that greeted Corbyn and Momentum at conference, it was not difficult to see why. The left appeared to own the future. On the floor, the Corbynites set about turning their popularity into political capital. Momentum and the trade unions marshalled their delegates to keep Brexit – the single issue on which the Corbynsceptics retained any hope of winning sympathy and support from members – off the agenda. Three additional seats for representatives of grass-roots members would be created on the party's ruling National Executive Committee. Nominations for any future would-be leader would be required from only 10 per cent of MPs, lowering the bar to entry from 15 per cent, which Corbyn had only just squeaked past in 2015.

Milne, Murphy and Fisher could permit themselves a smile when the changes passed overwhelmingly: the revolution set in train in Corbyn's office two months earlier was progressing as planned. They were certainly in no mood to tolerate dissent. As Len McCluskey delivered a tribute to Corbyn from the conference stage, James Asser, an argumentative moderate member of Labour's NEC, refused to join in a standing ovation for the union leader. Murphy, sitting behind him, bellowed in his ear, spittle flying: 'IF I HOLD YOUR COFFEE, YOU CAN STAND UP AND CLAP!' While some self-styled moderates appeared to have reached the final stage of grief – acceptance – others could not move beyond anger. Late one night, a well-refreshed Patrick Heneghan saw fit to confront a bemused Ian Lavery, who had been drinking with friends in the bar of the Grand Hotel, the favoured late-night watering hole for delegates and dignitaries. Irate, Heneghan accused Lavery of briefing the press that he had sabotaged Labour's election campaign. As MPs Gloria de Piero and Jon Ashworth attempted to restrain him, Heneghan shoved his finger in Lavery's face. 'We gave you the best advice based on what we were seeing,' he spluttered. 'And what we were seeing was not wrong.' Conscious that the scene was unfolding before the eyes of watching journalists, Lavery restrained himself and stared back glassily, with a mixture of pity and contempt.

There would be no more brutal an illustration of the Corbynsceptics' unhappy new reality than the speech Tom Watson took to the stage to deliver. The hard man of Labour's old right, feared by so many of his contemporaries as the bully boy of Brownism, appeared to have changed not only his tune, but his entire personality: 'I realised something as the crowd at Glastonbury's silent disco began to sing "Oh, Jeremy Corbyn!",' he said. 'As they sang, I realised it's actually better to be loved than to be feared. And that Jeremy has shown us that it's possible.' To the disgust of the MPs who had believed him to be their protector, Watson then broke into song: 'Oh, Jeremy Corbyn!' Though many viewed it as a capitulation, the deputy leader's allies took a different view. 'It was a tactic,' said one of Watson's senior aides. 'We had to get out alive. It was a signal that bygones should be bygones, and that we needed to get on with it. If we hadn't started singing "Oh, Jeremy Corbyn", they would have done.' Watson, unlike so many of his colleagues, had come to understand that for now, at least, Corbyn's internal opponents would have to acclimatise to a new political reality.

3

Him, Too?

In his two decades in Parliament, national newspaper journalists had seldom bothered with Kelvin Hopkins. Elected in the New Labour landslide of 1997, the MP for Luton North – easily identifiable by his bald head, pronounced stoop and white goatee – had spent his years in the Commons about as far away from relevance as it was possible to be. His Eurosceptic, unapologetically Bennite politics appeared to have no place in Tony Blair's Labour Party. Like Jeremy Corbyn, John McDonnell and Diane Abbott, he was a stalwart of the Campaign Group. The closest Hopkins, an accomplished jazz saxophonist, would get to power in the long thirteen years of Labour government was as an unpaid ad hoc adviser on yachting to Richard Caborn, a junior sports minister. Shunned by their own party, the likes of Corbyn and Hopkins had few friends in Parliament but each other.

That changed on the chilly evening of Thursday 2 November 2017, when the doorbell rang at Hopkins's family home. Did they have any comment on his suspension from the Labour Party over allegations of sexual harassment?

When Corbyn launched his long-shot bid to lead the Labour Party at a Campaign Group meeting, Hopkins had been the first MP through the door of the Parliamentary Labour Party office to nominate him. But even after his old friend's victory, he remained an isolated presence in Parliament until the coup. If Corbyn could rely on anyone in his moment of greatest need, it was his old comrade Kelvin Hopkins, whom he appointed Shadow Culture Secretary. But Hopkins's services were no longer required after the humiliation of Owen Smith, and he headed home to the back benches, having finally attained high office in the Labour Party at the age of 74. Few had noticed his promotion and fewer still mourned his departure in October 2016. There were, however, two significant exceptions: Ava Etemadzadeh, a 26-year-old graduate of Essex University, and Rosie Winterton, Nick Brown's predecessor as chief whip.

Two years earlier, in November 2014, Etemadzadeh had invited Hopkins to speak at a meeting of her university's Labour club. Having accepted, Hopkins drove to Colchester on the evening of 12 November and gave what by all accounts was a well-received talk. Afterwards, bidding Etemadzadeh goodbye, he gave her a hug. It was then, she alleged, that he 'held me too tight and rubbed his crotch on me'. Nearly three months later, on 2 February 2015, the pair reunited in the stately Strangers' Dining Room of the House of Commons, over-looking the Thames, for lunch. There, Etemadzadeh alleged, Hopkins asked her a series of intrusive questions about her personal life. Hopkins is even said to have suggested that if his staff had been away, he would have taken her back to his office. Several unanswered phone calls and two weeks later he sent her a text that read: 'A nice young man would be lucky to have you as a girlfriend and lover. I am sure one such is soon to be found. Were I to be young … but I am not.' The following January, she complained to Labour's Whips' Office, only to be told by Rosie Winterton that she would have to waive anonymity to advance a formal complaint. She was unwilling to do so, but Hopkins was nonetheless reprimanded by Winterton, a plain-speaking Yorkshirewoman with little time for the left. When Hopkins was promoted in late June 2016, she called Corbyn to remonstrate with him. Why had she not been consulted before the leader promoted an alleged sex pest?

The exchange would remain private – and Hopkins's public reputa-tion would remain intact – for sixteen months, when it would be forced into the open by events taking place in the most unlikely of places: Hollywood. The months of crisis that then ensued would force the leader's inner circle to confront just how little power they still had over their own party. The sexual harassment allegations that would hit Labour during this required the party to think and act as one: not only to contain the damage it was inflicting on them but to protect the vulnerable victims. But with its three most important organs – LOTO, Southside and the Whips' Office, whose inhabitants walked a delicate tightrope between their duty to Corbyn and sympathies with the PLP – in the hands of irreconcilable factions, the damage would be lasting and those victims would become pawns in a factional chess game. Corbyn's allies say now that it was this episode that exposed their relationship with Southside as unsustainable. It was time for LOTO to take back control.

*

When in early October 2017 the *New York Times* published its first exposé of Harvey Weinstein, the Hollywood producer and power-broker, Labour's chief whip Nick Brown was in no doubt that its reverberations would reach – and shake – their party. Like Corbyn, he was one of only three MPs left standing from Labour's 1983 intake. His last big job had been as chief whip in the government of another MP elected that year: Gordon Brown. Pot-bellied, squinting and softly spoken, Nick Brown's sphinx-like demeanour and gentle mien belied a ruthlessness that had led Corbyn to draft him to replace Winterton – whom most of the leader's office suspected was helping to coord-inate sedition by hostile MPs – which he did in October 2016. As Weinstein's accusers rose in number and women began to share their harrowing personal testimonies under the #MeToo hashtag, lobby reporters set a new scandal in train: Pestminster. On the morning of Monday 23 October, Weinstein was still dominating the headlines. A day later, the *Sun*'s Harry Cole filed a front-page story that revealed parliamentary staff had outed MPs and ministers as sex pests in a private WhatsApp group. By the time it appeared on news-stands that Wednesday, Westminster's reckoning had begun. Brown, with char-acteristic foresight, had begun preparations weeks earlier.

Corbyn's office and Southside were equally alive to the dangers the scandal posed for Labour. As one Shadow Cabinet official recalls: 'When the Weinstein stuff broke, people knew it was going to hit Westminster. There were conversations in all the different senior bits of the party: Parliament, Southside, LOTO, the whips. We knew it was going to be the focus.' Privately, most whips believed that bullying, rather than sexual harassment, was the primary issue when it came to MPs' misbehaviour, but they were well aware of what was coming – and that Kelvin Hopkins's name would soon make an appearance. 'Kelvin was one of the stories that we knew had been around,' a source says. 'LOTO had already been burned once by appointing him, and then there were questions of what Jeremy knew, what senior officials knew, or not, how it had been handled, and what the process was.' But as they braced for the impact of the Hopkins case, another was about to blindside them.

It was just after 5 p.m. on 31 October 2017 when Sam Matthews realised that the #MeToo scandal was about to engulf the Labour Party. The disputes sub-panel of Labour's NEC, originally scheduled to last an hour from 1 p.m., had continued all afternoon. For Matthews, who had ultimate oversight over every disciplinary complaint made about Labour members, elected representatives and staff, attendance was mandatory – and always dreaded. Before the Corbyn era, its meetings – at which officials and elected representatives would adjudicate on disciplinary matters and complaints against members – were barely ever quorate. The decisions taken there – to expel this councillor or that – were of little political significance. Then, younger officials from the party's right, like Matthews, viewed the NEC with a degree of irritation, particularly when it put meeting rooms at Labour HQ out of action. Once, older staff reminded them, the NEC had been the crucible of the party's civil wars. Tim Waters, the party's veteran head of data, was known to remark wistfully: 'Once upon a time, these meetings were reported on in the national press.'

Corbyn's election and the ensuing civil war meant that meetings like the disputes sub-panel, which had once been the preserve of party anoraks, suddenly assumed huge factional import. Just who the party disciplined, how, and for what became bitterly contested. And while the left did not yet control the NEC, they did their best to win every fight that they could. That inevitably led to meetings dragging on and on as the likes of Pete Willsman, a cantankerous left-wing activist who knew the party rulebook better than most, argued over the small print of each case. Those present recall the meeting of 31 October as particularly bitter and protracted. So much so that when BBC Radio 4's *PM* programme began at 5 p.m., its proceedings were still some way off a conclusion. What it broadcast would, in the words of one official present, 'turn #MeToo into #LabourToo'.

At the top of *PM*'s running order was an interview with Bex Bailey, a 25-year-old Labour activist who had herself once been a member of the NEC. Under gentle questioning from presenter Carolyn Quinn, she revealed that she had been seriously sexually assaulted at a party event as a teenager in 2011, only to be told by a senior Labour official that filing a formal complaint would 'damage' her some years later. Bailey's specific words would, according to one official, 'put rocket boosters' under a scandal whose impact had not yet been felt in Labour circles: 'I was raped.'

As her testimony hit the airwaves, the phones of NEC members began to light up. Matthews realised that something was seriously amiss when his boss, John Stolliday, left the room. As Labour's head of governance and legal matters, Stolliday, a gentle giant with a head of receding blond curls, had ultimate oversight over internal discipline, as well as the party's legal budget. Having worked for Labour since 2005, he was also one of the most seasoned – and senior – Corbynsceptic operatives at Southside. For him to leave a meeting of significance in the factional war of attrition, was unusual. Matthews began to worry. The news that awaited him when he finally emerged from the marathon discussion was worse than he had anticipated.

It was far from clear whether Southside was equipped to deal with a crisis of such sensitivity and magnitude. As general secretary, Iain McNicol was the party's most powerful official, but staff harboured doubts over his ability to lead. They also had trouble navigating his eccentricities. He spent much of his time in the office shoeless and was averse to using his computer. To his staff he was not the decisive presence they needed in a crisis. In those moments, they instead turned to Labour's executive director of governance, membership and party services, the steely Emilie Oldknow. She had cut her teeth running the party in the East Midlands, a region full of bitterly fought marginal constituencies, before her appointment as McNicol's effective deputy in 2012. Oldknow was seen by some Southside officials as their real boss. 'She had been running the party for five years,' one recalls. 'She was general secretary in all but name.' Another said: 'Iain had a role, but she had the brains. She did the thinking.'

She also had a knack for frustrating Corbyn's inner circle, whom she loathed. Though cordial in their face-to-face dealings, Oldknow spoke of them in private with hair-raising venom. Karie Murphy was 'Medusa'. One LOTO source said: 'Seumas and Karie believed they had a monopoly on everything, but they faced a brick wall with Oldknow.' As Bailey accused Labour officials of failing to investigate her rape live on national radio, Oldknow was precisely the person Matthews and

Stolliday felt they needed. Yet she was not in Southside but a hundred miles away in fancy dress, having promised her daughter that she would return home to Leicester – where her husband, Shadow Health Secretary Jon Ashworth, was MP – to take her trick-or-treating. In her absence, Southside was overcome by 'a monumental panic', as one official described it. The next day's papers made clear that it had been justified. On 1 November, *The Times* gave Bailey's account higher billing on its front page than its own exclusive on alleged sexual harassment by Damian Green, Theresa May's de facto deputy prime minister. The splash headline made for stark reading: 'Labour tried to cover up rape'.

For a fleeting period, the interests of Corbyn's office and Southside were aligned. In the immediate term, both needed to contain the scandal and prevent similar accusations of cover-up and conspiracy from rearing their head again. Labour also needed to show that it was taking Bailey's allegations seriously. Stolliday and Shami Chakrabarti, the Shadow Attorney General with whom he had frequently clashed, agreed that Karon Monaghan, a QC, should oversee an independent inquiry. The staff working beneath them had more pressing matters to attend to. Matthews, who was trusted by Oldknow as a 'disownable fixer' on difficult, factional projects like the Ergon House plot, took the lead. Alongside him was Sophie Goodyear, the party's head of complaints. By coincidence, she had spent the preceding months working up a new set of procedures for dealing with sexual harassment complaints – but they were only 'skeletal' by the time of the Weinstein revelations.

Matthews had a small staff. They were soon overwhelmed. Only one of his investigations officers, Nareser Osei, was a woman. With the bulk of complaints being female, she was soon burdened with most of the work. Before 2015, Labour's compliance unit would receive around five to ten complaints over alleged breaches of the party rulebook each year. Now they were processing a similar number of cases a day. Officials took the decision to set up a confidential hotline to allow victims of harassment to register their allegations with the party. But they needed staff. Regional officials were drafted in from parts of the country that did not have local elections the following May.

Rightly or wrongly, the Labour Party's MPs and members expected it to have institutional answers on sexual harassment ready: Labour was, after all, supposed to be the party of gender equality. But

Goodyear's new complaints procedures were as yet unfinished and had foundered on a set of questions that were about to assume a new urgency. 'We got stuck on knotty issues,' one Southside source said. 'How do you guarantee the difficult stuff that even the police aren't getting right? How do you guarantee anonymity and due process? How do you make sure that those named in complaints have a meaningful right to respond to applications, whilst also not creating a lot of barriers for people reporting this stuff? We haven't found the right answer yet as a society, and the Labour Party is expected to be better than all of this.' In the full glare of the national press, they struggled to find a way forward. 'It was dire for a whole host of reasons,' one Southside official says now. 'If you had a sexual harassment allegation to make about a Labour politician in the last fifty years, you made it in those two weeks.'

Some cases were relatively straightforward. Councillors and grassroots activists accused of harassment or inappropriate behaviour tended to be suspended from their Labour membership by officials immediately: their cases were unencumbered by political sensitivity. The same could not be said of those concerning sitting MPs and peers. Corbyn's office feared that Southside and the PLP would use the process as a pretence to exact revenge against the left, and vice versa. Whatever droplets of trust that remained between the two camps after the general election had evaporated. As one Corbyn aide recalls: 'It was a turning point because you can't handle these things unless there's total trust. It wasn't a good situation to be in. We always went into these things assuming our opponents were holding knives behind their backs.' Southside took the same attitude. 'We had a sort of grim view of each case,' said one senior official. 'If it was an allegation against a Campaign Group or Corbynista MP, then we would have to fight over how we were going to deal with it, whereas if it were against a moderate MP, we knew they would be demanding full sanctions immediately.'

They devised what they saw as an insurance policy. While Corbyn's office would have the final say on what disciplinary action to take against an accused MP or peer, they would have to put their judgement in writing: without a paper trail linking Karie Murphy or Seumas Milne to a disciplinary decision or lack of one, officials suspected they would be vulnerable to being stitched up. As one official recalls: 'We essentially instigate a process to protect us, to allow us to take some

action, but to remove some of our agency of making the final decision, and making them put it in fucking writing. Because otherwise
they would just do this by phone call: "No, you can't suspend him
and I'm not giving you a reason."'

Sources on the left remember it differently. Less than a year into
Corbyn's leadership, Angela Rayner had complained of a Southside
and Shadow Cabinet conspiracy to undermine the left, telling
colleagues to collect evidence of misconduct where possible. 'That
way, when it comes to sweeping them out, the evidence is there to
take action,' she wrote on WhatsApp. Ian Lavery agreed: 'There should
be an official written complaint sent to McNicol every time this behaviour occurs. This is a must, comrades,' he replied. By 2017, the
complaints had had little effect. At the start of the year, Andy
McDonald, the Shadow Transport Secretary, was repeating the same
strategy: 'We need the hard evidence and they then need to be nailed.'
Rayner joked in response: 'Send them on gardening leave or have
them work from JC's office to remove the problem. Send them on
fact-finding mission across the world to report on our foreign policies.
Anything to remove them from their current positions without firing
them.' Yet by the time that #MeToo exploded, the left could not wait
any longer to deal with Southside. Such was the potential for damage
from stories involving parliamentarians or a factional tit-for-tat that
LOTO needed immediate oversight of its conduct. The result was
that Murphy took on a role whose power vastly exceeded her formal
responsibilities. She would, in those frantic weeks, become the party's
de facto general secretary, wielding power well beyond her office
manager's remit and over the heads of Southside. Whips nicknamed
it the 'Karie Murphy Justice System'. Yet to LOTO its establishment
was imperative because it could no longer put its faith in Southside
to discharge its administrative duties. As Murphy had told comrades:
'Sabotage doesn't come close.'

In public, the leader's office had initially responded to stories of sexual
harassment in Westminster by seeking to make political capital out of
the revelations. In a speech at the UNISON union's annual policy conference in Aviemore on 28 October, Corbyn insisted that Labour would
not tolerate any inappropriate behaviour. 'The problem doesn't stop
with those who make unwanted advances on women, it extends to a
culture that has tolerated abuse for far too long,' he said. 'It's a warped

and degrading culture that also exists and thrives in the corridors of power, including in Westminster.' He urged any victim to come forward. At that time, it had appeared that the Conservatives would bear the brunt of the scandal. As Corbyn spoke, a spreadsheet detailing allegations against thirty-six Tory MPs was already circulating widely in Westminster and would soon leak in the press. By Thursday 2 November, however, it was clear that the Hopkins story was about to break.

As the whips had predicted, it was among the first Westminster journalists pursued. The previous Friday, *The Times* had published an anonymised account of Hopkins's case and had sent an agency reporter to his home. Now Etemadzadeh had gone on the record in an interview with the *Daily Telegraph*. In it, she detailed not just the alleged advances but her anger at Corbyn's decision to promote Hopkins to the Shadow Cabinet despite knowing of the accusations against him. Labour could no longer hide behind its holding line – that it did not comment on individual cases. That afternoon, a crisis meeting was convened in Corbyn's office in Norman Shaw South. Milne and Murphy were joined by Luke Sullivan, Nick Brown's baby-faced adviser, and officials from Southside. To the surprise of officials, both Murphy and Milne agreed that Hopkins, despite his closeness to Corbyn, must be suspended pending an internal investigation. The existence of text messages from Hopkins to Etemadzadeh made such a course of action unavoidable.

Just after 8 p.m., Sullivan was dispatched back to the Labour Whips' Office to brief journalists on the decision, in an effort to deny the right-wing *Telegraph* the satisfaction of a scalp. At 8.32 p.m., Laura Kuenssberg, the BBC's political editor, tweeted: 'Kelvin Hopkins, Labour MP, chucked out of the party after allegations of bad behaviour.' He was the first MP of any party to be suspended for alleged sexual harassment since the Weinstein revelations. Corbyn was privately distraught. Not only had he been compelled to suspend one of his oldest friends and allies in Labour politics, having promoted him despite being told of the harassment allegations, he now appeared to have been a willing participant in the Westminster culture he had decried. On Friday 3 November, the day after he had suspended Hopkins, Corbyn learned of an allegation against another of his own.

David Prescott had always divided opinion within the Labour Party. The son of John Prescott, the burly merchant seaman who rose to become Tony Blair's deputy prime minister, he was often referred to by journalists as one of the so-called Red Princes – the sons of prominent Labour politicians who harboured their own designs on elected office. Not only did David bear a striking resemblance to his father – give or take several stones in weight and decades in age – his alleged authorship of his father's tweets and newspaper columns was an open secret in Westminster. But unlike other Labour sons, Stephen Kinnock and Will Straw, the younger Prescott had failed three times to win selection as a Labour candidate in a winnable parliamentary seat and instead had to settle for a no-hope run in Gainsborough, a Tory stronghold, in 2015. After backing Andy Burnham's doomed campaign for the leadership in the months that followed, Prescott's hopes of success in Labour politics appeared to have been extinguished for good. By October 2016, however, he had undergone a Damascene conversion. Though never of the Labour left, Prescott became Corbyn's speechwriter and political adviser. He had not been LOTO's first choice, but in the months after the coup, Team Corbyn could barely populate its own office with supporters or even sympathisers, let alone the PLP or Southside. Its communications team was overburdened. What mattered to Milne and Murphy was that Prescott, an experienced public relations professional, was willing to do the job at all.

How he did it won him few admirers in LOTO. His attempts to enliven the leader's hitherto dry and earnest speeches were not always appreciated by colleagues. Even Corbyn, who seldom said a bad word about any of his staff, would complain about Prescott's style. Before long he was shunted to a less glamorous role coordinating communications for the Shadow Cabinet. If officials at Southside knew one thing about the opaque internal politics of Corbyn's office, it was that to some, Prescott had never been truly welcome. Some thought him overbearing. But the LOTO colleagues who disliked him felt he could rely on the overworked Murphy and Milne, who needed all of the support they could get.

That Friday afternoon, a young female MP met Corbyn and Murphy in secret. She had asked for anonymity and was, in Murphy's words, 'visibly distressed' as she told them she had been subjected to public and unwanted sexual advances by Prescott at a party event in 2014. She also informed them of two other disputed allegations. Though the first dated to 1993, it had long been the subject of Westminster rumour. Prescott was said to have relieved himself on the kitchen floor of a woman who refused to have sex with him. The second incident, in which Prescott allegedly propositioned two student members of the party to join him for sex, was said to have occurred only months earlier in 2017 – during his employment in Corbyn's office. He strenuously denied all of the accusations. Murphy subsequently wrote in an email memo to Emilie Oldknow: '[He] was forceful, rude, and aggressive when refused.'

Having heard the MP's testimony, Murphy told Oldknow that she had conferred with Milne, Prescott's line manager, and taken the decision to suspend Prescott from his job in LOTO: 'Under such circumstances, I considered it appropriate to speak to Human Resources and to request an immediate suspension . . . Please let me know what further information may be required and how this matter should proceed.'

Oldknow told Sam Matthews and John Stolliday of the case the following Monday. Both agreed that Prescott ought to be suspended not only from his job, but from his Labour membership: a measure that would have prevented him from attending party events and running in internal elections. Matthews was then instructed to draft a pro forma letter of suspension for Prescott, addressed to his home in the village of Collingham, Nottinghamshire, informing him that he was banned from attending party meetings and from running for selection as a Labour candidate. It was sent to Murphy and Milne for approval but did not go any further – and certainly not as far as Nottinghamshire. Some twenty-four hours later, on Tuesday 7 November, Murphy replied: 'I don't agree that DP's membership should be suspended. Until something is in writing, I don't think we have grounds to suspend.' Officials now say they were incredulous: far from signing off the decision as expected, she appeared to have intervened to save one of LOTO's own from a formal disciplinary process. They still claim that Murphy had invented the requirement for a written complaint to protect Prescott, who returned to work two weeks later. After a witness did not corroborate the accusations against him, a formal investigation could not proceed in the absence of a written complaint and no further action was taken.

But events imposed a new set of obligations on the party. Carl Sargeant, a Welsh government minister sacked over allegations of inappropriate behaviour the same day Murphy had suspended Prescott, had died by suicide. The last person he had spoken to before hanging himself in his downstairs utility room in an ex-council house in Connah's Quay, North Wales, was a Labour call-centre operative in Newcastle. The fact that Sargeant had not been given details of the accusations against him at the time of his death led to a shift in tone and emphasis in media reporting of harassment cases. One Southside official said: 'By the time the news broke about Carl Sargeant, the narrative had changed.' By the time Murphy refused to sign off on Prescott's suspension from the party, Labour officials felt they were under media pressure to protect the accused as much as their alleged victims.

Inevitably, the team at Southside suspected low politics was the real motivation for Murphy's intervention. Suspending Prescott would have kiboshed his run for the Labour candidacy in Mansfield, the Nottinghamshire mining town that had unexpectedly fallen to the Conservatives that June. It had since become a focus of Corbyn's campaigning efforts, and Prescott was his anointed candidate. Parliamentary selections were fiercely contested by Labour's warring factions, especially in marginal seats the party leadership believed it stood a chance of winning. Behind closed doors, staff were informed about Prescott's suspension from LOTO and told to send him texts of solidarity. His allies suspected a Southside stitch-up.

Southside's suspicions that Corbyn's staff were willing to bend rules and create new ones if it advanced their cause would intensify later that month. On 29 November, John Stolliday informed Milne and Murphy of a complaint against Pete Willsman, a 73-year-old member of Labour's NEC. His was not a name widely known beyond the Labour Party. Within it, Willsman enjoyed something approaching notoriety. Though he bore a striking resemblance to Melvyn Bragg, the avuncular broadcaster and Labour peer, he had little of the charm, as generations of Labour activists had learned first-hand. For more than four decades, Willsman had been agitating on behalf of the party's left: on the committees that determined the schedule for party conferences, in constituency parties, and on the NEC. Alongside Jon Lansman, who now chaired Momentum, Willsman had led the Campaign for Labour Party Democracy, whose defining mission was to make MPs more accountable to the grass roots. Its peak had come in 1981, when Tony Benn – assisted by Lansman – came within half a percentage point of ousting Denis Healey, the godfather of the

Labour right, as the party's deputy leader at its conference in Brighton. That conference saw Willsman enter Labour politics as a national player – and also marked the beginning of the left's slow retreat into the wilderness. Over the years and decades that ensued, modernisers, led first by Neil Kinnock and then John Smith and Tony Blair, took control of the party. The likes of Willsman were safe to ignore: the war was over.

Though Jeremy Corbyn's election as Labour leader in 2015 was heralded by many of his supporters as the birth of a new sort of 'kinder, gentler politics', one of its consequences was to give veteran activists like Willsman something they had not had for four decades: mainstream relevance. He was no longer fighting against a hostile leadership, but working for a leader whom he counted as a personal friend. Willsman could be relied on to fight his corner on the NEC more forcefully than anyone else. His loyalty to the man whom he eccentrically called 'Jerry', forged as it had been over nearly half a century in the political wilderness, was as good as total. In September 2017, he had told the NEC that MPs who criticised Corbyn 'deserved to be attacked'. Jo Cox, the MP for Batley and Spen, had been murdered outside her constituency surgery fifteen months previously, as a fellow NEC member reminded him. Even allies on the left were embarrassed by his outbursts: this was not the optimistic, inclusive politics that their leader appeared to have promised in 2015. But such pugnacity ultimately had its uses for a leadership that needed all the support it could get. Suddenly, Pete Willsman mattered – and so did the question of just how to deal with his often cantankerous behaviour.

Willsman's accuser, a former party member, had submitted a catalogue of allegations about his 'disruptive and inappropriate' behaviour towards young women at Southside. At one NEC meeting in 2016, he was alleged to have asked a young member whether she liked to twerk when she went clubbing – and boasted that women would often perform the highly sexualised dance move for him. To Southside it was precisely the sort of behaviour that would ordinarily be dealt with under the party's sexual harassment procedures. Willsman did not respond to the allegations when they were later reported in the press.

Murphy disagreed. Three hours after Stolliday alerted her to the complaint against Willsman, she replied via email: 'This is not in my view a complaint of sexual harassment. I am happy to discuss this matter with him directly if this is thought appropriate. This is not a matter to be managed under the sexual harassment policy.' Rather than employ the formal processes employed against MPs, she suggested she would 'have a word with PW instead'. Though she had no formal power over the party's disciplinary processes, Murphy was now not only deciding whether to apply the rules – but seemed to be rewriting them for the benefit of one of Corbyn's most reliable allies on the NEC. That, at least, was how Southside saw it. The LOTO view was that such cases could be more easily dealt with by being nipped in the bud by the likes of Murphy. To surrender the disciplinary process entirely to Southside was to ensure cases fell inside a black box over which the leadership, who would have to incur the political pain of any adverse consequences, had no control. And they had every reason to suspect that officials would take any opportunity they could to make their lives more difficult.

To the women and men who had spoken out about their experiences, however, LOTO's strategy perpetuated the toxic culture Corbyn had pledged to end. In initially failing to allow cases such as Prescott's and Willsman's to go forward under formal disciplinary processes, Murphy had left herself vulnerable to claims she put the Project first. That was certainly what her detractors thought. Some of those who had made allegations believed that LOTO's siege mentality had afflicted them with a wilful blindness, so long as the accused was one of their own. That was the view of activists like LabourToo, set up in the wake of the Weinstein revelations to seek testimonies from women in the party and 'build a compendium of the types of abuse women face which all too often are unseen, ignored or swept under the carpet'. Despite Corbyn's pledges to change politics, they believed his aides continued that cycle, rather than broke it.

By Christmas, Corbyn himself had concluded that the relationship between his own office and the party HQ that was supposed to serve its will was untenable. As 2018 began, LOTO would finally get its chance to take out the leader of the resistance. Over the festive break, Murphy had received a tip-off from John Bercow, the Speaker – and an unlikely personal friend of Murphy – that there would be openings in the Lords. Corbyn had always fiercely resented the cronyism of the Upper House and resisted perpetuating it by appointing peers of his own. Until then he had been persuaded to make only one exception, by nominating Shami Chakrabarti for a peerage and then appointing her to the Shadow Cabinet in 2016, when it was clear that the benefit to the left outweighed his principled objections to the institution. That was seldom the case.

Murphy had never been of the view that Iain McNicol should be bought off with a peerage. Her view was summed up to LOTO colleagues rather succinctly as 'fuck him'. Yet Bercow's approach made her reconsider. A peerage might be just the bauble to tempt McNicol away from Southside. A friendly appointment in his stead would not only hand control of the machine to LOTO but relieve the load on an exhausted Murphy.

Early one Monday morning that January she put the idea to Corbyn and McDonnell in a private meeting in LOTO. McNicol would be given a peerage and replaced by a woman of the left. McDonnell asked whether she had a candidate. 'No,' said Murphy. 'But I'm working on it.' She then did McNicol's old union, the GMB, the courtesy of telling them that their man was on his way out. They did not object, so long as she bumped him off gently.

Her next job was anointing a successor. LOTO's preferred candidate was Jennie Formby, an assistant general secretary of Unite and a close ally of Len McCluskey, as well as the mother of his oldest child. Yet Formby had no desire to do the job, and told LOTO as much. In response, Murphy deployed a stinging riposte she had previously used on Milne towards the end of his year-long sabbatical from the *Guardian*: if she declined the Project's call in its hour of need, she could never be their comrade in the same way. 'Her basic argument was that if you don't want to come, fine, but on the NEC, don't raise anything about changing the party for the workers,' recalled one confidant. Formby soon relented.

With a replacement lined up, LOTO set about organising the assassination. On Tuesday 20 February, McNicol and Julie Lawrence, his assistant, came to Parliament for what he assumed would be an expansive catch-up on Corbyn's desire for a team of community organisers and Southside's proposal to appoint compliance officers in each of Labour's regional parties, so that anti-Semitism complaints might be dealt with away from LOTO's prying eyes. Instead, it would be a summary execution. Murphy had drawn up his death warrant: a document that summarised his successes and failures as general secretary.

One person familiar with the paper described it as containing 'three sentences' of praise and 110 on his failures. Corbyn was furnished with a copy in advance. The plan was that he would produce it as evidence for why McNicol had to go.

Upon arrival at LOTO, McNicol was ushered into Corbyn's office alone for a private audience with McDonnell and Corbyn. Murphy made to leave but was beckoned to stay. The message the Project needed to impart was too painful for either of its greybeards to utter. Discussion kicked off with the formalities. McNicol made the case for his compliance officers; the two sides debated the merits of community organising. Corbyn waffled. McNicol was fidgety and defensive. Murphy, meanwhile, brimmed over with impatience and exasperation. As the conversation wound on and on, rudderless, she suddenly interjected. 'The detail isn't important. The detail isn't important!' Then came the *coup de grâce*: 'Iain, it's finished. You're gone.'

She pushed a pre-prepared statement in front of Corbyn. 'Jeremy, read that.' McNicol sat impassive as the leader read him his last rites, without looking him in the eye. 'We respect the work you have done as general secretary, what we'd like to do is offer you a place in the House of Lords.' He even dangled a front-bench post as inducement. 'I'd like to offer you Shadow ... Minister for Employment. No, no. I think I want to call it Employment Rights.' McDonnell stressed that the leadership wanted the story of his sacking to be a positive one. Yet McNicol resisted. He said he did not want to leave. It was then that Murphy informed him that she had already squared it with his old union. 'So you're finished. You're going.' With that he left. Two members of LOTO staff claimed to have seen him weeping in the corridors of Norman Shaw South.

Having despatched McNicol, LOTO's next task was to guarantee the succession. While they could anoint a candidate, the appointment was not solely in their gift. Formby would need to win the backing of Corbyn, Watson and the rest of the NEC. LOTO could neither afford a contest or a split in the left vote. Jon Lansman's entry into the race threatened to precipitate both.

Formby formally announced her candidacy on Monday 26 February, just three days after McNicol's resignation had become public. On 1 March, Lansman announced his candidacy himself. Having devoted his life to turning the Labour Party into a members-led organisation, he was not prepared to stand by and let the unions stitch the selection up. Corbyn, he pointedly said, had been twice elected on a promise to do the same – and that would involve 'sweeping away the old machine politics'. The target of his remarks was clear enough. That he felt compelled to make them in public exposed for the first time a tension that would continue to undermine the Corbyn Project. For Lansman, internal power was not an end in itself, but a means to a far nobler one: redistributing it among left-wing activists at the grass roots. Hand-picking Formby flew in the face of that aim. In defying LOTO's power games, he hoped to generate a proper contest. Only by taking a stand himself against the succession could he encourage others to believe that it could be done.

Corbyn and McDonnell did not agree, despite Lansman's pedigree as the grand old man of organised Bennism. Shortly after he declared, he received a call from a LOTO official who told him to hold the line for Jeremy and John. It was then that McDonnell told him in straight-forward terms that his candidacy was unwanted. Lansman promised to give their appeal due consideration. Ten days later, he pulled out with a further pointed appeal for Labour to end its 'command and control' culture. His intervention had the desired effect in the mean-time: several external applicants had thrown their hats into the ring. They ranged from Paul Hilder, the founder of election strategy company Crowdpac – whose references included David Cameron's barefooted svengali Steve Hilton and Lansman himself – David Sayer, the head of daytime programming at Channel 4, and a sixth-form-age WH Smith sales assistant who, having seemingly misunderstood the job description, had written their application in biro.

Formby's own application made innocent reference to her having heard of the job from the Labour Party website, despite it really having been a product of a twenty-first-century smoke-filled room. Len McCluskey and Emily Thornberry, then Shadow Foreign Secretary, vouched for her as references, and she paid fulsome tribute to Corbyn. Her aim, she said, was to reconnect the 'three pillars' of the party: voters, members and the unions. Formby need not have bothered, of course. With Lansman out of contention, she had a clear path to the succession. Despite her bumpy journey to the post and the later difficulties it would portend, the Corbynites were in a celebratory mood. On Tuesday 3 April, her first day in post, a beaming Ian Lavery introduced Formby to staff at Southside. Many were glum: the left was now in charge of the machine. Lavery took the opportunity to crow. In his distinctive Northumberland accent, he boomed: 'I'm so, so proud that we've got a lady general secretary!'

The price, however, had been to split the component parts of Corbynism. Lansman was ostracised. Momentum, whose millennial members would find themselves at odds with the LOTO machine with increasing frequency over the coming months and years, was no longer a subsidiary arm of the Project but something distinct. Lansman's relationships with its founding fathers changed irrevocably. The cordial conversation with Corbyn continued, but something disappeared in his moment of insubordination. His interactions with McDonnell, meanwhile, became frosty on the rare occasions they occurred at all. In breaching its ancestral ties with Lansman, the Project had put power before principle. It had muffled dissent and railroaded its own outcome with a ruthlessness that would have made New Labour's leading lights proud. Control of Southside justified the means, for the moment at least. But the cost had been the fracturing of the Project.

Formby had more pressing matters to deal with in the here and now: the purge of Corbynsceptics from Southside. First in the firing line was Emilie Oldknow, who, for reasons lost on the new general secretary, had been offered the chance to stay on and work with the new Corbynite regime if she so wished. Oldknow refused, and with their two leaders now gone the old order quickly followed them voluntarily. John Stolliday had long suspected that if he did not go, LOTO would see to his departure themselves. They had made their intentions clear over the Easter Weekend, just before Formby's arrival. During the 2017 general election campaign, Stolliday had received a complaint from a general election candidate's estranged wife, who alleged that he had beaten her. By way of evidence, she provided a council safeguarding report on the case, which named her children. Stolliday, having taken advice from a QC, concluded he could not do anything with the information – which, strictly speaking, he was not allowed legally to see – unless the woman submitted a formal complaint. She was unwilling, and her husband became an MP. Early in 2018, she told Jess Phillips, the campaigning MP for Birmingham Yardley, of the case. Labour's women MPs were incandescent to learn they were sharing the opposition benches with an alleged domestic abuser. But Corbyn's office blamed Stolliday's inaction and suggested his head would roll as a result. Phillips and others alerted him over the Easter weekend that preceded Formby's arrival: 'LOTO are trying to get you. They're trying to kill you.' Formby had already made clear she wanted him gone. When he arrived at the office on the morning of 3 April, he found Thomas Gardiner, the man who would later become his replacement, already sitting at his desk. Stolliday took the hint and handed in his notice five days after Formby's appointment.

With the process of clearing the stables well underway, LOTO could finally discuss the practicalities of making the Corbyn revolution permanent. For the best part of three years LOTO had been denied the ability to reshape the party in their own image – and that of its swelling membership. Now, finally, on 5 April, Milne, Murphy, Formby and Andrew Fisher met to plot out how Formby's new office might be used to future-proof the Project. They would use their new-found power to bring Southside to heel, and 'neutralise as much as possible' the vestigial power of the PLP. Tom Watson's staffing, it noted with some satisfaction, had been 'streamlined'. Overall, those present agreed: 'The key objective is to ensure lasting change to internal structures so they support a future left leader.'

Yet they did pause for thought. Would winning control of the party impede their mission to win power in the country? The minutes of the meeting asked candidly: 'Given that we are judged on our election results, would it be safer to employ someone with the relevant experience but who isn't necessarily completely aligned politically?' The PLP often complained that the leadership was preoccupied with power over the party rather than the compromises they believed were inherent in winning elections. But to them the coup had given them no choice but to suspect outsiders. For now, their priorities were clear.

Alternative power bases that had sprung up and proven so troublesome over the course of the #MeToo episode – like Stolliday's post of director of governance and legal, and Matthews' role as head of disputes – would either be abolished or forced to report directly to Formby. Intriguingly, there were hints too of LOTO unease at a cuckoo in its own nest. 'Any pressure for additional staffing resources for the Shadow Chancellor's office should be resisted,' the memo read. Suspicion that McDonnell was prosecuting his own agenda seldom spoke its name. But as 2018 began that distrust would rear its head with destructive frequency.

The changing of the guard at Southside had been swifter and more brutal than even the most pessimistic Corbynsceptics had anticipated. But a much more public humiliation was to come. On Friday 27 April, the *Daily Mirror* reported that Labour MP John Woodcock, a foreign-policy hawk who had emerged as one of Corbyn's most vociferous back-bench critics, was under investigation for sexual harassment. He denied any wrongdoing. The case had hitherto been kept from the public domain: his accuser, a former staff member of Woodcock's who complained of inappropriate text messages in November 2017, had requested her case be heard in private. For that reason, Woodcock had only been put under internal investigation. A suspension, by contrast, would have made the matter all too public. Yet somehow, the case had leaked. Officials suspected Murphy, who had been aware of the case from the outset. Over the weekend, Formby asked Sam Matthews for full details of the case. By Monday 30 April, she had resolved to suspend Woodcock from his party membership – a course of action Southside could not disagree with now the case had reached the newspapers. Formby informed officials of her decision via email that afternoon. Unsurprisingly, Murphy gave it her enthusiastic endorsement. 'Thank you for involving LOTO in this decision,' she replied. 'We completely support this move to suspend.' A minute later, Formby sent an intriguing response to Murphy alone: 'Can you ring??'

By then, however, events would force the Project to look outwards to a country that was altogether less sure of Corbynite wisdom.

4

From Russia With Hate

Gavin Shuker's career in Labour politics had started off well. The MP for Luton South, a gangly, fresh-faced former evangelical pastor with a puckish grin, had appeared destined for the top upon his election to Parliament in 2010. He had backed Ed Miliband for the Labour leadership and shared his politics. His reward had been a succession of Shadow ministerial jobs – ideal preparation for the real thing, which surely beckoned after the Labour victory he expected in May 2015. For a man who caught his break in national politics only because the parliamentary expenses scandal forced his predecessor, Margaret Moran, to resign, it was not bad going. But by January 2018, aged only 36, he knew in his heart that it was over.

Shuker began the year not with his own ministerial office in a Whitehall department, nor even in his party's top team, but at Fair Oak Farm, a luxury bed and breakfast deep in the East Sussex countryside. There a dozen Corbynsceptic MPs spent the evening eating home-made profiteroles – and chewing over what sort of a future, if any, they had in the Labour Party. All present had assumed that the 2017 election would be the end of Jeremy Corbyn, a man with whom they disagreed on more or less everything. None of them wanted him as prime minister, despite having campaigned for that very outcome six months previously. Shuker objected to what he saw as the political culture of the Labour Party, namely its bullying, factional fixing and machismo. Some, like Chris Leslie, an unreconstructed Brownite who had been unexpectedly elected aged just 24 in the landslide of 1997, believed that Corbynomics, with its steep spending increases and nationalisations, would bankrupt the country. Angela Smith, the Sheffield MP and a Rolling Stones fanatic, belonged in the same camp. Others, like Mike Gapes, the avuncular MP for Ilford South – a man with the look of a hatless Smurf who had once insisted that the only way he would leave the Labour Party was 'in a box' – believed the leadership's dovish stances on foreign policy were an existential threat to Britain's national security. All present had voted for Britain to remain in the European Union. They were also uncomfortable with Labour's handling of anti-Semitism allegations – and Corbyn's seeming inability to acknowledge it as a genuine problem.

Despite the hopes of the PLP, Labour's surprise electoral gains in 2017 had not made these problems disappear. Instead, it had hard-wired them into the politics of their party for the foreseeable future. Indeed, 2018 began with a series of rude reminders as to just who was in charge.

On 3 January, Tony Blair had published a 2,300-word essay on his own website, in which he warned Labour risked ending up as 'the handmaiden of Brexit' if it continued to prevaricate. Five days later, at the first PLP meeting of the year, Corbyn appeared to confirm his old enemy's fears. Addressing a hostile crowd, Corbyn disappointed Europhile MPs by ruling out membership of the EU's single market after Brexit. Remainers filed out of Committee Room 14 in a funk – although few were surprised. Corbyn, after all, had voted against more or less every EU treaty that had come before Parliament in his thirty-five years in the Commons. He insisted that his views were more nuanced than Labour MPs gave him credit for. 'I've always been in favour of social cooperation across Europe, I've always been in favour of better workers' rights,' Corbyn would insist when confronted with his voting record in an interview in November 2018 with Sophy Ridge of Sky News, remarks his allies always believed distilled the essence of his attitudes toward the EU over his three decades in Parliament. 'What I opposed is the element of free-market economics in Europe.' Nonetheless, some Remainers in the PLP were coming to the conclusion that they would never get their way under his leadership.

On 15 January the results of the elections to Labour's ruling NEC of three new representatives of the membership were announced. Momentum's slate swept the board, outnumbering the votes of their nearest competitor, the centrist comedian Eddie Izzard, by a margin of two to one. Soberingly for Corbynsceptics, Jon Lansman was among their number. Having spent a career agitating for the power to deselect

MPs whose views diverged from their members, he and two of his
followers now had their hands on the levers of Labour's ruling body.
Their opponents put on a brave face, pointing to a low turnout of
just 19 per cent. The few Labour members that did vote in such internal
elections had always backed left-wing candidates. Now, however, those
candidates were working with, rather than against, the party leadership – which enjoyed a majority on the NEC.

Opponents of the leadership, meanwhile, lacked clear leadership
of their own – or even a plan. Initially, they had looked to Tom Watson
who, like Corbyn, sat on the NEC *ex officio*. No leadership was forthcoming. 'The thing about Tom,' one NEC member said, 'is that he's
a bully. If you stand up to bullies, they don't know what to do. Corbyn
looked him in the eye in 2016 and effectively said: "Fuck off. I'm not
going." Then he did quite well. Tom didn't know how to cope with
it, so he just retreated.' Others took a more sympathetic view. A
diagnosis of type two diabetes in the wake of the 2017 election had
hit Watson hard, and inspired an eight-stone weight loss with the help
of 'bulletproof' coffee stirred through with butter, to stave off hunger.
He feared dying before his children came of age. With the stakes so
high, factional victories no longer carried the same existential import.
The physiological change was accompanied by a great mellowing. He
came to regret the viciousness of his past self. To bully and brutalise
in the name of a lost cause, as Corbynscepticism then appeared to
be, was to waste one's life.

Whatever the motivation, LOTO delighted in his disengagement.
One official often burdened with man-marking the deputy leader
through Shadow Cabinet and NEC meetings, lest he leak or coordinate
seditious activities, noted that he was still tapping frantically on his
phone – but rather than texting hostile journalists, he was taking notes
on his new diet of berries, bananas and cauliflower rice.

Unlike Watson, the MPs who had trooped to Fair Oak Farm at
Shuker's invitation retained an appetite for grand gestures. They were
unwilling to join in the chorus of 'Oh, Jeremy Corbyn!' Though they
shared Watson's conclusion that Corbyn was *in situ* for as long as he
wanted to be, they did not agree with his policy of accommodation.
Those at Fair Oak Farm had instead adopted what they referred to as
Plan A – staying and fighting to wrest control of the party from the
Corbynites. By January 2018, however, most of them had concluded

that that had failed – or was bound to. Now, at Shuker's behest, they set to work on a Plan B: a blueprint for life outside of the Labour Party.

Shuker had himself adopted Plan B six months earlier – specifically, just after 10 p.m. on 8 June 2017, when the exit poll revealed that Corbyn had led Labour not to a crushing defeat but to its best result in over a decade. The previous night, he had joined an awkward squad of fifty MPs – all of them hostile to Corbyn – on a conference call to discuss private polling that showed Labour on course for a net loss of seventy seats. A significant number of those on the call would be among the casualties. Yet they consoled themselves with the fact that a loss of such magnitude would doom Corbyn to an early exit too. The real result changed the calculus. 'At the moment when the exit poll came out,' Shuker recalls, 'I realised that I was not going to make it to the end of the Parliament as a Labour MP.' Like dozens of his colleagues, he had assured voters that they could vote to return him to Parliament, as there was no chance that a Corbyn-led Labour would get near power. The fact that Labour had made gains laid bare the hollowness of that calculation. It was at that moment that his thinking shifted from Plan A – 'stay, fight, grind it out, because there is no red line' – to Plan B, a course of action that would 'inevitably involve some form of split'.

Chris Leslie was Shuker's first port of call. Labour MPs of all political persuasions expected the member for Nottingham East to lead a split, and with good reason. Leslie loathed the Corbynites, and the Corbynites loathed Leslie. His dislike of the Project ran deep. In 2007, Leslie had run Gordon Brown's leadership campaign against a doomed but energetic challenge from McDonnell. In 2015, he had taken the opposite view to Corbyn of Labour's general election defeat that year: far from being too accepting of austerity, as Corbyn argued, he believed Labour's line on the public finances had simply not been tough enough. Departing to the back benches after Corbyn's first victory, he made no secret of his contempt for the leadership or its politics – especially not when journalists were listening. The shock of 2017 had not changed his view either. Despite having predicted a crushing defeat for Labour, Leslie condemned Corbyn for missing 'an open goal'. The leader's followers, meanwhile, revelled in having proved him wrong. At the end of July, Momentum activists had won control of his constituency party. By August, it was increasingly clear that Leslie, whose lilting West Yorkshire accent disguised an acid tongue, would be made to leave the Labour Party if he did not do so of his own accord.

One sunny afternoon that month, he drove down the M1 to Luton Hoo, a Georgian mansion on the outskirts of Shuker's constituency, for a discreet lunch of sea bass. Discussions over a formal split had begun in earnest. Shuker recalls: 'We began to sketch out really basic ideas: there were people who were Plan A, people who were Plan B, but it would have been irresponsible not to start work on that [Plan B], and to start thinking about it.'

Shuker spent the following months combing through a list of his parliamentary colleagues, entry by entry, identifying those who might be amenable to at least entertaining the taboo of leaving Labour. Some, like Alison McGovern, the Wirral South MP and chair of Blairite pressure group Progress, were surprisingly unwilling to even countenance the prospect in theory. She says now: 'There was a division between those of us who would be legitimately described as tribally Labour, versus those of us who said that it doesn't matter how we feel emotionally about the Labour Party, we have to do what's right for the country.' Shuker drew up a list of seventy-five MPs who he felt might be convinced. Over the autumn and winter of 2017, he met them for coffee in Westminster to sound them out. He also began to convene the chairs of the PLP's back-bench policy committees, at 5 p.m. on a Monday night. Traditionally, the committees had been powerless talking shop. Opponents of Corbyn had nonetheless taken control of them in the months after his election in a bid to exert a moderating influence over the leadership's policy agenda, dubbing themselves 'the Shadow Shadow Cabinet'. For Shuker, though, they were something more: a crucial means of building a network of sympathetic MPs ahead of a split. By the beginning of 2018, he had identified a core group of twenty would-be splitters, all of whom were added to a WhatsApp group called Mainstream, whose icon was a picture of an upper-case 'B' and a lower-case 'b' – for Plan B. The time had come to 'ask them to do something big'.

On Wednesday 17 January 2018, Shuker brought the group together at Fair Oak Farm. He had concluded that an overnight trip within easy reach of London, funded out of his own pocket and the office budgets of the invited MPs, was the only way that discussions over a split would be accelerated: 'Everyone's kind of dipping their hands in the blood to some degree. It's also a way to test people's appetite for doing something a bit more dramatic. The way I pitched that with people was: look, I can't tell you whether the Labour Party is "stay and fight-able", or whether we need a Plan B for a breakaway. But we at least need some smart people in the room to explore it.' That evening, they boarded a train at Southwark, bound for Sussex. Alongside Shuker and Angela Smith, Chris Leslie, Chuka Umunna and Mike Gapes were Liz Kendall, the Leicester West MP who had run against Corbyn for the leadership in 2015, Luciana Berger, the MP for Liverpool Wavertree, Ian Austin, the MP for Dudley South, Heidi Alexander, the MP for Lewisham East, Ann Coffey, the MP for Stockport, John Woodcock, the MP for Barrow, and Phil Wilson, who had succeeded Tony Blair as MP for Sedgefield. The logistics posed a challenge for the group. 'There were fifteen Labour MPs who hated Jeremy Corbyn piling onto the Tube under conditions of quite strict secrecy,' one recalls. 'What on earth were we going to say if we bumped into Sam Coates?' They were right to fear the mischievous *Times* deputy political editor – or any other lobby journalist in search of a scoop. By that point, the preliminary discussions over a split were an open secret in Westminster. But it would be months before their trips to Fair Oak Farm were rumbled.

Upon their arrival, the group gathered around a table in the farm-house kitchen to discuss – in many cases for the first time – their futures. Shuker drew on his experience as an evangelical pastor to guide the conversation. He asked the room a series of open questions: 'What are you carrying into this room with you? Is it distraction? Is it family? Do you feel concerned about being found out?' Shuker's chairmanship of the session also served a political purpose: several of the MPs in the room did not know each other well. Some were wary of the others' egos, particularly Umunna's and Leslie's. History loomed large too. Younger MPs like Shuker, Berger and Umunna were also intensely suspicious of Ian Austin, a political streetfighter who had cut his political teeth as a back-room operative for Gordon Brown. As an MP from the Black Country – a hotbed of factional warfare – he was close to another Brownite bruiser in Watson, who had deliberately not been informed of the discussions. One founder member explains now: 'If you feel like you're turning up to start Chuka's new party, or you're being controlled by Chris Leslie's revenge vendetta, it's an entirely different set up to a discussion led by a less high-profile honest broker trying to facilitate a discussion.'

Tentatively, the MPs began to vent. Angela Smith spoke through tears. After dinner prepared by a local chef, the group remained loyal to one aspect of Labour culture – excessive drinking. 'We're all members of the Labour Party,' one joked, 'so there was nothing else to do but drink.' Though not all were yet convinced that splitting from the Labour Party was the correct course of action, all agreed that things could not continue as they were. The trip concluded the following evening with an agreement to meet again in March to discuss the practicalities of a split in detail. Events in the intervening months would convince most of the group that they had taken the right course of action. But the Fair Oak Farm set were not the only group with a big decision to make that January.

*

As 2018 began, Corbyn and his aides found themselves under increasing pressure to take a concrete decision on Brexit – from within and without LOTO.

Labour had spent the previous year without a substantial position on the biggest issue facing the country. Its 2017 manifesto had pledged to end the free movement of people and leave both the EU's customs union and single market, but beyond that, precise details on what sort of trading relationship Corbyn would seek should he become prime minister had not been forthcoming. One LOTO official who worked on Brexit offered a straightforward explanation for the sluggish response: apathy. 'There wasn't a great opinion on the European Union. There was some in the office – quite prominent people were obviously quite anti the whole thing. But Jeremy doesn't get out of bed in the morning thinking about the customs union and single market.' Others thought Labour's failure to agree a detailed position was a product of presumptuousness. In the immediate aftermath of the 2017 election, Keir Starmer – who remained in post as the Shadow Brexit Secretary – had assumed that Theresa May, denuded of her parliamentary majority, would be forced 'to find a cross-party coalition' and seek a deal with Labour. Yet May did no such thing. Instead, buttressed by the DUP's ten MPs, she appeared on course to deliver a much harder Brexit than Labour would ideally have liked.

Besides, any deal May struck would almost certainly fail the party's six tests, devised by Starmer in early 2017 and signed off by Corbyn on 22 March that year – the same day that terrorist Khalid Masood had killed four pedestrians on Westminster Bridge with a rented car before fatally stabbing Keith Palmer, a police constable who had been guarding the entrance to Parliament. Starmer had put the finishing touches to the tests with Parliament in lockdown, and with fifty people taking refuge in his stuffy suite of offices in Portcullis House. They committed Labour to vote against any deal that failed to meet their criteria:

1. Does it ensure a strong and collaborative future relationship with the EU?
2. Does it deliver the 'exact same benefits' as we currently have as members of the single market and customs union?
3. Does it ensure the fair management of migration in the interests of the economy and communities?
4. Does it defend rights and protections and prevent a race to the bottom?
5. Does it protect national security and our capacity to tackle cross-border crime?
6. Does it deliver for all regions and nations of the UK?

Starmer's team saw the tests as 'a tool of opposition'. LOTO, meanwhile, believed – with some justification – that they had been designed to be failed, and later came to suspect that they had been devised with a view to forcing Labour into a Remain position further down the line. For Shadow Cabinet ministers in Leave constituencies, the tests spoke to everything that was wrong with the party's approach to the seats in its traditional heartlands. 'They were crap,' one reflected. 'They were unsellable in my constituency. We want the same rights in the labour market as we've got already? What the fuck does that mean? People voted against Europe because they think work is shit. LOTO didn't have the capacity to understand what was happening in held-back areas.' At one meeting of pro-Corbyn Shadow Cabinet ministers, Jon Trickett's frustration boiled over. 'These bloody tests, Jeremy,' he told Corbyn. 'Look at them. They're the status quo. We want everything we've got now! That's fine if you live in bloody Camden or Islington. There are 35,000 fucking graduates in your seat, and 9,000 in mine. This is a status quo test. We're not interested in the status quo. We want to get rid of it!'

By January 2018, John McDonnell and Diane Abbott had also reached the conclusion that the six tests alone would not suffice. Though they did not share Trickett's Eurosceptic analysis, both were concerned that Labour's gambit of strategic ambiguity could not hold. Labour appeared to have successfully dodged the issue of Brexit during the 2017 election with an anti-austerity campaign that focused on domestic issues, including social care. Whether or not Britain happened to be in the EU, questions of class and capital were far more significant. Milne openly dismissed those who prioritised Brexit as being caught in the crosshairs of 'culture wars'. Yet their analysis also overlooked an uncomfortable truth: that despite its manifesto position, Labour's surge in 2017 had been fuelled by Remain voters. And by 2018, the political reality had changed. May's Brexit talks with Brussels were in full swing. Labour needed to move. As two of Corbyn's oldest friends and political allies, McDonnell and Abbott had the authority to tell their leader to act – and did so.

Andrew Fisher, LOTO's head of policy, was dispatched to work up a plan. As the author of Labour's 2017 manifesto – a document that by now had the status of holy writ on the left – he was seen by some as the intellectual architect of Corbynism. Having worked as an aide to McDonnell during the Campaign Group's years in the wilderness, he had a deeper understanding of how Corbyn himself thought than most of his LOTO colleagues. The only person who knew the leader's mind better was Milne. But there was no way that any plan authored by Milne was likely to win the support of Shadow Cabinet ministers like Starmer, to say nothing of the PLP. 'Tactically, he [Milne] knew exactly where he wanted to go,' one aide to McDonnell recalls. 'His was basically the old Bennite position: socialism in one country.' On occasion, Milne had even been known to praise Tory Eurosceptics. Of Dan Hannan, the ultra-libertarian Conservative MEP, he remarked: 'This Dan guy is pretty good on Brexit, isn't he?'

Fisher, by contrast, had earned the trust of Team Starmer thanks to his intellect and work ethic – despite his history of salty Twitter attacks on the Corbynsceptics. As another senior aide to Corbyn explains: 'Fisher became much more significant because of the success of the manifesto, and also because Brexit became a much more detailed thing. It was less abstract. The question became: 'What kind of deal are you *actually* going to get?' Over the course of the next month, Fisher seized control of the pen and the process with uncharacteristic insistence, as was his right as head of policy. He drew up his answer, to which he gave a euphemistic title: 'Jeremy's plan'. In a major speech at Coventry University's National Transport Design Centre – a choice deliberately made to stress Labour's support for British manufacturing – Corbyn would commit his future government to leaving the single market and customs union. The plan would give Britain special access to European markets, whilst allowing the UK to pursue its own independent trade policy. The UK would no longer have to abide by Europe's state aid rules either – something which so-called Lexiteers had long felt would constrain a truly socialist government from nationalising the commanding heights of the economy if elected.

Though Milne was not directly involved in its initial drafting, its tone suggested otherwise – so much so that others in the room concluded that he may have written parts of it himself. Rather than taking a side in a fruitless Brexit culture war, Labour could offer a confident vision that shifted the debate onto territory on which it was most comfortable: jobs and public services. Milne had always been dismissive of those with an emotional attachment to the EU and its institutions. On one trip to Brussels, he jokingly derided EU officials as 'prophets of capital'. He had also been emboldened by internal polling which he claimed showed that most voters would prefer a deal that protected British jobs over one that preserved freedom of movement. In presenting its own distinct plan for Brexit, he hoped that Labour could move the conversation on. Keir Starmer, however, had other ideas.

On 12 February, Corbyn presented Fisher's plan to the weekly meeting of the Shadow Cabinet's Brexit subcommittee. Though it was nominally his own position, Corbyn was, according to several of those present, manifestly unfamiliar with the text – and read it off the page as though for the first time. Starmer, usually so straight-laced as to be almost robotic, reacted with uncharacteristic rage. 'It was basi-cally Boris Johnson's deal,' a source close to him reflects now. His anger was only exacerbated by the fact that he appeared not to have been given advance sight of Fisher's paper. A source said: 'They presented it at the meeting as "this is it", despite the fact that Keir hadn't seen it beforehand. It was so discourteous that they were just trying to bounce their version of Brexit through. He thought it was dishonourable and lacked principle. You just don't behave like that.' Starmer looked poised to quit. The prospect of his departure alarmed John McDonnell in particular. Though Starmer was no Corbynite, even the leader's closest allies admitted that he was second in import-ance only to Corbyn himself when it came to communicating the party's message on Brexit. Taken aback, McDonnell and Corbyn directed Fisher to return to the drawing board, and devise a plan that could win Starmer's support. In practice, that would mean a customs union at the very least. And this time, Starmer would be allowed input into the drafting process. He also took the opportunity to issue LOTO with an ultimatum. In future, only his advisers would be allowed into meetings of the subcommittee. The attempt to blindside Starmer had ended up increasing his influence – and losing what little trust he had in the leader's office.

Yet, unbeknown to Corbyn and McDonnell, Starmer had been given advance sight of the plan by Mark Simpson, who had slipped him a copy before the meeting. Though Simpson was employed by LOTO, he had forged a close working relationship with Team Starmer over summits at the Charing Cross branch of Nando's. In their company he found much clearer answers than among Corbyn's aides. On 18 February, he travelled to Leeds with Starmer for a meeting of Labour's National Policy Forum. There, in a hotel conference room, Starmer signed off on a new proposal: that the UK would join *a* customs union with Brussels after Brexit, rather than the existing EU customs union. Though he had hoped for a deal that also involved something akin to membership of the single market too, it was nonetheless a significant victory over Milne. The following day, the Brexit subcommittee met again. Unusually, they were joined by Tom Watson, who, though entitled to attend, did not do so regularly. The deputy leader had got wind of the previous week's bust-up and arrived with the expectation of fomenting more trouble for the Corbynites. He believed that the meeting would rubber-stamp a customs union, against Milne's wishes, and that sparks would fly. For Starmer, however, Watson's presence attested to all that was counterproductive about the deputy leader's modus operandi: he would only rear his head when an opportunity to cause drama arose. In any case, the deal with LOTO had already been brokered. Far from striking a killer blow, Watson's presence served only to highlight his own impotence, and lack of an overarching strategy to win policy battles. The lack of a row also offered a salutary lesson to those present: that, in Corbyn's Labour, real power was exercised not via formal structures such as the subcommittee, but via informal, ad hoc deals with Corbyn and his office.

But they were not yet home and dry. Starmer and his team feared a last-minute intervention from Milne, whom they suspected of wanting to excise any mention of a customs union from the speech entirely. Fisher was working under similar assumptions. So, to prevent Milne from interfering to change the content of the speech at the last minute, they made arrangements to practise the speech in secret, away from Westminster, in Corbyn's constituency office. If Milne was present, they suspected he might simply rewrite the speech to suit his own preferences. As Fisher and Corbyn gathered in Islington North on Saturday 24 February, just two days before the speech itself, only three people had seen its text in full: Fisher, John McDonnell, and 'Autocue Sue', the woman whose services the party retained to programme the leader's speeches to fit on autocues. Corbyn himself was unmoved by its contents. But nor was he ever enthused by the guts of Brexit policy.

Team Starmer, however, were facing questions of their own. The Sunday newspapers knew a major intervention from Corbyn was coming – and suspected they knew that it could involve a commitment to join a customs union. That Saturday, Tim Shipman, the *Sunday Times* political editor, phoned Ben Nunn, Starmer's head of communications, to smoke it out. 'I know what's in it,' he told Nunn, 'so just tell me.' Nunn could not oblige: neither he, Chris Ward, Starmer's chief of staff, nor Starmer himself knew whether Corbyn would allow a customs union to make the final draft of the speech. Ward, meanwhile, was badgering Milne and James Schneider, Milne's deputy, for a line to take on the following morning's *Andrew Marr Show*, on which Starmer was scheduled to appear. Schneider insisted that Ward did not need one: all that was necessary was to refer to the speech Corbyn was to give the following day. Starmer suspected a stitch-up, and took matters into his own hands. He told Marr that a customs union had 'unanimous support' within the Shadow Cabinet. In fact, only two of its members – Corbyn and McDonnell – even knew that it was about to become party policy. 'So it is a customs union,' Starmer said. 'But will it do the work of the current customs union? Yes, that's the intention.'

But far from enacting Milne's will, the speech that Fisher drew up and that Corbyn delivered in Coventry on 26 February was much closer to what the Shadow Brexit Secretary wanted than he and his team had expected. It certainly bore little resemblance to the lines Milne and Schneider briefed to the press in advance, which did not mention a customs union and instead talked up Labour's commitment to British manufacturing and the developing world. Instead, Corbyn promised that 'Labour would seek a final deal that gives full access to European markets and maintains the benefits of the single market and the customs union as the Brexit Secretary, David Davis, promised in the House of Commons ... We have long argued that a customs union is a viable option for the final deal. So Labour would seek to negotiate a new, comprehensive UK–EU customs union to ensure that there are no tariffs with Europe, and to help avoid any need for a hard border in Northern Ireland.' In a sop to Milne's preferred independent trade policy, he added: 'But we are also clear that the option of a new UK customs union with the EU would need to ensure the UK has a say in future trade deals.'

For hardened Remainers in the PLP, however, the policy was still not enough. After all, Britain would still be leaving the European Union. Nor did it satisfy the army of younger, pro-Remain Corbynistas at the Labour grass roots, who backed their leader to the hilt but believed Brexit to be an intrinsically racist and neoliberal project. Michael Chessum, the former treasurer of Momentum and national organiser of Another Europe Is Possible, the leftist pro-EU campaign, recalls: 'It was totally meaningless for our faction, and totally mean-ingless to most party members too. What people in the country really care about when it comes to EU membership, to the extent you can have a discussion beyond just staying in, is migrants' rights and free movement. They care about workers' rights, social protection and the environment. None of that's attached to the customs union – it's the least progressive aspect of the EU.' Team Starmer were nonetheless delighted. Nunn and Simpson, who stood at the back of the hall as Corbyn delivered his speech, quietly fist-pumped as they heard the words 'customs union'. European Commission officials were also pleased: though the British government did not have a workable plan for Brexit, the opposition finally seemed to be on the way there.

They had Fisher to thank. Though it was far from clear then, the most devout Corbynite in LOTO had struck a political marriage of convenience and taken the first steps on a journey that would eventually see him leave the orbit in which he had existed for a decade. Indeed, the episode had made clear that increasingly even the Corbynites were not united on what Corbynism should be. The following month, events in a sleepy Wiltshire cathedral city would throw those divides into even harsher relief.

*

Late on the afternoon of 4 March, the Southwestern Ambulance Service received a 999 call from a concerned pedestrian on Castle Street, in the centre of Salisbury. They had spotted a man in his 60s and a woman in her 30s apparently unconscious on a bench outside the city's Maltings shopping centre. The young woman's eyes were wide open, but her complexion was completely white. She was foaming at the mouth. By the time the two were transported separately to hospital, it was clear that the emergency services were dealing with an incident some way beyond their usual remit. When the pair were identified as former KGB spy turned MI6 informant Sergei Skripal, 66, and his daughter Yulia, 33, who had been visiting from Russia, their story assumed an international significance. The pair appeared to have been poisoned with a potent nerve agent and the hand of the Kremlin was immediately suspected.

Two days later, on 6 March, Boris Johnson, then Foreign Secretary, rose in the Commons just after 1 p.m. and appeared to blame Moscow for the incident. Though he claimed not to be 'pointing fingers', he made no secret of where the government believed responsibility lay. Threatening a boycott of that summer's football World Cup in Russia if the state's culpability could be proven, Johnson blasted the Kremlin

as 'in many respects a malign and disruptive force'. The Shadow
Cabinet appeared to agree with his analysis. Half an hour into
Johnson's statement, Diane Abbott echoed the broad thrust of his
words in a Sky News interview. 'We cannot allow London and the
Home Counties to become a kind of killing field for the Russian state,'
she said. Jeremy Corbyn would not find it so easy.

Over the coming days, it became clear that the evidence amassed
by police pointed squarely in the direction of Vladimir Putin. On 7
March, Marc Rowley, the Metropolitan Police's counter-terrorism
chief, confirmed that a nerve agent had been used to target the Skripals
specifically. But as consensus grew that Russia was indeed responsible,
the media's glare turned to LOTO as much as it did the Kremlin.
That, in no small part, was due to Corbyn and Milne. In his days as
a backbencher, Corbyn had frequently appeared as a studio guest on
RT, the UK outpost of Russian state broadcaster Russia Today. During
David Cameron's premiership, the satellite network had won a small
but loyal following on the British left for its willingness to challenge
the UK government's domestic policy, particularly on austerity. It
happily amplified the voices of politicians who were otherwise ignored
and impugned by the Fleet Street press and mainstream broadcasters,
including Corbyn, McDonnell and George Galloway, who presented
his own chat show on the channel. For that reason, it remained popular
with more hardline Corbynistas, and Shadow Cabinet ministers still
appeared on its programmes. Given the reputational difficulties that
inevitably beset any organisation linked to Vladimir Putin, RT also
paid handsomely for its guests' time – sometimes up to £750 per
appearance. Even in the days after the Skripals were poisoned, Labour
frontbenchers were still happily appearing on the network, even as it
dutifully broadcast the Kremlin's line on the poisonings. On 5 March,
Peter Dowd, the wisecracking MP for Bootle and McDonnell's Shadow
Chief Secretary to the Treasury, had appeared on the network. With
the Skripals still dominating the news agenda when the Shadow
Chancellor himself appeared on the *Andrew Marr Show* six days later,
McDonnell inevitably found himself questioned over RT. He was
categorical: he would be boycotting the channel. 'I think that's right
now and that's what I'll be doing,' he told Marr. 'Because what we're
seeing from Russia Today at times goes beyond objective journalism.'
Not only that, but he would tell Labour MPs to do so too. 'I've been

looking overnight at some of what's happening in terms of changes in coverage on Russian television in particular, and I think we have to step back now,' he said. Yet LOTO did not agree. Just hours after McDonnell's interview, he was upbraided in a terse statement from a spokesman for Corbyn – widely assumed to be Milne. There would be no boycott, they said: instead, they would be 'keeping the issue under review'. Uncharacteristically, Corbyn and his oldest ally were drawn into a very public war of words.

For Milne, just as for Corbyn, foreign policy was the real locomotive force of his leftism. Both understood their socialism in terms of global power, and who wielded it. In their view, the US was both a global hegemon and a force for ill in the world. They believed its imperialism ought to be resisted, and that resistance to its imperialism could almost always be justified. According to aides, Corbyn was wont to break off sensitive discussions at Shadow Cabinet to bend the ear of Emily Thornberry, the Shadow Foreign Secretary, 'about the Western Sahara or about West Papua. Self-determination for oppressed peoples was his driving thing when it came to foreign policy.' No matter how fractious relations between Thornberry's team and LOTO, Corbyn only ever wanted to talk about one thing. 'Emily always knew,' says a source close to Thornberry, 'that if she walked into the room, he would still want to ask: "Did you see that article by John Pilger about East Timor?"' Milne took a similarly Manichean view of geopolitics, and during his career at the *Guardian* had on several occasions ended up on the same side of the argument as Putin. In March 2014 he had defended Russia's annexation of the Ukrainian peninsula of Crimea, and praised its role as 'a limited counterweight to unilateral western power'. In October of that year, Milne – to the consternation of *Guardian* colleagues – attended the annual Valdai conference for Russia experts in the Black Sea resort of Sochi. There he chaired a lengthy question-and-answer session with Putin himself. Days later, he used his *Guardian* column to blame the crisis in Ukraine on the US's and EU's decision to support 'the violent overthrow of an elected if corrupt government'. Taken together with his back catalogue on Islamist terrorism – in the aftermath of the 11 September attacks, he had described the US as having reaped 'a dragon's teeth harvest' – it made him a convenient whipping boy for Fleet Street and Corbyn's internal opponents. Milne's views, particularly on Putin himself, were more nuanced than his critics were willing to give him credit for: most of his columns duly criticised the Russian government's authoritarianism, conservatism and abuses of human rights. Yet the eyes of the PLP were nonetheless trained on Milne as the story ground on. Though the Labour leader had a near-enough identical world view to Milne when it came to foreign affairs, it was his adviser who was widely – if inaccurately – considered the author of his foreign policy.

On 12 March 2018, Theresa May rose in the Commons to deliver a statement to MPs. In it, she revealed that samples of the substance given to the Skripals had been identified as a Soviet-era nerve agent, Novichok, that had originated in Russia. Corbyn did not respond in kind, or, indeed, blame the Kremlin for ordering the attack. Instead, he called for a 'a robust dialogue with Russia on all the issues currently dividing our countries, rather than simply cutting off contact and letting the tensions and divisions get worse and potentially even more dangerous'. Then, to the despair of MPs behind him, he turned his focus to the question of tax avoidance by the Conservative Party's Russian donors.

Worse was to come two days later, when May announced to the Commons that twenty-three Russian diplomats would be expelled from the UK over the attack. In reply, Corbyn again refused to condemn the Kremlin, instead criticising May's government for making cuts to the diplomatic service. He then asked a question that would enrage the PLP: had the government sent a sample of the nerve agent used on the Skripals to Moscow for testing?

Corbyn's intervention moved the PLP to the sort of open mutiny unseen since the early days of his leadership. Minutes after his speech, Pat McFadden, the MP for Wolverhampton South East, rose to address the chamber. A former Downing Street and enduring confidant to Tony Blair, McFadden – a thoughtful Scotsman and foreign-policy hawk – was a popular figure on Labour's back benches. He also had history with Corbyn. In January 2016, he had been sacked as Shadow Europe Minister for 'repeated acts of disloyalty' – namely a Prime Minister's Questions in the aftermath of the November 2015 terror attacks on Paris, in which he had asked David Cameron about the error of explaining 'terrorist acts as always being a response or reaction to what we in the west do'. It had been widely – and correctly – interpreted as an implicit attack on Corbyn. The leadership's decision to exact its revenge on McFadden for the comments had led to the resignations of three other Shadow ministers. Now, just over two years on, McFadden reprised one of his greatest hits. 'Responding with strength and resolve when your country is under threat is an essential component of political leadership,' he said. 'There is a Labour tradition that understands that and it has been understood by prime ministers of all parties who have stood at the Dispatch Box.' Ben Bradshaw, the arch-Remainer MP for Exeter who had served in the Blair and Brown governments, went even further, and explicitly praised May's response: 'Can I assure the prime minister that most of us on these benches fully support the measures that she has announced, and indeed some of us think they could have come a bit sooner.' On the airwaves, meanwhile, John Woodcock – a Fair Oak Farm attendee – went for Milne. He told the BBC: 'If you look at Jeremy Corbyn's long history on Russia and the views of key people around him, like Seumas Milne, they have been on the wrong side of very important arguments and disagreements that Russia has had with the UK over many years ... many of us thought Jeremy got the tone wrong.'

Corbynsceptics were not merely criticising the leadership for the sake of it. For many of them, a multilateral, Atlanticist foreign policy was at the very heart of their politics. As much as the left lionised Clement Attlee and Michael Foot, both had supported military action by their Conservative opposite numbers – during the Second World War and Falklands conflict respectively. That Corbyn was unwilling to even condemn what evidence suggested was an act of chemical warfare carried out on British soil in broad daylight by a hostile power was all the evidence that the PLP needed that their opposition to him was justified.

Following Corbyn's speech, Emily Thornberry told colleagues: 'Well, all right, we can talk our way around that.' Evidently, she held out hope that they would be able to salvage a more sensible position from the wreckage. But Milne soon went even further. After May and Corbyn had spoken, he addressed a huddle of journalists in the Commons Press Gallery. The briefing was routine: Milne, in his capacity as Corbyn's communications chief, took topical questions from reporters after every session of Prime Minister's Questions and any major statement by May to which Corbyn responded. The huddles were conducted under lobby terms – meaning Milne's answers could be used, but only on the condition that they were credited to a Labour spokesman rather than him personally. What he said on 14 March was deemed so remarkable by the parliamentary press corps that the Press Association, the most conservative of media outlets when it came to questions of style and convention, defied the unspoken rule and named Milne as the Labour spokesman in question. He had not only doubled down on Corbyn's suggestion that the government send a sample of Novichok to Russia for testing, but compared the incident to the build-up to the Iraq War. 'I think, obviously, the government has access to information and intelligence on this matter which others don't,' he said. 'However, also, there's a history in relation to WMD and intelligence which is problematic, to put it mildly. So I think the right approach is to seek the evidence; to follow international treaties, particularly in relation to prohibited chemical weapons, because this was a chemical weapons attack, carried out on British soil. There are procedures that need to be followed in relation to that.' The irony of the Press Association's decision was that Milne had considered giving statements as a named spokesman in the tradition of the White House at the beginning of his tenure. In the end LOTO had deferred to convention, on the grounds that MPs would have 'considered it an abomination'. Milne's judgement had been correct.

When news of the briefing reached John McDonnell's office, James Mills, the Shadow Chancellor's spin doctor, was so furious that he rose from his chair and kicked a bin across the room. Colleagues eyed him uneasily. 'That's fucking going to cost us the election!' Mills shouted. 'That's fucking stupid. Who the fuck does stuff like that?'

After Milne's address to the lobby, another Fair Oak Farm attendee broke cover to criticise LOTO's response. Chuka Umunna took to Twitter to condemn Milne by name. 'Mr Milne's comments do not represent the views of the majority of our voters, members or MPs,' he wrote. 'We'll get abuse for saying so but where British lives have been put at risk it is important to be clear about this.' Redcar MP Anna Turley, meanwhile, offered a barely veiled attack on Milne in the *Guardian* comment pages he had once edited. She wrote: 'There will be those who want to absolve Russia from any blame. Or those who want to construct elaborate conspiracy theories about the real culprits, and "false flags". Or those who hate the west, want to denigrate our security services and distrust the Tories. But now is not the time for such indulgences.' Every utterance from Corbyn's office seemed to strengthen the case for a split.

Andrew Murray describes the episode as a turning point: both for the Project's standing in the country, and LOTO's uneasy relationship with the PLP. He says now: 'The Salisbury attack is something we got wrong. When it happened, I thought, "Well, probably there's Russians behind this, because of the use of Novichok." I just thought it was Russian gangsters – some business interests, and so forth. I didn't think the Russian state was behind it. And we were wrong. The evidence that's emerged since is overwhelming. We misread that. I still think that the line Jeremy was trying to follow, which is, "Get the evidence first and then state sanctions, and so on, rather than the other way around," is a defensible position. You don't run into saying, "This is Putin's responsibility," when you haven't produced the evidence of it. In fact, this evidence has now been produced. Had we known then what we know now, we'd have taken a different view, I think. We just didn't think the Russian state would be so stupid and brazen as to do something like that – to carry out a poisoning attack on British soil. I know, given the Litvinenko precedent perhaps we should have done, but that never really got sorted out so clearly ... Up until then we'd still ha[d] a quiescent PLP. I wouldn't put it higher than that, but a quiescent PLP. We were doing all right in the polls. That started bringing all the doubts about Jeremy and LOTO to the surface again.'

The cry of despair from the PLP was the least of Corbyn's worries, however. Later that evening, Emily Thornberry was scheduled to give a lecture on human rights and Labour's foreign policy at an event hosted by Thompsons, the trade union law firm, at the Bloomsbury offices of the TUC. As the MP for Islington South and Finsbury since 2005, the Shadow Foreign Secretary knew and liked Corbyn personally: so much so that she had been among those to nominate him for the leadership in 2015. She had also served on his front bench for the duration of his tenure, which was more than could be said for her fellow travellers on the party's soft left. In one respect, Thornberry had much to thank Corbyn for. She had spent the year before his leadership in political purgatory, after tweeting a picture of a terraced home festooned in St George's crosses with a white van outside while campaigning ahead of a by-election in Rochester, Kent. The post was widely criticised as an act of snobbery: Thornberry was sacked from

Ed Miliband's Shadow Cabinet. Corbyn had not only invited her back into the fold, but in June 2016 had promoted her to shadow one of the most coveted offices of state.

Yet there was a limit to just how loyally she was prepared to serve. She opened her speech with a set of ad-libbed remarks that quite deliberately broke ranks with Corbyn. In the waspish tone for which she was renowned, Thornberry said: 'What could better sum up the challenge we face in protecting human rights and the rule of law around the world than the idea that a foreign state should launch an attack on British soil using an internationally banned nerve agent?' There was, she said, 'prima facie evidence' that Russia had been responsible. If Thornberry's intended target was not obvious enough already, then the speech's prompt appearance in both the next day's *Sun* and on PoliticsHome – the parish noticeboard for Corbynsceptics at Westminster – proved it beyond reasonable doubt.

The following morning, she was joined on the barricades by Nia Griffith, the Shadow Defence Secretary. Though an obvious misfit in the Shadow Cabinet, she had been one of the few MPs with sufficient front-bench experience who were willing to serve. Unlike Corbyn, she believed in retaining the UK's independent nuclear deterrent – an awakening she experienced only after her ascension. She saw it as her duty to undermine the leadership where necessary. In a meeting at the Estonian embassy soon after Griffith's appointment, Tiina Intelmann, the Baltic state's ambassador to the UK, expressed her alarm to the Shadow Defence Secretary at Milne's presence in LOTO and previous statements on Russia. Griffith wasted no time in dismissing Corbyn's chief adviser's views out of hand. The distrust was mutual. To LOTO she was 'NATO Nia' or 'Nukin' Nia'. Griffith's belief in multilateralism was so unstinting that she and her aides took it as a compliment.

She lived up to her reputation on the morning of 15 March, the day after Thornberry had fired her warning shot at LOTO at the TUC. First, in an interview with the *Daily Mirror* conducted just hours after Corbyn refused to blame Russia for the attack on the Skripals, she named the Kremlin as the culprits. Without LOTO's blessing, she also appeared to commit Labour to supporting Theresa May's policy of diplomatic expulsions. It had been intended as a valedictory. Before sitting down with the *Mirror* she had asked her team: 'Right, shall I resign now, or *after* I've given this interview?' She planned to quit and take two of her three Shadow ministers with her (the exception was Fabian Hamilton, the CND lifer appointed by Corbyn to serve as Shadow Minister for Peace). Griffith resolved to stay, but not to toe the line. She would chart her own course on defence policy, and LOTO could sack her if they wanted. She initiated the new approach when she told the *Mirror*: 'The message that the prime minister has conveyed to us is that this is an act of aggression. And that is why we are fully supporting the expulsion of twenty-three diplomats.' Unlike Thornberry, Griffith stressed that she was not merely freelancing, but setting out official Labour policy. Later that morning, she told the *Today* programme that Labour 'fully accepts that Russia is responsible'.

In a column for that morning's *Guardian*, Corbyn had warned of a 'McCarthyite intolerance of dissent' from the accepted narrative that the Kremlin was to blame. By that afternoon, however, he had been forced to change tune. He told the BBC: 'The evidence points towards Russia.' It was not the same line that Thornberry and Griffith had taken – but it was far closer to it than Corbyn and Milne would have liked. Support for the leadership was hard to come by. Of the PLP, only Chris Williamson – himself a regular on RT – was moved to defend Corbyn publicly. He blamed the furore on a 'tiny minority of irrelevant malcontents … fighting a proxy war'.

With Corbyn having been bounced into an unedifying climbdown, his enforcers within LOTO sought to reassert their authority. Amy Jackson, who had succeeded Katy Clark as Corbyn's political secretary and right-hand woman, contacted both Griffith and Thornberry. She asked Griffith if she was planning to resign – so Jackson could plan accordingly if so. Thornberry was ordered to report to the leader's office on the following Monday, 19 March, for a meeting of what Shadow Cabinet ministers referred to as 'the Star Chamber' – or, put more plainly, a ritual bollocking by Corbyn's most senior aides. Before either Griffith or Thornberry could face LOTO's summary justice, however, John McDonnell took to the airwaves himself, telling ITV's Robert Peston that he agreed with the rebels in the Shadow Cabinet. Surreally, he also went as far as to endorse Theresa May's handling of the episode. 'I agree completely with the prime minister,' he told Peston. His public U-turn gazumped the Star Chamber, who cancelled their meeting with Griffith. Off the hook, Thornberry took the opportunity to crow. She asked Jackson: 'Will John be coming to the meeting as well?'

Why did McDonnell, Corbyn's closest ideological ally and oldest political friend, defy him twice over? Their public rift over the Skripal case served to illustrate the defining difference between the two. McDonnell obsessed over the pursuit of power – for without it, Labour could never enact the genuinely radical socialist programme he had spent his career fighting for. Corbyn, on the other hand, prioritised principle, especially when it came to foreign policy, a subject on which he found it difficult to either compromise or say things he did not believe. McDonnell had never shared his comrade's passion for international affairs – and nor was he willing to let it derail the best chance the Labour left would ever have of forming a government on its own terms. He had already moderated his public persona in pursuit of his goal. The menacing McDonnell of old had been replaced by a twinkly, avuncular bank manager who imparted bad news in sorrow, and never with the anger that had once been his stock in trade. Isabel Hardman, the *Spectator*'s assistant editor, had put it best when she described the Shadow Chancellor's late style as akin to 'a man giving the eulogy at the funeral of a family pet'. In private, however, he had been livid at the whole affair. After James Mills's own outburst in the wake of Milne's lobby briefing, Mills called his boss to impart the bad news. Summoned to McDonnell's office, he arrived to find the Shadow Chancellor in a state of extreme agitation. McDonnell blamed Milne. He feared that LOTO and its political idiosyncrasies risked derailing the Project altogether, and resolved to take decisive action. As one aide to the Shadow Chancellor recalls: 'John was really worried, and wanted an alternative approach. He believed that, in a time of national crisis, regardless of anything, you have to roll behind the people defending the country.' With Corbyn and LOTO unwilling and unable to incur the political pain of compromise, that is precisely what he then did.

On 26 March, Corbyn and May faced off in the Commons for another debate on national security and Russia. The prime minister used her statement to confirm that both of the Skripals were critically ill, and went as far as to warn that neither might fully recover. She stressed that there was no longer any plausible alternative to the Russian state being responsible. Corbyn told the Commons that the

Kremlin was either directly or indirectly responsible, yet did not go as far as to say that Putin directly ordered the attack. Question after question rained down from the Conservative benches. Was the Russian government to blame? Irritable, Corbyn equivocated. His answers were met with jeers from all parties. So overpowering was the disgust of the Labour benches that Eleanor Laing, overseeing proceedings as Deputy Speaker, was forced to intervene: 'We can't have both sides of the House shouting at the leader of the opposition!' What the PLP did not know was that the speech had been written by one of their own in Damian McBride, the former spin doctor to Gordon Brown reborn as Emily Thornberry's chief adviser. Once such a vicious practitioner of spin against his own party as to be feral, McBride had mellowed in middle age. While LOTO did not trust him, they had a begrudging respect for his experience at the top of government.

The previous week, McBride had composed the words that Corbyn eventually spoke, for Thornberry had originally been supposed to front the debate for Labour. At the eleventh hour, however, Downing Street had subbed in May, forcing Corbyn to do so himself – such were the electoral profits to be gained in forcing him to face hostile questioning on national security. While LOTO happily took the speech off McBride's hands, there was a limit to the case they were willing to make. Andrew Fisher, the primary author of most of Corbyn's Commons speeches, and Milne, who had identical views on foreign policy to the leader, together sought to drastically dilute the tone. It was gutted of any statements levelling blame at Russia, support for NATO, or anything else that Corbyn might regard as unduly imperialist in its tone. Where Thornberry would have labelled Russia 'guilty as charged', Corbyn said: 'There is clear evidence that the Russian state has a case to answer, and it has failed to do so.' A section on the importance of seeking cross-party consensus on Britain's response – and committing Labour to supporting the government – was deleted entirely. Thornberry's full-throated endorsement of the government's reprisals against the Kremlin was replaced with the more restrained: 'We have supported actions taken.' A call for a European Court of Human Rights 'case against Russia' turned into a more general inquiry about whether the government would consider 'initiating or supporting' a wider examination of extraterritorial violations of human rights.

More striking still was the removal of all criticism of Russia's invasion of Crimea. McBride's original draft read: 'We will stand with them, as we did over Ukraine. To maximise the power of our collective action. And our collective sanctions against Russian aggression. And that our commitment to that collective action will not be diminished by Brexit.' It became: 'Now more than ever, it is vital that we stress to our European counterparts that their support is important in the wake of the Salisbury attack, that we wish to work with them to maximise the power of collective sanctions against violations of international law – whether from Russia or any other state – and that our commitment to such collective action will not be diminished by Brexit.' In an email to McBride, Fisher had set out his reasoning for disputing the point: 'I'm not sure the solidarity with Ukraine part is quite balanced enough – there's every reason to be wary of the Ukrainian government and the role some domestic forces played in the crisis – while not minimising Russian aggression?' Milne also chimed in, telling McBride that the language on Ukraine went 'well beyond our positions' and would 'exacerbate the current Shadow Cabinet split stories'. In a later passage, Fisher and Milne removed a commitment to NATO's Article 5 – that an attack on one member be taken as an attack on all. Instead Corbyn said: 'It is vital that the UK and all other NATO members make it clear to all our allies in the Baltic States and elsewhere that we want to protect peace and security on the borders, without ramping up tensions unnecessarily.' It was precisely the sort of equivocal language that had so worried the Estonian ambassador. Fisher had in one case beefed up McBride's language – replacing a reference to 'working with' Russia to the more detached 'engage'. He wrote in an email: 'I wonder if "work with Putin" sounds a bit too cosy at the moment – will [sic] malicious press headline with "We must work with Putin say Labour".' Yet his political intuition had otherwise failed him. Corbyn was again pilloried both for the restrained tone and for hedging the answer to the question of who was to blame.

By then the Corbynsceptics had met at Fair Oak Farm for a second time, on 21 March, a week to the day after Milne's disastrous lobby briefing. The Skripal episode ensured the case for a split now had 'a third leg' – the group's objections to Corbynite foreign policy. The nature of their discussions had stepped up a gear too. As the group dined on a Nigel Slater recipe of smoked mackerel, panzanella salad and chicken supreme cooked by Shuker they moved on from the why of leaving the Labour Party to the what and how.

Though the MPs had all ended up in the same place, each had their own reasons for contemplating a breach with their party. For the likes of Heidi Alexander and Liz Kendall, the point of the exercise was to work out how best they might make the argument for a centrist politics that was no longer welcome in the Labour Party. For Ian Austin and Mike Gapes, the Skripal incident had crystallised the extent to which a government led by Corbyn and Milne posed an existential threat to western security. For Luciana Berger – Labour's best-known Jewish MP – it was no longer morally defensible to prop up a party that had become a happy home for anti-Semites. But diffuse though they were, Shuker believed that each argument led inexorably to the same conclusion: 'We've just got to get out.'

The most committed around the table had also come to realise that LOTO were not for turning on the bigger question of a second referendum – the outcome many Corbynsceptics held out hope for. On the evening of 23 March, Owen Smith had been sacked as Shadow Northern Ireland Secretary after writing a *Guardian* column in which he called for the final Brexit deal to be put to a public vote. Upon his appointment in June 2017, Smith had promised to toe the party line on Brexit 'in his own way'. Now LOTO, if not Corbyn, had made its red line clear: the leader only mustered up the courage to call Smith to inform him of his sacking as a press release made its way to journalists' inboxes, so difficult did he find confrontation.

As the night wore on and the MPs polished off a cheeseboard and drained several bottles of Tesco Finest Argentinian Malbec, gin and prosecco, they sketched out how they might craft 'a single narrative, easy to explain, as to why we were going, because we needed to start making that argument before we went'. They also began to explore what the practicalities of a split might look like. Who would fund it? Would they quit and sit as independents, or start a new party altogether? When would they leave?

5

Labour Lives

Sadiq Khan was no Corbynite, but by the end of 2017 he was speaking like a true believer. Nowhere in the country had Labour had as good a night that June as in London. It had unexpectedly won Battersea from the Conservatives and slashed their majorities everywhere else. MPs in the capital had put Khan, rather than Corbyn, on their election leaflets: he was, after all, one of the few election winners left in the Labour Party. But the mayor had the good sense to be magnanimous.

Khan's speech to London Labour's annual conference on 25 November that year was one such occasion. He not only took the opportunity to lavish praise on Corbyn, but to make him a hostage to fortune. Elections to all thirty-two of London's councils were due the following May. Rather than hedge his bets, Khan set the bar high. 'There is now no corner of London where Labour can't win,' he said. 'With enough hard work, we can challenge the Tories even in their crown jewels of Wandsworth and Barnet.'

It was a lofty ambition. Both councils had been laboratories for Thatcherism, and had proved impervious to Labour even in Tony Blair's pomp. But in the wake of 2017, their voters looked more receptive to Corbyn than ever before. All three boroughs had voted to Remain and were home to tens of thousands of EU nationals. LOTO's number-crunchers were less convinced. 'It was the least helpful thing in the world for anybody to have said,' one recalls now.

Khan was not alone in his optimism. In the months before polling day, Momentum raised the bar even further. Not only did they believe that Corbyn could deliver historic victories in Wandsworth and Barnet, but in Westminster too. Throngs of activists corralled by Momentum descended on streets that had never elected a Labour councillor – still less a majority of them.

In the early hours of 4 May 2018, the prophesied gains in London failed to materialise: not one of Barnet, Wandsworth or Westminster fell. The picture was even bleaker outside of London. After 2017, Seumas Milne had told the NEC that Labour had to consolidate its general election vote – whilst making inroads into the places they had performed most badly: among voters in the English north and Midlands, among the elderly, and in Scotland. The week before the poll, Southside officials briefed *The Times* that the real test of Labour's success would be its performance in what was then not yet called the Red Wall: the councils that overlapped with small-town seats in the north and Midlands that Labour had held since 1997 or longer.

On all counts they failed. Despite the pre-poll excitement and gains in Trafford and Plymouth, they ended the night in control of as many councils as before. More ominously, both Derby and Nuneaton and Bedworth – home to precisely the Midlands marginals Corbyn would need to hold and gain at an election – stayed blue.

Historically, opposition parties tend to win local elections in the middle of any government's term in office – let alone one punctuated by the calamities that had befallen May. In late April, only a matter of days before the elections, the Home Secretary, Amber Rudd, had also been forced to resign over the Windrush scandal, in which dozens of elderly Commonwealth migrants – many of them born in Britain or residents for most of their lives – had been wrongly deported. But far from taking flight in the country, Corbynism appeared to have stalled.

On the morning of 4 May, the prime minister rocked up in Wandsworth. Unlike Corbyn, May had lost several councils – albeit far fewer than expected – but nonetheless struck a triumphant tone. 'Labour thought they could take control, this was one of their top targets and they threw everything at it, but they failed,' she crowed.

Fleet Street shared the prime minister's assessment. Corbyn, they concluded, had flunked his first major test of public opinion since the 2017 general election. LOTO believed they had good reason to disagree. Some blamed Khan for raising expectations. 'We were slightly fucked in the run-up,' one official said. 'We suffered in London because the benchmark had been raised so high.' John McDonnell also bemoaned the 'hype' that had been allowed to build up in the weeks before polling day. It was a view shared by Corbyn's aides who subsequently crunched the numbers and concluded that they had not lost ground since 2017. One recalled: 'The locals were framed in the context of Windrush starting to break and the Salisbury attack. But both of those things at that stage seemed to have been priced into people's views of the political parties.'

LOTO tended not to worry themselves with the opinions of what Seumas Milne liked to call the 'hyena class' of the mainstream media. Nonetheless, the narrative was in danger of slipping from their grasp. Labour's claim to be a government-in-waiting was looking rather less convincing than it once had. That summer his team would make a bold bid to recapture the spirit of 2017.

★

Most people blame Ian Lavery for Labour Live. In December 2017, six months after Corbyn had been feted at Glastonbury, officials from the leader's office and Southside met in the LOTO boardroom in Norman Shaw South. There was only one item on the agenda. Lavery was still flush from the success of the general election campaign that he had overseen, and wanted to maintain its energy. He told the room that Labour needed to put on a show for its activists the following summer, be it a festival of political education or a concert. There were only three criteria. Excitedly, he told colleagues: 'We wanna do something that's full of energy, that's exciting, and big!'

Lavery cast his mind back to June for inspiration. On the eve of polling day, Corbyn had addressed six mass rallies across the country simultaneously via a satellite link. At each, he had shared a bill with some of Labour's many celebrity supporters. In Birmingham, Steve Coogan had quoted Shelley before welcoming Corbyn to the stage. In Warrington, indie also-rans Reverend and the Makers and the actress Maxine Peake had teed up Rebecca Long-Bailey. John McDonnell and Ben Elton shared a stage in Croydon.

They were precisely the sort of events that set Labour's campaign apart from Theresa May's. Faced with evidence of Corbyn's ability to pull in a big crowd, his internal opponents bitterly quoted the late MP John Golding, the self-anointed 'Hammer of the Left'. Ahead of Michael Foot's disastrous showing at the 1983 election, he confronted his leader with opinion polls that showed Labour on course for a heavy defeat. 'You're wrong!' Foot told Golding. 'There were one thousand people at my meeting last night, and they all cheered.' Corbynsceptics still quoted Golding's reply: 'There were 122,000 people outside who think you're crackers.'

Yet 2017 had been different. LOTO had concluded that voters did not think Corbyn crackers. Many of them even appeared to think he was *cool*, something that could not be said for Theresa May. Meanwhile, 2018 would be the first summer Corbyn had enjoyed since becoming leader on his own terms: 2016 had seen a leadership challenge and 2017 a general election. What better way to celebrate – and to thank the foot soldiers who had made the result possible – than for Labour to host a festival of its own?

So began the journey to Labour Live – which the press would soon be calling JezFest – a one-day festival for members to be held in North London in June 2018. It would later be framed in the media as a Corbyn vanity project, but the leader – whose aversion to partying was such that aides feared coming into work hungover – was not involved. Though the project was Lavery's baby, the job of realising his vision was delegated to two officials: LOTO's Marsha-Jane Thompson, a Momentum activist who had arranged merchandise for McDonnell's leadership campaign in 2007 and then Corbyn's eight years later, and Carol Linforth, Southside's head of events and a veteran of the Blair and Brown years.

With a date pencilled in for June, the big task before them was assembling a line-up capable of convincing members who could otherwise see Corbyn deliver a stump speech for free at a rally to travel to North London and pay for the privilege. Thompson, like other supporters of the project within LOTO, assumed it would be relatively easy. After all, a constellation of cultural luminaries had come out for Corbyn over the course of the general election campaign, and the real Glastonbury was on one of its fallow years. One official who worked on the festival recalled: 'In 2017, we had so many celebrities endorsing Jeremy – I think people just thought that would translate into them wanting to perform for free.' Thompson set her sights high – perhaps too high. At the top of her wish list were Ed Sheeran and Stormzy, the biggest names to have publicly backed Labour in 2017. Both declined. Stormzy, despite being the most vocal Corbyn supporter in pop, was not even asked to play until after a date for the festival had already been announced. In February, the plan for the festival was leaked to the *Sun* – a briefing that bore all the hallmarks of Southside sabotage. 'It got out super-early,' one LOTO official complained. The leak denied them the opportunity to cancel quietly and gracefully.

After Stormzy and Sheeran said no, Thompson looked instead to another decade, and invested what remained of her hopes in UB40. The reggae legends had supported Corbyn's 2016 leadership campaign and Thompson hoped they might bail him out again. Younger LOTO staff assigned to work alongside her were bewildered by her obsession with what they derisively referred to as a 'shit old-people band'. Eventually a junior leader's office staffer entrusted with minuting the meetings snapped. They told Thompson: 'Fucking let UB40 go! Nobody fucking likes UB40!' For the millennials who were the backbone of LOTO's administrative operation, Thompson's fixation was evidence that Labour Live was doomed to fail. 'We were dealing with people who were not that into popular music,' said one. Ticket prices were also the subject of torturous debate. Members were eventually asked to pay £35 a head, but not before an extended negotiation over the course of several meetings. Together with the wrangling over the line-up, it delayed the big reveal. It was not until 18 March that the party confirmed it would be hosting Labour Live at White Hart Lane Park, in the Tottenham constituency adjacent to Corbyn's Islington North seat – and even then the biggest name on the bill was the leader himself.

As was so often the case during a crisis, Karie Murphy then took charge. Conscious that details of the festival's planning – or lack thereof – were regularly appearing in the press, she banned phones from the Thursday meeting. There were two problems: the line-up – and the number of people buying tickets. By mid-May, Labour Live's headline act was still slated to be the Magic Numbers, a half-forgotten indie band whose only top-ten single had come under Tony Blair's premiership. The *New Statesman* put it bluntly on 15 May, with a blog that asked: 'Why is the line-up at Labour's musical festival so bad?' Nor were they anywhere close to a full house. Only 1,800 tickets had been sold, despite the venue's capacity of 20,000. Corbyn's star power appeared to have waned precipitously since the real Glastonbury. In an email sent to the PLP the same day, MPs were urged to promote the festival to their members: few bothered. It was beginning to look as if only divine intervention could save the project from humiliation.

Two weeks later help nonetheless came in the form of Len McCluskey. On 29 May, Unite announced that it would buy 1,000 tickets – notionally to distribute among their members. In reality, it was a bailout. It did ensure more punters turned up, though it came too late to spare LOTO's blushes. In the weeks leading up to the festival on 16 June, Labour Live's teething troubles were so widely known that the comedian Tracey Ullman – who did an uncanny impersonation of Corbyn – was riffing on them weekly in her prime-time BBC One sketch show. They also inspired a stand-up routine from Theresa May. 'I've heard the Labour leader is trying to organise a music festival,' she said, to peals of laughter during Prime Minister's Questions. 'I'll pass over the fact it will have a solidarity tent which will have no MPs in it. I don't know if all members are aware of the headline act – the Shadow Chancellor and the Magic Numbers – that just about sums them up!' Unite's intervention could not and did not prevent the festival from becoming a laughing stock in Westminster and beyond – but that was not the point.

On Saturday 16 June, the reality of the festival was more forgiving. Acts dealt the bum hand of playing early, like original Sex Pistols bassist Glen Matlock and Levi Roots, the inventor of Reggae Reggae Sauce, played to crowds that in places were only two deep. For long stretches of the afternoon it was Unite's ice-cream van, whose chimes played 'The Red Flag' and whose Mr Whippy machine was manned by McCluskey himself, which drew the biggest crowd. But LOTO were relieved: they had managed to shift 13,000 of the 20,000 tickets thanks to discounts and freebies. The day itself passed largely without incident, though not for want of trying from would-be mischief makers. Sophie Nazemi, a junior press officer, was given the job of man-marking Ross Kempsell, a reporter from the muckraking Guido Fawkes blog who had come armed with a camera and a simple brief: to present the event in the most embarrassing light possible.

As Corbyn strode onto the stage in a natty outfit of cream chinos and grey short-sleeved shirt, and began a reprisal of his customary homily about decency in politics, pro-Remain activists in the ground unveiled a banner and began chanting the message it carried: 'STOP BACKING BREXIT'. Their protest was ostensibly a response to

Corbyn's decision the previous week to whip his MPs against an amendment to Brexit legislation that would have kept the UK inside the EU single market, but it also threw a bigger problem into harsh relief. Europe was driving a wedge between the leadership and a portion of its supporters at the grass roots, a majority of whom voted to Remain. Perturbed, Corbyn stopped speaking while the anti-Brexit picket was ejected from the crowd. Later, Corbyn's staff celebrated a disaster-free day over free beers in a tent hosted by the Communication Workers Union. But the signs were unmistakeable: Brexit was beginning to isolate some of the Project's most loyal supporters.

*

Two days before JezFest, a routine by-election in Lewisham East had also raised the alarm. On 8 May, its MP Heidi Alexander, the first Shadow Cabinet minister to quit in the 2016 coup, had resigned her seat to take up a post as one of Khan's deputy mayors at London's City Hall. For LOTO it was a free hit. The Labour majority in Lewisham East might as well have been weighed rather than counted. Replacing Alexander, a Fair Oak Farmer, with a true believer would mean a lifelong indenture for a Corbynite.

But Corbynsceptic organisers also sensed opportunity. Alexander's resignation would indeed offer the left an opportunity to remodel the PLP in its own image. But the resistance to the Project believed they might ensure that it was not taken. Progress and Labour First, the last bastions of Blairism and Brownism at the grass roots, believed that the leadership had mistaken a pro-Corbyn party membership for an ideologically Corbynite one. While the grass roots had voted overwhelmingly for Corbyn twice, their belief in the Project was not unshakeable or unconditional. Only in two leadership elections conducted in uniquely rancorous circumstances – the aftermath of the 2015 election loss, the outset of five more years of Tory austerity, and in the wake of the coup – had he inspired members. Most of his electors, organisers on the right calculated, did not care for the hard grind of factional politics at the level of the Constituency Labour Party – and even if they did, their priorities would not necessarily align with the ideological hang-ups of the leadership. Just as Corbyn had driven a wedge between members and the party establishment with his unapologetic leftism in 2015 and 2016, the resistance now hoped to use Brexit to do the same.

Plenty on the left were alive to the risk. Richard Burgon, Corbyn's Shadow Justice Secretary, says now: 'None of us ever thought that the lion's share of Labour Party members were ideologically Bennite. Jeremy became leader when we'd just lost a general election where we'd promised austerity-lite and when the party had backed abstaining on the horrendous Welfare Bill. I know plenty of Labour members who don't even consider themselves on the left of the party at all, who back in 2015 voted for Jeremy to be Labour leader. People from a range of political views in the party wanted change. They wanted the party to be anti-austerity and principled. They wanted the party to reject illegal wars and drop the politics that led to the "Controls on Immigration" mugs. Jeremy becoming leader was a product of a particular set of historical circumstances and he and we recognised that.' But when it came to select a candidate to succeed Alexander, not all of Burgon's comrades did.

The NEC moved quickly to fix a timetable for Alexander's replacement that would favour candidates of the left, who would find funds and support altogether easier to raise than the Corbynsceptics. A candidate would be selected in just ten days – and with the Corbynite NEC handed responsibility over the local party, it seemed that the left would get its way whatever the outcome. An all-BAME woman shortlist was imposed so as to winnow the field to exclude the overwhelmingly white, Corbynsceptic men who dominated politics locally. Progress and Labour First cried stitch-up. Yet they could not agree on a candidate. Splittism, the left's congenital defect, took over. Momentum threw its weight behind Sakina Sheikh, a local councillor. She had announced her candidacy within an hour of Alexander announcing her resignation and immediately launched the sort of polished social media blitz that was the millennial left's specialty. LOTO and Unite, the two other power brokers of the Corbynite left, did not follow, however. Instead they rowed in behind Claudia Webbe, a former aide to Ken Livingstone and NEC member who applied for nearly every vacant candidacy as one of the Labour left's perennial candidates. John McDonnell, meanwhile, kept his options open. He flirted publicly with backing either Sheikh or 'Lady' Phyll Opoku-Gyimah, a left LGBT activist. The Project's constituent parts were moving in different directions. But, faced with toothless internal opposition, it did not seem to matter that much.

Complication came on 13 May, the eve of nominations closing. Two days earlier the Guido Fawkes website, which paid closer attention to the social media feeds of Labour candidates than the activists themselves, uncovered a Facebook post in which Opoku-Gyimah had compared Israel to the Nazis on Holocaust Memorial Day 2017. She subsequently withdrew, which forced the NEC to extend the selection process by another three days. It was then that Matt Pound, Labour First's bearded full-time organiser, spied opportunity – and a Trojan Horse for Corbynscepticism in Janet Daby, the deputy mayor of Lewisham who had also thrown her hat into the selection ring to little fanfare.

Daby, on paper, was a left candidate. She had voted for Corbyn twice. Yet still she found herself overlooked in the selection in favour of the younger Sheikh, whom she had mentored. Part of the problem was her unabashed opposition to Brexit. She had campaigned not for the LOTO line but against leaving the single market and customs union. It was as close to a continuity Remain position as the circumstances allowed and unquestionably a promise to defy Labour policy on the biggest issue of the day for the duration of her time in Parliament. Her independence of mind did not endear her to the left. But to Pound and the resistance on the right, Daby's iconoclasm on Brexit was not a weakness but her biggest asset. Despite Progress telling him that they had things under control, Pound turned up in Lewisham without warning and told Daby he would take control of her campaign. The rearguard had begun. Daby squeaked onto the shortlist.

The campaign Pound then ran for her relied on shoe-leather campaigning. He corralled forty activists into a church hall and instructed them to proselytise Daby's pro-Corbyn but anti-Brexit message to the membership. Momentum, meanwhile, pulled in stars of the left to campaign for Sheikh. Its campaign machine was formidable. Owen Jones and other prominent leftists turned out to campaign for her. On social media her presence was near-ubiquitous. Yet Daby's canvassers found overwhelming support for their candidate. Said one: 'We would be 2–1 ahead and I thought my numbers are fucked up, I was literally losing my mind being like, oh, I've fucked it up because clearly those numbers aren't right.' Yet they were. Come the selection meeting on Saturday 19 May, Daby beat Sheikh overwhelmingly.

To the left, Daby's pedigree as a two-time Corbyn voter was a sign that they had lost the battle but won the war: even the Corbynsceptics were now having to coalesce around supporters of the leadership. But to the right it proved something important. Said one Corbynsceptic organiser: 'That was the point at which I realised: oh shit. These people are beatable. It's all a lie.' And even while Daby breezed home to a predictable and comfortable victory in the by-election, the seat saw a substantial swing to the Liberal Democrats, powered by disenchantment over Labour's failure to back Remain. Yet Brexit had already wrought more significant change in British politics in disrupting the Corbynite succession. In one short week, the Project's soft underbelly had been exposed in Lewisham and at Labour Live. The Corbynsceptics, meanwhile, had written the playbook with which they would eventually kill it.

6

For the Many, Not the Jew

On 2 October 2012, Mear One, a street artist from Los Angeles, had taken to Facebook to vent about Tower Hamlets Council. Its officials had threatened to paint over his latest work – a mural of lurid conspiratorial imagery criticising the so-called New World Order. Posting an image of the artwork to his followers, he wrote: 'Tomorrow they want to buff my mural Freedom of Expression. London Calling, Public art.' In the comments below, Jeremy Corbyn, then still a backbencher, had offered his support. 'Why? You are in good company,' he wrote. 'Rockerfeller [sic] destroyed Diego Viera's [sic] mural because it includes a picture of Lenin.' The answer to Corbyn's question was immediately obvious. Mear One's mural depicted hook-nosed bankers playing Monopoly on the backs of the poor. By his own admission, they included Lord Rothschild and Paul Warburg, both of them Jews. It was, by any reasonable definition, anti-Semitic.

Questionable rhetoric and overt hatred towards Jews had always found a happy home on the outermost edges of the organised left, where anti-imperialism often meets conspiracy. Under Corbyn's leadership, Labour's membership had swollen to half a million – and those fringes were subsumed into the party's official structures. It was often said that Labour's transformation into a mass movement under Corbyn had transformed its finances and campaigning power. But the consequences of an influx of members whose prejudices for so long went unchecked in little-read pamphlets and poorly attended meetings were just as significant.

Half a year after becoming leader, Corbyn sought to acknowledge the problem by commissioning Shami Chakrabarti, the esteemed human rights activist and barrister, to conduct an independent review of the party's handling of accusations of anti-Semitism after complaints from Jewish members. LOTO knew that to be seen as tolerant to any form of racism was to contradict the promise Corbyn had made upon his first election as leader in 2015. 'Last summer, I called for a kinder, gentler politics,' he said in June 2016 on publication of Chakrabarti's report, which, to the consternation of the Jewish community, concluded that anti-Semitism was not endemic within the Labour Party. 'Sadly I have to report that is still a work in progress.' Yet many in the PLP believed that Corbyn was himself the problem. Though only a handful would go as far as to say that he himself was anti-Semitic, they believed that his anti-imperialist world view, and the sometimes questionable company he had kept during his decades of advocacy for Palestinian statehood, had blinded him to the problem.

Shadow Cabinet ministers who sought to lance the boil themselves came to the same view. On 2 November 2017, Emily Thornberry took the bold decision to tell an event held to commemorate the centenary of the Balfour Declaration – which had committed the British government to a Jewish state in Palestine – that Corbyn supported Israel's existence and was, in effect, a Zionist. He had not signed off on the remarks and nor had LOTO. Amy Jackson summoned her for a ceremonial hauling over the coals the following day. It was there that Thornberry broached the subject of anti-Semitism. Concerns had been raised to her about Corbyn's handling of the issue. Her intervention, as well as falling within her wheelhouse as Shadow Foreign Secretary, had been intended to quell tensions. The reply was blunt: 'That's none of your business.'

Matters escalated the following month, when Thornberry suggested an urgent question on Donald Trump's decision to move the US embassy in Israel from Tel Aviv to Jerusalem. LOTO reacted enthusiastically. But when she accidentally missed the deadline to table the question, she was summoned for another dressing-down and left LOTO in a state of distress. A senior LOTO staffer, Thornberry told friends, later sought to reassure her by visiting her office and explaining: 'They're saying the Jews have got to you.'

It was a comment which reflected an awkward truth. Many Corbynites saw the anti-Semitism allegations as yet another proxy for factional squabbling – and a way for the Jewish community's mainstream bodies to punish him for his opposition to Zionism. Despite its presence on a public Facebook page, Mear One's Facebook post had remained largely unnoticed for half a decade. It had been circulated online by critics of the Corbyn Project, but it had failed to attract any mainstream media attention. In 2017, the post had even been the subject of a formal complaint to the Labour Party, but no action was taken. But on 23 March 2018, the morning after her second trip to Fair Oak Farm, it came to the attention of Luciana Berger.

Like most of those present at Gavin Shuker's awaydays, Berger's career in Labour politics had turned from a lifelong dream to a living nightmare. As the great-niece of Manny Shinwell, one of eleven Polish Jewish children from an East End family, who rose to become a Cabinet minister in Clement Attlee's post-war government, she was a scion of one of the party's great dynasties. As an old friend of Tony Blair's son Euan and a prominent student activist, she had been marked out by the party establishment in the New Labour years as a star in the making. Her ascent to Westminster had been as straightforward as any aspiring MP could wish for: in 2010, aged just 28, she had been elected to Liverpool Wavertree, one of the party's safest seats. Initially, she had no links with the city – and could not identify Bill Shankly, Liverpool FC's legendary manager, when quizzed by the *Liverpool Echo* ahead of her election. To some local activists, she represented everything that was wrong with New Labour's attitude to its heartland seats: that they were little more than launching pads for careerists with no ties to the communities they ostensibly represented. In the years that followed, however, Berger made her home in Liverpool. She could not become a Scouser – but she married one. By 2015, she was on the party's front bench. Like Shuker, she was destined for ministerial office once Ed Miliband put David Cameron out of office.

Corbyn's election had put Berger on an altogether different path. Initially, she had been among those willing to at least try and make the new political reality work. As part of the leadership's mission to do politics differently, a new role had been created for her at the Shadow Cabinet table: Shadow Minister for Mental Health. Yet the election of an unembarrassed left-winger to the leadership had empowered the most reactionary elements of the Labour Party in Liverpool – once run by Militant, the city had always had a strong organised hard left, who already saw Berger as a Blairite carpetbagger. More troublingly for Berger, it had also seen anti-Semitism move out of the shadows and into the open.

When Berger posted the picture of Mear One's mural to Twitter at 2 p.m. on 23 March 2018, even Corbyn's closest allies could not deny what was immediately obvious: their leader, inadvertently or not, had defended an anti-Semitic artwork. That morning, Berger had contacted LOTO to seek an explanation for Corbyn's comments. None had been forthcoming. After she went public, the leader's team scrambled for a line to take. That evening, it issued a statement that acknowledged the obvious offensiveness of the mural but did not admit any culpability on Corbyn's part. 'In 2012, Jeremy was responding to concerns about the removal of public art on the grounds of freedom of speech. However, the mural was offensive, used anti-Semitic imagery, which has no place in our society, and it is right that it was removed.' Dissatisfied, Berger shot back: 'The response from the Spokesperson is wholly inadequate. It fails to understand on any level the hurt and anguish felt about anti-Semitism. I will be raising this further.' LOTO was then forced to go a step further, and issue a personal apology from Corbyn himself, which explicitly described the mural as anti-Semitic. 'I sincerely regret that I did not look more closely at the image I was commenting on, the contents of which are deeply disturbing and anti-Semitic. The defence of free speech cannot be used as a justification for the promotion of anti-Semitism in any form. This is a view I've always held.'

It was not the first time Corbyn's Facebook account had raised questions about his attitude to anti-Semitism. It was not even the first time that month. Earlier in March, Corbyn had been found to have been a member of Palestine Live, a group in which anti-Semitic material had been repeatedly shared. He had pleaded ignorance: 'Had I seen it, of course, I would have challenged it straight away, but I actually don't spend all my time reading social media.' James Schneider, Milne's deputy, had attempted to put a lid on that story by asking Southside to suspend any Labour members found to have also been part of the group, so as to allow the leadership to say it had taken decisive action. The mural, however, was a crisis of much greater magnitude. Stories about Corbyn and anti-Semitism had always depended on a degree of guilt by association, and tended to revolve around the activists with whom he had shared a platform and the groups of which he had been a member. Now, for the first time, MPs and journalists had evidence of what Corbyn himself thought – and in this case, it was that he saw no reason why a seemingly obviously anti-Semitic mural ought to be taken down. One aide who immediately grasped the significance of what had happened was Andrew Fisher, whose relationship with the rest of LOTO had already been strained by the previous months' drama over Brexit. For the first time in his career, he told colleagues, Corbyn had done something that he could not defend.

On Sunday 25 March, LOTO attempted to get a grip on the situation with another statement from Corbyn, this time on video. Uncharacteristically, he did not link the subject to the situation in the Middle East and took his hardest – and most contrite – line on the issue yet. 'I want to be clear that I will not tolerate any form of anti-Semitism that exists in and around our movement. We must stamp this out from our party and movement. We recognise that anti-Semitism has occurred in pockets within the Labour Party, causing pain and hurt to our Jewish community in the Labour Party and the rest of the country. I am sincerely sorry for the pain which has been caused.' It did little to quell the anger of the PLP and Jewish community, 1,500 of whom rallied in Parliament Square the following evening. Their placards carried a stark and simple message: 'Enough is Enough'.

Yet the problem ran much deeper than Corbyn himself. The following week, his critics received yet more evidence to bolster their view that the leadership's tolerance of anti-Semitism was a feature, rather than a bug, in its political world view. On 29 March, Christine Shawcroft, a veteran left-winger and close ally of Ken Livingstone, quit as the chair of the Labour National Executive Committee's disputes panel – the internal party body responsible for determining how to sanction alleged anti-Semites. Leaked email correspondence had revealed that she had opposed the suspension of Alan Bull, a council candidate in Peterborough who had posted an article on Facebook that suggested the Holocaust had been a hoax. Though Shawcroft quit, she was unrepentant. The following day, she posted a lengthy defence of her conduct to her own Facebook account. 'I am not a Holocaust denier and I would not support a Holocaust denier,' she wrote. She nonetheless added a caveat that confirmed the worst fears of Jewish community groups: 'This whole row is being stirred up to attack Jeremy, as we all know. That someone who has spent his whole life fighting racism in all its forms should find himself being accused of not doing enough to counter it, absolutely beggars belief.' She resigned from the NEC entirely the following day – but her departure could not undo the damage done. The case had raised a troubling question for the PLP and Jewish community: how could LOTO be trusted to resolve the anti-Semitism problem when Corbyn did not always recognise it, and many of his proxies in the party machine did not believe it to be a genuine problem?

More controversy followed. On 2 April, Corbyn attended a Seder dinner hosted by Jewdas, a radical left Jewish fringe group, in his constituency. Mainstream Jewish community groups interpreted it as a calculated snub. Jewdas, whose members were mainly millennial and maintained an anarchic social media presence, had previously described Israel as 'a steaming pile of sewage which needs to be properly disposed of'. They expressed their anti-Zionism in bawdy and deliberately provocative terms. Such politics – and irreverence – were well within the Jewish tradition. It was not an illegitimate stance, but one outside of the discourse of mainstream British Jewry and antithetical to its representative bodies. Unbeknown to Corbyn, the evening had very nearly seen him break bread with one of Britain's most eminent rabbis. Laura Janner-Klausner, senior rabbi to the Reform Judaism movement, had been at the Seder, but fled upon spotting Corbyn. Unlike other Jewish community leaders, she was not hostile to his party. Not only was she a lifelong Labour voter, but her father, Greville Janner, had been a Labour MP and peer. She had also forged an unlikely friendship with Jennie Formby, Labour's general secretary, offering private counsel on the issue of anti-Semitism. But relations between Corbyn and the Jewish community had reached such a low ebb that Janner-Klausner, sensing news of the event would leak and could be photographed, furtively left. Even the left-wing leader of progressive Jewry could not be seen in public with Corbyn. Jewdas had their fun regardless. They later listed a pickled 'anticapitalist beetroot' that Corbyn was said to have 'blessed' at some point in the evening on eBay, where bidding briefly reached £45,000.

His critics in the PLP did not share their amusement. Wes Streeting, the combative MP for Ilford North, said: 'This demonstrates either extraordinarily bad judgement or a deliberate affront to the majority of British Jews. Probably both.' Jon Lansman, Corbyn's most prominent Jewish ally, offered the somewhat tenuous defence that the Labour leader had attended the Seder 'on his night off' and had not told staff of his whereabouts. Once Corbyn returned to LOTO the next morning, arrangements were immediately made for him to meet with the Board of Deputies and Jewish Leadership Council without preconditions – with a view to agreeing how anti-Semitism in the party might finally be addressed.

By now, even the leadership's most unyielding enforcers knew they needed to do more to repair Labour's strained – if not by now non-existent – relationship with the mainstream of the Jewish community. Having identified the question of anti-Semitism as one to which Corbyn struggled to give an answer, the press were all too happy to pose it again and again and again, with frequent reference to Corbyn's extensive back catalogue of past speeches and writings. Upon her appointment as general secretary, Jennie Formby had stressed that dealing with anti-Semitism was her foremost priority. But Karie Murphy knew that LOTO would have to take the initiative itself if it were to reclaim an overwhelmingly hostile narrative – and soothe the nerves of a minority community spooked by the prospect of a Corbyn government.

In furtive calls and texts, she sought the counsel of Michael Levy, the millionaire Labour peer whose support for the Project's old adversaries had been so generous as to earn him the nickname 'Blair's ATM'. Their discussions taught Murphy that the problems Corbyn faced were grave but not insurmountable. To overcome them he needed to show that he understood the difference between questions of foreign policy and the practicalities of life as a Jew in the Britain of 2018. Having offered thousands of mostly ill-received words on anti-Semitism in film and in print, now was the time for action. That much, to cool heads in LOTO at least, was a 'no-brainer'.

Some of Murphy's suggestions were mundane: a round-table summit with community organisations, a series of meetings with Jewish Labour activists and MPs, outreach to Jewish communities outside of London, and a new strategy for rebutting stories in the media. Others were far more striking, if not genuinely radical by LOTO's standards. Corbyn would visit Auschwitz. He could meet children at London's Jewish Free School, with Dan Carden, Laura Pidcock and Rebecca Long-Bailey undertaking similar visits elsewhere. *Haaretz*, Israel's liberal broadsheet, would get a set-piece interview.

Congregants at a progressive synagogue and residents of a Jewish care home would get to mix with Corbyn too. Any one of the proposals would have made for an eye-catching and potentially groundbreaking gesture of reconciliation.

All but one of them came to nothing. Comms aides in particular cringed at the thought of Corbyn braving a hostile crowd of teenagers at a Jewish school, lest they pull pranks and humiliate him in public – or, worse still, on social media. The one proposal from Murphy's paper that *was* enacted, at the recommendation of Shami Chakrabarti, was that Labour's code of conduct be amended to 'comprehensively rule out all forms of prejudice'. The way in which Corbyn interpreted those words would convince much of the Jewish community that he was incapable of grasping another recommendation from the paper: 'Ensure members understand what is anti-Semitism.' Many of his own team agreed. At times over the course of the summer it would feel that Corbyn and the Project were not only under attack from the media – but from within.

★

Corbyn's meeting with the Board of Deputies and Jewish Leadership Council (JLC) took place on 25 April. He left with one request ringing louder in his ears than any other. Both organisations wanted Labour to incorporate into its code of conduct the full definition of anti-Semitism given by the International Holocaust Remembrance Association (IHRA), an intergovernmental body of which the UK was a member. By September, 'IHRA' would become a shorthand for all that the Jewish community distrusted and disliked in Corbyn. 'IHRA was a consequence of the Enough is Enough rally,' said Peter Mason, the national secretary of the Jewish Labour Movement. 'The rally was a consequence of Muralgate. Everything in between Muralgate in March to the IHRA was a turbocharged period where things just deteriorated.'

The definition itself, which had first been published in 2005 before its adoption by thirty-one governments (including the UK's) in 2016, was relatively uncontroversial: 'Anti-Semitism is a certain perception of Jews, which may be expressed as hatred toward Jews. Rhetorical and physical manifestations of anti-Semitism are directed toward

Jewish or non-Jewish individuals and/or their property, toward Jewish community institutions and religious facilities.'

As much as their critics often spoke as if the party leadership disputed those words, Labour had already accepted the definition itself, in May 2016. But the Board of Deputies and the JLC had asked that it go further and adopt the IHRA's eleven illustrative but non-exhaustive examples of anti-Semitism too, which provided a framework by which the definition could be applied. Without them, the IHRA would later insist that an organisation could not be said to have adopted their definition.

As was the case with the definition itself, most of the examples were also uncontroversial: next to nobody disputed the assertion that calling for or aiding the murder of Jewish people, blaming the entire Jewish community for crimes committed by one of their number, denying the Holocaust, or accusing Jewish people of dual loyalty were all examples of anti-Semitism. But having adopted seven of the eleven examples into the new code of conduct verbatim, LOTO chose to exclude four, of which three were reworded. These, the party would later tell the Equalities and Human Rights Commission's inquiry into its handling of anti-Semitism, were 'added to and contextualised'. All of them related to the foreign-policy issue that animated Corbyn more than any other: Israel.

Critics of the definition – be they academics, politicians or journalists – had always contended that these examples were an attempt to police legitimate criticism of the Israeli state's conduct in Palestine, if not proscribe it altogether. Corbyn had always seen himself as part of the vanguard of that struggle. Unsurprisingly, those who know him best say he harboured the same aversion to the definition. Crucially for the events to come, though Labour's code of conduct would say that denying the Jewish people the right to self-determination was anti-Semitic, LOTO's proposal, which would be taken to the NEC for a final vote on its adoption in July, was that the code would not include the IHRA's remaining words: that 'claiming that the existence of a State of Israel is a racist endeavour' was anti-Semitic too.

The PLP and media would lay the blame for this ultimately disastrous decision at the door of Seumas Milne. They seized on a 2009 *Guardian* column in which he had contended: 'Throughout the Arab, Muslim, and wider developing worlds, the idea that Israel is a racist state is largely uncontroversial.' Their criticism was not entirely fair: Milne had also written of the fine line between anti-Zionism and anti-Semitism. But even if, as critics of Milne in the Shadow Cabinet contended, his intellectual influence on Corbyn was decisive, if not overpowering, those familiar with Corbyn's thinking at the time argue that the amendment was not imposed on Corbyn by Milne, but imposed on the party by Corbyn. A senior LOTO official says now: 'Jeremy was particularly worried about that phrase.' Indeed, from the moment the full IHRA definition and its examples became a topic of debate, LOTO aides attest that Corbyn himself was unequivocally against its adoption. 'When it comes to IHRA in particular,' one said, 'Jeremy – not Seumas – *Jeremy* had dead-set ideas that he wanted.' He believed – as so often in his long career – that he was defending the rights of the Palestinian people to self-determination. He refused to yield to what he saw as attempts by his political opponents to undermine that mission. Another aide who worked closely with both men said: 'Jeremy resisted, and Seumas resisted, because of the fear it would be used in a racist and bigoted way to discriminate against Palestinians . . . Karie and Seumas weren't strong-arming him into that position.' Murphy herself states: 'I did not persuade Jeremy on IHRA. That was his decision and I always respected his decision as leader.'

To strategic thinkers in LOTO, Corbyn's position was absurd. They shared his desire to protect and advance the Palestinian cause but feared his prescriptivism might have the opposite effect. 'Not getting a Labour government elected is letting the Palestinian people down,' said one. 'This is a fight we didn't need, shouldn't have had and couldn't win.' Yet Corbyn's politics did not permit any other course of action. For that reason, IHRA failed the most fundamental test of any prospective Labour policy: if Corbyn did not believe it, he could not say it aloud convincingly – or, indeed, at all.

Amending the examples was not, in fact, without precedent. In 2015 the House of Commons' Home Affairs Select Committee – a majority of whose members were Conservative MPs – had recommended that bodies that adopted the examples include caveats to protect the right to free speech on Palestine. But beyond his own convictions, the most significant influences on Corbyn's thinking were to be found not in LOTO but in Islington North. There he frequently canvassed opinion

from Jewish leftists, old friends whose steadfast support had a significant impact on his thinking – or rather its inability to change. Jewish
Voice for Labour (JVL), a radical left group set up to provide a coun-
tervailing voice to the Jewish Labour Movement (JLM), the party's
official but overwhelmingly Corbynsceptic Jewish affiliate, offered the
sort of counter-narrative that Corbyn could buy into. Its members
were led by Jackie Walker, who was born a Catholic but claimed
Jewish heritage, and had been expelled from Momentum after claiming
Jews had been the 'chief financiers' of the slave trade. Alongside her
was Naomi Wimborne-Idrissí, who had accused Luciana Berger of
confecting the mural row to 'suit her anti-Corbyn agenda'. Most of
its membership opposed the Zionism of the Board of Deputies. To
JVL, the anti-Semitism storm was a malicious fiction designed to fulfil
the political purpose of undermining Corbyn.

Other friends from Islington formed a kitchen cabinet to which he
would often defer on anti-Semitism: Asima Shaikh, an Islington councillor and member of the Campaign for Labour Party Democracy,
Sue Lukes, an activist from JVL, and David Rosenberg, the leader of
the Jewish Socialists' Group. To them, the communal organisations
demanding the adoption of full IHRA – like the Board of Deputies
– were firmly of the right, and therefore too unrepresentative to dictate
policy in the community's name. Said one senior LOTO official: 'Jewish
activists were saying to him: you're basically pandering to the right-
wing control in the community, which doesn't represent most Jewish
people, the Board of Deputies has always been a Conservative body.'
They were, his aides complained, not only 'constantly in his ear', but
hard-wired into his strategy on the issue. Corbyn would refuse to so
much as tweet about anti-Semitism without the green light from Lukes
in particular – who Jack Bond, his social media manager, would have
to liaise with before pressing send to Corbyn's more than 2 million
followers. One person recalled: 'Jeremy was scared to say no to her.'

Another LOTO aide sums up the nub of the counsel provided by
Corbyn's Islington set: 'Don't give an inch, don't give in, you're right,
this is bad, don't give them anything, you're doing the right thing.'
For Lukes, there was nothing wrong with showing sympathy with the
Jewish community and learning about their history and religious
customs. But there was nothing to be gained by behaving as though
he had himself done anything wrong.

On one occasion, Murphy and Shaikh had come to verbal blows in a conversation conducted on loudspeaker as Murphy drove. Shaikh contended that history would judge Corbyn if he folded on IHRA. 'No,' Murphy had said in reply. 'History will judge him on whether he gets into Number 10.' Yet Corbyn seemed to value their advice more than anyone else's. When aides proposed a course of action on anti-Semitism, he would sometimes respond: 'Well, what does Sue Lukes think?' It was at those moments that aides felt most frustrated. What progress they could make in moving Corbyn towards a compromise position was undermined by his conversations in his constituency. 'Often, we would have a sense … he was engaging with the issue better and then he'd go back and talk to people, mainly old Jewish Trotskyists in his constituency or elsewhere, who'd tell him, "There's no problem. This is all capitulating to Zionism."' The problem for LOTO was not so much that their views were illegitimate, but that they were foreign to the majority of British Jews.

Perhaps the most profound influence aides discerned was that of Corbyn's wife, Laura Alvarez. LOTO sources believe she was horrified by the growing consensus in the media that her husband, whose anti-racism was the very core of his identity, was at best tolerant of racism and at worst a racist himself. According to them, she felt that LOTO had not done enough to defend him. In compromising, they would be seen to concede the legitimacy of such charges. Aides noted with some concern that she regularly read the hyper-partisan Canary website, which took a similarly uncompromising line against opponents of the Project – real or imagined. She had also forged an unlikely friendship with Shraga Stern, a Haredi activist whose sect, the Satmars, believed that Judaism and Zionism were diametrically opposed on the grounds that the state of Israel had not been delivered by the Messiah. Some in LOTO feared that the effect of Alvarez's love and solidarity was to embolden Corbyn into his 'rebel mode'.

On 8 May, the Labour NEC's Anti-Semitism Working Group met to discuss the code of conduct. The group had been set up by Formby on 17 April, soon after her arrival at Southside. Corbynites believed its existence and membership – which drew from both wings of the party – was evidence that the leadership had approached the problem in good faith. Activists from the Corbynsceptic JLM took the view that it was a Potemkin body packed with leadership stooges. Peter

Mason, its national secretary, said: 'The people who were on the Anti-Semitism Working Group were Jon Lansman, Chakrabarti and basic-ally just a collection of people who didn't appear to care about the impact of anti-Semitism on people or at least certainly didn't commu-nicate.' The 8 May meeting would confirm that impression.

The JLM had been invited but Mason could not make it to Victoria in working hours and told officials at Southside that two other JLM officials – Adam Langelben, who had blamed the loss of his seat on Barnet Council the previous week on anti-Semitism, and Ella Rose – would attend in his stead. Like Mason, Langelben was slight and softly spoken but fought his corner ferociously. Colleagues knew him as 'the Syringe': it was his job, through combative tweets, to 'draw out the poison' from online anti-Semites. But twenty-four hours before the 8 May meeting, Langelben's and Rose's invitations were rescinded. The official grounds were that Mason had been invited in his capacity as a member of Labour's National Constitutional Committee, its quasi-judicial disciplinary body, and not as a representative of the JLM. He suspected the real reason was Langelben's reputation as a scrapper. Mason instructed them to head to Southside anyway. They sat in reception, visibly frozen out, as the cameras rolled. The meeting ended up making the sort of headlines that Formby had made it her mission to avoid.

There was, however, a member of JLM on whom Formby could rely. Sharp-suited and shaven-headed, Ivor Caplin had once been a Labour MP – albeit the sort that Corbynites loathed. Elected in 1997, he had spent his eight years in Parliament as an enthusiastic servant of New Labour, including as a defence minister during the Iraq War. Now, when not lobbying for corporate clients, he chaired the JLM. It was in that capacity that Formby invited him to discuss the new code of conduct on 2 July. The rest of the JLM leadership grumbled that Caplin – who made frequent use of the access to the parliamentary estate accorded to former MPs – had delusions of grandeur. He had already met Formby once before in private. This time they insisted he had to be accompanied. But with Mason, their expert on discip-linary processes, indisposed at a Local Government Association confer-ence in Bournemouth, Caplin was instead accompanied by Neil Nerva, an eccentric Brent councillor known to wear Crocs to Labour meetings. He happened to have been the only other member of the JLM executive available to attend at short notice. They met Formby in her Southside office and were both given sight of the code. Despite having been told not to agree to anything, neither raised any objections, nor did they propose any amendments to the text. Having received no push-back from the leadership of the JLM, Formby informed the organising subcommittee that the code could be adopted without further emendation. The full NEC would meet to do so formally two weeks later, on 17 July.

Formby had drawn the wrong conclusion. Emboldened by Caplin's response, she subsequently shared their planned measures for combating anti-Semitism – including the new code of conduct – with the Board of Deputies and Jewish Leadership Council. In her letter, she noted that Caplin and Nerva had signed off on them. She very quickly discovered that they had not been speaking for their own organisation, let alone the Jewish community as a whole. On 4 July, Formby received a terse letter of complaint from the JLM. They claimed not to have approved the code of conduct and demanded Labour adopt the full IHRA definition and examples immediately. Pointedly, it said that the JLM leadership would 'have to resign for betraying our members' if they approved the Corbynite code. Yet that is exactly what Caplin and Nerva had inadvertently done.

The backlash to the new code of conduct from the Jewish community was as swift as it was unambiguous. Both the Board of Deputies and Jewish Leadership Council condemned it in a joint statement. 'It is impossible to understand why Labour refuses to align itself with this universal definition,' they said. The JLM, meanwhile, threatened Formby with legal action for claiming the code had their endorsement. Their ferocity spooked moderates in the Shadow Cabinet. On Sunday 8 July, Keir Starmer laid down the gauntlet. In an interview with the *Andrew Marr Show*, the Shadow Brexit Secretary called on the leadership to adopt the IHRA definition and examples in full. For Starmer, the issue was partly personal: his own wife, Victoria, was the daughter of Polish Jewish émigrés, for whom he would host regular Shabbat dinners at his North London home.

While LOTO had hoped the NEC meeting on Tuesday 17 July would be a straightforward rubber-stamping exercise, the days leading up to it made clear it would be anything but. The day before, sixty-eight rabbis from almost every Jewish denomination signed an explosive letter to the *Guardian*, demanding Labour rethink the decision. 'The Labour Party's leadership has chosen to ignore those who understand anti-Semitism the best, the Jewish community,' it read. 'By claiming to know what's good for our community, the Labour Party's leadership have chosen to act in the most insulting and arrogant way.' The gulf between some of the rabbis' interpretations of their faith was so great that several of them did not believe every signatory to the letter was a rabbi. Yet their aversion to the new code was enough to induce a symbolic truce. Ephraim Mirvis, the chief rabbi, was not a man given to intervening in national politics, but he too wrote a letter to Labour, warning the NEC not to show 'unprecedented contempt' for British Jews.

The PLP also made its views clear. At its weekly meeting the same evening, it overwhelmingly passed a motion, tabled by Jewish MPs Luciana Berger and Alex Sobel, calling for IHRA to be adopted in full. Corbyn did not attend. The leader's closest allies feared that to back down on the question of the definition would be to leave the leader vulnerable to even starker demands. One said: 'As if it would have stopped there? The idea that if you satisfy one demand, there won't be another one ... to prove that you're opposed to anti-Semitism, you need to expel Jeremy Corbyn from the Labour Party. Quite a lot of the people we were dealing with on these issues were not acting in good faith, and were using it politically. You can see this with everything.' They believed they had two choices. 'Under any pressure in any political situation, you need to decide either whether you're absolutely going to hold the line, or whether you're not absolutely going to hold the line. Then you should give in and try to draw a new line. The areas where it was difficult were the ones where we fell between those two stools.'

On 17 July the NEC voted unanimously to adopt the new code of conduct but to keep its provisions under review and consult with Jewish community groups on how it might be improved. It had been a tense and, for some in the room, unbearable meeting. Despite the sensitivity of the issue at hand, some Corbynites went on the attack. In remarks that were secretly recorded and later leaked to the *Jewish Chronicle*, Pete Willsman fumed that the sixty-eight rabbis were 'Trump fanatics'. Raising his voice, he barked: 'I think we should ask the rabbis: where is your evidence of severe and widespread anti-Semitism in this party?' He then put the same question to the room, challenging his colleagues to raise their hands if they had indeed seen anti-Semitism in Labour. When several did, he spluttered incredulously: 'I'm amazed. I've certainly never seen any.'

The fallout from the decision would highlight just how many people took the opposite view.

★

Margaret Hodge took the news personally. Though the daughter of Holocaust refugees who had fled Germany for Egypt and then Egypt for London because of anti-Semitism, the veteran MP for Barking had always worn her Jewish identity lightly. Indeed, for most of her parliamentary career she had resented being cast as a Jewish MP at all. At the 1994 by-election which had seen her elected to the Commons, the *Jewish Chronicle* had asked Hodge for an interview. 'I don't want to talk to them,' she had told the Labour press office. 'I have nothing to say.' She eventually relented. 'So,' Hodge was asked, 'what are you going to do for the Jewish community?' The truthful answer, she admits now, was: 'Not a lot.' A quarter of a century on, she was talking about little else.

In the hours after the NEC decided not to adopt IHRA in full, Corbyn returned to Parliament for votes on the EU Withdrawal Bill, the legislation that would transfer European law onto the British statute book. Tensions within the PLP were already running high, as was always the way when it considered the question of Brexit. The news from Southside inflamed them. As Labour MPs filed through the division lobbies time and time again, discussion inevitably focused on the afternoon's events.

Hodge found herself in conversation with Gavin Shuker and Ian Austin, two fellow conspirators from Fair Oak Farm, behind the Speaker's chair. It was then she spotted Corbyn. Turning to Shuker and Austin, Hodge snapped. Using the sort of language she would never utter in public, she told them: 'I'm going to tell this guy he's a fucking anti-Semitic racist.' Austin reacted with almost childlike glee. 'Go on Margaret!' he said. 'Go and do it!' With that, she made a beeline for Corbyn.

It was not a decision Hodge took lightly. As a former leader of Islington Council, she had known Corbyn for the best part of forty years. The two were not friends but had always enjoyed a warm professional rapport: Corbyn's interests meant his sights were often trained beyond Islington. As such he had never caused her much trouble at the council. She knew that to confront him would be to blow up whatever relationship they had left. In 2016, egged on by Chris Leslie, she had tabled the motion of no confidence in Corbyn that had led to Owen Smith's doomed leadership challenge. But this intervention was of a different order.

As she approached Corbyn, Hodge made a promise to herself: she would not swear, lest she undermine the potency of her argument. Unbeknown to her, however, Austin – summoning the skills he had honed as a Brownite spin doctor – would brief the industrial language she had used in their conversation to Paul Waugh, the veteran political editor of the HuffPost website. Waugh already had his headline when Hodge began her verbal assault on Corbyn. 'It's outrageous, the decision you've taken,' she told him.

Seemingly impassive, Corbyn began to quote the new code of conduct in reply. 'You're making Labour a hostile environment for Jews to belong to,' Hodge shot back, before calling him 'an anti-Semite and a racist'. The Labour leader said little in reply. By the time their four-minute conversation had finished, Hodge was shaking. 'It wasn't a little deal,' she recalls now. Her fellow Labour MP Caroline Flint accompanied her for a glass of water. Having composed herself, Hodge then headed to the Young Vic to see a musical production of Alison Bechdel's *Fun Home*. As she left the theatre, her phone exploded: news of the confrontation had spread far and wide. Just after 11 p.m., she briefed the Press Association with her account of the row and retired to bed.

That was not the end of the matter. While Hodge had been at the theatre, the Corbynites had attempted to redefine the narrative. Andy McDonald, the Shadow Transport Secretary, had witnessed the argument and submitted a formal complaint to Southside. Hodge did not find out until the following morning. She arrived in Westminster a heroine, and was feted by colleagues only for the celebration of her clash with Corbyn to be cut short by toothache. Midway through the dentist's appointment her parliamentary researcher burst in. Luciana Berger had called. 'I can't talk to her right now,' Hodge said. Yet Berger was insistent she take the call. The dentist stopped to let Hodge take her phone. 'They're going to suspend you from the party,' Berger told her.

Hodge's heart sank. Her hope had been that Corbyn might listen. Instead, LOTO was on the warpath. That afternoon, Theresa May took the opportunity to salt Labour's wounds, and told Corbyn at Prime Minister's Questions that he should adopt the full IHRA definition. Addressing lobby reporters at their weekly huddle afterwards, however, Milne said action would be taken against Hodge. 'The behaviour was clearly unacceptable under Labour Party rules,' he said, suggesting that Berger's dire prediction could yet come true. The next day, Hodge received a letter formally placing her under investigation.

The decision would trigger the most profound breach between Corbyn and McDonnell the Project would ever experience. Some in LOTO argue that it was never repaired. At its heart, the dispute was political. Would Labour discipline a septuagenarian Jewish MP who had vented about racism, albeit aggressively, as it would any other member? Or would it compromise by having the issue dealt with off the books of the formal disciplinary system – and away from the keen eye of Hodge's lawyers – by entrusting the response to Nick Brown and the whips?

Corbyn backed the former option. He was supported by his wife, who was appalled. Alvarez felt that her husband had been victimised and that they could not give an inch to Hodge. LOTO opinion, jaundiced as it was from the 2016 coup, broadly fell behind Corbyn. One Shadow Cabinet minister described the overriding view among senior aides thus: 'Margaret Hodge has to behave like any other Labour Party member, and if she doesn't, then we've got a system.' Those who saw the obvious political danger in following the letter of the rulebook rather than conceding in the interests of the Project were exasperated. John McDonnell was among them. With Formby on holiday in Turkey, he turned to Murphy and urged her to cancel the disciplinary action. Murphy, whose personal affection for Formby was matched only by her trade unionist's reverence for the office of general secretary, refused.

In the subsequent days, Hodge enlisted the services of law firm Mishcon de Reya. She was not backing down. To McDonnell, that the LOTO hierarchy would not do so itself was incomprehensible: he did not see the point of jeopardising Labour's standing for the sake of winning an argument with an elderly Jewish MP on a point of principle that was to most voters beyond arcane. Having vented privately to friends and to Corbyn himself, he broke cover on 22 July, five days after Hodge's row with Corbyn, to demand Labour drop the investigation. Adopting his avuncular register, he told Sky's *Sophy Ridge on Sunday*: 'I've worked with Margaret over the years ... She's got a good heart. Sometimes you can express anger – I'm one of those people who has in the past – and basically you have to accept that people can be quite heated in their expressions. Let's understand that, and just move on.' Not for the first time that summer, Corbyn found himself publicly at odds with his oldest friend in politics.

LOTO aides say McDonnell lobbied Corbyn obsessively over the decision. To them, it appeared to be a classic McDonnell manoeuvre: a short-term tactical compromise for the sake of the Project. Some complained that his tendency at times of crisis was to immediately over-correct in the face of any difficulty. 'If you're attacked for being soft on Russia and Putin, John would then immediately ask for the suspension of diplomatic relations with Russia and the expulsion of its diplomats,' one said. In the case of anti-Semitism, his preference was that Corbyn should take the symbolic – if drastic – step of visiting Jerusalem. A member of the Board of Deputies had proposed he should visit the Holy City's Hadassah hospital, where Jews and Arabs received treatment side by side. 'He would have had Jeremy in Jerusalem on the next plane,' a LOTO aide said. But McDonnell's reaction was motivated by a deep anger as much as it was a cool political pragmatism or a desire for control. A friend of the Shadow Chancellor said: 'They could have drawn a line under it at that point, and John felt passionately that that was the case. The other issue was that Jeremy wasn't listening to him and was listening to other people, when John felt he had a long bond with Jeremy.'

In any case, Corbyn gave the impression of a man unwilling to budge for the sake of his own pride. In an interview at the Tolpuddle Martyrs festival in Dorset on the same day, Corbyn was asked about his reaction to Hodge's tirade. 'I felt upset about it,' he said. 'But, as always, I am very calm and treat people with a great deal of respect. I don't shout at people. I just listen to what they have to say. A complaint has been registered and that will have to be dealt with by the party, but that is independent of me.' A LOTO adviser suggests

the feelings ran deeper: 'Why did Jeremy dig in? Well, all of his politics have been about supporting the Palestinians. He was absolutely
affronted by Hodge's attack on him. That led him to dig in.' Unlike
McDonnell, he did not see the row in terms of the Labour left's quest
for power. It struck at the very core of his sense of self. He was a
politician who existed to defy the stultifying constraints of polite
opinion. 'He was reluctant to dance to somebody else's tune ... to
overcome this you must go to Israel, or you must do this, or you must
do that. For him it was difficult, because he felt so personally under
attack [and] upset about that.'

Things came to a head the next day, Monday 23 July, when the
Shadow Cabinet met for an awayday at the offices of the Local
Government Association on Smith Square. Witnesses describe
McDonnell as gripped by an almost biblical temper at the decision to
proceed with action against Hodge. So forcefully did he make his case
that even Andrew Fisher, his old protégé, stormed out of the discussion early. As the meeting wound up, Corbyn reached an aide to
express his anxiety that his Shadow Chancellor had lost his temper.
The sheer extremity of McDonnell's reaction had given him pause
for thought. Later that day he phoned Murphy and appeared to suggest
that it might be time to call off the disciplinary action. She told him
in no uncertain terms that it was Formby's decision alone.

Later that same day, the PLP chose to escalate hostilities. Having
already called for the party as a whole to adopt the IHRA definition
and all of its examples, at its last meeting before Parliament broke for
the summer recess it voted unanimously to write them into their own
rulebook – in a direct show of defiance to the leadership and NEC.
Two days later, the Jewish community's three biggest newspapers, the
Jewish Chronicle, *Jewish News* and *Jewish Telegraph*, all ran the same
front-page editorial, suggesting that a Corbyn government would pose
an 'existential threat to Jewish life'. Some thought the rhetoric over-
heated. To many Jewish leaders, allowing Israel to be characterised as
a racist project *did* pose existential questions. If a Labour government
adopted the same position, could Jewish bodies with links to Israel
lose their charitable status? Would the government continue to fund
Jewish security charities which had links to the Israeli embassy? Could
Britain become a cold home to its Jews, the vast majority of whom
did support Israel's existence? To most MPs, such questions remained

remote. Yet the headlines in Jewish newspapers served as a clear warning sign: Corbyn should cut his losses and admit defeat.

The broadcaster Paul Mason, holidaying in Greece, made a vain attempt to convince LOTO to change course. While on the beach he had received a call from an official in the leader's office, seeking advice. Conscious that he was surrounded by British holidaymakers who might recognise him from his days on *Channel 4 News* or *Newsnight*, he waded out to sea. 'Sign the goddamn IHRA definition right now,' he said. 'It's a governmental thing. If you want to change it when you're the government, you can make some changes, but you lose nothing by doing this now.' Bob Kerslake agreed. He told McDonnell: 'This is not going to go away, it's a serious issue. You need an independent review, somebody outside the party or outside the political sphere. You need to strengthen your capacity to deal with these complaints. You need to accept the international definition, even if it's a flawed document in some ways.' He went as far as to offer to conduct the review himself, but was never taken up on the offer.

On 30 July, the tape of Willsman's rant at the NEC meeting at which the IHRA definition had been discussed was reported in excruciating detail by the *Jewish Chronicle* and was swiftly condemned by Luciana Berger and Tom Watson. Willsman begrudgingly apologised, but that was not the end of the matter. Jon Lansman took the decision to boot him off Momentum's slate for the upcoming elections to the NEC. He also demanded that Labour launch disciplinary action against Willsman, warning Murphy via WhatsApp that not to do so would be a 'massive tactical mistake'. LOTO refused.

The row over Willsman forced divides within the Shadow Cabinet – and between Corbyn and McDonnell – into the public domain. On 31 July, *The Times* got wind of McDonnell's private entreaties to his friend. LOTO staff suspected the hand of Andy Whitaker, the Shadow Chancellor's new spin doctor, whom LOTO comms staff derisively referred to as 'the booking agent', such were the number of interviews to which McDonnell agreed. Some in LOTO chalked up the public shows of defiance to lingering resentment on McDonnell's part. Having twice run for the Labour leadership as the hopeless standard-bearer of the Campaign Group, the Shadow Chancellor had given an interview in December 2015 in which he said that Corbyn did so merely because it was his 'turn'. Though not inaccurate, Corbyn bristled at the suggestion that his victory was a mere happy coincidence. Since 2016, Corbyn had made the office his own, and his authority and stature in the public eye, not to mention his popularity on the left, had eclipsed McDonnell's. So too had his confidence. No longer was he quite as reliant on McDonnell, the organisational and strategic mastermind of the Bennite left, to hold his hand. 'He never approached the reputation Jeremy had, or the support that Jeremy had, or the loyalty that Jeremy had,' said a senior Corbyn adviser of McDonnell. 'That's the reality of it. By 2018, Jeremy had been through two leadership elections which he'd won with large majorities, and the general election.'

The working relationship was no longer so close, nor on an even keel. To Corbyn's aides, it looked at risk of emulating the two partnerships the two men had sought not to emulate: the rancorous and wholly dysfunctional Blair–Brown duo, and the partnership between Ed Miliband and Ed Balls, who could be courteous but neither trusted nor wholly agreed with each other. Corbyn had defied the advice of Unite, who had preferred the New Labour veteran Angela Eagle or Owen Smith, to appoint his friend to the Shadow Chancellorship. They agreed on everything. But by 2018 the foundations of the partnership had been undermined. The effect of the lost summer of anti-Semitism was to explode a bomb beneath them.

A question that preoccupied aides in LOTO, as well as members of the Shadow Cabinet, was whether McDonnell and Corbyn were comrades or personal friends first. For a period that summer it was painfully clear that they were neither. After McDonnell's explosion over Hodge, one senior LOTO aide said, 'They never spoke for months. Never spoke the whole summer.' McDonnell's usually compulsive communication with LOTO aides also suddenly desisted. Said a senior LOTO adviser: 'We would normally get hundreds of calls from John Mac ... so he'd phone really early in the morning, he'd also phone really late at night, then all of a sudden he disappeared.' They found their own texts to him blanked. Another LOTO source said: 'He just wasn't around any more ... He never came to meetings any more, he wouldn't talk to us, he refused to have meetings with me, refused to have meetings with Karie, he just disappeared.' A third senior LOTO source said: 'Stories of John and Jeremy splitting, and John manoeuvring, were all rubbish for most of the four years. But not in this summer.'

As McDonnell sought to reclaim the initiative himself, Corbyn's reluctance and low moods saw LOTO's attempts to do so fall flat. Aides were by now desperate for the leader to make the speech of his life at a Jewish organisation or museum. In April, he had written for the *Evening Standard* on his efforts to 'banish' anti-Semitism from Labour. It had been loosely modelled on a *Guardian* column Milne had written at the height of the Second Intifada in Gaza, and cautioned the left against falling into conspiratorial tropes about capitalist elites and overstepping the fine line between anti-Semitism and anti-Zionism. According to Andrew Murray, Corbyn paid a high price for putting his name to the piece: 'He got a lot of grief from a lot of people about that, saying, "You shouldn't have said that, you shouldn't apologise." And then, of course, he felt maybe he shouldn't.' Yet even then, well-intentioned but arid political education was not enough. LOTO had come to realise that huge sections of the Jewish community did not merely dislike Corbyn, but saw him as an existential threat. Milne had been particularly affected by a television vox pop with an Orthodox Jewish family on a Manchester street who said they were scared of the Labour Party. Dispelling those deeply held fears would require Corbyn to show the quality that defined his activism on behalf of other oppressed peoples: empathy. Words were one thing. Being seen to believe them was quite another.

Some in LOTO wondered whether he did. His condemnations of anti-Semitism were always suffixed with the caveat: 'and *all* forms of racism'. In internal discussions Corbyn and supportive junior staff would sometimes ask whether to single out the Jewish community would be to afford them special treatment. Milne and Murphy gave the suggestion short shrift. Murphy explained: 'I would be like, fucking yes. There's a reason for it, we have a problem in this community, and we need to address the problem. Yes, we are [paying particular attention to the Jewish community], but if we don't stand up for a minority then nobody on the left should vote for us. Why would they? We have to stand up for the minority here and we are being told we've got a problem, we've got a fucking problem.' A question that troubled others was whether Corbyn categorised anti-Semitism as the same kind of racism as those he had always set himself against. Said Andrew Murray: 'He is very empathetic, Jeremy, but he's empathetic with the poor, the disadvantaged, the migrant, the marginalised, the people at the bottom of the heap. Happily, that is not the Jewish community in Britain today. He would have had massive empathy with the Jewish community in Britain in the 1930s and he would have been there at Cable Street, there's no question. But, of course, the Jewish community today is relatively prosperous.' For Murray, the fact anti-Semitism and economic exploitation were not necessarily entwined posed a difficult question for many on the left: 'Racism in British society since the Second World War – what does it mean? It means discrimination at work, discrimination in housing, hounding by the police on the streets, discrimination and disadvantage in education, demonisation and mischaracterisation in the mass media. That is what has happened to Afro-Caribbean and Asian immigrants and their descendants. It is not, mainly, what has happened to Jewish people. The fascists I knew in the 1970s didn't go out Jew-hunting, they went out Paki-bashing. For a whole generation – that's now quite an influential cohort in the Labour Party and around Jeremy personally – that is what racism is. They would say, "Of course, Jewish migrants to Britain in the first half of the twentieth century – they lived in appalling conditions. They had it rough, they were attacked by the fascists. But, you know, that was then. The Jewish community's moved on. It's developed, it's integrated and ... " This is where the failure to understand comes in – that, actually, anti-Semitism has different aspects to other forms of racism.' Many wondered, therefore, not *whether* Corbyn would empathise, but whether he *could*.

His inner circle nonetheless saw a speech – a show of the deep and genuine humanity that had won him legions of admirers – as the best vehicle for rehabilitation. Interviews on the subject seldom ended well. They showcased the worst of Corbyn. Accusations would be levelled and rebuttals would be given irascibly. A defensive exercise was not what aides in LOTO had in mind. Almost every senior member of the leader's office urged him to make a speech. They told him he would have the opportunity not only to repair Labour's frayed bond with the Jewish community, but to reassert its support for a two-state solution to the Palestinian conflict. According to one of the putative authors of the speech, it would have argued that fighting anti-Semitism 'had nothing to do with supporting the Palestinians completely ... you didn't have to pull the brakes on your support for Palestinian rights because you were militantly against anti-Semitism'. But those who made the case describe Corbyn as uneasy with the plan: he did not veto it directly, but instead made his discomfort clear in a 'Jeremy-ish way'. On 3 August there was nonetheless a breakthrough, when LOTO briefed plans that Corbyn – who was nervous about the politics of any gesture – would deliver a speech at Camden's Jewish Museum the following week. After a communal backlash, however, the museum cancelled. With that, the chances of the speech ever happening disintegrated. Corbyn had been nervous about making the gesture in any case. 'What he didn't want,' said one senior aide, 'was for it to turn into some kind of demonstration ... He didn't want it to turn into something where it became counterproductive by becoming a conflict.' The point of the intervention in his eyes was to soothe rather than escalate tensions. That his planned appearance at the museum had met so much opposition was, aides say, evidence enough that it would inevitably make matters worse. 'He didn't want to do it after that,' said another senior adviser. 'He felt comfortable about doing it there. But when that started to unravel, he didn't want to do it somewhere else.'

Instead the vacuum was filled by bad news stories. The same day as plans for the speech collapsed, 3 August, Corbyn wrote for the *Guardian* in an attempt to defend the by now widely discredited code of conduct. That afternoon Southside offered to drop its disciplinary action against Hodge, on the condition that she apologised. She publicly ridiculed the demand as absurd. By the time it finally did so (without an apology of their own) on 6 August – more than two weeks after McDonnell first urged LOTO to move on – the damage was done. Two days later, Lansman admitted defeat, and urged Corbyn to adopt the IHRA definition in full in order to repair his relationship with the Jewish community. Yet Corbyn's reputation still had new depths to plumb.

On 10 August, photos from 2014 emerged that appeared to show Corbyn laying a wreath at a Tunis cemetery for dead members of the Palestinian terrorist group Black September, who had been responsible for the murder of the Israeli Olympic team in Munich in 1972. Despite the pictures showing him carrying a floral tribute the size of his own torso, two days later Corbyn insisted, to much ridicule, that he had been 'present, but not involved'. Berger gave his explanation short shrift. 'Being "present" is the same as being involved,' she said. 'When

I attend a memorial, my presence alone, whether I lay a wreath or not, demonstrates my association and support. There can also never be a "fitting memorial" for terrorists. Where is the apology?' Sajid Javid, the Conservative Home Secretary, demanded Corbyn's resignation.

On the same day, the *Daily Mail* had unearthed footage from 2013 which appeared to show Corbyn violating the IHRA examples himself. Speaking at an event in Parliament, he had suggested that Palestinians in the West Bank lived 'under occupation of the very sort that would be recognised by many people in Europe who suffered occupation during the Second World War'. Though LOTO insisted that he was not comparing Israel to Nazi Germany, the comments were inevitably interpreted as such. On 13 August, Benjamin Netanyahu, the Israeli prime minister, felt impelled to wade in. He tweeted: 'The laying of a wreath by Jeremy Corbyn on the graves of the terrorists who perpetrated the Munich massacre and his comparison of Israel to the Nazis deserves unequivocal condemnation from everyone – left, right, and everything in between.' Corbyn responded to Netanyahu in kind: 'What deserves unequivocal condemnation is the killing of over 160 Palestinian protesters in Gaza by Israeli forces since March, including dozens of children.'

But despite Corbyn's public pugnacity, LOTO was preparing to accept the IHRA definition in full. On 16 August, Len McCluskey offered a clue as to which way the wind was blowing in a column for HuffPost. Despite accusing Jewish community leaders of 'truculent hostility' and 'refusing to take yes for an answer', he backed the adoption of IHRA and all its examples. Further revelations from Corbyn's past would underline the extent to which LOTO had no choice but to do so. Yet more archive footage emerged on 23 August, in which Corbyn described two British Jews who had heckled a speech by the Palestinian Authority's envoy to the UK as 'Zionists', and said: 'They clearly have two problems. One is that they don't want to study history, and secondly, having lived in this country for a very long time, probably all their lives, don't understand English irony.' To his critics, the speech was yet more evidence that Corbyn himself – and not just those he associated with – had a problem with Jews. He insisted that he had used the word Zionist 'in the accurate political sense'.

Jonathan Sacks, the former chief rabbi, did not agree. In an incendiary interview with the *New Statesman* five days later, Sacks described the 'English irony' remarks as the most offensive by a British politician since Enoch Powell's 'Rivers of Blood' speech. Though LOTO dismissed the comparison as 'absurd and offensive', much of the PLP were of the same mind.

Corbyn took the stories badly. According to his closest aides, his response was to withdraw: emotionally and professionally. 'He just couldn't deal with it,' said one. 'And so he just behaved in a way that made him seem like he didn't care, and he 100 per cent cares – he just looked like he didn't.' To LOTO it appeared that he had lost sight of his responsibilities as an emotional and existential funk set in. 'He couldn't see he was the leader of a political party any more, he had a responsibility to reach out and represent people and to reassure people ... it was just silence, and political mistakes.' Corbyn was physically present but emotionally absent. His office longed for the return of 'the 2017 Jeremy'. To see him suffer and struggle under the weight of the accusation that he, too, was capable of indulging or indeed perpetrating racism was almost too much to bear. That there were no easy options did not help him out of his hole either. Even if he and LOTO acted decisively, they were resigned to the fact that the attacks – from the press, the PLP and the Conservatives – that so demoralised him would have continued. Murphy recalls: 'Jeremy was shocked and saddened that anybody could think that about him. It broke my heart for him, and I was so sad for him ... I know what it must feel like to be accused of something you've not done, so publicly and so unfairly. I don't use the word weaponised, but it felt to me as if we'd been stabbed from every angle at the time. You know, I was just like, "oh my God this is horrendous".' The activists who had Corbyn's ear took the same view. They told him that to apologise would be to encourage further attacks. Above all, a friend describes him as having been 'at a loss to think that people would actually believe that about him. You know, it could bring me to tears from thinking about it, and it brought Jeremy to tears.'

Emotions continued to run high between Corbyn and McDonnell. 'It was clear they were estranged,' said one senior LOTO aide. The leader refused to contact the man to whom he had once been a lone friend in politics, or to broker a peace. By the end of the summer, neither was answering the other's calls. 'It was absolutely true that they weren't talking,' said another LOTO staffer. 'They were walking past each other in the corridor and blanking each other, it was that level of not talking.' For the situation to continue into the looming parliamentary term, with a vote on Theresa May's Brexit deal and a potential split in the PLP a live prospect, would be not only unsustainable but politically suicidal. So it was that Andrew Fisher was dispatched to Norfolk, where McDonnell spent his summers boating on the Broads with his grandchildren, to negotiate a settlement. His boat had served as an ad hoc leadership campaign headquarters for Corbyn in the summer of 2015. Now it would be the venue for peace talks for a war between two men who were once politically inseparable.

Having worked for McDonnell himself, Fisher was the ideal person for the task. There was, according to other LOTO aides, a personal motivation at play too. Relations between the two had not been the same since the Hodge debacle. The trip served the purpose of rekindling both relationships.

After seeing relatives in the area, Fisher paid a visit to a brooding McDonnell. After a cordial conference call from the boat with Corbyn and LOTO's senior management team, he agreed to bury the hatchet upon his return to Westminster, where a cathartic summit with the aides who had caused him so much fury that summer was scheduled. Those present for the meeting describe it as an exercise in 'bloodletting', at McDonnell's suggestion, and it quickly degenerated into a slanging match between him and Murphy, who interjected with profane challenges at every turn. McDonnell, intensely frustrated by what he saw as the chaos and wastefulness of LOTO, laid out his grievances. Blanching at the hostility, Corbyn intervened to encourage others to speak. But Murphy wanted a fight. In an exchange that got to the heart of the disagreement, McDonnell said: 'Karie, the way I see it is this: I'm the elected politician and you're the officer.' Murphy replied: 'Well, here's the difference. You're my comrade, and I don't fucking work for you.' For all the hostility, however, the outcome was positive. 'We did then start to make progress,' one attendee said.

While relations between LOTO and McDonnell began to return to some form of normality, the same could not be said of the relationship between Jeremy and John. Often it had fallen to Seb Corbyn, caught in the uncomfortable position of working for McDonnell while owing his ultimate loyalty to his father, to play the pained intermediary. LOTO would often prevail on him to influence McDonnell. 'It didn't suit Seb for his dad and John not to be talking,' said a LOTO source. In the wake of the lost summer, Laura Alvarez and McDonnell's wife, Cynthia, were also entrusted with making peace between the warring families. They went to the theatre together to clear the air. It did not lead to the full reconciliation that some had hoped for. 'Laura never, ever changed her mind about John after that, never,' said one senior Corbyn aide. 'So the friendship between the families didn't recover.' There was little surprise at the continued frostiness among LOTO staff. They believed McDonnell had behaved dishonourably. 'He damaged a lot of relationships,' said one. 'You don't just fuck off, refuse to talk to anyone, and then swan back in like nothing ever happened.'

Those who experienced the fallout from the row contend the biggest stumbling block to a full and proper reconciliation was that neither man could admit that they were wrong – or, as they approached their eighth decades, change as people. Corbyn, while cognisant that a problem existed, continued to deny its scale and seriousness. More pertinently, he believed that it was his right, not McDonnell's, to direct the party's response. His Shadow Chancellor, as the self-appointed godfather of the Project, would continue to bypass LOTO when he disagreed with them. His calculation was that he was a more convincing evangelist for the Project than Corbyn and a superior strategist to Milne.

On 4 September, the NEC met to consider IHRA again. By then it was almost too late to mitigate any of the damage the summer had inflicted on the Project. The previous week, McDonnell's worst fears about the future of the party had been partially vindicated by the resignation of back-bench stalwart Frank Field from the PLP, and rumours in the press of plans for a more formal split of the kind planned at Fair Oak Farm. On the eve of the NEC meeting, McDonnell had taken to the *Andrew Marr Show* sofa to implore MPs not to go.

Yet Corbyn entered the meeting determined to make one last quixotic stand for his cause. By September, there was a clear majority for the full IHRA definition and its examples on the NEC: each of the major trade unions had come out in support of the plan over August. Murphy and Jackson both told him that he would lose. But still he persisted. He told Murphy he had made up his mind. 'OK, you want to die in a ditch, Jeremy, you die in a ditch,' she told him. 'But you're going to get beat.'

Corbyn rarely addressed the NEC, but was moved to do so this time. Reading from a page-and-a-half statement, he urged its members not to adopt the examples without an accompanying caveat that would have clarified: 'It cannot be considered racist to treat Israel like any other state.' Having seen the steep cost the party had paid for his inflexibility, the NEC made clear it would not do so. The saga ended as it had begun: with an expression of Corbyn's intransigence.

With Labour's party conference now looming, it had an even bigger definition to agree on.

7

Days of Remain

Keir Starmer never intended to become Labour's Remainer-in-Chief. His ambition upon becoming Shadow Brexit Secretary in October 2016 was not to thwart Britain's departure from the European Union but see it delivered, albeit with a minimum of pain. To Remainers like Alastair Campbell, he was the patron saint of disappointment. In the summer of 2018, Starmer visited the sultan of spin in his North London kitchen to disabuse him of the idea that Brexit could be stopped. 'I don't know why you're doing this,' he told Campbell. 'We've had the referendum. You know you can't stop this. It's got to happen.' Though LOTO suspected Starmer's aim was to obstruct and delay, in private his sympathies were aligned with theirs. Starmer wanted to make Brexit happen.

David Davis trusted this to be the case, even if LOTO did not. Away from the Dispatch Box, and the thrust and parry of Commons debate, the Brexit Secretary felt he had an ally in Starmer. They might not have agreed on the *how* of Brexit, but Davis could at least be sure they ultimately agreed on the *what*. He made sure his opposite number was appointed to the Privy Council, and could enjoy the confidential government briefings accorded to its members. In Brussels, too, he opened doors for Labour: with the UK's ambassador to the EU, Tim Barrow, and Michel Barnier, the EU's chief negotiator. The strictures of party politics demanded they did not acknowledge it, but Davis and Starmer came to like one another. In the square-jawed lawyer from North London, the grand old man of Tory Euroscepticism saw someone on whom he could depend.

Starmer strived to project the same image to Europe. The former Director of Public Prosecutions had not left a storied career as a barrister to posture in opposition. He wanted to govern. Often he would behave as if he already was. If the May government did indeed collapse, Starmer would come to save Brexit, not to bury it. A Shadow minister recalled: 'Keir was always determined to act like he was in government, and could be negotiating with the EU. It did seem like a possibility at times: the government could have fallen at any point, we had close votes, it was a hung parliament. He wanted to take things forward that could be the basis of a negotiation with Brussels. We weren't, just for the sake of the internal politics of managing the PLP, going to declare for things that we knew didn't stack up.'

May and June 2018 saw MPs and peers chew over the EU Withdrawal Bill, the meatiest piece of Brexit legislation to come before Parliament since the referendum itself. Its legal function was to transfer European law onto the domestic statute book. For Remainers in Labour, Corbyn's speech in Coventry, in which he committed to 'a' customs union with the EU, had been a marginal gain. But it had not gone far enough. Now the PLP's most vocal Remainers, chief among them Chuka Umunna and Chris Leslie, saw the EU Withdrawal Bill as their ticket to a Norway-style Brexit of continued single-market membership: with help from Conservative rebels, they expected to amend the bill to lock the government into negotiating membership of the European Economic Area (EEA), and with it the same access to the single market that the UK enjoyed as an EU member state. To all intents and purposes, it would be as if Brexit had not happened. All they needed was Starmer's support.

It was not forthcoming. When the Lords amended the Withdrawal Bill with a proposal to keep Britain in the EEA, Starmer did not ride to the rescue and throw his weight behind it. He had never believed in Norway: better to be a rule-maker, he said, than a rule-taker. Besides, MPs in the faded coalfield towns that had fuelled the 2016 Leave vote in the first place would not have let him go there even if he had wanted to. To accept membership of the single market was to accept the free movement of people, and their constituents would not wear it, as the likes of John Mann and Gareth Snell reminded their colleagues at PLP meetings. With MPs in his view 'too divided' to accept the EEA, Starmer instead proposed a soft Brexit of his own – expressed in the sort of opaque, lawyerly language that was his stock-in-trade. The United Kingdom would have 'full access' to Europe's internal market and 'shared institutions and regulations'. Remainers believed he was obfuscating. And in any case, May's Brexit legislation passed without a blemish. Five Labour MPs who did back the EEA amendment were summarily sacked from the front bench.

MPs like Leslie had come to expect disappointment when it came to LOTO and Brexit. But what did Starmer *really* want? They did not know. Apart, perhaps, from the fact that he was happy to leave the European Union. Yet the facts were about to change – and with them, Starmer's mind.

On 6 July, exactly a month after Starmer set out the broad brush-strokes of Labour's preferred trading relationship with Brussels, May did the same at a Cabinet awayday at Chequers. She had faced a choice between maximising either Britain's sovereignty post-Brexit or its access to the EU's internal market – and had chosen the latter. Though far from a soft Brexit, it was not the decisive breach from Europe's economic structures that Brexiteers like Davis had hoped for. Within days, he and Boris Johnson resigned. Before long, dozens of Conservative MPs joined them in demanding a clean break from Brussels. A debate that had hitherto been conducted on fairly nebulous terms began to polarise – and both LOTO and Starmer needed a plan. Now May had finally published her own blueprint, Starmer could say with certainty that it failed his six tests. Labour MPs would vote it down. He and LOTO knew that much. What remained to be agreed was what they would do next.

In the left's imagination, party conference, where delegates elected by the grass roots adjudicated on the issues of the day alongside the unions, was their bulwark against leaders inclined to lurch to the centre. But now pro-Europeans on both the left and right of the party wanted to play the leadership at its own game. With Corbyn seemingly unwilling to move towards a decisive answer on Brexit of his own accord, they planned to use conference to move him themselves.

While LOTO had managed to keep Brexit off the conference floor in 2017, the change in the political climate meant they would now not be so lucky. In ordinary times, the compositing process was easy enough to fix. Motions submitted by local Labour parties or unions on any given policy issue were collated and haggled over until a compromise wording for approval by the conference floor could be agreed. If consensus could not be reached, then delegates would vote on more than one motion. Democratic though the latter outcome might have been, it was seldom in the interests of any leadership – even one that prided itself on fostering grass-roots democracy – to allow it to happen. Rather, the point of the compositing meeting was for LOTO to ensure it was pointless. Their objective in the months before the party decamped for a long weekend in Liverpool was to ensure that friendly unions and constituency parties submitted the motions that might make up the eventual compromise. Though they knew Labour policy needed to evolve in response to the new political reality at Westminster, they neither wanted nor expected to take an explicitly pro-EU position. But an unlikely alliance of left and right had other ideas.

To LOTO's right were the People's Vote campaign, whose objective was to secure a second referendum – with Remain on the ballot paper – on any Brexit deal that the government secured. Theirs was not a staff schooled in the art of grass-roots democracy. New Labour's greying alumni network pulled the strings. Peter Mandelson and Alastair Campbell's presence lent the operation the conspiratorial energy of a gang of old lags reassembling for one last heist. Tom Baldwin, the former *Times* journalist and Ed Miliband aide who had once been Campbell's favoured court journalist, headed up its spin operation. In the pages of the *Thunderer* he had helped amplify the Blair government's case for war with Iraq. Now he and Campbell worked to force Labour into adopting a policy that in the eyes of some Corbynites would make for an even bigger breach of trust with the electorate.

The arrival of Corbynsceptic refugees from Southside had changed the political complexion of the organisation from Liberal Democrat yellow to a deeper shade of Labour red. John Stolliday and Patrick Heneghan bolstered its ranks in early May. Its spokespeople on the green benches of the Commons, meanwhile, were moderates to a man and woman. Mandelson and Campbell would meet pro-refer-endum MPs every Monday in the Commons. Umunna and Leslie were the most vocal on the airwaves. Stephen Doughty, the feline MP for Cardiff South who had quit as a Shadow minister live on the BBC in protest at Corbyn's sacking of Pat McFadden in January 2016, served as its de facto whip alongside Alison McGovern, the chair of Progress. Like the left-wing entryists they abhorred, they knew that the only way to effect the change they wanted was to amend the policy of the

Labour Party. Yet they were hobbled by a rather obvious problem: Corbyn himself might have struggled to assemble a group less compatible with his inner circle, whom Remainers had for months tried and failed to influence.

Baldwin had discovered just how inhospitable LOTO would prove to their advances first-hand shortly after his appointment in December 2017, when he met Jon Trickett in Portcullis House. Trickett was 'shifting miserably' from foot to foot when he told Baldwin: 'Karie wants to see you in LOTO.' Upon arriving in his old workplace, Baldwin was confronted by an irate Murphy. She jabbed her finger in his chest, and barked: 'Who the fuck are you? What the fuck do you think you're doing?' He later recalled: 'It was a full-frontal attack. I hadn't really met Karie before. I never had anything to do with her. I just thought she was magnificent. I was sort of slightly laughing. Initially that wound her up, and then eventually I think she saw what it was and I said, "I'm a Labour Party person. I'm not going anywhere." She softened a bit to me after that.' Trickett later told Baldwin: 'The reason she hates you is because of Falkirk. You worked for Ed. She's never forgiven anyone.' But even without the historical baggage, the People's Vote campaign stood little chance of wooing Murphy. She and others believed the outfit was essentially a Trojan Horse for Umunna's leadership ambitions. They had no intentions of letting it through the gates of Corbyn's office, no matter how sincere its emissaries seemed in their loyalty to the Labour brand.

Unable to wield influence via the informal networks that they had ruled in the days of sofa government, they instead turned to the democratic structures that Blairites had traditionally neglected. They pinned their hopes on the compositing meeting and set to work on one of the biggest exercises in grass-roots democracy ever undertaken on the British left: corralling hundreds of friendly Constituency Labour Parties to submit pro-EU motions ahead of the compositing process. Heneghan was put to work ensuring that local parties did so. As factional foot soldiers of the old school, he and Stolliday did what Baldwin and James McGrory, another senior People's Vote official who had worked for Nick Clegg in government, were either unwilling or unable to do: game Labour's byzantine internal democracy. They also knew how to deal with the unions. In a very meaningful sense, the People's Vote crew were – for that summer, at least – the living embodiment of the vision Corbyn had set out in his first leadership campaign for a vibrant, bottom-up, member-led party. The irony, of course, was that they had been among those who had done all that they could to prevent that vision ever becoming reality at Southside.

So it was that the Portcullis House office of Chris Leslie became a hotbed of Corbynism – at least as far as internal party democracy was concerned. Having spent much of the year drawing up a plan to leave the Labour Party altogether, he was now making one final attempt to force a change of course. He gathered Stolliday, McGovern and Frances Grove White, another former Labour staffer recruited to the People's Vote campaign, to thrash out the wording. Stolliday, who knew the intricacies of the process from his days in Southside offi-cialdom, was entrusted with the pen, while Leslie paced the room, dictating sentences in his lilting West Yorkshire tones. Umunna, whose office was next door, popped in intermittently with contributions to the creative process. As one of those present recalls: 'We kept the phrase "people's vote" out of the motion itself, because there was already a sense that campaign was a bit toxic, and seemed a bit of a Blairite, Mandelsony operation. We called it a "public vote" instead.' It was a phrase that would assume a new significance by the time they arrived in Liverpool. MPs who attended Campbell's and Mandelson's Monday night meetings returned to their constituencies to spread the gospel, with Stella Creasy leading the push to have the People's Vote motion submitted via as many Constituency Labour Parties as possible.

If the People's Vote had a spiritual opposite, it was Another Europe Is Possible. On everything but Europe, their politics were Jeremy Corbyn's. Their operation was nimble, millennial, and run on a shoe-string: not for them the millions in funding provided by the PR mogul Roland Rudd, brother of Amber. Yet LOTO's refusal to engage had driven them to the same place as the Blairites whose legacy activists like Michael Chessum, Another Europe's national organiser, had come into politics to exorcise from the Labour Party. They had lobbied hard for LOTO to adopt a soft-Brexit position that retained the free move-ment of people and single-market membership. But they had already had their fingers burned by LOTO's connivance to keep Brexit off the conference agenda in 2017. Corbyn's team had subsequently radicalised them with the same kind of intransigence that met their factional enemies in Umunna and Baldwin. As Chessum recalled: 'The response we got from LOTO was, at best, silence, and at worst: "You're sabotaging Jeremy, you're sabotaging the Project, and you're in league with the Blairites to undermine the left." We'd tried. We really tried to compromise.' By the summer, they had adopted an overtly and aggressively pro-Remain posture and began to campaign as the Left Against Brexit. For the first time in decades in Labour politics, the likes of Stolliday were grateful for them.

LOTO, on the other hand, were not. It was apparent by September that they would have to move to support a public vote in some form or another at conference – lest they be moved further still. They devised a 'two-pronged process' to manage the shift. Amy Jackson and Mark Simpson were assigned to work up a text for the compositing process that Milne and Murphy could live with. Starmer, meanwhile, set about schmoozing the unions, who would agree their own common position at a special TUC conference in the weeks before Labour headed to Merseyside.

Starmer sought to kill any opposition with candour. He told the executives of each union: 'Look, this is my problem. This is going to be *our* problem if we don't act.' In fact, the TSSA, the Corbynite rail union, had long been pushing for an explicitly pro-referendum and pro-Remain position. They were joined by the GMB, whose support for a second referendum belied its reputation as a spiritual guardian of Labour's heartlands. Its general secretary, Tim Roache, was in regular contact with the People's Vote team. Though other members of his executive were less keen, its membership was more pliable than Labour MPs imagined. In 2017, the GMB had polled 10,000 of its members on the prospect of a referendum vote on Brexit. It found that, with the right question, they were ready.

Though Len McCluskey's own views were never knowingly underexpressed, Unite were much harder to pin down. LOTO aides observed that its huge membership was 'all over the place'. Neither McCluskey nor his dyspeptic deputy, Howard Beckett, wanted to adopt a policy that would alienate white working-class voters. To those triaging the process from LOTO, Beckett's obstructionism was 'a nightmare'. He would invariably greet suggestions of a second referendum with a blunt dismissal: 'The working class voted Leave. Listen to the working class.' Yet those listening to Unite could not discern what they did want, beyond acknowledgement of their grumbles. As strident as they sounded, its leadership was ultimately happy to move towards a compromise. 'They didn't want to look too Remain-y, they didn't want to look Leave-y,' a LOTO aide said. They certainly did not want to be seen to work with the People's Vote campaign, who instead sought to influence the union from 'the bottom up' with covert meetings with industrial activists at Millbank. UNISON was an even tougher nut for Starmer and LOTO to crack. In principle, it was prepared to move towards a compromise that placated the Remainers in its own ranks, but its leadership insisted on involving its members in a protracted conversation on the way forward, and like Unite's, its membership was divided. Nonetheless, as September approached, the big unions appeared to be moving to precisely the place Starmer wanted them.

Ian Lavery and Jon Trickett followed developments from their constituencies – at first with trepidation, then with anger. Like McCluskey and Beckett, they feared what a shift to Remain might mean for Labour's standing in seats like theirs: the sort of towns the party had been established to defend. They made their displeasure clear to LOTO. As had been the case in Coventry, Andrew Fisher took Starmer's side: supporting some sort of public vote at conference was necessary. Milne, too, had accepted that the party had little alternative but to make some gesture of support towards a second referendum.

Within the Shadow Cabinet, Trickett and Lavery had already lost the argument. Emily Thornberry had been first to fold. The Shadow Foreign Secretary's big compromise had been accepting the result of the 2016 referendum *at all*. Internally, she had always been the most vocal proponent of efforts to soften the party position – much more so than Starmer. In due course, she would be the first to agitate for a conference motion that explicitly committed the party to holding a second referendum. As a result, LOTO had been intensely suspicious. Milne, Murphy and Jackson combed her media interventions for evidence of perfidy. On occasion, Thornberry would refer to Labour's support for *the* customs union, rather than *a* customs union – the letter of its policy – in interviews. Shortly after leaving one studio or another, her phone would buzz with a reprimand from LOTO. She would inevitably respond: 'What's the difference? It's the same thing. I usually say *a* customs union, but on *this* occasion, I didn't. It wasn't a deliberate thing.' Her LOTO interlocutor would insist that it really was deliberate, and really did matter. 'It's very different,' the reply would come, 'people see it very differently, and you must not say *the* customs union.'

The people who saw it differently, of course, were LOTO. They feared, rightly, that the Shadow Cabinet was fragmenting. Indeed, Corbyn's position had been not to take one – so as to ensure the Shadow Cabinet and his own inner circle were united around the same one, whatever it was. He would be a mere conduit for consensus. But his oldest allies were wobbling around him. Once a strident Eurosceptic, Diane Abbott had mellowed with the times and took the same line as Another Europe and voters and Labour activists in her constituency: the Brexit vote of 2016 was the result of a racist, right-wing project that all good progressives should resist. She had a debilitating headache on the day in 2017 the Commons voted for Article 50 that formally began the withdrawal process. The impact a Tory Brexit would have on migration weighed particularly heavily on Abbott. At meetings of the Brexit subcommittee she argued alongside Thornberry and Starmer in opposition to Trickett's and Lavery's axis of blokeishness. A LOTO aide recalled: 'Emily and Diane wanted it to go the other way – into proper referendum mode.'

At times the dialogue was about as constructive as Christmas dinner conversation between *bien pensant* students and their parents. In one meeting Lavery, who abided by the same working-class honour code that had governed behaviour in the miners' welfare clubs of Northumberland, was even moved to break his self-denying ordinance on swearing in front of women. Abbott had appeared to suggest that northern Leave voters were racist; Starmer gently nodded, seemingly in assent. Lavery exploded, ranting at length at Starmer, the only man available to absorb the fusillade. 'If you fucking agree, do you want to fucking try that again, son?' His rage did not cow Starmer, whose manoeuvres in the lead-up to conference would give Lavery his answer.

Even John McDonnell appeared to be wandering off the reservation. As was the case with anti-Semitism, his priority was protecting the Project at all costs. If government was the aim, there was no such thing as an unholy alliance. He would later ask Tom Baldwin: 'Are you people who will help us win power? Or are you people who are going to stop us winning power?' He applied that analytical framework ruthlessly – and in doing so found himself strange bed-fellows indeed. One People's Vote source said: 'John got it early. He's married to a pollster.'

Yet as the tide turned slowly in their favour, Remainers were still unsure of themselves. Not only was it far from clear whether Starmer's lobbying campaign would deliver a commitment to a second refer-endum, but Starmer himself was still reticent. In the midst of his meetings with the unions Starmer met Tom Baldwin for the first of what would become regular clandestine encounters at a Kentish Town café whose often deserted upstairs room the Shadow Brexit Secretary would frequent for orange juice and avocado on toast. To the People's Vote campaign, Starmer was a disappointment. He remained committed, first and foremost, to negotiating a Brexit deal – no matter how popular endorsing a second referendum would prove among many Labour members and voters. 'If it meant that Britain got a worse deal,' Baldwin recalled, 'he said he wasn't prepared to do that.' Michael Chessum agreed: 'Keir's mythology now is all about how he was always a Remainer from the start, he was always on our side. As the person who was negotiating on our behalf . . . I didn't have a single meeting with Keir Starmer or anyone in his office, or anyone who was passing a message from me to him or from him to me. There was no sense in which Keir Starmer was cooperating with the Remainers who had gotten those motions to conference.'

Starmer was not yet the spiritual leader in Parliament that Labour Remainers yearned for. At times, he barely seemed like an ally. But in private, he urged his critics to be patient. One People's Vote official said: 'He said he could only go as far as the rope will let him. He was constantly seeking to increase the radius in which he could roam. But it was incremental. He is a cautious, careful politician – but what's impressive is that he was pursuing an overall objective and direction.' For now, that objective and LOTO's – was that conference should end with Labour committed to push for a general election, and failing that, a 'public vote'.

The Trades Union Congress gathered in Manchester on 9 September. Hours of at times testy deliberation saw them end up roughly where Starmer and LOTO wanted. The agreed position was almost impos-sible to disagree with: the unions would at first seek a general election, and failing that, a 'popular vote on the terms of Brexit'. It was just strong enough to satisfy those who wanted a commitment to a second referendum – but ambiguous enough to sustain the idea that Labour would still deliver Brexit. But cajoling the unions into agreeing a position among themselves was one thing; ensuring the fragile new consensus did not combust upon contact with conference delegates was quite another. Starmer's real work was only just beginning.

In early September, Starmer and Mark Simpson had been given advance sight of the hundreds of conference motions submitted by local parties on a trip to Scottish Labour's headquarters. Most demanded the same thing: a second referendum. Some even wanted Labour to commit to campaign for Remain. Wary of the fight over the wording that awaited in Liverpool, Starmer read every last one. Only by emulating the Corbynites in speaking for the grass roots, not himself, would he have the authority to win the day.

LOTO knew what they were up against almost as soon as they arrived in Liverpool. 'Literally everyone,' a senior adviser recalls, 'was wearing a "Love Corbyn, Hate Brexit" t-shirt. That was the problem we had: they were loyal to Corbyn, but saw no problem with taking both positions.' Even the porter at the Hilton hotel – temporarily home to Len McCluskey and Unite's delegation – was wearing one.

The People's Voters understood the dynamic intuitively. On 23 September, the Sunday afternoon of conference, they unleashed their opening salvo. Thousands of marchers thronged to Liverpool's iconic Pier Head for a rally painstakingly choreographed by Campbell and Baldwin. If the object was to detoxify their cause once and for all in the eyes of the Labour grass roots, the method was to keep Umunna as far away from the stage as humanly possible. The line-up would instead be 'very, very left wing' – at least by the old Blairites' rather genteel standards. Manuel Cortes, general secretary of the TSSA, was among those coaxed into speaking. The Gibraltarian giant's Corbynite bona fides could not be questioned: he had been the first union leader to throw his weight behind Jez in 2015, and the TSSA's Euston offices had at one time or another served as the headquarters for both Corbyn's leadership campaign and Momentum. 'He gave us a veneer of left-wing authenticity,' one recalled. Campbell also enlisted Peter Reid, the simian Everton FC legend reborn in late middle age as an aggressive anti-Tory tweeter, to lend a certain Scouse verité to proceedings. 'Johnson, Gove, Rees-Mogg,' he spat.

'Absolute dopes!' So thick were the crowds that they briefly brought traffic to a halt.

LOTO watched with trepidation. Their path to a compromise that could unite the party was narrow. Excitable Remainers were the last thing they needed. And even if LOTO's preferred wording passed, would the rump of members who loved Corbyn, yes, but did *not* hate Brexit split from the rest of the grass roots and revolt? Every alternative route led to disaster. Worse still, it would be played out in full view of a media primed for a Labour split on Brexit.

It took close to seven hours for Labour to agree to disagree on Brexit. At 6.30 p.m. on the Sunday evening of conference, more than a hundred delegates piled into a stuffy meeting room in Liverpool's ACC, a glass-and-steel behemoth on the banks of the Mersey, to thrash out the compromise that Starmer and LOTO had spent months brokering.

The Shadow Brexit Secretary chaired proceedings. His aides Chris Ward and Ben Nunn acted as his enforcers, as did Simpson, shuttling between union representatives and delegates as the night ground on. Karie Murphy slipped in and out. The People's Voters enjoyed no such institutional advantage: Stolliday instead paced the corridor outside, attempting to orchestrate a Remain rearguard via WhatsApp.

Cortes moved quickly to spike his guns. He wanted a motion that favoured Remain but did not completely isolate LOTO. His people had flanked the entrance to the meeting room like bouncers, distributing copies of a proposed motion that both the TSSA – and ultimately Corbyn – could accept. Once discussions kicked off, he ensured he was first to speak. His passionate, wild-eyed oration made clear that he would not leave the room without a form of words he could live with.

The question that divided delegates was just how strong a commitment to a second referendum Labour should make. Would it support a public vote on Brexit itself? Or would it offer its backing only to a public vote on a Brexit deal? Or would it, as LOTO hoped, support all options, including but not limited to a public vote on either? Michael Chessum and the Corbynite Remainers were confident that the meeting would plump for the first option – a vote on Brexit itself – for which they had the backing of the unions. But the deal had collapsed as Chessum made his way into the meeting. UNISON pulled out, and the GMB followed. Ian Hodson, the mop-haired president of the Bakers' Union, blundered into the meeting late. Furious that he'd been persuaded by LOTO to table a motion he did not support in order to bring on board the other unions who were now deserting, he demanded the floor. 'THE BAKERS MUST BE HEARD!' he barked. Before his rant could begin in earnest, however, a delegate familiar with the small print of the process had him evicted: only those who had been present for the start of the meeting were allowed in the room. He was not the only one. Richard Corbett, the hyperactive Remainer who led Labour's MEPs, was asked by Starmer to leave lest his enthusiasm derail progress towards a compromise. He was left to stand, neck craned to the door, with the BBC's Laura Kuenssberg and Ross Hawkins.

Corbyn himself was barred from entry by aides. As the night wore on, he had asked one aide: 'Would it be a good idea if I just pop in?' Those present recall the answer was expressed in two short letters. Having been actively disinterested in the difficult gestation of Labour's Brexit policy – or lack thereof – only the prospect of witnessing the byzantine workings of the party's internal democracy had piqued his interest. For Starmer, the arrival of a higher power risked upsetting the room's delicate balance of forces.

By 8.24 p.m., two Corbyn-free hours into the session, his team were confident they were in control. Stella Creasy sent a brusque message to the WhatsApp group set up by Stolliday to coordinate pro-Remain efforts. 'Keir's people briefing they have the room.' But if anyone was in control of the room, it was tedium. Delegates became restless as hours passed without agreement – or tea and biscuits, which had been withheld deliberately in an attempt to accelerate proceedings. One rather melodramatically complained that to be denied a break was a violation of their human rights.

Cortes, meanwhile, was building consensus for a new form of words. Labour would keep 'all options on the table – including a public vote'. Though uneasy, both the Corbynite Remainers and the People's Voters came to begrudgingly accept that it was the best they could do. Just before 1 a.m., an exhausted room was on the brink of passing the motion. Unanimity was required, but one particularly zealous Europhile held out. By that point, however, the rest of those present were ready for bed. The lonely dissenter was ignored. Unanimity was declared. Labour would 'support all options remaining on the table, including campaigning for a public vote'. It fell well short of what Remainers had initially hoped for, but they still found cause for celebration. 'What a night,' was Stolliday's verdict. 'Small, incremental progress.' Starmer's team were delighted. They had, as planned, avoided all-out civil war and inched Labour, crab-like, closer to a pro-referendum position.

*

In the week before conference, Starmer had met a friend for lunch. They were not of the Labour Party but were nonetheless familiar with its internal politics. The conversation turned, in time, to the task that awaited the Shadow Brexit Secretary in Liverpool. 'You should say in your speech that Remain is an option,' they said, 'because the party needs to hear it.' Starmer demurred. 'LOTO clear the speeches, and they just won't let me say that.' But his lunch partner was insistent. 'For good or ill, people see you as the leading pro-Remain voice in the Labour Party. You've got to show some guts and do it. If you don't, it will really damage you.'

Starmer might not have taken that advice were it not for a mistake by John McDonnell early in the morning of Monday 24 September, mere hours after Starmer and the compositing meeting had put the new policy to bed. McDonnell had drawn the short straw and would be appearing on that morning's *Today* programme. Predictably, he was asked about Labour's new Brexit policy – and with it the prospect of a second referendum that cancelled Brexit. McDonnell was categorical: the 'public vote' would not include the option to Remain. 'If we are going to respect the last referendum, it will be about the deal, it will be a negotiation on the deal,' he said. The same day, McCluskey sought out the *Guardian* and rubbished the idea. 'The referendum shouldn't be on: "Do we want to go back into the European Union?" The people have already decided on that.'

Starmer and the People's Voters interpreted it as a calculated slight at best – and at worst an attempt to cut the new policy off at the knees. With the ink barely dry on the page of a compromise which had taken months to negotiate, LOTO and its allies had summarily ripped it up.

Yet McDonnell had not intended to do so at all. Friends maintain he was badly briefed. It was the first conference in three years he had attended with his new spinner Andy Whitaker. In any case, neither accompanied him to face *Today*'s Nick Robinson: instead, he went with a young press officer from Labour's regional office in the north-west. By accident, not design, he had laid down the gauntlet for Starmer, who took to the conference stage the following afternoon.

It was there that Starmer, for all his reluctance and caution over the preceding months, would cement his status as the standard-bearer of Labour's Remainers. As he reached his peroration, his hands gripped the lectern. His gaze shifted from the teleprompter to his paper notes. 'Our preference is clear, we want a general election to sweep away this failed government. But if that's not possible, we must have other options. That must include campaigning for a public vote. It's right that Parliament has the first say, but if we need to break the impasse our options must include campaigning for a public vote and nobody is ruling out Remain as an option.'

First, silence. Then a standing ovation. In the front row, Karie Murphy sat stony-faced and silent, as did Dennis Skinner, the cantankerous old goat of the Campaign Group. If some in LOTO had not quite understood the significance of the Brexit policy that had been agreed at conference, they certainly did now. The reaction among Corbyn's aides was one of fury. Amy Jackson asked Andrew Fisher a simple question: 'What the fuck?' Fisher, who others in LOTO increasingly saw as a de facto Starmerite, demurred and even defended the ad lib. In the absence of back-up, Jackson took unilateral action. She stormed backstage, phone in hand. It had taken only eleven minutes for the Tory press office to clip the offending phrase for Twitter. 'CONFIRMED', its post screamed. 'Labour will not respect the result of the referendum #Lab18.'

'What have you done?' Jackson asked Starmer, applause still ringing in his ears, as she brandished the tweet. 'Look at what you've just done!' Before their exchange could begin in earnest they clocked the impish broadcaster Michael Crick observing them at close quarters. They retired to a side room to have it out. Jackson accused him of deliberately undermining Corbyn. He had gone well beyond the policy that had been so painstakingly brokered the night before. Starmer immediately blamed McDonnell's earlier intervention. 'John had said

Remain won't be on the ballot,' he said. 'I had to correct it.' His voice raised in self-righteous indignation, he asked: 'What did you want me to do?' The row broke up inconclusively. But Jackson was not yet finished. LOTO colleagues claim they later saw one of Starmer's aides weeping after receiving a similar upbraiding.

But it was Team Corbyn who had suffered real upset. One LOTO aide sitting in the audience spoke for many that day when they dead-panned after Starmer's speech: 'He's completely fucked us.' In staking his claim to the Remain mantle, Starmer had certainly screwed his rivals for the Labour leadership. He had also screwed LOTO and the Project. In Corbyn's own speech the following day, he made no attempt to steer away from Starmer's words. All options were on the table. And now Labour's options included cancelling Brexit altogether. By making legitimate what had once been taboo, Starmer would hasten divisions not just within the PLP, but inside a leader's office where tensions were already at boiling point.

8

A Deep State

Jeremy Corbyn did not have a preferred candidate to succeed Laura Parker as his private secretary. In fact, he had not wanted to hire another private secretary at all. When Seumas Milne and Karie Murphy presented a shortlist of fourteen applicants to their leader in December 2017, he vetoed every single one. He bristled at what he saw as an imposition on his autonomy, of which there had already been rather too many. But after Corbyn vetoed a second shortlist, Murphy and Andrew Fisher went ahead and interviewed candidates anyway. If Corbyn would not choose, they would have to choose for him. They found that Iram Chamberlain was an imposition Corbyn could live with.

LOTO aides often joked that their colleagues could be divided neatly into two categories: people who knew Jeremy, and people who knew Karie. Chamberlain was a member of the first group. Her husband, Iain, had been a leading light of the Stop the War Coalition. They shared an anti-imperialist, pro-Palestine politics that were very much to Corbyn's taste. He had even attended the couple's wedding. If he had to have a private secretary, a comrade would do.

The affection was mutual. Even before she came to join the LOTO payroll Chamberlain wore her allegiance to the Project loudly and proudly. In her interview Fisher noted her laptop bore a Corbyn sticker. Senior male aides saw her as a 'fan' or 'groupie' whose enthusiasm might prove a hindrance rather than a help. Fisher was wary, but Murphy pushed ahead. Above all, appointing a private secretary would make her own life easier – and with it the Project's. She could not have been more wrong.

Chamberlain and Murphy disagreed on more or less everything from the moment her employment in LOTO began. It did not help that they could not agree on what she had been hired to do. In

Murphy's eyes, Chamberlain's job entailed making decisions for the benefit of Corbyn and the Project. Often that might mean making decisions that Corbyn himself did not want to take. That was certainly her approach to managing LOTO.

Chamberlain saw it differently. As far as she was concerned, she worked for Jeremy Corbyn, not Karie Murphy. She was there to give effect to Corbyn's will and Corbyn's will alone, even if that meant blocking out three hours in his diary on a Monday morning to visit his favourite Turkish barber. Orders issued by others were irrelevant. A LOTO adviser said: 'It became so evident that she was managing things the way Jeremy wanted it done, and not the way the Project *needed* it done.'

What Murphy saw as insubordination, Chamberlain saw as loyalty. At times she felt like the only member of Corbyn's staff who respected his sovereignty as leader. On occasion Corbyn would directly instruct her to do one thing, only for Murphy to arbitrarily veto it and flatly insist on another. 'We're not going to do that.' Chamberlain had expected to be Corbyn's wing-woman, staying close to his side at key events and dispensing political counsel. Instead, she found him – and herself – frozen out by Murphy from key decisions, as were John McDonnell and Diane Abbott, to her eyes. She found the power of the chief of staff to be incomprehensible and unjustifiable, and she took to telling Corbyn so.

She also clashed with Murphy over anti-Semitism. Chamberlain was a stout defender of Corbyn's refusal to budge on points of principle and believed that the anti-Semitism allegation was cynically being used to shift his position on Zionism. Murphy believed in the sort of compromises with political reality that the leader found particularly painful.

Chamberlain's ambition was not only a source of irritation for Murphy, but an existential threat. Since the attempted coup of 2016, her modus operandi had been to protect the leader at all costs. As far as his most senior allies were concerned, Corbyn, a man well endowed with idealism but not guile, was incapable of doing so himself. To Murphy, that meant exercising extreme control over whom he met and what he knew. Said one hostile staffer: 'She was selectively choosing what information was given to him. It meant he was quite removed from the office.' Another friend of the leader described the result as:

'A Fort Knox on Jeremy. People would try and get to speak to him, and they wouldn't be able to get there.' Chamberlain's sin had been to attempt to prise open the doors.

Chamberlain's employment posed another problem for life in LOTO. More than three months into the job, she had still not received security clearance for a parliamentary pass, only issued after counterterrorism vetting by the Home Office. Instead, she trooped through the airport-style scanners at the entrance to Parliament every morning and was furnished with a paper visitor's pass. From there she would be escorted to Norman Shaw South by a colleague. It was a cumbersome state of affairs, not to mention one that contravened parliamentary rules. It also posed a question with no clear answer: what was taking so long?

To Chamberlain, who was from a Muslim family, the cause of the delay was obvious enough: Islamophobia. She told colleagues of her suspicions. Murphy did not disagree that some form of racial profiling was the likeliest reason. But she was unwilling to rule out another motive – or Chamberlain concealing an inconvenient truth about her past. She took her concerns to Milne and Corbyn, and asked what the leader knew about his private secretary. He attested to their friendship and little more. 'There is a problem here, Jeremy,' she told him. 'And we're going to have to get to the bottom of it.'

It was when Murphy confronted Chamberlain directly that she concluded there was more to the case than the new staffer was willing to admit. Murphy asked her to come clean about anything that might have impeded her security clearance. Chamberlain insisted she had nothing to tell. Murphy, whose early working life had been spent as a psychiatric nurse, later told a colleague that Chamberlain had struggled to make eye contact. She became convinced there was a problem.

Milne and Andrew Murray were dispatched to make inquiries. Both had been involved with Stop the War and had links to Chamberlain's circle that Murphy did not. They returned with the news that Corbyn expected but had not wanted to hear. Chamberlain's brothers had awkward CVs – and might be on the radar of the security services. One of them, Mohammed Basith, had travelled to Syria in the wake of the Arab Spring, albeit as a blogger and not to fight. He denounced ISIS. The other brother, with whom Chamberlain was not close, had been an active participant in online extremist circles. In online posts on Islamic forums, he had expressed sympathy with al-Qaeda and armed jihad – and openly pondered the question of going to Syria to wage holy war.

Murphy resolved to confront Chamberlain with what she had learned. For the first time she threatened to sack her. 'You've failed to disclose something to me that you should have disclosed,' she said. 'And I want to know what it is. And if you don't tell me what it is, you're finished, because you're working here illegally.' It was then that Chamberlain acknowledged that her family background might have posed a problem. She declined to go into further detail, but soon after made her case directly to Corbyn and Milne. Citing the fact that her brothers were religious Muslims and dressed conservatively, she asked rhetorically: 'Might they have raised the suspicions of security services?' One witness to the exchange claimed: 'It was an open-ended question, not a statement of fact.'

Afterwards, Murphy returned to Corbyn and Milne. 'What do you think?' the leader asked. His chief of staff found the potential dishonesty more perturbing than the substance. Murphy warned that were Chamberlain found to have been economical with the truth, Corbyn would be in a difficult position. The potential for an avoidable controversy was frighteningly obvious. But together the three resolved to leave the ultimate judgement to the parliamentary security services. Chamberlain, after all, had done nothing wrong herself. To allow guilt by association to influence their decision would be to bow to the establishment Islamophobia which all believed to varying degrees was at play. One source familiar with their discussions sums up their thinking: 'These Islamophobic bastards are stopping her getting her pass, and it must be institutional Islamophobia.'

Senior figures in LOTO, not least Corbyn himself, had always had difficult relationships with the security service. He, Milne and Murray were children of the Cold War. Milne's journalistic magnum opus, *The Enemy Within*, had revealed the extent of MI5's involvement in efforts to suppress the miners' strike. From Greenham Common to the War on Terror, they had long been critical of the very arms of the state that now took a close interest in the workings of Corbyn's office.

Those at the heart of the Project suspected that interest was rather too close. Upon John McDonnell's appointment as Shadow Chancellor, one of his aides had suggested that their suite of offices in Norman

Shaw South be debugged. Those present recount the incident with amusement but during the early days of Corbyn's leadership certain LOTO officials approached sensitive discussions with similar caution, choosing to leave the office to speak outside, rather than within the potential range of listening devices.

Murray, like Chamberlain, had been denied a security pass himself, and faced the indignity of queuing up with tourists to enter the parliamentary estate. MI5 had followed Murray's career, which had begun in the Parliamentary Press Gallery as a reporter for Novosti, the USSR's state news agency, with close interest. During his stint at the *Morning Star*, Britain's own communist daily, his father had been drinking at the Travellers' Club on Pall Mall when he was approached by an old acquaintance. 'Ah, Peter,' he said. 'I've just been looking at your son's security file.' Their motivation for withholding approval for Murray's pass was a matter of public record, unlike Chamberlain's. But it did mean that she was not alone.

As 2018 ground on, LOTO came to suspect that MI5 was airing the grudge it held against the Project in public. On 2 September came an attack on Corbyn from the security services in the shape of a well-briefed scoop from Tim Shipman, the political editor of the *Sunday Times*. 'Jeremy Corbyn has been summoned for a personal briefing by the head of MI5 on the terrorist threat to Britain amid questions about his approach to national security,' read its suggestive top line.

The *Sunday Times* reported that Milne, Corbyn and Diane Abbott had been invited to their first briefing with Andrew Parker, the head of the agency, so that they could 'begin to understand the facts of life' when it came to Islamist terror and Russian espionage. Just as embarrassing – and well sourced – was the revelation that Corbyn had apparently snubbed the invitation, citing the demands of an all-day NEC meeting on anti-Semitism on 4 September. When Shipman offered LOTO a right of reply on the story, James Schneider reacted humorously. 'Of course' Corbyn, devotee of Labour democracy that he was, would spend the day at the NEC rather than MI5. 'What else would you expect him to do?' Readers were led to infer that Corbyn and his aides were not only disinclined to get to grips with national security, their party was too disorganised for them to even try.

There were competing theories in LOTO as to how the information had leaked. Milne suspected that Conservative ministers were the paper's sources. Others believed it had been briefed directly by MI5. In either case, the spooks had been the ultimate source of the information, even if it had been conveyed indirectly. 'It originated somewhere,' one LOTO aide joked, 'and it wasn't the Labour Party.' Two weeks later, the *Mail on Sunday* revealed that Murray had been banned from entering Ukraine, information he suggested had been briefed by agents of the 'deep state' in a subsequent column for the *New Statesman*.

The attacks on Corbyn and his staff reinforced long-held LOTO suspicions that the security services applied different standards to the Project than to politicians of the mainstream. Corbyn's radicalism on foreign affairs had been tempered by the responsibilities of his office but he still represented a breach from business as usual when it came to foreign affairs and defence policy. In 2015, just before a contentious vote on airstrikes against the Islamic State in Syria, a serving general had even gone as far as to brief the *Sunday Times* that they would stage a mutiny if a Corbyn government dared tinker with the armed forces. A LOTO aide reflected: 'All of these things were breaches in the protocol in the independence of the Civil Service, the independence, impartiality of the security services, of the military – it was just another reflection that the same rules of the game didn't apply.'

Shami Chakrabarti, whose once exalted reputation as a civil liberties campaigner owed everything to her willingness to take on the security services, was among the most indignant. She described the MI5 story to colleagues as 'constitutionally outrageous'. As LOTO's designated point person on security and human rights, she wrote to Andrew Parker herself. Her letter was at once a show of defiance and an attempt to normalise relations. She cast Parker as the inheritor to a rich lineage of establishment smears. To Chakrabarti, the suggestion that Corbyn had snubbed MI5 deliberately was a Zinoviev letter for the twenty-first century – he would, she insisted, be happy to meet them. She hoped that the security services were not seeking to undermine him as they had Harold Wilson.

Chakrabarti signed off with a warning. She told Parker that she had instructed her staff to neither brief nor leak the letter, and that she expected his staff to do the same. She insisted that Labour, for all the Corbynites' historic grievances with the state, wanted a constructive relationship with the security services. But for that to be feasible they needed minds in MI5 to remain open to that possibility too. That the newspapers did not get wind of the correspondence suggested that it was received in good faith.

But taken together with the prolonged foot-dragging over Chamberlain's parliamentary pass, LOTO's public and private clashes with MI5 did fuel a nagging discomfort – even among those who were not conspiratorially minded by politics or disposition. At best they raised serious and troubling questions about the security establishment's attitudes towards the left and Britain's Muslim community. At worst, they proved – as Andrew Murray wondered aloud – that the deep state was actively conspiring to undermine the Project.

On 4 September, the day Corbyn had been due to meet Parker, Murphy and Chamberlain instead met the Parliamentary Security Department to resolve the issue of the missing pass once and for all. Murphy had sought Chakrabarti's counsel in advance, who advised her to lay out their concerns calmly and methodically. Why had Chamberlain's pass taken so long? Were they briefing the press? Murphy, who suspected the room might be bugged, impressed upon Chamberlain the importance of honesty. Yet two sources familiar with what occurred in the meeting describe Chamberlain's attitude in it as defensive and taciturn. After an uncomfortable discussion about recent leaks to the press, the official asked if there was anything in her background that might be causing delays to her counter-terrorism check. She responded: 'No.' She had a good employment and education record, no criminal past, and her credit rating was sound. The official then pointedly asked whether she knew anyone who might be problematic. Chamberlain braced herself to say no. She later told a colleague: 'My instinct was to do so rather than invite suspicion.' It was then that Murphy said to the room: 'Time out.' She requested a brief recess, to which the security personnel agreed.

It was at that point she again threatened to sack an emotional Chamberlain if she did not provide the clarity they were seeking. Under duress, she is said to have obliged. The officials revealed that they had known far more than they had originally let on. According to one source, they explicitly asked her about her brothers. They then explained that the rigmarole it had taken to secure that basic disclosure might require the case to be escalated to the Clerk of the House – the chief administrator of the Commons – and the Speaker. Yet for all of LOTO's misgivings, the reaction of the officials was – in the words

of another source familiar with the case – 'the opposite of Islamophobic
... they understood why she would conceal it, and that it didn't necessarily make her a bad person or a threat herself'.

Neither Chamberlain nor her husband were as understanding. She
left the meeting in a state of some distress and called Iain, who was
of the view that she should not have confessed. So angry was he at
his wife's treatment at the hands of LOTO and state authority that
he came to Parliament to make his case to Murphy in person. Their
discussion quickly degenerated into a heated row. Yet for all their
differences, Murphy was still willing to face down the establishment
on Chamberlain's behalf. That evening she met Corbyn to discuss the
case. He resolved to defend Chamberlain, who was not alone among
Muslim staff of Corbyn's in having had a less than straightforward
relationship with parliamentary security. On his behalf, Murphy
composed a short email to security officials to reaffirm his support
for Chamberlain.

On 11 September, however, HuffPost reported that Chamberlain
was working in Parliament without security clearance and hinted that
her pass had not been approved 'due to questions over known associates'. In response, the parliamentary authorities played down suggestions that Chamberlain had been a special case, insisting in *The Times*
that it was 'not unprecedented for cases to take several months'. The
same day, however, Eaman Awan – whose married surname happened
to be the same as Chamberlain's maiden name – and Zeyn Mohammed,
two LOTO advisers of Muslim heritage, received emails from those
same authorities demanding further references. LOTO suspected an
orchestrated plot against its ethnic-minority staff. In an email to the
parliamentary authorities on 18 September, Murphy put the charge
of Islamophobia on the record for the first time. Forwarding the
pointed requests for information that Awan and Mohammed had
received, she wrote: 'Your email was sent the day after another member
of LOTO staff was publically [*sic*] humiliated when a story about her
pass application was leaked to the press. You will note that they share
the same surname. Please can you let me know why Eaman has
received this random request?' Then, noting that Mohammed had
been given security clearance and a pass within four days of applying
seven months earlier, she added: 'I am sure you will see the pattern
here. I look forward to your response.'

Corbyn was similarly convinced of institutional racism. Having been forwarded the correspondence by Murphy, he wrote in reply on 18 September: 'I see a pattern here as I am sure you do. Three people with Islamic-sounding names get asked for additional information. It never happened to Laura Parker or anyone else I can recall. We need to be very stern with these people and support our team. Thanks, great letter, JC.'

Chamberlain had finally received her own pass the previous day, and posted a selfie with Corbyn to Twitter as a memento. Yet it was not the end of the office drama – merely the first act.

*

Later that week, at 3 p.m. on Thursday 20 September, Corbyn, Abbott and Milne headed to MI5's HQ at 12 Millbank for their postponed briefing with Andrew Parker. The ninety-minute conversation was not the no-holds-barred lecture on the 'facts of life' that had been bullishly briefed to the *Sunday Times*. Nor were Corbyn and Milne read the Riot Act.

Instead, officials were at pains to stress that they were no longer in the business of flushing out reds from under the bed. LOTO's past associations – be they with Irish republicans or the Soviet Union – were in the past. They disavowed the hostile briefings to the newspapers. Proceedings were altogether more sober and serious, they insisted.

Milne was most struck not by the security services but by a last-minute addition to the LOTO delegation: Chamberlain. Before the meeting began he texted Murphy to ask whether she had signed off her attendance. She explained, using industrial-strength language, that she had not.

Just over a month later, Milne and Murphy had the same conversation again. At 3 p.m. on 30 October LOTO's initiation into securocrat circles continued with a meeting at MI6 in Vauxhall. Murphy had returned from a holiday on the morning of the meeting. When LOTO's delegation – Milne, Murphy, Corbyn and Emily Thornberry – departed from outside Portcullis House, she found that Chamberlain was accompanying them all the way to Vauxhall, not merely to Corbyn's car. Murphy's body language changed immediately. Chamberlain could see that she was angry but, as Corbyn's closest personal aide, did not believe her presence merited any debate. Besides, she insisted that Corbyn had granted her express permission to accompany them. Murphy, unaware whether Corbyn had given Chamberlain's presence his blessing, yet unwilling to air her burning grievance in front of Thornberry, sent a group message to both the leader and Milne. 'Who signed off Iram?' she said. 'This is not appropriate.' Corbyn did not read the message, but Milne did. He implored Murphy to speak out. Still unsure as to whether Corbyn had approved Chamberlain's attendance or not, she held back.

Her delayed explosion came upon their arrival at MI6, where their appointment was with Alex Younger – the director general, known in the parlance of spooks as 'C'. In the lift up to Younger's office Murphy spotted a Palestinian badge pinned to the lapel of Chamberlain's jacket. Before they entered Younger's office, she staged an intervention.

'I don't think this is appropriate for you to come in here,' she said, gesturing towards the badge. Chamberlain snapped back: 'Jeremy thinks it's OK.' Murphy looked to Corbyn, who was clearly in no mood for a confrontation. Murphy removed Chamberlain's badge herself. 'These people think we're fucking idiots,' she said. 'Why prove it to them?'

Chamberlain went on to advertise her politics to Younger and his team anyway. She took the floor in the meeting to ask about far-right extremism in the UK and internationally, and whether more could be done to combat Islamophobia abroad. It was not an irrelevant question. The previous year had seen a far-right extremist drive a van into a group of Muslim pedestrians near a mosque in Finsbury Park, at the heart of Corbyn's constituency. The issue was deeply personal for Chamberlain herself, too: the father of a close friend, a Muslim, had been killed by a neo-Nazi from Ukraine. Younger reassured her that the threats were being taken seriously.

Thornberry, who had met Younger for a preliminary discussion a fortnight earlier, was irritated but unsurprised. Despite her attempts to patch up the relationship between LOTO and MI5, Chamberlain's intervention had only highlighted the differences of world view in the two offices. Thereafter the conversation that ensued was 'very anodyne', with MI6 apparently unwilling to disclose confidential information in front of Corbyn's staff.

Once the meeting was over, an incandescent Murphy and Milne cornered Corbyn to demand an explanation for Chamberlain's presence. His response was one of boyish innocence, likened by one witness to the young Jesus lost in the Temple. 'I thought you'd agreed it,' he said. Other LOTO staff who learned of the conflagration put it down to Corbyn's idiosyncratic approach to management. One reflected: 'Jeremy said to her: "You should come to this meeting." Iram said: "Yeah, I will." Whereas if Jeremy said to me "Why don't you come for Sunday dinner with my family?", I'd say "Yeah, of course." But I wouldn't go, because it's not appropriate.'

When Shami Chakrabarti learned the following day of what had happened at MI6, she responded with a degree of fury that, according to one LOTO aide, would have broken the Richter scale. Chakrabarti viewed Chamberlain as a member of administrative staff who had no right even to attend such a high-level meeting, let alone take the director general of MI6 to task on behalf of the official opposition. The mere fact of Chamberlain's presence at the summit had the potential to fatally undermine the leadership on national security. She made representations to Corbyn to that effect. She later met Murphy and Diane Abbott to make clear that she thought the situation had become untenable. They agreed. John McDonnell was also made aware of the issue.

Chakrabarti then escalated the issue to Jennie Formby, who quickly concluded that Chamberlain's behaviour amounted to gross misconduct. If she could not accept that she had done wrong, then she would be sacked. At the general secretary's behest, Murphy called Chamberlain. Rather than engaging with their concerns, Chamberlain simply reminded Murphy that she worked for Corbyn. Formby concluded that Chamberlain's time was up. 'Well, you phone Jeremy,' Murphy warned Formby. 'Because he'll not want it.' It proved a prescient judgement. Corbyn was indeed unwilling. It also emerged that Iain Chamberlain had gone as far as to ask him to line-manage his wife directly. 'Look, I know there's a problem with Iram,' Corbyn said to Murphy, before revealing details of the men's conversation. Her reaction was volcanic. But Corbyn had inadvertently shone a light on a truth that he would soon have to confront: LOTO functionaries distrusted his chief of staff even more than she distrusted them.

It took an intervention from Chakrabarti before Corbyn was convinced of the case for dismissing Chamberlain. As far as the Shadow

Attorney General was concerned the case was simple. It was unacceptable that an objectively junior member of staff – no matter what Chamberlain believed her own status or relationship with Corbyn to be – should book themselves into a meeting with the leaders of MI5 and MI6, having at best obfuscated and at worst lied about her family to the security services. Chamberlain appeared incapable of understanding her own job or of comporting herself with honesty.

For Chamberlain, issues of national security were a red herring. She felt the real issue was the enmity that had been generated by her willingness to challenge the Cult of Karie. Both Chamberlain and her husband suspected that Murphy was the ultimate source of the stories that had drawn attention to her battles for security clearance. Iain even went as far as to contact Paul Waugh, the veteran political editor of HuffPost, and Laura Murray, LOTO's head of stakeholder management, in an attempt to smoke out the source. Waugh insisted that Murphy had not been the source of his story, yet the Chamberlains were unconvinced. They reached the conclusion that Karie had been a willing accessory in the security services' attempts to repress not only the left, but the British Muslim community. They also accused her of spreading the false rumour within LOTO and McDonnell's office that Chamberlain's brothers had joined Isis.

Matters came to a head on 1 November, when Murphy confronted Chamberlain in a side room in LOTO. A discussion about a relatively insignificant disagreement soon mutated into a nuclear conflagration over the events of the previous weeks.

'Why were you there?' Murphy asked of the meeting at MI6 two days previously. 'Why did you go to that meeting?'

'Because I'm Jeremy's private secretary,' Chamberlain said. 'His [Alex Younger's] private secretary was there, so it's completely normal.'

'That's not going to happen again,' Murphy said. 'You're not coming to any other meeting unless you run it past me first.'

Chamberlain dared to defy her. 'Yes, it will happen again,' she said. Murphy was incredulous. Chamberlain ploughed on, insisting that her post gave her the right to attend any meeting Corbyn was happy for her to. Murphy did not so much reply as erupt. Again she insisted that Chamberlain could only attend meetings with her approval. Her voice was raised to a shout that was audible not just to the rest of LOTO but to passers-by in the adjacent corridor. Again and again

Chamberlain refused to yield. In the face of her defiance, Murphy convened what friends of Chamberlain recall as a kangaroo court of senior LOTO staff. She called Chamberlain in to see them and told her that all present had complaints about her conduct and warned her that they would meet the next day so that she might better understand what exactly her role entailed. In the interim, Murphy instructed Chamberlain not to speak to Corbyn. Her job was merely to serve him with papers.

Chamberlain assented, but only on the condition that she would be allowed a trade union rep alongside her. Murphy, despite her own labour-movement pedigree, is said to have reacted with furious disbelief. 'Do you really want to formalise this?' she asked. Chamberlain then spoke to Corbyn, having taken the opportunity to consult her union rep. The rep had advised that she should indeed submit a formal complaint, but Corbyn insisted that they could work things out as friends. 'We'll talk this through,' he told her. 'There must be some sort of misunderstanding.'

Six days later, LOTO decamped en masse to the Leicestershire village of Quorn for an awayday. Chamberlain was about to begin a session with the correspondence officials who worked beneath her when Amy Jackson and Andrew Fisher beckoned her into another room. Other LOTO staff noted with some curiosity that a member of Southside's HR team was present that day. Chamberlain then learned why. Fisher and Jackson served her with a charge sheet outlining her professional failings. It had led the LOTO hierarchy to the conclusion that she must be suspended, they explained. Initially, Chamberlain assumed she was the victim of a *Candid Camera*-style prank. 'Is this some sort of joke?' she asked. It was not. She stormed back into the room where the rest of LOTO's staff were gathered to collect her things, and left accompanied by a junior correspondence official who returned in tears, shaken by the brutality of Chamberlain's sacking.

All the more distraught was Chamberlain, who found herself effectively jobless and alone more than a hundred miles from London. Colleagues took pity on her and ordered her a cab home. Over the course of the journey she made another call to Corbyn. 'Do you know this has happened to me?' she asked. Again he claimed ignorance and played peacemaker. 'We'll figure this out,' Corbyn limply replied. 'We'll work it out.' Within twenty-four hours, fearing an inquisition led by acolytes of Murphy, Chamberlain had handed in her notice.

*

The battle to shore up the Project's weaknesses on national security had exposed another: the relationship between staff at LOTO and the woman Corbyn had delegated his entire authority to.

'You became like Voldemort – the name that can never be mentioned in the office,' a friend of Chamberlain's at LOTO told her in the wake of her departure. The great irony of Murphy's alleged conduct towards her was that it engendered a greater level of class consciousness within the leader's suite at Norman Shaw South than the Project would ever manage in the country. 'People thought: "God, if she can get rid of someone on basically no basis whatsoever, then she can do it for any of us,"' said a former LOTO staffer.

The Labour staff branch of Unite was led by Rory Macqueen, John McDonnell's chief economic adviser, together with Bell Ribeiro-Addy, Diane Abbott's political adviser. It was Murphy who had installed Macqueen in the post; until then Labour's staff unions had been overrun and controlled by disciples of Iain McNicol. Neither Macqueen nor other staff knew the specifics of the previous month's controversy over Chamberlain and the security services. All they did know was that several of Murphy's staff felt ruled by fear and loathing. Now Macqueen began a month-long process of drafting and seeking signatures for a letter of complaint against his former mentor. It was LOTO's equivalent of Zola's *J'Accuse*.

Milne and Fisher were also targets. Whereas some of Murphy's accusers claimed to be victims of over-management, theirs complained of a lack of professionalism and basic support. To some, it was a matter of vague amusement that Milne arrived at work late, often emerging with pastries or a steaming English breakfast from the Debate cafeteria in Portcullis House. Others found it less endearing. Fisher was felt to be mercurial and absent. 'By the end of the year, the senior management team had completely lost the confidence of more junior staff,' said one aide. 'Karie was far too aggressive. Seumas and Andrew were simply inadequate and created the vacuum for Karie to fill.' For junior staff in LOTO, the time had come to confront Corbyn with the senior team's failures.

Murphy and Jackson suspected McDonnell had encouraged Macqueen to canvass opinion against them. 'It was pushed by John. They worked together. He gave them the legitimacy to do it.' That theory is scotched by sources close to McDonnell, who say that he had 'zero' role in the genesis of the letter. What few dispute is that the initial impetus came from the bottom up. Macqueen spent November acting as a conduit-cum-counsellor for the staff who worked beneath Murphy, Milne and Fisher. Meanwhile, Murphy's followers kept her updated on the manoeuvres against her. Jack Bond and Laura Murray, two aides they privately derided as 'posh kids' and 'spoiled brats', helped Macqueen corral junior staff to put their names to a letter that collated more or less every grievance any member of staff had ever expressed about Murphy, some of it true, some of it rumour, and much of it derived from her clashes with Chamberlain.

Murphy was accused variously of attempting to discredit a staff member by spreading the fact the staff member had suffered a miscarriage, of pushing a member of staff by the neck and pinning them against a wall, and of inaccurately telling colleagues that other staff were alcoholics – allegations she categorically denied. Junior female staff complained about one impromptu meeting Murphy convened in the LOTO boardroom in which she told them that their clothing was inappropriate and recommended a more chaste dress code. That intervention in particular drew the ire of millennials who believed Murphy to be acting with a grubby political machismo at odds with the ideals of the Project. Her supporters nonetheless insist she had a point. 'What the fuck do you do when you're a manager and you have employees dressed inappropriately? What do you do when you tell them over and over and over again to stick to the dress code? You are suddenly a bully.' Andrew Fisher was the subject of lurid allegations too. Himself married to a black woman, the previous year he had apologised to a young black aide after responding to the apparent shortage of dark rye bread at a work dinner by declaring, 'Once you go black, you never go back.' Yet the primary complaint against him and Milne was not unconscious racial bias but incompetence and an inability to lead. One person in Fisher's team claimed that the majority of his subordinates signed the letter.

Doubts lingered among some of the prospective complainants until 12 December, when LOTO hosted its office Christmas party. Midway through the evening, festivities were brought to an abrupt halt by an irate Murphy, who had caught wind of unwelcome guests. A junior LOTO staffer had invited a handful of Liberal Democrats to the fifty-strong gathering. While cross-party friendships are an inevitable fact of life for parliamentary staffers, to Murphy the presence of the enemy at a LOTO event was an act of inexcusable recklessness. She marched the staffer to a private room and, in the words of one horrified witness, gave her 'the bollocking of a lifetime'. Another member of staff drew the blinds to obscure the grisly scene but Murphy's raised voice was audible through the walls. To Murphy's supporters, she was merely protecting the Project's young servants from their own worst instincts. To the recipient's colleagues, it was an act of unnecessary and wanton aggression. Jack Bond, Corbyn's social media manager, made a vain attempt to intervene. The staffer left in floods of tears.

Eight days later, Macqueen delivered the missive. It was 20 December, the day of the Christmas parliamentary recess. Corbyn was given a copy by hand, as were each of LOTO's executive directors – Milne, Murphy and Fisher – as well as Jennie Formby. When Murphy was served with her copy, she summoned Macqueen for a private discussion. He took notes of the confrontation, which record Murphy describing the group's actions as 'childish', 'immature' and 'reckless'. In any case, she insisted that it was impossible for Macqueen to have amassed the number of signatures he claimed because half of the staff had already disavowed the letter to the management. It was then she returned the letter unopened to Macqueen, claiming not to have read it.

Had she done so, she would have found her and her colleagues' alleged failings denounced in their own vernacular: the language of class solidarity, socialism and workers' rights. The complainants began by pledging their support for the Project, and a Jeremy Corbyn govern-ment, and then explained at length why it would be Murphy, Milne and Fisher who would prevent it from happening. 'As committed trade unionists, we are raising concerns, and directing them in writing to only the very few people who have the authority to do anything to address them – the Executive Directors in the Leader's Office and the General Secretary,' it read.

The charge sheet was as long as it was unedifying, ranging from 'bullying and intimidation ... including shouting in the office and berating staff in front of colleagues, either in person, over email or over WhatsApp', 'a divisive and toxic culture fostered in the office ... creating unnecessary animosity', 'lying about colleagues', 'sexist behaviour, including comments made in front of colleagues about female members of staff's appearances or clothing, inviting only female staff to a meeting where they were lectured on how to dress and conduct themselves', 'race discrimination', and 'bad recruitment processes'. It demanded 'wholesale change in the culture of the office' via management and equality training, a gender and race pay audit, independent mediation between senior management and those with whom it had fallen out, and a guarantee that rules on staffing and grievances would be followed properly.

The most pointed comment on the state of affairs within LOTO was the anonymity of the letter's signatories. It came from '20+ members of staff from the Leader's Office'. By way of explanation, they wrote: 'We all regret the need to send this letter anonymously: something which unfortunately reflects a widespread culture of fear in the office meaning staff are afraid to speak up or even discuss problems they are having in the office. We believe even more colleagues would have signed if we had felt comfortable discussing it more widely without fear of repercussions.'

As if to prove its central point, far fewer would admit to signing the letter publicly. Several LOTO staff made private approaches to Murphy to disavow the letter, and when its existence was later leaked to the press, twenty-one LOTO staff went on the record with a public reply professing their support for her. The tone was one of unconditional devotion. One declared: 'I have never ever witnessed her behaving badly in any way.' Jennie Formby gave it short shrift. First, she texted Macqueen to ask if she could send it to her private email address. Then she rebuked him for using the word 'we' when describing the letter's signatories. He later wrote: 'I got the impression she thought this is something I've cooked up maybe with a couple of discontented individuals.' It took until 8 January for her to reply formally. 'As the allegations made are anonymous it is impossible to ascertain whether or not they are true,' she wrote. 'This is not only worrying in relation to members of staff who may be feeling anxious or unhappy; it is also very unfair to the SMT [senior management team], against whom the complaints have been raised but who are in no position to explain or defend themselves ... A significant number of individuals in LOTO have made contact wishing to distance themselves from the letter, with several of these people saying that they do not recognise the behaviours that have been outlined ... I would therefore strongly urge you to pass on the message to any individual who has a specific concern to follow the formal grievance procedure.' Murphy's rearguard had prevailed. The letter had effectively been dismissed.

Another question remained, however: what would Corbyn do about the unease among his own staff? Between New Year's Day 2019 and the return of LOTO staff to Parliament, he convened a crisis meeting in his constituency office of his senior staff, including Fisher, Milne and Murphy. 'Jeremy was very frustrated and angry about the insurrection in the ranks,' another senior adviser present said. They engaged in heated back-and-forth over whether Formby or Murphy should reply to the allegations in any detail, if at all. To sceptics, the discussion proved the folly of his most senior appointments: 'Seumas and Karie don't know how to be professional,' said one senior LOTO aide. 'It's not that they don't want to [be]. They just have no experience.' A consensus quickly developed that the allegations themselves did not need to be dignified with a formal response on the grounds that they were mostly fabricated. The meeting broke up having resolved to manage the issue politically, rather than treat it as a matter for HR.

But it had become painfully clear to those present that the power that underpinned Murphy's regime – Corbyn's confidence in her leadership – had begun to crumble. 'Karie was very wobbly,' one witness said. 'It was the point at which the relationship between Jeremy and Karie began to disintegrate.' The fraying of their once unconditional trust would see the Project unravel in uniquely unedifying fashion in the final months of its final year. Before then, however, Corbyn and LOTO would have to reckon with the very public collapse of another relationship – that between the Labour Party and its MPs.

9

The Split

Ian Austin was characteristically blunt. 'Look, Tom. You're not going to be a Secretary of State in a Corbyn government.'

The deputy leader of the Labour Party affected not to know what his closest friend in politics could possibly be talking about. 'Why not?' he replied.

Austin smiled: 'Because I want to do everything I can to stop him getting into power.'

By the summer of 2018, both men had gone further in that aim than either could ever have foreseen in their days as two of Gordon Brown's closest and most vicious lieutenants. For a start, they were now breaking bread with Peter Mandelson – quite literally. In the dog days of New Labour's civil war, the only reason either man would have had to visit the Regent's Park mansion of the Prince of Darkness might have been to slash his tyres. The enmity was mutual. Blairites like Mandy once spoke of the likes of Watson and Austin as if they had gone feral. 'Working for Gordon does something to people,' they would say incredulously. Working beneath Jeremy Corbyn had done quite another. It had seemingly induced changes of personality and temperament in the most fanatical servants of New Labour's warring courts. It had even convinced Ian Austin to spend a warm July evening at a barbeque in Peter Mandelson's garden. No longer were the Blairites and Brownites fighting one another for control of the Labour Party. Their aim now was to save it. If they failed in that objective, Austin readily admitted that he would rather try to kill it.

His host was not yet willing to go so far. Mandelson, sat at the centre of his garden table, was surrounded by Labour MPs from two new tribes. In his day, the party had mainly been divided by questions of personality, with broad consensus on policy. Now they were united by personality and divided by policy. Alongside unapologetic Remainers – Alison McGovern, Wes Streeting, Anna Turley – were colleagues who wished they would shut up and accept a Brexit deal. Austin, who had come within twenty-two votes of losing his seat in 2017, was the most vocal. Ruth Smeeth, the Jewish MP for Stoke-on-Trent North, was in a similar boat, as was Gloria de Piero nursing a majority of just 441 in the once safe seat of Ashfield in Nottinghamshire. What they *did* agree on made that difference in opinion seem much less fundamental. All of Mandelson's guests longed for the day Corbyn was no longer leader of the Labour Party, regardless of whether the sweet release came inside of the EU or out. To Mandelson, no stranger to a schism for schism's sake, that is what really mattered. It pained him to see the anti-Corbynistas blinded by questions of customs unions and single-market alignment. New Labour's *enfant terrible* adopted an avuncular pose. He was now in the business of bringing a new generation of squabbling children together.

Opposite Mandelson, at his instruction, sat Watson. Theirs was a peace that rivalled that of Ian Paisley and Martin McGuinness for its discombobulating implausibility. At times, the hatred had seemed just as atavistic – at least for Watson. In 1986, Mandelson, then director of communications, had stared glassily through the young Watson as he toiled over his photocopying in Labour headquarters. The younger man had reminded his old adversary of his aloofness. Mandelson pleaded insanity: he had been in the grip of a breakdown. Ten years later, and in sound mind, Mandelson had waltzed once more into HQ and sacked Watson as the deputy coordinator of Labour's general election campaign. Another decade on, Watson the minister, the Brownite bulldog, had had his revenge, corralling MPs to oust Blair from office. The mutiny he fomented forced the prime minister to name his exit date and cleared the way for Brown. Mandelson had departed Westminster by then, exiled to the European Commission. As soon as he returned as Lord Mandelson in 2008, Watson wanted him gone again. During his campaign to succeed Brown as leader, Ed Miliband sought Watson's counsel on what he ought to say if journalists asked about Mandelson's future at the top of Labour politics. Watson told him: 'Say you believe in dignity in retirement.' Not that he believed Mandelson deserved it. Even then he tweeted, blogged and sniped at his old adversary. To torment the Blairites was to exist.

One former Cabinet minister said: 'You have to remember that Tom was an absolutely frightful, vicious thing.' Watson took the same attitude to them as Roosevelt had towards opponents of the New Deal: 'They are unanimous in their hate for me – and I welcome their hatred.'

Now they welcomed one another, and worked together. To what precise end they did not yet know. Yet Mandelson did know that he could not salvage *his* Labour Party without Watson. Over the course of 2018 Watson had lost seven stone and with it much of his vestigial loathing for the old order. Those energies were instead directed to the new one. Corbyn's inner circle believed Watson's mission was 'to destroy us, by whatever means possible'. For Watson and Mandelson, that was the first step to rebuilding a party they recognised.

In 2018 they began to meet regularly. Their past was disinterred, aired, and buried again. Endowed with his own mandate from the members who had elected him alongside Corbyn in 2015, Watson could be the 'sheet anchor' for a disenfranchised PLP, or so Mandelson thought. If MPs recognised Watson as their leader, then any meaningful split without him would never succeed.

'I'm never going to let you down,' Mandelson told Watson. 'I'll always help you. I'll always be there.'

'We will go on this journey together,' Watson said. 'Everything that we decide to do, we'll decide to do together.'

Where once Mandelson had been the power behind the throne of Labour leaders past – Kinnock, Blair, Brown – now he plotted a regicide.

There was only one problem. Unlike the rebels of Fair Oak Farm, Mandelson and Watson did not know what to do. Nor, other than Austin, did their audience know either. Only among a few had opinion hardened irrevocably. The buffet exhausted, each MP addressed the gathering in turn. Most harboured doubts about the Plan B that had taken shape in the Sussex countryside and was now being worked up by Gavin Shuker, Chris Leslie, Chuka Umunna, Angela Smith and Luciana Berger into a plan for a formal breakaway. Those doubts could be summed up with three letters: SDP. In the Labour mythos, at least, the Gang of Four had been the midwives of Thatcher's 1983 landslide. One attendee insisted that a new party would simply repeat its mistakes. Austin, once tribal to the point of derangement, demurred.

'Well, you could argue that the SDP were helping the Labour Party back to common sense.'

For Mandelson, the longer Jeremy Corbyn remained leader, the further they would be from government. But the question was not so much whether to stay and fight; it was how to win. It would be a long march home. Mandelson wanted Watson to lead it. In his view, nobody else could.

On that point, Mandelson's old master Tony Blair disagreed. 'Tony developed a view, which he held very strongly, and very deeply, that the Labour Party was finished – that it was irrecoverable,' a friend of Blair's recalled. He had always believed that the great tragedy of British progressivism had been the rupture between its two radical traditions: Labourism and Liberalism. Whenever they split, they failed – and under Corbyn, they were not only split, but irreconcilable.

Blair's conclusion that Labour was all but lost to the Corbynites was debatable. That his reputation among them was irrecoverable was not. The election of Corbyn had been a repudiation of Blair's premiership and the sins the left believed it to have committed: its spin, its acceptance of Tory orthodoxies on the free market, its authoritarianism, its support for US military intervention. Admirers of his could still be found in the PLP, albeit in the same place Corbyn had once been – on the back benches, isolated from the new mainstream. Some would take the short walk from Parliament, up Broadway, to the offices of Blair's Institute for Global Change, the think tank he had established to campaign against the rise of populism in the wake of Brexit and Trump. The grandiloquent branding belied a rather more frustrating truth: he could not even change his own party. MPs adjudged to share his despair came at his invitation. New Labour was reunited in grief, as dysfunctional families tend to be.

Watson had been to see Blair at Mandelson's instruction, to sue for peace. 'Look, there's nothing I can say in mitigation. I just apologise for the role that I have played. I am sorry. But there we are,' said Watson. Blair did not attempt to relitigate the past. He accepted the apology graciously, but not Mandelson's optimism. A friend of both men said: 'Peter was rock solid. He wasn't leaving. With Tony, what he wanted would depend on the month.' Cynical observers of Blair's rapprochement with Watson took a different view. If to Mandelson Watson was the lynchpin to *prevent* a mass exodus, to Blair he was the man to lead it. 'If Tom had any relevance and usefulness to him at all, it was to raise the number of people who would leave the party.'

Blair now explains his calculation thus: 'The difference between people like Jeremy Corbyn and myself is fundamental, and actually the difference between Jeremy Corbyn and Lisa Nandy is fundamental, it's just a different type of politics ... My view all the way through was very simple, that if Corbynism took a grip on the Labour Party that couldn't be removed then the party was finished.'

Brooding at his home in North Queensferry, meanwhile, Gordon Brown sought vainly to influence events. His self-imposed exile in Scotland had left him far removed from the machinations of the other grandees of New Labour. At first he appeared more relaxed at what had become of the party. Brown's legacy as Chancellor, in the domestic sphere at least, was one that Corbyn and McDonnell felt comfortable embracing. But by the summer of 2018 he had come to share Blair's and Mandelson's analysis: the Corbyn era needed to end. 'Gordon was appalled by the anti-Semitism,' said one Brownite survivor in the PLP. He responded, as he had so often when his long war of attrition with Blair was at its ugliest, by summoning Watson. Out of the blue he would dispense orders via phone to his old enforcer, like a Caledonian capo ordering a hit from his safe house, apparently oblivious that arrangements were being made in his absence. 'You've got to get Corbyn out. You've got to organise.' Old friends viewed his efforts with scorn: they had already tried and failed. 'It was classic GB-ery,' one said. 'No warmth. *You've got to get Corbyn out.* Thanks, but me and whose army?'

Blair's abiding charm could not hide the fact that he was similarly desperate. From his young guests he sought scraps of information on the Labour Party like a divorced father seeking news of estranged children. 'He was never vitriolic, or even interested in going over what was going wrong. It was what we could do to get things right,' one MP said of their audiences. He did so calmly and plaintively, as if haunted by what had become of the party that was once his. What was the mood in the PLP? Might anything change? Wouldn't somebody *do* something?

Most of those who had been at Fair Oak Farm visited Tony in turn. In Chuka Umunna and Chris Leslie he found men more than willing to feed his pessimism. When Blair came to learn of what they were planning to do, he did not discourage them. 'They didn't get a green light from Tony,' a confidant said, 'but they didn't get a red light, either.' Cherie played Lady Macbeth to her equivocal husband, at least in the Corbynsceptic imagination. The former first lady of Downing Street had gravitated towards Jess Phillips, whom she would love-bomb with messages and articles. The Fair Oak Farmers believed Cherie was geeing Phillips up to fulfil the promise the younger woman had once made to stab Corbyn 'in the front', and leave Labour. Those familiar with their correspondence insist Cherie offered nothing more than sisterly encouragement via the subject lines of otherwise blank emails.

*

Even if the Blairs had given the splitters a red light, most of them would have driven through it. Five of the Fair Oak Farmers – Shuker, Umunna, Leslie, Smith and Berger – had spent the months after their last country rendezvous working out a detailed plan for the coming split. As early as March the previous year, at the height of the media storm over the Mear One mural, Luciana Berger had called Gavin Shuker out of the blue and told him she was resolved to leave. They had never been close, nor had Shuker seen her as a core member of the group, but Berger was exhausted. 'Look,' she had told him, with remarkable candour. 'I'm done.' Shuker calmly talked her down from the ledge. 'I absolutely understand that,' he told her. 'But you know that I'm building out this process, and we need to make sure that when you go, we have as many people around you as possible.' Those who attended the final meeting on 23 May had been given an ultimatum: it was time for them to make a decision on their futures. Over a barbeque of beefburgers, peri-peri chicken fillets and salads prepared by Shuker, they had agreed that the exploratory phase of talks was over. For the Fair Oak Five, Plan B had become their Plan A.

Shuker preferred to speak of the task before them in an idiosyncratic and often impenetrable mixture of space-age and biological metaphor. In internal documents the quintet was referred to as 'the I-Group', a cell of irreconcilables who would determine when to move from the 'first trimester' of planning to the brave new world of the 'second trimester'. Or, in plain English, when exactly they would quit. They would not immediately become a new party – that would come in trimester three – but a coalition of independent MPs. Nicola Murphy, Leslie's wife, was leader of 'PreCo', a group of civilian staff who busied themselves with logistical questions of office space, staffing and data. 'At that point I'd be establishing a company called Gemini,' Shuker recalled. 'Why Gemini? Well, the Fair Oak phase was, in the language of the US space programme, Mercury. Then we need a period where we're The Independent Group, not a political party – that's Gemini. Then, when you do become a political party, that's Apollo.' Before lift-off, however, they needed a crew.

There had been plenty of discussion at Fair Oak Farm about the circumstances in which Labour MPs would not quit – or events that would doom any split to failure. Chat around the table in the Fair Oak Farm kitchen had thrown up three nightmare scenarios. The first was Corbyn's replacement by another true believer from the left: any changing of the guard, however superficial, was likely to convince Labour MPs that there might be jam tomorrow. The second, even more harmful to a split's chances, was the prospect of a successor to Corbyn whom the mainstream of the PLP actively liked and agreed with. The third was positively lethal: Corbyn's replacement by what the Five's internal strategy papers pithily referred to as a 'moderate woman'. That would have put a bomb beneath their case against the machismo, bullying and extremism of the Labour Party. But it wasn't going to happen.

There was also the risk that their departures would not look voluntary. Each faced unrest in their local parties and the spectre of deselection. In leaving, each would to a certain extent look as though they were jumping before they were pushed, which would appear cynical at best and cowardly at worst. Chris Leslie was among those who believed that LOTO would go as far as to orchestrate moves against them in their local parties from afar, a somewhat paranoid assumption that his colleagues did not share.

In planning their breach with the Labour Party, they did at least honour one of its traditions: setting tests in lieu of answering a difficult question. As Keir Starmer had done on Brexit and Brown had done on euro membership before him, the Five laid out six tests that Plan A – staying and fighting – would have to fail, and six tests that Plan B – splitting – would have to meet to be viable. Unlike Starmer's and Brown's tests, which had been drafted with failure in mind, the

Five's tests for Plan B were designed to be passed whatever the circumstances. Shuker put it explicitly in a memo circulated among his co-conspirators at the start of the long summer: 'Our challenge, frankly, is to design a series of tests which we are sure to meet; and to shift the model in the minds of colleagues away from "red lines" to "green lights".'

By the time the Commons broke for its summer recess in July 2018, Plan A had already failed its first test. Despite a series of Tory rebellions, MPs had not secured a soft Brexit via amendments to any of the three pieces of Brexit legislation that had come before them that summer. Much to LOTO's displeasure, an attempt to amend the Trade Bill to force Theresa May to negotiate a customs union with Brussels was scuppered by the votes of four pro-Brexit Labour MPs. If only briefly, the left's ire was turned to the misfits of Labour's old right – Kate Hoey, Frank Field, John Mann and Graham Stringer – rather than the more telegenic cast of young villains from Fair Oak Farm. Momentum called for members to deselect them. Field, the ageing maverick, resigned the whip six weeks later, in a characteristically lonely protest against anti-Semitism and the leftism of his own local members. Yet it was the Five who had been pushed one step closer to the exit.

The second Plan A test was failed in September. Momentum and the Campaign for Labour Party Democracy had run a joint slate in that summer's elections to the NEC in the hope of solidifying the left's control over the party apparatus: the #JC9 or, as the Five preferred to call them, 'the nine NEC Trots'. Despite their very public disavowal of Pete Willsman over his rant on anti-Semitism, all nine were duly elected on 3 September. Nothing, it seemed, could shake the membership's attachment to Corbyn. The PLP was always able to console themselves with the results of internal elections, no matter how insignificant. As Ian Austin recalled: 'People were always looking for reasons not to leave. You'd talk to people on the traditional old right and you'd be told, "Have you not heard about the AGM in some obscure local branch somewhere, where the moderates won the vote by seven to five, and that Corbyn is on the verge of collapse because of it?"' Even the desperate among them had to acknowledge that the balance of power on the party's ruling body was impossible to spin.

What vestigial power to influence the party's future the PLP retained withered further. Later that month, the NEC drove the Five even closer to departure when on the eve of conference it came to deliberate on the contents of a long-feared review into Labour's internal democracy. Commissioned by Corbyn and conducted by his then political secretary Katy Clark, it made a series of bold proposals to devolve power from Labour's elected representatives and officials to its members, as Corbyn had promised in both of his leadership campaigns. Several of Clark's ideas were rejected but the two that gave Corbynsceptics most cause for distress were approved. The first was that future candidates for leadership of the party would have to secure nominations from only 10 per cent of MPs, reduced from 15 per cent, and would furthermore be required to secure 5 per cent of local parties or two trade unions and another affiliate. In other words, MPs were no longer the sole gatekeepers of the leadership. (Officials jokingly referred to the reduction in the threshold as 'the purge of the Chrises', on the grounds that Chris Leslie and Chris Williamson were the only two MPs unpopular enough to fail to meet the new thresholds.) The other was that deselecting an MP became easier, with only a third of an MP's local party branches being required to endorse a contest, down from half. Ironically, nobody was more disappointed with that result than Momentum, who had demanded completely open selections for candidates ahead of each election. Yet it still amounted to a doomsday scenario for the MPs who had set themselves against their politics.

By the time they had arrived in Liverpool, Shuker had already lost a vote of no confidence in his CLP. So febrile was the atmosphere on Merseyside that Berger, despite being in the city she represented as an MP and had come to call home, was flanked by police as she made her way to and from the conference venue. Leslie had even made the audacious suggestion that the group resign at conference, even though three tests proving Plan A was dead remained to be met. 'That was a potential flashpoint,' said one former MP. 'Should we do it at conference? Should we use that platform to make the break? Other people were and weren't ready.'

One man who was almost ready by September was Blair. Having arrived at the conclusion that Labour was now probably beyond saving, he wrote a column, destined for the *Times* comment pages, calling for the centre-left – in the words of one confidant – 'to completely rethink the future'. The Labour Party was irrelevant, finished. It was time to move on.

He circulated a draft among his intimates, all of whom had at one time or another worked at the heart of Labour's last government. According to one, the verdict was unanimous. 'This is not the right thing to be saying. It's not the right time, and if it were, it would be best not said by you.'

Blair chose to say it anyway. On 7 September, a week after Frank Field had resigned the whip, three days after the NEC had finally adopted IHRA and its examples of anti-Semitism in full, two days after Gordon Brown had spoken of a battle for the party's soul in a speech to the Jewish Labour Movement, Blair sat down for an hour's podcast interview with the BBC's Nick Robinson. Warming up, Robinson needled his old sparring partner on what it all meant for Labour's future. Blair, employing heavy, Pinteresque pauses, replied that he was more interested in the #JC9's victory in the NEC elections four days previously. 'It's a profound change,' he reflected. As the hour progressed, he offered his analysis of the Corbynite world view, at every turn deferring to his successor's authority as leader of the party but emphasising the extent to which it departed from his own. 'You can agree or disagree,' he said. 'But this is a *different* Labour Party.'

Robinson waved to his own 21-year-old son, sitting on the other side of the studio glass. Would Blair recommend he joined the Labour Party? He would. But he did not know whether it could be taken back from the Corbynites. The conversation then turned to the prospects of an organised breakaway.

'I've been a member of the Labour Party for over forty years,' Blair said. 'You do feel a strong loyalty and attachment, but at the same time it's a different party. The question is: can it be taken back?'

'And that's an open question,' said Robinson, nudging Blair in the direction of news.

'And that's a pretty open question.'

'And if not?'

Blair dialled up the candour to eleven. 'If not, then I think you've got to distinguish between the individual choice, which you might make on tribal grounds, to stay ... but I think the more pertinent question, in a way, is the type of politics that people like me represent – which I would describe as more moderate, progressive politics – if that isn't represented by the Labour Party, it doesn't really matter what I think, or what these MPs think.'

He proceeded to tell Robinson what he did think. 'I don't think the British people will tolerate a situation where, for example, the choice at the next election is Boris Johnson versus Jeremy Corbyn. I don't know what will happen, I don't know how it will happen, but I just don't believe that people will find that, in the country as a whole, to be an acceptable choice.'

'Something will fill that vacuum?' Robinson asked knowingly.

'Something will fill that vacuum,' Blair replied, as if in prayer.

There was a flatness to Blair's voice. He was, after all, resigned to the party's fate, and was only repeating the sort of conversation he had been conducting in private ad nauseam. Robinson was nonetheless rapt. 'It's not often that an answer makes me pause,' he reflected in his introduction to the podcast. 'But that answer from Tony Blair did. I knew that he and his supporters, those who look up to him, have been contemplating whether they've got a life in the Labour Party. What I've not heard him do before is reflect on it in public. On tape.'

The comments were less dramatic than the words he had wanted to commit to print, although Blair denied that he had at any point concluded that Labour was beyond saving. 'If I ever felt that it really got to the stage where it was irretrievably lost, I would have said so, and in the interview with Nick Robinson, I was just saying, it may not be possible, and that's literally what I thought,' he said.

The comments still electrified the news cycle, much to the consternation of those who had warned him against intervening. When friends confronted him, he protested his innocence. Given what Blair knew about the intentions of the Corbynsceptics in the PLP, it was a wholly unconvincing line to take. It also had the effect of irritating both factions of his disciples. To those like Mandelson who wished to prevent a split – or at least delay one – it was a deliberate incitement to Labour MPs to accelerate efforts to break away. To those convinced of the strategy's wisdom, it made failure more likely.

Blair's former chief of staff Jonathan Powell led the latter camp. A lanky patrician from a Civil Service dynasty and best known for his role in mediating the Northern Ireland peace process, Powell now spent much of his time flying from war zone to war zone, dispensing his wisdom in sonorous tones. But in Corbyn's Labour he found a conflict that he could only conclude was insoluble. Powell believed a negotiated peace between the leadership and Blair's heirs in the PLP was neither preferable nor possible. Instead, he told them, they had to declare independence unilaterally. Together with Emily Benn, grand-daughter of Corbyn's hero Tony, he had set to work on preparations for a new party, an infrastructure that the Fair Oak Farm splitters could eventually slot into.

Emily, as her uncle Hilary had once quipped, was a Benn but not a Bennite. In 2010, aged just 20, she had been a Labour parliamentary candidate. She ran again in 2015, when Andrew Fisher urged left-wingers to vote for a Trotskyite candidate instead. It had only been downhill from there. The Benn name was no inoculation against the righteous anger of the left, for the Tony whose politics she hugged close was Blair. In the wake of the EU referendum, it was Hilary who had attempted to drum up support for a Shadow Cabinet coup against Corbyn. His niece was prepared to go even further. Online trolls monstered her as an apostate. Emily made no secret of where her political allegiances lay, nor of her distaste for the politicians who had set about transforming the Labour Party in her grandfather's name.

Though Powell kept his old boss availed of his plans, he did not want his new enterprise to have a Blairite face, and under no circum-stances could Blair front their breakaway himself. 'For Tony to lead that effort would be the kiss of death,' Powell told friends. The reason was simple. The only man ever to have led Labour to three consecu-tive general election victories polled lower among his public than Trump.

Among Blair's apostles, however, Powell was in a minority. People's Voters like Alastair Campbell were absorbed by the struggle for a bigger prize: EU membership. He and Tom Baldwin believed the Labour Party was the only vehicle capable of taking them to a second referendum. Neither could afford to be dragged into the weeds of factional warfare. As Baldwin had assured Karie Murphy in their first meeting, they were Labour men.

'In lots of ways, Alastair is not a caricature Blairite,' Baldwin said. 'It's fair to say Peter [Mandelson] and Tony don't always come across as being particularly Labour people. I guess that was part of the appeal of New Labour to some. But Alastair stinks of the Labour Party. Part of his thing is about Burnley FC, comprehensive schools, being northern, hating poshness. He doesn't revel in being elite or aspire to be part of the establishment.'

Internally, much of Campbell's and Baldwin's time was spent fighting a rearguard against the political arrivistes they worked alongside, like Roland Rudd and Hugo Dixon, an Old Etonian contemporary of Boris Johnson, to prevent them from using the People's Vote machine to campaign against Labour. In any case, it was a machine staffed by refugees from Southside, like Patrick Heneghan and John Stolliday, whose politics started and ended at a visceral loathing for Corbyn. Despite Murphy's suspicions that they were a Chuka Umunna leadership campaign by another name, those People's Voters would not join a breakaway either.

The Five would have to go it alone.

*

If Shuker was fond of speaking in metaphor, Umunna's critics complain he spent most of the period that preceded his departure from the Labour Party speaking out of both sides of his mouth. In public, the man LOTO had long suspected of harbouring ambitions to lead a split insisted he had no such plans.

On 7 September, he told members of his constituency party in Streatham: 'I have not made plans to launch a new political party. I am a Labour member and a Labour Member of Parliament. I do not want this to change, and ultimately I hope the people that will decide if I remain a Member of Parliament are the constituents who elect me.' Of course, he did want it to change, and change it would. But if change was to mean success, then he could not be blamed for his own departure. 'The Labour Party has always been a broad church of views, opinions and traditions. For the Labour Party to continue to be a radical and transformational movement, I firmly believe that must remain the case ... The issue of whether there is a split in the Labour Party or whether members leave, is therefore ultimately in the hands of Jeremy Corbyn and the Labour Party leadership.'

The following day he kicked off the blame game in earnest with a speech to Progress. 'My message to our leadership: it is within your power to stop this, so call off the dogs and get on with what my constituency, one of the most diverse communities in the nation, demands we do – without equivocation, fight this Tory Brexit.' It had the desired effect, which was to bait the Corbynites into spluttering rage. An irate Ian Lavery took it literally: 'Calling anybody a dog is totally outrageous in the extreme. Chuka Umunna of all people should know that.' LOTO briefed reporters that the speech was 'incoherent and inaccurate'.

John McDonnell took a different approach. Unlike others on the left, the Shadow Chancellor reacted not with antagonism but anxiety. A split, he calculated, had the potential to cause even more damage than the unseemly rows over Skripal and IHRA. He was, according to aides, haunted by the role the SDP had played in splitting the vote in his own constituency in the 1980s. On 1 September, he had taken to the pages of the *New Statesman* to play conciliator. 'Talk to us … We've got an open door on that. If it is anti-Semitism, we've got to resolve it and will, and that's it. I don't see these as fundamental issues that would encourage a split. I'm worried and I'm saddened.' LOTO aides took a dim view of his concerns: 'John was very worried about a bigger split, very worried about the PLP and so on, and I think if you spend too much time worrying about them you don't do anything correct.'

Yet McDonnell continued to fret. Speculation over just when Umunna and others might jump had reached a new pitch over the summer months. On 7 August, the *Daily Express*, not a newspaper known for its Labour Kremlinology, had revealed the existence of the Fair Oak Farm summits. Curiously, it described the meetings as 'secret awaydays … to make plans to oust Jeremy Corbyn'. Anyone with even a passing acquaintance with any attendee knew that in fact their purpose was to plan for their own ousting. Stephen Kinnock and Conor McGinn, two divisive Corbynsceptics with no plans to leave the party, were also wrongly fingered as attendees. Spooked, actual attendees suspected the hand of Austin, who had joined them, and Watson, with whom he was in daily contact. Both pleaded ignorance, but it would not be the last time that the deputy leader and his acolytes were accused of trying to strangle the split at birth. Regardless of the leaker's identity – all involved agree that the likeliest candidate was one of the MPs in the PLP who had taken a dislike to Kinnock – the *Express* story underlined the extent to which the splitters' plans had become an open secret in Westminster.

Proponents of Plan A were trying and failing to talk them out of it too.

On 22 August, Progress director Richard Angell had written to
Shuker to make a passive-aggressive case for staying and fighting.
'Having spoken to a number of colleagues I understand that you
actively support the idea of an alternative path for progressive politics
other than the Labour Party. If not, please do let me know.' There
was no public demand for a new party, he insisted. They risked splitting the progressive vote and might hand scores of marginal constituencies to the Conservatives. Worse still, it would gut the Labour
Party of Corbynsceptic MPs and members and gift the Labour leadership to the left in perpetuity. 'I hope this is a misunderstanding, and
you are on board with the aim to win back Labour. If not though, I
wanted to make clear the strength of opposition from Progress to a
new party, and appeal to you to leave this idea to die, and remain on
the only practical path for the centre-left.' Angell's missive was treated
less as a warning than as a source of light relief by the Five, who saw
Progress and its confinement to the margins of the party as evidence
that staying and fighting was pointless. But his words did portend the
resistance that would await them.

First they would have to overcome themselves. Over the summer
recess, the Five had been enrolled on a course of personal development coaching with Maggie Ellis, a psychotherapist beloved of
FTSE100 executives and known to Shuker from his days as a pastor
– all the better for deprogramming them after over a century's
combined service in the Labour Party. Upon their return in September,
they had devoted themselves nearly full time to preparing for a split.
Initially, the conclave met at 5 p.m. every Monday in Umunna's and
Leslie's office to nail down the unglamorous technical details on which
a split would live or die: its rules and standing orders, its finances, its
governance structure. Uneasy, Shuker took to booking meeting rooms
in Norman Shaw North instead.

Months away from the earliest likely launch, they already faced a
larger challenge. Umunna's and Leslie's hold over the project was already
deterring would-be asylum seekers from the PLP. Most Labour MPs
had come to one unflattering conclusion or another as to the purpose
of the proposed breakaway – it was either Chuka's vanity project, or
Chris's revenge mission. The thought of being enlisted as cannon fodder
for either enterprise, neither of which matched the blue-sky pitch
Shuker had spun to colleagues, filled most MPs with dread.

'Chuka's very difficult to socialise and put into a group,' one moderate organiser said, 'because he's incapable of behaving in a collegiate way, having a rather large ego.'

Chris Leslie's insatiable appetite for bitching had also begun to repel potential conscripts. The twenty-five-strong WhatsApp group that had been set up to coordinate trips to Sussex became his digital dartboard. Wes Streeting, the Corbynsceptic member for Ilford North, was more often than not the target for Leslie's verbal attacks: his sin was to talk in the uncompromising language of an MP signed up to Plan B while remaining committed to Plan A. He was not in the group, but plenty of his friends from the 2015 intake were, namely Jess Phillips and Peter Kyle. They did not take kindly to Leslie's negativity.

Nor did the trust so painstakingly built up over awkward small talk and late-night boozing sessions in the Fair Oak Farm kitchen survive the leak of a plan for another vote of no confidence in Corbyn, floated briefly by one member of the group, to the *Sunday Times* at the start of September. Leslie was again assumed to be the culprit. One disgruntled co-conspirator recalled: 'Already, around the edges, people were starting to say: "Hang on a minute, this is meant to be a confidential space." So things had already started to fragment.' Leslie had pulled off the remarkable feat of convincing waverers that Corbyn's Labour might just be less toxic than a political party that did not yet exist.

To succeed, the Five knew that they would have to pull off not one split but two: a first wave of defections would have to be followed by a second, as had been the case with the SDP. Yet Leslie's strengths lay in burning bridges rather than building them. By the end of the summer, his behaviour had already shrunk the pool of defectors. Said one of the Five: 'If you keep on going after Wes Streeting as though he's your personal punchbag, what do you expect is going to happen?'

Luciana Berger elicited strong emotions in the PLP too, albeit of a different kind. She was unquestionably the Five's biggest asset. They knew it, and LOTO knew it. Unlike her co-conspirators, she united rather than divided opinion. Nobody was willing to justify the abuse she received. On one occasion, Andrew Murray had even personally intervened to order a Unite activist in Berger's constituency to stop abusing her. Berger was also a rarity among the splitters in that she was admired by Milne. She had been a diligent Shadow Cabinet minister in the first year of Corbyn's leadership and, while a Blairite by pedigree, had at least tried to make an accommodation with the left. That was more than could be said for the other splitters. Andrew Murray said: 'David Owen and Shirley Williams would never have spoken to Michael Foot in the way these people did to Jeremy Corbyn.' Unbeknown to the splitters, the Corbynites had not always sought to alienate them. In the summer of 2016, LOTO had even considered sacking Jon Ashworth as Shadow Health Secretary and replacing him with Berger. Angela Smith, a fellow Fair Oak Farm attendee, had been another option, alongside Lisa Nandy and Dawn Butler. A LOTO aide recalled: 'Whenever we talked about "reaching out" to the PLP, Luciana was right up there.'

Both LOTO and the Five believed that the departure of Labour's most prominent Jewish MP would seriously damage Corbyn. As such, she was vital to any split. For the Corbynsceptics who knew her as a friend and colleague, she also functioned as a canary in the coal mine. Jess Phillips was among those who had told Berger that she would follow her if she felt compelled to quit. 'You just say the word,' she had told Berger over a drink in Parliament some months before the split. 'Because I feel like if you can't stay, then I can't stay.'

Berger's restlessness had already inspired a one-man split. On 18 July, John Woodcock, the hawkish MP for Barrow and Furness, had resigned his Labour membership. His motivation had been twofold. Suspended for alleged sexual harassment in April, Woodcock told friends from Fair Oak Farm that he could not afford to keep throwing money at legal representation for his case indefinitely. He was also convinced that LOTO, whose politics he opposed with religious zeal, had conspired to rig the disciplinary process against him. But as regards the timing of his departure, it was his belief that Berger was preparing to quit that had been decisive. Just before his resignation, she had told Woodcock that her Labour membership had one more month to run at most. Said one of the Five: 'When John left, he left with the expectation that everyone else was coming.'

On 29 September, Chris Leslie's local members followed Shuker's in passing a vote of no confidence in their MP. Leslie responded using the same language Umunna had deployed in his warning shot to local members, writing in the *Guardian* that Labour was 'no longer a broad church'. The ire of the grass roots was to be welcomed, for it helped the Five fulfil one of their tests for launching Plan B – making the case against staying in the Labour Party as it currently existed. Berger's ordeal presented it in the worst possible light. On 3 November, it emerged that the party had failed to tell Berger or the police of a violent threat made against her by a party member. As autumn turned to winter, it became obvious to Berger's colleagues that neither she nor the rest of the Five could wait much longer.

Shuker thought in terms of opening and closing windows. By his calculation, the window through which defectors would jump would open after the meaningful vote on Theresa May's withdrawal agreement. At that point they would need quitters to commit. The window would close behind them by May or June 2019 at the absolute latest, ahead of an expected new parliamentary session. It was considered especially important for would-be splitters to know when they would cease to be Labour MPs. Leaving the timeframe open-ended was unlikely to force hands and calm minds.

The Five knew that their own departure would likely come earlier, for Berger was pregnant. That imposed an even harder deadline of March. Leave it too late for Berger and the split risked crashing and burning. Shuker said: 'It was like trying to build a runway while the plane is taxiing down it. So I was always pushing: can we go later? Equally, Luciana was fit to burst. We were thinking about how we do it if she went into labour.'

When Parliament returned in January, the window opened. Three MPs committed to climb through alongside the Five. Two were veterans of the right's modernising mission. Mike Gapes, the MP for Ilford South, had been one of Neil Kinnock's most devout disciples. As a student activist in the 1970s and 80s he had revelled in campaigns against the left. Now they were in charge, in his view peddling a foreign policy at odds with his muscular Atlanticism.

In the dying days of summer, Gapes had told the eighty or so members of Birthday Club, the Corbynsceptic WhatsApp group in which the increasingly bitter debate between the splitters and stay-and-fighters was litigated, that his time as a Labour MP was coming to an end. 'I am not prepared to support the racist anti-Semite. Period. It's over for me.' All that remained, he added, was 'the timing of my announcement'. Alongside Gapes was Ann Coffey, the owl-like member for Stockport. She had been Blair's parliamentary private secretary in his first term as prime minister and shared his conclusion that the party was beyond redemption. At Leslie's behest, it had been Coffey and Margaret Hodge, another Blairite of long service and advancing years, who had tabled the motion of no confidence in Corbyn's leadership in 2016. The third was the former Shadow Scottish Secretary Ian Murray, the MP for Edinburgh South and sole survivor of Labour's 2015 wipeout north of the border.

The outer circle of the Fair Oak Farm set clung on. Some had been turned off by Leslie and Umunna. Others had never intended to go in the first place. One attendee recalled: 'I felt cross with Chris and Gavin. When I went, originally, it was a really brilliant forum for us to think, strategise, bring the party back. They just wanted to leave. I didn't.' All of the hold-outs hoped to influence Corbyn's position on Brexit.

On 10 January 2019, Corbyn gave them a firm reminder of whose side he was on. With the meaningful vote on May's deal looming, he travelled to Wakefield to set out why Labour would oppose it in the Commons. He also took the opportunity to articulate Labour's own vision, and dutifully rehearsed the policy agreed in Liverpool: a customs union, close relationship with the single market, EU rights and protections, and failing all of that, a public vote. But unusually, it also included an extended riff authored by Corbyn himself, rather than Milne or Fisher:

> I would put it like this: if you're living in Tottenham you may well have voted to Remain. You've got high bills, rising debts, you're in insecure work, you struggle to make your wages stretch and you may be on universal credit, and forced to access food banks. You're up against it. If you're living in Mansfield, you are more likely to have voted to Leave. You've got high bills, rising debts, you're in insecure work, you struggle to make your wages stretch and you may be on universal credit, and forced to access food banks. You're up against it. But you're not against each other.

As one LOTO aide put it, Brexit speeches seldom amounted to more than a 'public update on a private row'. But this was pure Corbyn. The passage, inspired by an impassioned monologue he had given at a strategy meeting, distilled his personal perspective on Brexit unlike any of his speeches before or since. It confirmed that Labour's mission

as he saw it was to reconcile Britain's warring tribes rather than champion one over the other. That, not the second referendum mentioned
in passing, was his aim. To the Five it was a sign that another of their
tests had been passed. Efforts to chivvy the leadership into supporting
a referendum had manifestly failed.

On 15 January came the meaningful vote. True to Corbyn's word
in Wakefield, all but three Labour MPs voted against May's deal. They
were joined by 118 Conservatives in the no lobby to inflict the largest
defeat of modern parliamentary history on the prime minister. Corbyn
responded by tabling a motion of no confidence in her government
the following day. That too failed. In response, the prime minister
appeared to discover a well-concealed appetite for working across
party lines. She invited Corbyn and the other opposition leaders to
talks on a compromise. He declined. Remainers in the PLP demanded
he begin to agitate for a second referendum – after all, he had failed
to secure a general election and all options were on the table. But he
would do no such thing.

In a series of Commons votes over the following weeks on the
government's own Plan B – to reopen negotiations with Brussels
– the Labour leadership refused to push for a second referendum as
a first rather than last resort. Quite the contrary. On 29 January,
Corbyn signalled to May that he would be willing to thrash out a
compromise deal should one be on offer. 'We are prepared to meet
her to put forward the Labour Party's points of view about the kind
of agreement we want with the European Union in order to protect
jobs, living standards, and rights and conditions in this country.' A
public vote might have been on the table, but LOTO was reaching
for Brexit.

On 11 February, Angela Smith took the Brexit debate into the realms
of physical theatre. In an attempt to demonstrate that Corbyn would
not be moved even by grass-roots opposition, Smith had set up an
online petition urging him to back a referendum. He had ignored
Smith's attempts to intervene to make the argument in the Commons
that afternoon. She had been so persistent that Julian Smith, the
Conservative chief whip, had fashioned a handwritten sign for Corbyn's
benefit and waved it from the government front bench: 'ANGELA
WANTS TO ASK ABOUT A SECOND REFERENDUM'. Snubbed in
the chamber, she trooped to Southside with the petition printed and

packed into a dozen cardboard boxes. Officials rejected the delivery on security grounds, giving her her headline.

By then, the splitters had settled on a date: a week later, on 18 February, they would leave the Labour Party.

One of the tests Plan B had to pass was that the media was primed for what was to come. At the beginning of February, it became apparent that Smith approached the task with gusto when a curiously detailed account of their plans had appeared on the front page of the *Observer* under the headline: 'Rebel Labour MPs set to quit party and form centre group'. It was at that point her colleagues discovered that she had enjoyed a lunch with Toby Helm, its political editor, earlier in the week. Lunching with an ITV reporter that week, another of the Five found themselves furnished with details of their plan before they had ordered their starter. All of Westminster knew what was coming.

The Five, who had taken to ostentatiously dining together in the Members' canteen, did nothing to disabuse colleagues of their suspicions. Their calculation was that it made no difference if the bubble knew their plans. If anything, it would only increase the media's appetite to cover their departures. They made several visits to the London Bridge offices of Winckworth Sherwood, the law firm where Umunna's mother Patricia was a partner, for secret rehearsals of the press conference at which they would do the deed.

In January, Shuker had met Blair, who knew of the plan and made no attempt to dissuade them from it. Instead, he wanted numbers, and advised them to set out a policy platform. He knew that to present a bland, content-free alternative to politics as usual was to fail before one had even begun. Blair says: 'I remember having a discussion with some people from outside of the Labour Party, saying they want to start something new, I said to them, so what's your position on Brexit, they said, ah, we don't really want to get into that. OK! Yeah, well, that's a great start!'

In the week before the split, Mandelson paid a similar visit to Umunna. 'Have you got something planned?' he asked. Umunna answered in the negative. 'Rather than think you can leave the Labour Party and create a new one, it might be better for you to consider joining the Liberal Democrats,' Mandy counselled. Umunna roared with laughter.

In public Leslie adopted an almost coquettish tone when quizzed by the media. Suggestions of a split, he insisted, were 'pure speculation'. Then came the teasing chaser: 'A lot of people's patience is being tested right now. I think there are some questions we are *all* going to have to face, especially if Labour enables Brexit.' Addressing another Commons Brexit debate on Valentine's Day, he made that very charge. 'The idea that the Labour Party is not together and arguing against this disaster is, for me, entirely heartbreaking ... Our party political system is shattered, it is broken, and it is letting our country down at a crucial time.' It would be the last time he spoke as a Labour MP. On *The World At One* the same day, Watson was asked whether a split was unstoppable. 'I hope it isn't.' But both he and Corbyn knew what was coming.

*

The splitters were not alone in preparing for the inevitable. LOTO had known a split was coming since 4 February, when the PLP overwhelmingly passed a motion demanding 'action on anti-Semitism'. Tabled by Ruth Smeeth and Catherine McKinnell, two outspoken Corbynsceptics, it gave Jennie Formby, who was in attendance in her capacity as general secretary, a week's notice to supply a report on all outstanding disciplinary cases. If not, they warned, Labour would be seen as 'institutionally racist'. A LOTO source said: 'It was very clear from that point on that there was going to be a split, and that the ground was being prepared.' Corbyn's inner circle needed to beat them to the punch – or at least prepare to roll with them.

On 9 February, Ian Lavery was dispatched to fire a warning shot on HuffPost. In typically pugnacious style he hammered home the case for the prosecution. A breakaway would split the vote. They would let the Tories and their hard Brexit come through the middle. They would have no members, no union backing, no nothing. 'Only the likes of Boris Johnson and Liam Fox would be cheering – it would untie their hands to impose their ideological fantasies unimpeded by a strong and united opposition,' he wrote.

Lavery was reading from a playbook written by Andrew Murray. In a confidential strategy paper circulated among LOTO colleagues the week before the split, he derided the split as a 'Plan C' – an unknowing retort to Shuker's terminology. 'First, they thought the PLP could dismiss Jeremy at will, but that failed in 2016. Second, they hoped for an implosion of our project at first contact with the electorate – that was confounded in 2017. So this is their third roll of the dice.' The tone was bullish – but not to the point of complacency. While a pessimistic McDonnell fretted that as many as seventy MPs could jump, LOTO expected only ten to fifteen of the PLP to break away. 'It is not a powerful initiative – it divides the right wing of the PLP, whereas the "coup" of 2016 united it. There is no obvious leader, and certainly none with the standing and record of the famous Gang of Four. However, we should not underestimate the potential for damage. The chances of a new centrist outfit establishing a permanent and powerful presence in politics is very small. But the chances of it obstructing the election of Labour at the next election – its central objective – are greater.' He dismissed their supposed concerns over anti-Semitism as 'inflated' to make up for the weakness of their arguments on Brexit. 'It gives MPs a sort of moral "cover" for leaving. However, it is unclear what electoral impact these smears have, if any; and opposition to anti-Semitism is not a very strong basis for a new political party, since it is hardly a line of demarcation from every other party.'

On this, Blair agreed. He says now: 'I said to people, look, anti-Semitism's a reason for being furious with the leadership of the Labour Party, it could be a reason for breaking with the Labour Party if the Labour Party as a whole obviously moved into an anti-Semitic position, but opposing anti-Semitism on its own doesn't amount to an entire political philosophy.'

To Murray, an old fellow traveller of the USSR, the splitters' complaints over foreign policy – 'Venezuela, Russia, Hamas, NATO, etc., etc.' – showed them up as political illiterates. 'Attacks on this issue have little public traction; however, our calls for a new approach on foreign affairs have significant resonance and Trump makes "business as usual" a hard sell in this area of policy.'

Finally, he predicted that they would cry bullying, and 'use any incident in CLPs, real or imagined, and any democratic initiative to present a false picture of the party'. He nonetheless warned: 'It again provides a rationale for MPs leaving with a degree of public sympathy. It intersects with a defence of "parliamentary sovereignty/supremacy" against agitators and activists.'

What could LOTO do to mitigate the damage? Murray provided an arsenal of counter-narrative. 'This would be a centrist, no change, millionaires' initiative. We should emphasise its essential conservatism at a moment when people are wanting alternatives and change.' It would keep the Tories in power. It would be 'indistinguishable' from the 'anaemic' Lib Dems. The MPs owed 'their seats and their careers to the Labour Party', if not Jeremy Corbyn himself. They would make a hard Brexit more likely and fail on their own terms. And not one union would support them. Tempting though it would be to engage in 'social media rejoicing along "good riddance" lines' at the sight of Chris Leslie resigning his Labour membership, Murray insisted they should avoid gloating. The Shadow Cabinet should start taking the fight to the defectors in their speeches. LOTO should prepare 'anti-split statements by Jewish activists'.

Most striking was his suggestion Corbyn should meet potential splitters. 'It may be difficult/unpleasant, and some may decline, but it is important to be seen to make the effort.' The invitations were not issued – Corbyn's aides knew he was too averse to confrontation. In any case, it was much too late.

*

On the evening of Sunday 17 February, the Labour MPs who would the next morning become The Independent Group were in a meeting room at St Martin-in-the-Fields church in Trafalgar Square. Shuker had pulled in a favour from a fellow man of the cloth. Only seven were present. Ian Murray had been so close to defecting he had his speech ready, but he pulled out, having decided he should stay and fight rather than gift his seat to a Corbynista at the next election. 'I didn't want to hand my seat to someone from the Corbyn wing of the party and felt loyalty to all the people who had worked so hard to help me win over the years,' he told friends. Murray's speech was thus divided up and folded into those of the other splitters. They had prepared scripts and, as Blair had advised, a 'Statement of Independence', their answer to the Gang of Four's Limehouse declaration. Drafted over the course of several tedious meetings at Umunna's mother's office, it sketched out what the group were for: a market economy, a rules-based international order, and Remain.

Lobby reporters who knew the Seven well were met with radio silence. 'Been trying Chuka for hours and no response,' Kevin Schofield tweeted. 'Ominous.' It was not like Umunna to decline the opportunity to speak to the media. The only journalist who knew for sure what was coming was the BBC's Laura Kuenssberg. She had been holidaying in the countryside when she received word from Umunna and Leslie that she should be at County Hall, across the Thames from Parliament, on Monday morning. Leslie had worried that reporters would not turn up if they were not given advance notice of what was to happen. His anxiety was misplaced. At 8 a.m., lobby journalists received an email from Stuart Macnaughtan, Umunna's chief of staff, notifying them that a group of Labour MPs would make an announcement about 'the future of British politics' in two hours' time. They knew exactly what the invitation meant.

Just before 10 a.m., the Seven sent their letters of resignation via email to Nick Brown and Jeremy Corbyn, who would later send each a curt reply demanding that they call by-elections. Having been waylaid momentarily as Umunna struggled with his iPad, they strode silently, like a family filing into a hushed church behind a coffin, to face the massed press. All that was audible was the sound of camera shutters.

One by one they made their case against Corbyn's Labour. Berger, heavily pregnant, began by introducing herself as a Labour MP, before pausing to nervous laughter from journalists. Four days earlier she had nearly derailed the launch with an unexpected trip to hospital. She told the room that she and all six of the MPs alongside her on stage had resigned. 'For my part, I have become embarrassed and ashamed to remain in the Labour Party ... I cannot remain in a party that I have today come to the sickening conclusion is institutionally anti-Semitic.'

'We did everything we could to save it,' Leslie said of the party he had spent the best part of a year plotting to leave. 'In all conscience, we can no longer knock on doors and support a government led by Jeremy Corbyn or the team around him. The evidence of Labour's betrayal on Europe is now visible for all to see.'

Gapes, voice cracking, thundered: 'I am furious that the Labour leadership is complicit in facilitating Brexit, which will cause great economic, social and political damage to our country.' Coffey spoke of her 'great sadness' of leaving after twenty-seven years in Parliament.

Smith said: 'Our politics is broken and all the main parties are incapable of inspiring confidence in the future.'

It fell to Umunna, the man most people in the room assumed would end up leading the effort, to close with a sales pitch. 'If you are sick and tired of politics as usual, guess what? So are we. That's why we have done what we have done today and why we commit to do things differently. We don't have all the answers, so we will treat people like adults and be honest about the tough choices facing Britain ... If you want an alternative, please help us build it. The bottom line is this – politics is broken, it doesn't have to be this way. Let's change it.'

The media's attention then turned to two men who were not in the room: Blair and Watson. In the script the splitters had pre-prepared, Umunna insisted that Blair had no knowledge of what they were doing *that day*. Blair confirmed as much to a nonplussed New Labour grandee, whom he called in the wake of their announcement. 'What are these people doing?' Blair said. 'They never told me. They never consulted me – it's a complete surprise.'

Watson, meanwhile, launched his rearguard. With help from the *Times* columnist Philip Collins, Pat McFadden and his communications aide Sarah Coombes, he wrote a speech setting out his position. Staring down the barrel of a camera in his parliamentary office, he said the Seven had not been wrong to leave – merely that they had done so too soon. 'The instant emotion I felt, when I heard the news this morning that colleagues were leaving Labour, was deep sadness. I've devoted my life to this party and I'm proud to serve it, I am hugely disappointed about what has happened. This is a sad day for all of us. I think our colleagues have come to a premature conclusion. But this is a moment for regret and reflection, not for a mood of anger or a tone of triumph.'

Watson offered Corbyn advice that he and the PLP knew would be ignored – to recruit his adversaries to the Shadow Cabinet so that 'all the members of our broad church feel welcome in our congregation'. More significantly, he signalled to MPs that he would build the political equivalent of a nonconformist chapel for the dissenters. 'Social democratic and democratic socialist traditions, which has always been the mainstream of Labour's political thought, is where we can find the answers to the current crisis. That is why in the coming weeks and months I will be working with Labour MPs to develop policies within that tradition to address the challenges of the future. I believe the much-needed modernisation of this nation must come from there.'

He and Mandelson had been planning for the moment they would need to ordain Watson as the spiritual leader of the stay-and-fighters for months. In November and December, they had come to the conclusion that they would need a space to organise – and know they were supported. They conceived of a caucus within the PLP – a party within a party – that would enable them to exchange ideas, air the policy proposals that the leadership ignored, and learn how they might defy deselection.

Shuker watched with annoyance. Watson had been the first person he called after leaving the stage. It was time to tell the de facto leader of the Corbynsceptics to put up or shut up. He received no reply. Though Shuker interpreted the snub as a calculated attempt to strangle The Independent Group at birth, the reality was that Watson missed the call and did not have Shuker's number saved to his phone.

The Corbynite response initially smacked of anger, rather than sorrow: McDonnell called for The Independent Group's MPs to face by-elections and LOTO dispatched Lavery – for many MPs the face of the politics they hated – to address the PLP. He denied that Labour had become institutionally anti-Semitic, and one by one the party's Jewish women – Hodge, Smeeth and Louise Ellman, Berger's constituency neighbour – rose to say they would not be joining The Independent Group. Only one MP present would. Joan Ryan, the member for Enfield North and chair of Labour Friends of Israel, left the meeting early. She had already told *The Times* that she would be joining the splitters, which came as news to The Independent Group. Two days later, their numbers swelled to eleven with the arrival of three Conservative Remainers in Heidi Allen, Anna Soubry and Sarah Wollaston. The Independent Group was building up a head of steam.

On 21 February, Gordon Brown called Ian Austin, who would be next to jump. Brown attempted to talk him off the ledge but Austin was no longer as biddable as he had been in Downing Street. He had already explained his decision to his local newspaper. 'Look, Gordon, I've done my interviews. This is happening. Even if you persuaded me not to, there's nothing I could do about it now. There's no point discussing this.' Brown persisted, but to no avail.

It soon became clear that the splitters did not have anything like the number of MPs Austin had envisaged – nor any big beasts as the SDP had done. It did not help that the left's anger gave way to pity. The day after their announcement, Angela Smith was forced to apologise after appearing to refer to people of colour as having a 'funny tinge' on live television. That incident would later see them nicknamed in LOTO as 'CUK Tinge PLC', a dig at their corporate politics, Smith's gaffe, and their status – in the eyes of the online left at least – as the 'cucks', or weak-willed, servile moderates of British politics. Yet Corbyn would make major concessions in order to prevent any further defections. On 25 February, Corbyn returned from a trip to Brussels and announced that, unless its Brexit plan passed the Commons in the latest round of Brexit votes two days later, Labour would support a second referendum. Outside of the Labour Party, the splitters appeared to have taken only a week to effect the shift they had wasted the best part of a year agitating for inside it. LOTO denied the decision was a sop to their opponents. Yet given an inch, Emily Thornberry grabbed the opportunity to take a mile on behalf of the Shadow Cabinet's Remainers. To LOTO's consternation, she claimed that both she and Corbyn would be campaigning to stay in the EU. On anti-Semitism too, LOTO quickly learned the art of compromise. When the Corbynite provocateur Chris Williamson was revealed to have told a Momentum meeting in Sheffield that Labour had been 'too apologetic' on anti-Semitism, he was suspended from the whip. To many in the party, it served as proof of a vital sentiment: dissent worked – especially when expressed in public.

By 11 March, when Watson and Mandelson gathered 150 MPs in Committee Room 14 for the inaugural meeting of their Future Britain Group, it was clear that their worst-case scenario had been averted. Most of the PLP had concluded, however reluctantly, that a split was not the answer. But that did not mean LOTO's problems had gone away. With no end to the Brexit crisis in sight, they would soon have to contend with a split of their own.

Deal or No Deal

'We need to get this right, because there's gonna be blood on the walls.' Ian Lavery was a man who made no compromises, not even in metaphor – and when it came to Brexit he was surer of himself than ever. Theresa May's Brexit withdrawal agreement would come before the Commons in January 2019, a few short weeks away. Labour had already resolved to vote it down. Yet its chairman, an unapologetic class warrior from the Leave-voting pit villages of Northumberland, sensed political danger. He made his case to the well-heeled Remainers of the Brexit subcommittee with characteristic bombast. 'Move an inch this way, you'll have blood on the walls. The other – BLOOD ON THE WALLS!'

Jeremy Corbyn recoiled. 'Ian,' he said. 'Can you just calm down a bit? Calm down.' This, in essence, was Corbyn's view of how Labour ought to respond. Rather than shed blood by lurching one way or the other, could they not mediate a middle way?

Yet 2019 would not be the year that Lavery, his Shadow Cabinet colleagues or indeed the country calmed down.

Theresa May's withdrawal agreement, the fruit of more than eighteen months of torturous negotiations with Brussels – and her own party – had just landed in Westminster with the force of an artillery shell. It now fell to Starmer, who had read all 599 pages of the document in his loft on the night of its publication, 14 November 2018, to decode its contents for the edification of his colleagues. Starmer had been in full flow before the Shadow Cabinet's Brexit subcommittee, doing precisely that, when Corbyn asked quizzically: 'What's this backstop?'

Close reading was not required to know that the proposed deal had gone down badly among Conservative Brexiteers. May had emerged from a four-hour meeting of Cabinet that evening and declared she had won unanimous backing for her deal. Here, finally, was the agreement that would remove the UK from Europe. Over the course of the next twenty-four hours, minister after minister popped up to clarify that it was not. The following morning, Starmer and Nick Brown had been interrupted midway through a private tutorial on the contents of the deal from Olly Robbins, May's chief adviser on the EU, and Gavin Barwell, her chief of staff. Brown's adviser Luke Sullivan burst in. 'Just to let you know,' Sullivan deadpanned in his West Country brogue. 'Dominic Raab has resigned.' Raab was the second of May's Brexit Secretaries to quit in the space of four months. Esther McVey, the Work and Pensions Secretary, Shailesh Vara and Suella Braverman, two junior ministers, followed in short order. For a brief moment, the government looked as though it might fall before lunch.

The quitters' objections to the deal were shared by hardliners on the back benches and could be boiled down to two words: Irish backstop. Downing Street had agreed, at the behest of Brussels and Dublin, that unless and until it could find a way to leave the EU without imposing a hard border between Ireland, which would remain in Europe, and Northern Ireland, which would be leaving with the rest of the UK, then the whole UK would remain in a customs union with the EU. To Conservative Leavers, Brexit would not mean Brexit after all.

The liberal commentariat often worked itself into a frenzy about Corbyn's apparent Euroscepticism. Yet the truth was that he was unmoved by the definition Westminster was tearing itself apart over, and showed little desire to get to grips with it. In the months that followed, as the Brexit paralysis deepened, so did Corbyn's own withdrawal. To his closest aides, he had fallen into something of a funk and become either unwilling or, as time went on, psychologically incapable of leading. It would fall to his warring court to articulate exactly what Brexit meant to the Labour Party.

In LOTO there had long been a belief that they need not reckon with the question. Two assumptions had underpinned the leadership's approach since June 2017. The first was that May would yield to the pressure of a hung parliament, bend her red lines, and strike a deal that enjoyed the support of a majority of MPs. The second was that her grip on power had become so tenuous that Labour would soon be in Downing Street, whatever their Brexit policy. Precise questions of trade and diplomacy could wait – for it was the job of the government to answer them, not the opposition.

But when forced to address the question – and it was only when forced upon them that it took up significant headspace – they took divergent views. Seumas Milne, who has never denied voting Leave in 2016, had taken advice from a team of QCs, who told him that the 2017 manifesto was inoperable within the EU. Andrew Murray, who as a good communist might have thought the manifesto rather weak beer anyway, believed the 2017 programme was just about doable within the strictures of Brussels legislation – but that a more radical manifesto for a second or third term could quickly set a Corbyn government on a collision course with the European courts. Andrew Fisher, the manifesto's chief architect, was altogether more relaxed, and dismissed any notion that EU membership presented a block to his policy platform. Corbyn himself was conflicted. 'He felt that they had been dishonest throughout the referendum campaign,' a senior LOTO aide said. 'He had an argument that, while leaving the EU might, under some circumstances, be all very well, to leave while you had a Tory government would be a big risk, because they might tear up the protections that the EU *did* offer us.' He certainly did not approach the subject with the Bennite fervour his critics in the PLP and press attributed to him. First and foremost, he wanted to heal a divided nation. The other questions were academic. They could be dealt with later.

Such indecision meant that LOTO's detractors were free to describe the party as they wished. To Remainers, Corbyn was a Brexiteer. To Brexiteers, he had been corrupted by Remainers. In December 2018, May had been forced by opposition within her own party to postpone the first meaningful vote on her deal until the New Year, and had then faced a vote of no confidence from her own MPs. Yet somehow it was Corbyn who had headed into the Christmas recess looking winded by events. At the final PMQs of the year on 19 December, May had baited her opposite number across the Dispatch Box. Where was his Brexit policy? Why, if he so wanted to force a snap election, had he not tabled a motion of no confidence in her government? The Conservative backbenchers that had sought to oust her only a week earlier hooted with delight. Corbyn mumbled in irritation.

It was to the *Guardian* that he rushed to clarify that he did in fact have a plan, telling the paper on 21 December that a Labour government could take the UK out of the EU in time for the Article 50 deadline at the end of March. 'You'd have to go back and negotiate, and see what the timetable would be.' But on the question of which way Labour would campaign in a second referendum he would not be drawn. In a characteristic show of deference to the sovereignty of the grass roots, he said: 'I'm not a dictator of the party.' That much was certainly true.

Julian Smith, Theresa May's chief whip, had spent Christmas Eve and Boxing Day on the phone to Labour MPs whose constituents had backed Leave in 2016. It was obvious by then that no negotiated Brexit would pass the Commons without the support of at least a chunk of the Labour Party. Not a single MP had passed through either division lobby to pass judgement on the withdrawal agreement. But by December, he had lost enough sleep and hair to realise that Conservative Eurosceptics were not for turning. Holed up with his family in a one-bedroom flat in the Barbican, he spoke to each of the Labour MPs in turn, making his case. May's deal was a softish Brexit but nonetheless a decisive one. Backing it was not only in their constituents' interests, but in *their* interests. Yet one by one the Labour MPs said no. As much as many of them wanted Brexit to happen, next to none of them were prepared to incur the political pain of making it so. Excuses came thick and fast. The deal was not soft enough. Workers' rights were not sufficiently protected. The government would renege on its promises in negotiations on a future trade deal. There was just enough wrong with what Smith was offering for them to say no in good conscience.

It took Theresa May's massive defeat on 15 January to rouse LOTO out of its collective slumber. The scale of it – a yawning 230-vote margin – made clear that, in one form or another, Labour would have to license some form of Brexit if it was ever to occur. Whether it was May's deal, a compromise deal or indeed no deal at all, Corbyn and his team would have to decide and say what Labour wanted – or didn't. That would mean reckoning with Labour's irreconcilable coalition in the country. It would, as Lavery predicted, mean blood on the walls.

★

In the wake of the general election of 2017, Andrew Murray had launched a one-man mission for collaboration with the government over Brexit. He spent much of 2019 operating at reduced capacity, having suffered a severe heart attack and undergoing bypass surgery, but in his absence, his arguments grew more pertinent.

'Is it time for us to take a powerful initiative relating to Brexit?' he wrote in a memo to LOTO colleagues. 'The inept and incoherent Tory government is increasingly perceived as being incapable of agreeing what it wants from the talks with the EU, let alone delivering it. The mood of impending calamity is growing.' May, he argued, was 'cocking this up Olympic-style'. It was time for Corbyn to stop the 'regular opposition thing' of needling the government and offer to pull the prime minister out of the hole she had dug herself. 'We should offer to forge a common national position and take responsibility for delivering it in talks with Brussels.' He proposed Corbyn make a speech naming the price for a grand bargain. There were risks to any form of collaboration with the Tories, he acknowledged. Yet it was worth the gamble: 'In the here-and-now, I think the JC leadership has enough credit in the bank. Our radicalism in general would remain undiluted.' Though couched in the language of the national interest, Murray's paper set out the political prizes on offer in the event his colleagues were brave enough to grasp the nettle. He was not a man given to hyperbole but drew an explicit comparison with Clement Attlee's decision to take the party into coalition with Winston Churchill's Conservatives in 1940. 'It would make Labour look states-manlike, confident, national, patriotic and government-ready,' he wrote, acutely aware of the damage done to the party. 'We would be seen to be acting to put the country first at a moment of mounting concern and alarm.' Labour could leave the sidelines and line up on the pitch as a government-in-waiting. It might also unite a PLP and Labour electorate in a country increasingly riven by differences of opinion on Europe. Leavers would see a Labour Party not only defer-ring to the 2016 mandate but ensuring it was delivered in orderly fashion. Remainers would acknowledge it was 'erecting a firewall against a cliff-edge, crash-out Brexit'. And Corbyn would be leading in doing so, rather than being dragged in the wake of right-wing backbenchers. The mere fact of the offer promised to divide the Conservatives too. Any prospect of collaboration with LOTO would disgust their right wing. Were that groundswell of opposition to lead May to reject Corbyn's entreaties, Murray calculated that Labour would still benefit. 'More than ever they [the Tories] would exclusively carry the can for Brexit.' Most alluring, Murray believed a deal 'would mean that the balance of argument could shift from the course of the negotiations with the EU towards the contrasting visions for a post-Brexit vision'. It would unite the bulk of the PLP around the leadership's domestic policy, which most MPs found inoffensive and in some cases genuinely exciting. Unsurprisingly, given his status as Len McCluskey's emissary to Planet Corbyn, Murray also argued that the unions would line up behind it too.

Corbyn would demand that his jointly negotiated Brexit was immediately followed by the general election he had been calling for, so that voters could choose between his and May's versions of the peace. It could, Murray suggested, be Corbyn's 1945.

Back in the present, he could not resist playing to the baser instincts of his audience with a dig at Chuka Umunna. 'Above all, it would block the road to an anti-Brexit centrist realignment. The driving force behind this – the Chuka-ists – would be gazumped at a stroke. It would marginalise the Blairite/Lib Dem position in terms of public opinion, or at least reduce it to that much smaller group that oppose *any* Brexit on any terms and agitate for a second referendum. We're not going there.'

Unfortunately for Murray, John McDonnell had begun to show a tentative interest in the opposite: a second referendum. As Smith schmoozed Labour MPs, Remainers outside of Parliament sought to woo McDonnell. Alastair Campbell was chief among them.

Two years earlier, McDonnell had violated a gentlemen's agreement brokered backstage by Seb Corbyn by viciously attacking Alastair Campbell on *Question Time*, describing his opposition to the Project as 'nauseating'. Campbell later derided the Shadow Chancellor as 'a man who hates anyone who helped Labour win'. Now, though, Campbell had decided that McDonnell was the *only* person in Corbyn's inner sanctum who cared about winning. The pair forged an improbable friendship after bonding over football. 'Alastair is a big Burnley fan and John went to college there, so he knew a bit about the background of the club,' said one friend of Campbell. From there flowed a stream of texts and the 'odd phone call' making the case for Remain.

In parallel, left Remainers started to address the PR problem caused by New Labour's old masters of spin. The pro-EU cause, in the eyes of LOTO at least, was associated with enemies of the Project. Murphy had grown used to telling the likes of Heneghan, who had sought asylum with John Stolliday and other Corbynsceptics at the People's Vote campaign, that she would only countenance a second referendum 'over [her] dead body'.

As 2019 began, left Remainers began the process of reclaiming it from them. It was headed by Manuel Cortes, the gruff TSSA leader who had got his way with the composite motion at party conference in Liverpool the previous September. Now his objective was to ensure the leadership followed it through to its logical end point – a referendum in which Labour campaigned for Remain. Together with Hope Not Hate, the anti-racism campaign, the TSSA would show Corbyn just how damaging equivocation – or, worse still, facilitation – on Brexit could be. Sam Tarry, Cortes's enforcer and a former campaign aide to Corbyn, and Laura Parker, the former LOTO aide turned Momentum apparatchik, were deployed to preach the gospel of Keynes: 'When the facts change, I change my mind.'

The facts made for grim reading indeed – and flew in the face of what Murray had agitated for within LOTO. 'If there is an election in 2019, Labour will get a lower share of the vote in every seat in the country if it has a pro-Brexit policy than if it has an anti-Brexit position.' Core demographics who had voted Leave in 2016 and Labour the following year had shifted to Remain: working-class voters, young voters, and Muslim voters. Labour Leavers as a whole cared more about austerity than they did about the vagaries of Brexit itself.

Their figures claimed, contra Murray, that a deal would not lance the boil of a new centrist party but inflame it. 'Our polling suggests that 19 per cent of current Labour voters would be very likely to support a new centrist party that is committed to opposing and/or overturning Brexit. Amongst Labour Remain voters this rises to 27.6 per cent.'

Brexit equalled electoral zugzwang for Labour. Calamity awaited Corbyn no matter what direction he jumped in. The only question was of scale. Block Brexit and Labour would lose eleven seats in its old north and Midlands heartlands. But were they to follow Murray's advice and implement it, they would lose forty-five – sixteen of them in London, and five of their seven seats in Scotland. Splitting the difference would no longer cut it electorally. The circumstances demanded a bold choice.

Cortes zeroed in on McDonnell, knowing that his hunger for electoral success at almost any cost more or less guaranteed them a fair hearing. Those who know the Shadow Chancellor credit the paper as inspiration for a Damascene conversion to the Remain cause, or at least the makings of one. Here, it seemed, was evidence that the Project could not survive association with Brexit.

*

In the wake of the first meaningful vote, the prime minister, thanks to procedural chicanery from the donnish backbencher and former Attorney General Dominic Grieve, had been required to set out her Plan B. When MPs voted to amend it on 29 January, two months to the day before Brexit was still scheduled to happen, the Conservatives and DUP united around a proposal to send May back to Brussels to negotiate a replacement for the backstop. The only other proposal to muster a majority was an amendment from Labour's Jack Dromey and the former Tory Cabinet minister Caroline Spelman, calling on the prime minister to rule out no-deal. The vote gave Corbyn sufficient cover to meet May and relay the demand in person.

Their meeting, subsequently described as 'serious', was the first of many between the oddest of couples. While May knew what her party did not like – the backstop – she lacked the means to do anything about it. The only thing that united her MPs was a solution that, in the eyes of Brussels and Dublin, did not exist. Yet nothing else appeared capable of commanding a parliamentary majority. So it fell to the leaders of the largest parties to chart a way forward and begin the tentative first steps of Murray's plan.

Those accorded the dubious privilege of accompanying Corbyn to his sporadic one-on-ones with May over Brexit spoke of them as Tinder dates from hell. Neither had the hinterland to sustain a conversation beyond the dry matter at hand, which Corbyn had little interest in anyway. Instead, they would make pained small talk about their constituencies and May's churchgoing. On his way out, Corbyn, as if suggesting a nightcap, asked May: 'What are you up to now?'

'I don't know, I do whatever my people tell me to do,' the prime minister replied.

Karie Murphy shot back: 'I wish you were a bit more like that, Jeremy!' On her return to LOTO, she even told colleagues that May was surprisingly 'nice' and 'really genuine'.

But May's post-date verdict was withering. In response to Corbyn's central and indeed only demand she tweeted: 'The only way to avoid No Deal is to vote for a deal.' As a statement of fact, the logic was self-evident, but it had only a tenuous relationship to political reality. Her deal not only fell short of what Labour had demanded, it was so loathed by Conservative MPs as to have no chance of passing anyway.

Corbyn was not a politician built for the Brexit age. It demanded that he exercise executive power with a regularity and force that seemed beyond him. The interminable cycle of votes and amendments kept him chained to Westminster. Gone was the spirit of 2017, its heady insurgency and the clarity of message. Aides say Corbyn still believed in delivering Brexit, but how Labour might get there – and precisely what kind of Brexit it might deliver – seemed to be beyond him. His instinctive response, according to those present, was to withdraw. At his best he was Delphic, at his worst he was gnomic. It fell instead to his team to decode and debate what little he did say, in the hope that they might claim it as a victory for their own conflicting agendas.

On one occasion Milne, Murphy and Fisher were forced to do just that, arguing over the meaning of what Corbyn had said as he sat in silence. Another aide recalled: 'Jeremy was sat there, and didn't speak to offer any clarity whatsoever on what he'd meant. So he was just there, and I remember thinking, "this is mental". They were interpreting his words in front of him, while he wasn't saying anything. And he'd just sit there and he'd always have his notebook and just ... It was like he didn't feel the need to clarify or to take control of the situation.' Increasingly Starmer took charge of the Brexit subcommittee, with Corbyn limiting himself to cursory greetings and instead devoting himself to his phone, checking his diary and scrolling through Twitter as the battle raged around him.

In the leader's self-enforced absence, Starmer could prosecute his plan for the softest of Brexits – and a referendum – while enjoying a latitude that came close to impunity. On 7 February, Corbyn wrote to

May with a list of demands that would need to be met before any cross-party deal could have lift-off. The wish list spoke to Starmer's growing influence: it included a customs union, close alignment with the single market, continued membership of European agencies and cooperation on security, and guarantees that the UK would stick to EU rights and protections even as they were changed by Brussels. Politics abhors a vacuum as nature does, and Starmer filled that left by Corbyn.

But May was not yet at the point of compromise and neither was Labour. The following day, LOTO officials met to cook up plans for the snap general election many of them assumed would solve the Brexit conundrum. Andrew Fisher led the discussion, describing his vision for a campaign that would treat Brexit not as the most divisive policy proposition ever visited upon the electorate but a means of uniting the country behind Labour's domestic platform. The consensus was that Labour should simply tell voters the same things it had told them in 2017. It was summed up by the slogan 'Transforming Britain and Bringing Us Back Together' and the attack line 'Austerity Isn't Over'. The session even spawned a secret website, failingthemany.com, which would have highlighted the depredations of Tory rule. It was a campaign that neither events nor his own party would permit Corbyn to fight.

As LOTO dreamed up how it might best attack the Tories, a motley band of Labour MPs to their right were working out how they might best work with them. On 12 February, May welcomed the Labour MPs John Mann, Caroline Flint and Gareth Snell into her Commons office for a discussion of what might induce them to support her deal. Each of the three was about as far from Corbynism as it was possible to be, and each sat for constituencies that, despite their deep ancestral ties to the Labour Party, had swung heavily behind Leave in 2016. Mann, the PLP's patron saint of righteous indignation, had voted Leave in 2016 and subsequently appointed himself leader of those MPs who wanted to help a deal pass. To nobody's surprise he had been one of only three Labour MPs to have voted for the withdrawal agreement at the first time of asking, and made it his mission to cajole more of his colleagues through the aye lobby with him. He promised the chief whip that he could deliver the government the numbers they needed.

Flint was similarly convinced that a deal must pass. Though elected as one of Blair's Babes in 1997, nothing less than Brexit would do. Both she and Mann represented coalfield constituencies whose bonds with the party that had been established to represent them were fraying. From their surgeries and canvass sessions they relayed to colleagues dire warnings of electoral oblivion if Labour was seen to block Brexit. Flint's office became the nerve centre of a new faction in the PLP: the Respect the Vote group. Its thirty or so members included Jon Trickett and Ian Lavery.

Snell, making up the numbers in May's office that evening, was in some ways an unlikely presence. Balding, bespectacled and baby-faced, he had been an MP for only two years. He had only squeaked into the Commons in the by-election for Stoke-on-Trent Central, another Brexit hotspot in early 2017, after his back catalogue of questionable tweets was unearthed by the press. Most embarrassing for Snell was not his description of a female *Apprentice* contestant as a 'gobby bird' but a stanza of self-authored verse about the choice nearly 70 per cent of his prospective constituents had taken in 2016: 'Soft Brexit, Hard Brexit, Massive pile of Shit. Sloppy Brexit, Messy Brexit. Quit, Quit, Quit.' He had since come to the reluctant conclusion that Labour needed to deliver precisely that if he was to keep the job on which he had such a precarious hold. Starmer's team found Snell's furious lobbying for a deal followed by indecision in the division lobbies so insufferable that aides joked that he should quit the PLP to become Speaker. One aide had messaged colleagues: '#Snell4Speaker'.

Snell and his comrades told May that evening that they would need legislation that bound the government to sticking to EU standards on workers' rights if they and like-minded colleagues were to back a deal. In doing so they set a bar that neither they nor the government would ever clear.

Not all of Corbyn's advisers agreed that MPs should be dissuaded from breaking the whip to back a deal. A frustrated Andrew Murray told colleagues in LOTO: 'Why are we working so hard to stop Labour people rebelling? We should just let them … because if this deal goes through, it will be the best thing for us politically.' The problem was that to allow it would be to give the deal Corbyn's tacit blessing. Hours before May's meeting with the Labour dealers, Remainers had staged a protest half a mile from Corbyn's home, accusing him of precisely that.

Led By Donkeys were a gang of self-styled guerrilla advertisers who had made a name for themselves on social media by plastering billboards with the promises of Conservative Brexiteers such as Gove and Johnson made during the referendum campaign of 2016. Hindsight revealed them to have been utterly hollow. Now they had rented a prime advertising spot next to Arsenal's Emirates Stadium and given Corbyn the same treatment. Except that his picture was accompanied not by words but by a blank space. To the young progressives who had invested their hopes in his leadership of the Labour Party twice over, it summed up the fundamental disappointment of Corbyn's approach to Brexit: here was an injustice he was unwilling to stand up to. Armed with a stepladder, Shakira Martin, the president of the National Union of Students, joined activists in daubing the blank space with criticism of Corbyn. 'You have let down the mandem,' was her charge.

In mid-February, Corbyn took a trip to Brussels to discuss plans for breaking the deadlock with Michel Barnier. LOTO's policy team had invited Starmer to join him. Murphy, distrustful of the Shadow Brexit Secretary's agenda, reacted furiously. 'Jeremy doesn't want Keir there,' she told them. 'You've got to respect Jeremy. He doesn't want him there.' Eyebrows hit the ceiling when she instead proposed Corbyn be accompanied by Richard Burgon, a plan that was guaranteed to generate headlines about closet Brexiteers at the heart of Corbyn's team. More pertinently, it would have left Corbyn adrift in a meeting at which even his admirers in LOTO admitted he was ill-equipped to hold his own. The idea died a swift death after Starmer made his objections clear to Corbyn – he eventually attended the talks alongside Burgon.

Starmer liked to behave in meetings abroad as if he was already in government. His objective was to return from Brussels with the outline of a negotiating strategy that could inform Labour's approach if they were in power. Starmer's aides, all of them white men, defined themselves against what they saw as the chaos and disorganisation of LOTO, who in turn likened them to supercilious civil servants. Starmer's team were particularly horrified by Corbyn's seeming inability to absorb any of the torrent of detail as the Brexit crisis developed. In the days before their trip to Brussels, Corbyn and his delegation had first visited Madrid for a meeting of the Party of European Socialists. At a round-table of national leaders he lavished vigorous praise on Antonio Costa, the Portuguese prime minister. Thanks and congratulations were in order, Corbyn said, for a Brexit amendment on EU citizens' rights that Costa had tabled at Westminster. Lisbon's interpreters translated the speech for Costa, whose bafflement grew in direct proportion to Corbyn's enthusiasm. Corbyn was some way into the monologue before Starmer's team realised why he was so excited. As they explained to the bemused premier in the aftermath, Corbyn had assumed that his hero, who had shown that it was possible to win power on an anti-austerity platform, was somehow the amendment's author – and not the Conservative MP Alberto Costa.

They also felt that Milne primarily saw the talks as an opportunity to put on a show of statesmanship. For reasons of ideology he was opposed to the institutions of the EU, but he also appeared to enjoy the pomp and ceremony accorded to Corbyn on his visits. There he was given a status that the British establishment seldom dignified him with. Corbyn's presence in Brussels alone was evidence that he was an alternative prime minister. By the time of the February meeting, he had grown bored of Barnier – despite the EU27 having entrusted him with negotiating on their behalf – and instead began agitating for an audience with Emmanuel Macron, Angela Merkel or the president of the European Council, Donald Tusk.

What Labour would have hoped to secure from such a powwow was less clear. At the end of February, May put another motion on her plans before the House, which Corbyn again amended. MPs voted against both the motion and the amendment by a decisive margin of eighty-three votes. After the defeat, Corbyn told MPs that Labour would keep pushing for the vision of Brexit they had just rejected, but added: 'We will back a public vote in order to prevent a damaging Tory Brexit or a disastrous no-deal outcome.' It was as strong an endorsement as Corbyn himself had ever given to a second referendum but it was laden too heavily with caveats to satisfy its intended audience.

It was increasingly obvious from John McDonnell's public appearances that he was more than happy to pick a side. Speaking to ITV's Robert Peston in the immediate aftermath of the votes, the Shadow Chancellor went a step further than Corbyn and committed Labour to amending May's deal to allow for a second referendum when it came before the Commons again in March. Asked by Peston which side he would campaign for, McDonnnell declared for Remain. Minutes later, Labour MP Lisa Nandy – speaking on behalf of those who wanted a deal – criticised the party's rush towards a referendum.

There, in a nutshell, was Corbyn's problem. Party policy obliged him to support a public vote. But to much of the PLP that was a bridge too far. And so the deadlock continued.

★

The second meaningful vote on 12 March was defeated by a margin of 149 votes, and on 14 March the prime minister brought forward her motion on extending the Article 50 period, which duly passed. Despite McDonnell's gung-ho prediction that Labour would then go full throttle in its endorsement of a second referendum, Corbyn did not go quite that far. MPs were instead whipped to abstain on an amendment that called for a public vote. Five frontbenchers whose constituencies had voted to leave in 2016 could not stomach it. Ruth Smeeth, Gareth Snell's constituency neighbour in Stoke, was joined by Stephanie Peacock, Justin Madders, Emma Lewell-Buck and Yvonne Fovargue, all of whom quit the front bench to vote against the amendment. Despite their protests, most Labour MPs followed the whip to abstain. The amendment was easily defeated.

In private, many within LOTO sympathised with those who had quit. On 20 March, they had even taken the step of deliberately leaking polling to the *Sun* – a publication whose very existence was anathema to many Corbynites – that warned that by refusing to block a second referendum, Labour risked losing a decisive working-class voter. Its story was delicately worded, relying on the view of an unnamed 'senior figure', so as to disguise the fact that comrades were conspiring with a Murdoch tabloid to undermine their own.

By 21 March, the Brexit extension had been agreed. It came with a built-in guillotine. If MPs approved the prime minister's deal by the original deadline of 29 March, then the delay would run until 22 May and the UK would have to take part in elections to the European Parliament. If MPs rejected her deal for a third time, then the reprieve would run for only two weeks, until 12 April. At that point, the UK faced a choice between a deal, no-deal, an even longer delay, or cancelling Brexit altogether.

On 27 March the Commons were given a choice between no less than eight different options in a round of indicative votes. This time, Labour MPs were whipped to vote for a second referendum, a customs union, and Labour's own plan. None passed. By now not even the Shadow Cabinet could be relied upon to maintain discipline. Remainers demanded heads roll after Ian Lavery, Jon Trickett and Andrew Gwynne defied the whip to abstain on Margaret Beckett's proposal that any deal passed by Parliament be subject to a referendum. Trickett and Lavery believed that to back Remain would be to risk a fundamental breach with the English working class. On Mothering Sunday, Lavery had been tending to his mother's grave when he was confronted by three constituents who accused him of trying to thwart the will of the people. Leavers in the Shadow Cabinet saw Beckett's plan as a trap. For starters, it had not been her brainchild at all. Instead, she had been drafted as a unifying grandee to front a plan devised by Peter Kyle and Phil Wilson, the Blairite backbenchers who had kept Tony and Mandy well abreast of their plans.

The Kyle–Wilson proposition was something of a Faustian bargain. Labour MPs would approve May's deal on the proviso it was pitted against Remain in a referendum. Neither Trickett nor Lavery could live with either option.

Suspecting their rebellion would be weaponised to undermine the left, Trickett and Lavery headed to LOTO the next morning to offer their resignations.

'We've come to resign,' Trickett said.

'I thought that might be what this is,' replied a weary Corbyn.

'We're trying to protect you,' Trickett went on. 'You're our comrade, we love you, but we think we should fuck off.'

Invited to sign their death warrant, Corbyn instead granted them a reprieve. 'You've put me in a tricky position. The chief whip's really annoyed. But I won't mind if you don't do it today. I'll give you a call tomorrow and let you know.'

Lavery accepted it with gratitude. 'Well we don't really want to, you're our mate.'

Trickett began to squabble. 'Well, how can he keep us, Ian?'

It fell to Corbyn to keep the peace. 'Don't go today.'

They never did go. Both would later rue the latitude their leader had granted them as a missed opportunity to walk out and mobilise the left and Labour Leavers in opposition to a second referendum. Behind the scenes, however, even Andrew Murray had reached the conclusion that the game was up. After the first round of indicative votes he told the Brexit subcommittee that it was time to back a referendum as a first resort if they could not pass a deal.

Corbyn himself was gripped by indecision. He had been ground down by the tedium of the parliamentary schedule – by the late nights and long, rancorous sittings. The process demanded qualities with which even his closest allies and admirers admit he was not endowed. He was not by nature decisive or confrontational. Nor would a radicalised parliamentary party, whose relationship with discipline and loyalty was by then wholly selective, allow him to be. His Shadow Cabinet and MPs were riven by a difference of opinion so fundamental as to be irreconcilable, as were their voters. To Corbyn, leadership was not to impose the answer but to facilitate agreement. Some grew frustrated by his reticence.

Lavery longed for Corbyn to defend his position more aggressively. If in doubt, his preference was always to wage class war. In Shadow Cabinet and Brexit subcommittee meetings he would demand a more combative approach. 'Ian, I don't want to get in the gutter,' Corbyn would sigh. His party chairman wanted to scrap: 'Well, can I get in the fucking gutter for you?' Yet Corbyn always declined the offers. Loyalists in the Shadow Cabinet had been dealt a vexing hand. Their leader was a man whose promises to do politics differently and eschew the conventions of Westminster had won him the adulation and devotion of the left, if not of a generation. To a divided nation, however, they feared that looked like indecision. Said one Shadow Cabinet minister: 'A lot of people loved him for that, but the general public weren't terribly enamoured.'

In LOTO, those who worked most closely with him began to doubt Corbyn could impose his will even if he tried. He tired as the long nights wore on. His daily break, sacrosanct in his day's schedule, was frequently violated. 'The man couldn't even go to the toilet in peace,' one LOTO aide recalls. On occasion the placid exterior would buckle. He complained to Murphy of being shoved from appointment to appointment with no opportunity to breathe. In weaker moments he sought respite wherever he could. Aides recall how Ayse Veli, his diary secretary, provided him with pillows and a duvet, encased in navy blue sheets, for use in his office for naps when the demands of the late votes proved too much. He availed himself of the bedding on at least two occasions. Those snatches of sleep were the only occasions on which he would be left alone. 'He slept like a baby,' recalled an adviser.

Like most issues around Corbyn's health, the arrangements were not discussed openly in LOTO. Instead they were contemplated in hushed tones in private conversations. By 2019 it had become office policy to keep Corbyn accompanied at all times, for reasons of security and political management. The risk otherwise was that he might wander off piste, making the conversation with ordinary people he so relished, or be bounced into decisions with which he was uncomfortable. Yet rumours swirled in LOTO of more serious incidents, including an occasion on which Corbyn had been tended to by a close aide after abruptly blacking out. The rumours bubbled under in Westminster, never quite reaching the press. On 24 March, however, Corbyn was forced to acknowledge to the *Sunday Times* that he had been receiving treatment at Moorfields Eye Hospital, and had been prescribed thick, Buddy Holly-style glasses to correct a muscle weakness on his right side.

The physical changes that were outwardly discernible led to allegations that a 'tired and fed up' Corbyn was ready to resign. He went as far as to rebut them, but the central charge was true. Tired and fed up he indeed was. Aides felt his demeanour change subtly but significantly after he suffered an assault via egging in his constituency on 25 March. The strains of his eye condition had also forced him to moderate his routine. Out went the autocue and in came speeches printed in point size 20, as the half-blind Gordon Brown had preferred. On one occasion the business of LOTO was disrupted for several days after he left the glasses in Lisbon. He was encouraged to take breaks to rest his eye – which served the welcome secondary purpose of liberating him momentarily from Murphy and Milne. Above all, he was exhausted. At 70, he had given his life over to what one close aide described as 'the hamster wheel of leadership', which some days he would be forced to ride from 6 a.m. to 11.30 p.m. Attempts to gloss over the issue were singularly unconvincing: that Corbyn was unhappy and out of sorts was plain to see. It did not stop the SKWAWKBOX blog from trying. On 27 March it published a bizarre story that contended Corbyn had been 'preparing for the demands of office with regular runs of up to 15 kilometres'. An anonymous LOTO official was quoted speaking in terms so effusive as to be positively North Korean: 'Jeremy is as fit as a fiddle and does these runs as often as his schedule allows – a lot of his staff get worn out just thinking about it!'

By June, newspapers were willing to make darker allegations in public. On 25 June, *The Times* published allegations from unnamed civil servants that Corbyn was too frail to become prime minister: 'He's obviously not well and it's not just ageing, something has happened – he just doesn't seem all there sometimes.' Another blamed Murphy: 'He looks old and exhausted. He's 70 years of age, she is putting him through a programme that would be exhausting for a 40-year-old person. They think he's at his best when he's on the stage speaking to rallies but the crowds are getting smaller and smaller.' LOTO moved the story on by demanding an inquiry into the leaks. The focus shifted to the conservatism of the Civil Service and its breaches of impartiality. But the reality was that aides were concerned by Corbyn's low moods and irritability.

The stories and rumours would persist. Only Guido Fawkes dared to report the most pervasive rumour, for which there was no evidence: that Corbyn's glasses had been prescribed in the aftermath of a stroke. LOTO did not dignify the claims with a response.

*

The government whips and LOTO had both doubted what good indicative votes could do. Rather than encouraging MPs to coalesce around a compromise, it radicalised them. Remainers who on 24 June 2016 would have bitten the hand off anyone offering them a customs union – or a plan that looked like Corbyn's – instead found themselves drawn to the extremes of a second referendum and the revocation of Article 50. A LOTO aide lamented: 'What we thought was going to happen is exactly what happened. Everyone went into their own camp. You had pro-Europeans who weren't voting for a customs union because they knew what that meant. Everyone pitted themselves

against what they believed was their nearest rival.' Softening Brexit
was no longer enough for back-bench Remainers, who opted to take
votes away from a customs union lest it give oxygen to the idea that
leaving the EU was somehow legitimate.

On 29 March 2019, the day Britain was supposed to have left the
EU, May brought back the withdrawal agreement for a third time –
albeit detached from the political declaration on a future trade deal,
to satisfy the Speaker's edict that they could not ask MPs to vote on
the same proposition repeatedly. Over the previous weeks, Julian Smith
and his special adviser, Lilah Howson-Smith, had cooked up a plan
with Gareth Snell and Lisa Nandy, both of whom wanted to back a
deal, to secure Labour votes for the agreement. To the quiet bemusement of government whips, Snell in particular had become fixated on
the idea that he would vote for the deal at the last possible opportunity.
But Labour MPs needed cover to do so. They also needed a guarantee
that they would not be the midwives of a hard Brexit. Together Snell
and Nandy, with the connivance of Smith, proposed a sort of legisla-
tive prophylactic: an amendment whereby the government would not
be able to negotiate a trade deal without first winning Commons
approval. The wandering hands of a future Conservative prime
minister would be bound by Parliament.

Yet Speaker Bercow did not allow amendments to the deal.
Though the Attorney General Geoffrey Cox rose to assure Snell that
the government would abide by it anyway if the deal passed, his
word alone was not enough to get Labour MPs through the lobbies.
Only four Labour MPs joined John Mann in voting with the government, far fewer than he had suggested to Julian Smith. That morning
May had met the putative dealers for the last time, in a last-ditch
attempt to convince them to jump. There she had found a positive
reception from the likes of Snell, Nandy and Melanie Onn, the MP
for Grimsby.

As the day wore on they began to falter. Snell began the day saying
he would vote for the deal, then that he would abstain, and ended
it by voting against it. Some would-be dealers made up their
minds upon seeing Conservative MPs and the DUP heading for the
no lobbies. Though Brexiteer Tories began to fold after May said she
would not lead the next round of negotiations – an implicit promise
that a Leaver willing to pursue a more severe breach with Europe

would – twenty-eight hardliners, led by the idiosyncratic Steve Baker and christened 'the Spartans', held out. So too did the DUP.

One source from the Respect the Vote group sums up the attitude taken that afternoon: if Labour MPs voting for a deal 'were more in number, then they probably would have felt more protected, but it never really felt like the number was the issue. It was more that DUP factor. If they weren't going to do it, then why should we have bothered?' The electorate would later answer that question for them.

Another round of indicative votes bore no fruit on April Fool's Day, a sitting which was interrupted by a nude protest from climate activists Extinction Rebellion in the public gallery of the Commons. Such were the divisions at the heart of the leadership that Labour had not even submitted its own proposal for consideration by the Commons. Amy Jackson, assigned to draw the proposal up, had attempted to water down Labour's commitment to a second referendum in defiance of Starmer and McDonnell. Intending to circumvent them, she had sent it directly to Corbyn for his approval. She had had the misfortune to do so while he was sat beside both men in the Commons chamber. They had then exercised the very veto Jackson had been hoping to avoid. LOTO could no longer concoct a form of words to bind the party together.

The following day, after a seven-hour Cabinet meeting, May again turned to Corbyn. That evening she invited him to talks, in a televised address live from Downing Street in which she also revealed she would seek another delay to Brexit. 'A decisive moment in the story of these islands … requires national unity to deliver the national interest.' It was time, she said, for the big two to work together to strike a deal that respected the result of the referendum. The odd couple of political Tinder were rekindling their romance.

On 3 April Corbyn and May met for a pre-date sharpener at Prime Minister's Questions, where MPs on both sides fretted aloud at what was about to ensue. Labour Remainers believed Corbyn was walking squarely in the direction of an open manhole. Ben Bradshaw, the Blairite greybeard, spoke for many of his colleagues when he tweeted: 'It is clearly a trap designed to get May's terrible deal through, which some people have fallen for, but Labour mustn't.'

Accompanied by Milne, Starmer, Nick Brown and Rebecca Long-Bailey, Corbyn headed straight from the chamber to see May in her

Commons office. After two hours the Labour delegation emerged blinking into the light. Corbyn said that the talks had gone 'very well'. Downing Street sang from the same hymn sheet, describing the conversation as 'constructive, with both sides showing flexibility and a commitment to bring the current Brexit uncertainty to a close'.

Minutes before the Shadow Cabinet met to discuss the talks, Emily Thornberry emailed colleagues to demand they be given a vote on whether any deal agreed would be put to a second referendum. LOTO's reprisals were swift and brutal. Days after her act of insubordination, Amy Jackson told Thornberry that she had been banned from visiting NATO's annual summit later that year. Though LOTO cited budget issues, the real reason was revenge. Yet attempts by LOTO to freeze her out did little to dissuade Thornberry: her demand for a second referendum was a sentiment that would scupper not only the talks, but May's premiership too.

Talks began at the Cabinet Office in Whitehall on 4 April. Neither Corbyn nor May was present: indeed, neither possessed the requisite authority over their negotiating teams to take ownership of the process. Civil servants, exhausted by two years of fruitless wrangling within government, were nonetheless so excited by the prospect of an imminent deal that they had procured luxury sandwiches that even members of the Cabinet had not seen before. 'It was the nicest spread I had ever seen,' one minister recalled. 'The Civil Service was *that* desperate to make it work.'

Yet they found a Shadow Brexit Secretary seemingly unwilling to countenance any avenue that might lead to a negotiated Brexit at all. Sir Keir had become Dr No. What May's team had assumed to be the broad basis for agreement Starmer dismissed before detailed talks had even begun. 'On the pure question of trade,' he said, 'we have started from single-market membership, whereas you seem to have started from WTO, and you're working up. We are shaving off, you are building up. Those differences of approach reflect different political models. They show in the end result.'

Labour had four basic demands. The first was a customs union. That was the bare minimum, though Corbyn's negotiating team knew that the government could not offer one in name. 'We needed to get around the political fact that, if we'd gone backwards on a customs union – even if they said we've not – if the words aren't going to be there in some form, then we'd struggle to sell them to the PLP.' The others were a close relationship with the single market, agreement on workers' rights and environmental standards.

Gavin Barwell offered, hopefully, that there might be common ground elsewhere. 'So it seems we aren't far away on security and agencies. We *could* reach an agreement.' Starmer slapped him down. 'Maybe.' By the time discussion had turned to workers' rights, the Shadow Brexit Secretary was even less convinced. 'Let's be honest – Boris Johnson has said that we should junk half of this stuff!'

The prospect of a Johnson premiership played heavily on the minds of both sides. Barwell and his colleagues knew that the talks were the last realistic opportunity they would have to force through Parliament a deal that broadly resembled May's.

Starmer had warned them: 'The politics of this, in selling an outcome to the PLP, we are going to find hard.' The politics for May were even harder. Strike a deal that was too soft and she risked the ire of a parliamentary party with an even more selective attitude to discipline than Corbyn's. Fail to strike a deal at all and she faced taking the Conservative Party she loved to the polls having reneged on the promise she had staked her career on. In either outcome, it would be springtime for Johnson, who hoped to ride to the leadership as a tribune of back-bench discontent.

It was exactly that scenario that so worried Labour. No matter what May's emissaries offered now, they feared a future government could simply rip up any cross-party agreement – and the mere existence of any compromise deal would only aid the cause of Johnson or any other Conservative Brexiteer, like the zealous Dominic Raab, that thought May's withdrawal agreement itself was too soft to countenance. John McDonnell had grumbled to colleagues on the way to talks that dealing with May was like negotiating with a company going into liquidation.

Barwell insisted that the amendment Julian Smith had helped Gareth Snell and Lisa Nandy write the previous month was the answer: it would give Parliament the right to determine what sort of deal government was negotiating. Milne sensed a trap. What would happen if a Conservative prime minister found themselves with a majority of their own? 'The European Commission have indicated the political declaration could be changed in very quick time,' he said. Barwell exchanged a knowing look with May's chief EU adviser Olly Robbins, a man well practised in diplomatic obfuscation. 'You are both correct and incorrect,' Robbins said, elliptically.

But by the time both sides were deep in the weeds of technical discussion, it was painfully obvious to Downing Street that their Labour counterparts did not know the answer to their own parliamentary party's existential question – whether any deal they now negotiated would have to be put to a referendum and potentially rejected. Both sides told the press that the first day had gone badly. Downing Street briefed that they were serious and prepared to make wholesale change to the political declaration. After all, the last thing May wanted was to lead a Conservative Party that had promised to deliver Brexit by 29 March into the European elections, by then just nine weeks away. Her aides made clear to reporters that a second referendum was equally toxic as far as she was concerned. Any attempt from Labour to force the issue would sink negotiations.

On 6 April, May upped the stakes in a speech. 'If we can agree a deal here at home, we can leave the EU in just six weeks.' The next day she offered the same message once more with folksy feeling in a video message filmed from the sofa of her living room in 10 Downing Street, in which she urged MPs to vote for a deal – or rather *her* deal. But it was increasingly clear that her own party was unlikely to be able to stomach anything that might emerge from the talks. An extensive account of them appeared in the *Mail on Sunday* under the headline: 'Is May set for total Brexit SURRENDER?' Tory MPs suspected that their ministers were about to give Labour everything they wanted: a customs union, a parliamentary lock on whatever deal they had agreed, and a vote in Parliament on a second referendum. Philip Hammond, whose most significant constitutional role was no longer that of Chancellor of the Exchequer but bogeyman to the hard Brexiteers, did nothing to disabuse them of that suspicion when he openly admitted from a trip to Romania that the government had no 'red lines'.

Labour's negotiating team struggled to take him at face value. By the same token, the Tories feared Labour were merely indulging the talks as a charade. When the two sides met again on 9 April, Milne sought to firefight. 'There have been some reports,' he said, obliquely. 'I want to assure all here that we are not engaged in can-kicking. The issues we are covering are broad, we have opened out from the starting point, and it is a complicated set of disputed matters.' Starmer added, deadpan: 'And then there is Liam Fox.'

The EU27 would give the can an almighty boot the following day when it granted May an extension until 31 October, much longer than she had hoped. The cliff edge of no-deal had receded. Nonetheless, Downing Street – whose increasingly nervous eyes were fixed on the European elections – wanted things wrapped up by 22 May.

But Labour was not thinking in those terms. Foremost on the minds of its negotiating team was the looming recess and with it a chance for a holiday. Both Sue Hayman, the Shadow Environment Secretary, and Rebecca Long-Bailey were reluctant to be drawn into further talks over Easter. 'I'm due to go on holiday!' Hayman wrote on WhatsApp. Long-Bailey suggested flying back from a holiday in Cornwall in the 'worst-case scenario' that her services were required.

'Don't knock yourself out over this Becky,' McDonnell wrote. 'I can cover any meeting tomorrow or Monday. Don't worry as the Tories will be desperate to fly out to their gîtes to inspect their vineyards.'

Corbyn gave a characteristically eccentric blessing to a pause. 'I reslise [sic] Tory desperation but our team … ALL OF THEM … need a break so we can try and finish pre Easter discussions today to free up Friday and next week?'

McDonnell offered a friendly concession to his old mate's authority. 'Will definitely try but only on the basis that you have a break too comrade!'

Corbyn assented. 'Yes of course!'

Labour's seeming aversion to intensive talks did not go unnoticed by Smith and Barwell. By 23 April, Corbyn was describing them in public as a sham. He accused the government of 'just regurgitating what has already been emphatically rejected three times by Parliament'. By week 'two or three', Corbyn was asking how Labour might escape the talks. Fisher and McDonnell appeared to have persuaded him they were bound to fail, regardless of whether the Conservatives agreed to a referendum. A senior LOTO aide said: 'I think in Andrew's calculation, and probably John's too actually, you don't need to get to a referendum bit. If they moved on workers' rights, if they move on the customs union or single market, it'd be the death of her.'

They were not wrong. On 30 April, the Foreign Secretary Jeremy Hunt – limbering up for the imminent contest to succeed May – warned Downing Street publicly that a customs union would cost them the votes of more Tory MPs than the Labour MPs it would gain. 'Jeremy Hunt clearly on a mission to detonate the talks as part of his pitch for the Tory leadership,' Fisher wrote in the WhatsApp group that morning.

He was not the only one with an ulterior motive. 'Seumas was just bloody useless,' said one LOTO aide, 'because it was all about looking statesmanlike and being there and convincing people that didn't think Jeremy Corbyn could be in government that now, all of a sudden, his top people were in Number 10.' Milne's preference was to leave meetings at the Cabinet Office via the front door, onto Whitehall and the scrum of photographers, while McDonnell preferred to slip out of the back. Chris Ward, Starmer's chief of staff, similarly moaned of Milne's preference for the 'circus' of meeting in Whitehall rather than in May's Commons office.

Starmer was most frustrated at their negotiating team's lack of strategy. His unease was matched by Number 10's desperation. On 3 May the electoral price for their failure to deliver Brexit was starkly illustrated when the Tories lost control of forty-five councils and more than 1,200 council seats. Labour, unlike most oppositions primed to win a general election in mid-term, lost control of six. That the Liberal Democrats finished the big winners with eleven gains offered a warning sign for both parties.

Barwell responded to the electoral humbling by attempting to expedite a deal. That Monday, 6 May, he sent Fisher a document that he hoped might form the basis of an agreement at a meeting the following day. McDonnell and Starmer were not convinced. 'We need a full strategic meeting before we engage any further,' wrote Starmer. 'We should not be bumped or rushed by the government and we need a clear and agreed position going forward.' In public, Starmer described the 7 May talks as 'crunch time'. In private, he was already agitating for a way out. While Long-Bailey said there was 'of course' a point in ploughing on, Starmer's team briefed the lobby: 'What was on the table was politically and legally worthless.'

Nonetheless, one person believed a deal remained to be done. At the outset of the process, Karie Murphy and the Shadow Chancellor had rowed over her exclusion from the negotiating team. She believed she had been patronised by McDonnell, which he denied. That most of the meetings were scheduled for Fridays, when Murphy visited her sick mother in Glasgow, only heightened suspicions that she had been deliberately frozen out. Now, with Corbyn's approval and behind McDonnell's back, she prevailed on Milne – who was in frequent contact with Robbie Gibb, Downing Street's head of communications – to organise a secret summit in the LOTO boardroom with Barwell and Robbins.

There was none of the passive aggression and politesse that defined the mood of talks in the Cabinet Office. 'I don't come from the same background as you all come from,' Murphy told them. 'I don't come from the same class as most of you. So I'm going to call through all the shit and just tell you, I'm a negotiator. I'm a trade union negotiator.' Over the course of her weekly train journeys from London to Glasgow and back again, her fellow travellers had told her they never wanted to hear the word Brexit again. 'Forget the technicalities,' she said, 'they only want it over and fucking done with.' Her attempts to talk the men she saw as the 'posh boys' of both sides into agreement bore no fruit. Fisher told her that the PLP would not wear a deal.

Starmer's frustration also appeared to be boiling over. Yet another round of talks was suggested on Friday 10 May, and he wrote: 'Again I'm not sure why we're meeting them on Monday? We are not in a position to deliver our promised document and risk getting sucked further in despite strategic decision this week?' By then, the decision had been taken to pull out. On 8 May, Corbyn's operations manager Janet Chapman circulated a note to colleagues, summing up the conclusions of a LOTO senior management team meeting that day. It noted that the departure would be 'choreographed ... due to disarray of government'. It also betrayed the deepest anxieties of LOTO's Remainsceptics when it argued pulling out of the talks would 'reassert Labour as insurgent, anti-establishment cause'. They would pull out of the talks. The only questions were how and when. If Brexit was to happen, Labour would not be helping.

May ploughed on regardless. On 14 May she summoned Corbyn for a meeting in her Commons office. As Starmer's and McDonnell's exasperation with the process grew, so did a childish excitement on Corbyn's part. In the stench of decay emanating from Downing Street he scented opportunity. 'Any signs of Government meltdown?!' he had written to the negotiating team the day before.

Over the course of a long hour, the PM told Corbyn that she would bring back her deal for a fourth time in the first week of June, this time in the form of the Withdrawal Agreement Bill. In doing so she set a hard deadline not only on the talks with Labour but on her premiership. He made clear that Labour would not be supporting the deal unless it got the changes that had been discussed for the best part of six weeks.

McDonnell saw her intransigence as the ideal pretext for collapsing the talks. 'We can use this as an added reason for withdrawal tomorrow, in that contrary to our advice that we need the deal largely agreed with the EU and her own side consolidated before putting largely the same deal before Parliament and risking another defeat, she is determined recklessly to press ahead. If she does lose again we can say later we warned her.'

Barwell hammered the final nail into the coffin of talks on 16 May, when he sent Fisher the text of the government's proposed legislation on customs – which did not amount to a customs union at all. Corbyn, anxious that the European elections were only a week away, was firmly of the view that talks should end by that evening. A LOTO aide recalled: 'He said: "Shut this down, this is nonsense, this is mad."'

Corbyn's team decided to announce the cessation of talks via a pre-recorded speech the next morning. It would be recorded at 9.30 a.m. and released abruptly, pulling the rug from beneath May. LOTO would seize the initiative; the government would take the blame.

The plan was to meet at Girasole A Taste of Italy, a café around the corner from Corbyn's home, at 8.30 a.m. From there, they would make the short journey to the location for the recording, Wray Crescent, a park a stone's throw from Corbyn's constituency office. There would be plenty of time to prep Corbyn, both for his tele-prompted speech and any media questions that might follow. An easy victory over a fragile government was within their grasp.

It was at 8 a.m. that the plan began to disintegrate. Jack Bond, Corbyn's social media manager, was en route to the café when his phone rang. LOTO had forgotten to book Jeremy's car. Might Bond ring his dad, a cab driver often prevailed upon to rescue Corbyn in his moments of maximum disorganisation, and ask him to drive the group from the café to the park instead? Bond obliged, as did his father. By 8.30 a.m. they were at the café as agreed, alongside spinner Jack McKenna. Bond's phone buzzed again with more unwelcome news from LOTO. 'It's looking more like Jeremy and Seumas will arrive at 9 a.m.'

The appointed hour came and went. Labour's leader and head of communications were nowhere to be seen. At 9.10, head of press Anjula Singh rocked up. Corbyn followed ten minutes later, fifty minutes late and with only ten to go before his statement was to be committed to film. He did not rush the group but instead ordered a breakfast quiche, which he munched peaceably throughout a briefing from Singh, who appeared not to be fully aware of the script. She asked for guidance on the points Labour wanted to land. McKenna too was none the wiser. The party's videographer sat alone in the park. It would be 9.55 a.m. – some twenty-five minutes after the clip was due to be filmed – before Milne appeared. Only at 10.10 had they finally finished the job. The pre-recorded message had to be cancelled. Patience among the waiting press pack had worn thin over the course of the hour they had been kept waiting. Corbyn was given an accordingly rough ride. He emerged from the mauling in a huff, and snapped: 'That was terrible.'

Corbyn was quite right. In the absence of the promised televised statement, LOTO left a vacuum that Downing Street had gladly filled. According to May, the talks had failed because of a lack of a 'common position in Labour about whether they want to deliver Brexit or hold a second referendum which could reverse it'.

Defeat, as so often, had been snatched from the jaws of victory.

11

Boris

Jeremy Corbyn led with his chin. 'It's said that Labour is trying to offer something to everyone over Brexit. I make no apology for that. Labour will never be the party of the 52 per cent or of the 48 per cent.' The launch of Labour's European election campaign was a speech that neither he nor LOTO had expected or wanted to have to make. A week before the Wray Crescent debacle, with just two weeks to go before polling day, he had stood before his audience in Kent and sought to make a virtue out of the gaping hole that clarity might otherwise have filled.

That the elections were happening at all was primarily the fault of Theresa May, and it would be she who was punished most harshly by the electorate. But the prospect of a proxy second referendum – as the poll would very quickly become – was hardly ideal for Labour either. Optimists in LOTO had always consoled themselves that, come a nationwide election, they would be able to shift the agenda away from Brexit and onto more hospitable ground: domestic policy, the economy. Elections to the European Parliament afforded them no such luxury.

At the beginning of May, the NEC had taken the decision that Labour would campaign on its conference position: only if it could not secure changes to May's deal or a general election would the party back a public vote. As a device for holding together the PLP, it was a form of words that had proved itself over the previous months. But as an election slogan, it was too chewy and conditional to get a fair hearing. LOTO knew it. Instead, Corbyn made a valiant attempt to recast the election as a referendum on racism and the far right. 'It is Labour that wants to bring our country back together,' he said. 'So whether you voted Leave or Remain in 2016, I urge you to vote Labour, the party that is determined to bring the many together and take on the entrenched power of the few.' Unity was the watchword, damage limitation was the aim. 'We could allow ourselves to be defined only as "Remainers" or "Leavers", labels that meant nothing to us only a few years ago. But where would that take us? Who wants to live in a country stuck in this endless loop?' Corbyn's speech was sincerely meant. The problem was that most voters *did* think in those terms and they would punish him just as harshly as May for failing to deliver on either Leave or Remain.

One of the most piquant ironies of the European Parliament elections was that Labour had initially been slated to win them. On 10 April, the first poll of the campaign had put Corbyn well ahead of both the Conservatives and Nigel Farage's Brexit Party. Farage preached a gospel of betrayal to an impatient Tory electorate, and immediately cannibalised much of May's support in the country. Having failed to fulfil the foundational promise of her premiership – delivering Brexit by 29 March 2019 – talks with Labour had been the prime minister's last chance to escape a mauling by Farage. Seditious elements in May's parliamentary party now wondered aloud if she might be returned with no MEPs at all.

The same, however, was true of Labour. The stakes were not existential as they were for the Tories, but it nonetheless faced a reckoning. While disgruntled Brexiteers had Farage, Europhiles in the country – or, indeed, progressives who cared little for Europe but less for Corbyn – had Vince Cable, the septuagenarian leader of the Liberal Democrats. For the best part of a decade, the sagacious economist had yearned to lead, yet he had the misfortune to ascend to the leadership in 2017, at precisely the moment both he and his party had gone out of fashion. Now, campaigning under the unapologetically provocative slogan of 'Bollocks to Brexit', he was the culture warrior that Remainers had wanted but could not find in Corbyn.

Nor did the Greens have any compunction in campaigning along similar lines. They targeted 'squeamish' Labour voters on the basis of the two big progressive concerns of the day: yes to Europe, no to climate change. The fear in LOTO was that their resurgence might be more than a blip. Corbyn's road to the leadership – and, indeed, to 40 per cent of the vote in 2017 – had run through disenchanted voters of both parties. Now it appeared that Brexit could begin a great unspooling of the Corbyn coalition.

As the short campaign unfolded, Labour struggled to find its metier. Outspoken Remainers like Andrew Adonis, the Blairite peer and hyperactive tweeter, Eloise Todd, the chief executive of anti-Brexit campaign Best for Britain, and Laura Parker had been selected as candidates. Yet none enjoyed a plum position on the party's list. Corbyn, meanwhile, struggled to find himself. The flight of the Europhiles who had sustained him in office, both as an MP and leader of the Labour Party, had hit him hard. Friends and aides observed him develop an all-encompassing obsession with a 6-million strong parliamentary petition demanding the immediate revocation of Article 50. He watched the signatures in Islington North tick up and up and up. His estrangement from his constituency was as public as it was painful. In conversation with aides he turned to irritable self-pity, inviting them to blame him for Labour's misfortunes. 'It's all my fault,' he would mutter.

A senior LOTO adviser said: 'I think Jeremy was shocked by the extent of the shift in his own area among his own voters ... He's a very acute reader of public opinion.' Another described it as an assault on his sense of self: 'He still refers to that petition ... He's represented that seat since 1983 and for a long time, of course, he had no aspiration or expectation of ever doing anything more than being a constituency MP.' In Shadow Cabinet discussions over Brexit, Diane Abbott, Emily Thornberry and Keir Starmer also raised the number of signatures in their own North London seats. Others around the table believed their political horizons, already narrow, had been constrained by Brexit to the point of self-parody. Andrew Murray liked to remind attendees of the Brexit subcommittee that it would take him less than an hour to walk through Corbyn's, Abbott's, Thornberry's and Starmer's constituencies from his office in Unite. Lavery, meanwhile, had his own axe to grind. 'Look how many signatures there are in *my* seat!' he moaned. The answer, as in so many other Labour redoubts in the north and Midlands, was not very many. At its peak, the number of signatures in Corbyn's seat was 27,000. In Lavery's backyard, a mere 4,300.

Late on in the campaign, Corbyn appeared to crack. Under pressure not only from Keir Starmer and the other usual suspects in the Shadow Cabinet but leftists like Clive Lewis, he told the media in heavily caveated terms that Labour would become the party of a second referendum. It would not be enough. The clarity of message at both poles of the debate proved more attractive to voters. Farage swept to victory with twenty-nine of seventy-three MEPs at the Brexit Party's first attempt. The Liberal Democrats shot from one to sixteen. While not quite as ignominious a performance as the Conservatives – reduced from nineteen to just four MEPs – Corbyn found Labour's representation in the European Parliament halved at a stroke from twenty to ten. Welsh Labour slipped to third, behind the firmly pro-EU Plaid Cymru. In Scotland, it came a risible fifth with just 9.3 per cent of the vote, a result that pushed the Project's loyal emissary to Edinburgh, the Scottish Labour leader Richard Leonard, into apostasy. He demanded that Labour respond by becoming a 'Remain party'. Light relief came in the number of seats won by The Independent Group, now rebranded as Change UK: zero. But while Labour voters had not abandoned their party for the splitters, they had found a happy home in the embrace of the Liberal Democrats, Greens and SNP.

The result upended the strategic calculation that had underpinned nearly every pound Southside had spent on campaigning since 2017. LOTO had concluded in the wake of 2017 that Remainers, as Peter Mandelson had once breezily remarked of the working classes, had nowhere else to go but Labour. Corbyn's path to a majority, they believed, ran through the towns of the English north and Midlands that it had once held but had since surrendered to the Conservatives. In short, Corbyn would have to win over Brexitland were he to ever become prime minister. On that basis, resources – and Murphy's community organisers – had been pumped into seats like Mansfield. The devastation wrought upon Labour by Remainers and Leavers alike blew a hole in that electoral logic. Europhiles did have somewhere else to go. From then the question changed. In treating Remainers as banked, LOTO had in effect driven them away.

On 27 May, Paul Mason, a stalwart friend of the Project in the media, vented his spleen in the *Guardian* with a column that stated Corbynism was in crisis, perhaps terminally so. He too argued that it was time for Labour to abandon its hopes of winning back Mansfield and become a Remain party. Before polling day, he had drawn up a spreadsheet to gauge just how aggressive his post-match intervention would need to be. If Labour fell below ten seats, he had decided to call for Corbyn's head. In the event he only demanded those of Milne and Murphy, incurring a furious reaction from Howard Beckett, Len McCluskey's deputy at Unite, in the *New Statesman*. The Project's constituent parts were moving in different directions – and hurling insults at one another as they did.

LOTO was glad to see the back of one Remainer. On the morning of 28 May, Alastair Campbell revealed his Labour membership had been terminated. The case against him was, procedurally at least, open and shut. On the night of the count he had gone on national television and revealed that, for the first time in his life, he had voted Liberal Democrat in an act of anti-Brexit, anti-Corbyn protest. To publicly support an electoral opponent of the Labour Party was a sackable offence as far as the party rulebook was concerned. The political case for going nuclear was much weaker, if not non-existent. Campbell was merely articulating an unease felt by millions of Labour voters, which Remainers in the Shadow Cabinet had acknowledged by calling for Corbyn to endorse a second referendum in all circumstances in the wake of the result.

Campbell immediately became a martyr. 'I am and always will be Labour,' he said in a series of tweets. 'I voted Lib Dem, without advance publicity, to try to persuade Labour to do right thing for country/party. In light of appeal, I won't be doing media on this. But hard not to point out difference in the way anti-Semitism cases have been handled.' Jess Phillips noted that he had been expelled more swiftly than a Holocaust denier in her constituency party. LOTO had reaped a whirlwind of its own making. Having lost Remainers in their droves at the ballot box the previous week, it seemed determined to drive them away for good.

The plan to humiliate Campbell had been sanctioned from the very top. Its execution was a typical tale of unforced errors, conflicting motives and duff communication between the leaders of the Project. Corbyn, his closest aides say, had explicitly approved the expulsion. 'He wanted to do it,' said a senior LOTO source. Yet once the news broke, he and his staff found themselves at odds with John McDonnell. The Shadow Chancellor had found in Campbell and the other New Labour luminaries of the anti-Brexit cause comrades, if not friends. He rightly argued that to expel him would be to compound the Project's woes among Remainers. In a terse text to Karie Murphy, he demanded that Southside contact Campbell and tell him that his membership had been reinstated.

But there were limits to Murphy's power. She insisted that to do so was not in her gift. Only Jennie Formby, as general secretary, had the power to overturn the decision unilaterally. She had refused, and Gordon Nardell, LOTO's go-to QC, agreed with her. Politics and law stood in the way of a compromise. It was immediately clear in any case that Campbell would sue to regain the place in the party that, despite it all, he still saw as his rightful home. Andrew Murray, an improbable contact of New Labour's master of spin, had made a vain attempt to convince Campbell not to tweet about his expulsion: to do so only risked complicating his legal case for readmission. He took the stand regardless.

His case immediately became a cause célèbre among Remainers and prompted a round of Spartacus tributes from Blairites of a certain age. In the wake of Campbell's resignation, the former Cabinet ministers Charles Clarke and Bob Ainsworth revealed they had voted for Remain parties in the Liberal Democrats and Greens. Cherie Blair too said she was 'happy for it to be known' that she had backed the Liberal Democrats, the party that had turned criticism of her husband into a populist artform. Tony, who had made an enthusiastic appeal for Remainers to back Labour in the days before the vote, would not be drawn. Campbell went as far as to suggest that unnamed aides in LOTO had secretly recommended Labour voters take their support elsewhere. The episode was not so much tragedy as self-inflicted farce. Corbyn found himself at the eye of the storm. Aides saw him overcome with rage. To one he remarked angrily that the idea had been 'fucking stupid', in defiance of his rule of not swearing. McDonnell's obvious displeasure had left him spooked and irritated, but he could not decide on which of the dissonant voices of his inner circle to listen to. In those moments, the man who had promised to pull a warring country together could barely unite the Project.

The Campbell controversy provided a momentary, destructive distraction from an altogether more significant departure. May's humiliation at the ballot box had coincided with her enforced resignation from office. Despite the failure of the talks, in the days before polling day Downing Street had announced that it would table the Withdrawal

Agreement Bill, the legislation that would give legal effect to the deal. If passed, MPs would get a vote on a second referendum. Even that indirect endorsement of cancelling Brexit was too much for her party to bear. On the eve of polling day, Commons leader Andrea Leadsom – in an act of almost karmic retribution for her own failed leadership bid in 2016 – sealed May's fate by resigning from Cabinet. Two days later, May appeared on the steps of Downing Street. Choking back tears, she announced she would be gone as Conservative leader by 7 June and out of Downing Street by the end of July. Her voice cracked as she began the long goodbye.

As May wept, Corbyn's tweet offered not condolences but a call to arms. 'Theresa May is right to resign,' he wrote. 'She's now accepted what the country's known for months: she can't govern, and nor can her divided and disintegrating party. Whoever becomes the new Tory leader must let the people decide our country's future, through an immediate general election.' Those closest to him began to confront the new reality. If they could not find an answer on Brexit, then somebody else would. And in all likelihood, that person would be Boris Johnson.

Theresa May had at times been an unwitting ally to Corbyn. Her ungainly presence on the campaign trail had helped catalyse the shock of 2017, when her ambitious plans to convert swathes of Labour terri-tory to Toryism for the first time in their history had largely failed. Her haplessness as a party manager – and her inflexibility when it came to her discredited and thrice-rejected deal – had allowed Labour to exploit Tory divisions in the Commons to delay Brexit and avert a dangerous no-deal, an outcome she herself had never been comfort-able with anyway. In LOTO's collective memory, Corbyn had out-campaigned her once. In the event of a snap election, many were confident that he could do so again.

Johnson was an altogether different quantity. Twice a winner in the mayoral elections in liberal London, he had since the EU referendum – and his resignation from May's Cabinet – reinvented himself as the patron saint of an altogether harsher strain of electoral Conservatism. He was also a harsher human, to Labour eyes at least. Few on the opposition benches had doubted May's Anglican sense of duty, decency and devotion to public service. John McDonnell had been known to remark in private that Johnson was 'evil'.

Then there was the question of competence, or at least relative competence. While not renowned for his organisation or grasp of detail, LOTO aides rightly feared that Johnson's operation would be a much slicker machine than late-period May's. 'This ain't going to be the same election,' one recalls thinking. 'There's no way. He will be a formidable campaigner. She was fucking shit, we couldn't believe how bad she was. He won't be. We knew. We needed to get the policy right or he was going to beat us. His tanks were on our lawn, sticking up a mile.'

To Tory MPs terrified by the prospect of a Farage tsunami at a general election Johnson offered a simple solution: he would deliver Brexit, deal or no deal, by 31 October – and whatever deal he did strike would not contain the Irish backstop that had proved so fatal to May's premiership. As far as Brussels and Dublin were concerned, however, that was a deal that did not exist. It was with some trepidation that EU leaders watched Johnson rack up endorsement after endorsement from Conservative MPs, many of them Remainers otherwise deemed sensible.

Leo Varadkar was chief among those EU leaders. On 30 May, the Taoiseach received Corbyn, Milne and Tony Lloyd, the Shadow Northern Ireland Secretary, in Dublin. Varadkar only really wanted answers to three questions. How would Corbyn deal with a Johnson premiership? Would Labour support a second referendum? What, if anything, would Johnson support? One member of the party's delegation recalls the discussion that ensued as not only the most embarrassing meeting of their life, but a decisive moment on Varadkar's own journey towards compromise with Johnson on the Irish border. 'I don't think they saw any great trust or belief that Labour wanted anything or could push anything through ... in Ireland we felt a deep frustration from them in particular that we were just wasting people's time by that point.'

If Varadkar had expected clarity on Labour's own intentions, he would not get it. The Taoiseach wanted to know how Ireland and the rest of the EU27 might be able to help a Labour government get a deal over the line. What would he need to offer? Corbyn could not give a straight answer on just how seriously he was taking a referendum for there was not yet consensus within LOTO. While Andrew Fisher had been among those who pushed for a shift to a second referendum in *all* circumstances in the wake of the European elections, Milne remained unconvinced. Nor were answers forthcoming on whether a Labour government might accept a Norway-style settlement, and with it membership of the single market. Corbyn instead filled the vacuum by stressing his desire to protect the rights of the Irish community in Archway, at the northernmost edge of his constituency. One observer described Varadkar as visibly irritated by the Labour delegation's lack of the hard answers he sought.

Yet LOTO could always reverse-engineer a case for the status quo. The following week, Labour would pip the Brexit Party to victory in a by-election in Peterborough, a traditional Tory bellwether, despite a campaign marred by accusations of anti-Semitism against its candidate, Lisa Forbes, and the fact that its previous MP had been recalled after being imprisoned for perverting the course of justice. That the Conservatives had fallen into third with Labour clinging on in first was cited by Corbyn as a vindication of his Brexit policy. It would be no coincidence that Johnson would choose the city to launch his own leadership campaign.

When the discussion in Dublin turned to Boris Johnson, Milne had offered a humorous dismissal. 'Don't worry about Boris Johnson,' he said. 'He'll flip-flop.' Other attendees were aghast. 'He couldn't flip-flop,' said one. 'It was a miscalculation. He had to go hard on Brexit. Even if Seumas knew that, it created the impression we weren't serious.' At the outset of the Tory leadership campaign, some in LOTO *had* consoled themselves that Europe would be Johnson's undoing rather than his making. Such optimism would not survive Johnson's ascent to the premiership – and his uncomplicated pledge to deliver Brexit come what may. Karie Murphy became so convinced of his talents that she bet Corbyn and three other LOTO aides £20 each that he would end up as the victor. His two mayoral victories over Ken Livingstone loomed large in Team Corbyn's collective consciousness. Johnson was a formidable opponent. He had beaten the left not once but twice in a Labour city. Their usual attack lines would not suffice.

On 23 July, Johnson's succession was confirmed. Having won convincingly among Conservative MPs in every round of voting, he clobbered Jeremy Hunt, the Foreign Secretary, among members by a yawning margin of 66 per cent to 34 per cent. Addressing his first crowd as leader of the Tories at the QEII Centre in Westminster that afternoon he was characteristically irreverent. In places it was not so much a speech but a revue. For much of it, Corbyn was the butt of the joke. 'We know the mantra of the campaign – in case you have forgotten it – it is deliver Brexit, unite the country and defeat Jeremy Corbyn and that is what we are going to do,' Johnson bellowed. 'Some wag has already pointed out that deliver, unite, defeat was not the perfect acronym for an election campaign since unfortunately it spells dud. But they forgot the final "e", my friends, "e" for "energise". And I say to all the doubters: Dude! We are going to energise the country.' An endorsement of his populist credentials duly came in a tweet from Donald Trump: 'Congratulations to Boris Johnson on becoming the new prime minister of the United Kingdom. He will be great!'

The next day he took to the steps of Downing Street to put meat on the bones of that ambition. Milne and LOTO's communications staff watched the address in Norman Shaw South. Johnson spoke neither the language of Cameron nor May, but something distinct. His, it seemed, would be a communitarian, statist – even Gaullist – conservatism. 'My job,' he said at breakneck pace, 'is to make your streets safer – and we are going to begin with another 20,000 police on the streets and we start recruiting forthwith. My job is to make sure you don't have to wait three weeks to see your GP and we start work this week with twenty new hospital upgrades, and ensuring that money for the NHS really does get to the front line … My job is to make sure your kids get a superb education wherever they are in the country and that's why we have already announced that we are going to level-up per-pupil funding in primary and secondary schools.'

Austerity it was not. To hear a Conservative leader extol the virtues of a strong state so enthusiastically was a novelty in LOTO, and not a particularly pleasant one. Aides recall Milne's reaction to the police commitment as one of terror. Reversing cuts to policing budgets had been LOTO's way of combining Corbynomics with conventional mores. 'Not good, not good,' he said, turning to colleagues. 'He's stealing our lines. We can't attack him on austerity.' The following day, Corbyn's first clash with Johnson in the Commons chamber only compounded Milne's fears. Alongside predictable gibes on Corbyn's 'terrifying metamorphosis' from Bennite Eurosceptic to Remainer, his alleged palliness with 'the mullahs of Tehran' and McDonnell's leftist

economics came an unashamed populism whose potency Milne immediately recognised: 'We are the party of people. We are the party of
many, they are the party of the few. They will take this country backwards. We will take it forward.' Aides recall Milne's face dropping.
'This is really worrying, really worrying for us,' he said.

For all the worry, LOTO had not prepared a communications plan
to respond to Johnson's election. Initially, they had not intended for
Corbyn to respond at all. When Jack Bond, Corbyn's social media
manager, pre-booked a slot to film a piece to camera immediately
after Johnson's election, he found it was cancelled. It had instead been
ordained that Ian Lavery, a man about as far from an Old Etonian as
it was possible to be, would lead Labour's response. By the time LOTO
had changed its mind, Corbyn's diary was full. His video response
came a day late as a result.

McDonnell's team also recognised that they were not dealing with
a conventional Conservative. It had become a truism on the left to
say that Corbynism had broken the mould of British politics, but there
had been little anticipation of the Tories responding in kind. Said one
aide to the Shadow Chancellor: 'We failed to reckon with the fact that
Boris Johnson was an exception. It's true that centrism is dead. There's
no future in Cameron Conservatism or Blairite Labourism. But when
you break the mould and open up the populist box, there's no guarantee it's going to be the left – or left populists – who benefit.'

Having inherited a hung parliament and imposed upon it a Brexit
policy far more divisive than May's, all of Johnson's political roads
eventually led to an election. In demanding a deal that the EU had
no intention of offering, he all but guaranteed a no-deal Brexit. In
signalling his willingness to accept the latter outcome, he put a
Commons in which a majority of MPs were opposed to no-deal on
notice to conspire against him. His Cabinet also appeared to have
been selected not on merit but on the grounds of industrial-strength
Euroscepticism, as Andrew Fisher noted in a strategy paper circulated
among LOTO colleagues on 31 July: 'Boris Johnson's new Cabinet is
clearly trying to attract working-class Leave voters in the north and
Midlands. We need to show we have real policies and real connection
with people's lives – not just sound bites and phoney announcements
of failed policies ... Boris Johnson has appointed a staff and a Cabinet
that is for campaigning not delivering. The position of the EU,

Johnson's own red lines, and the parliamentary arithmetic all make it likely that a general election is imminent.'

For all the acknowledgement that Johnson did pose a serious threat, some in LOTO could not see much work being done to insure Labour against it. Niall Sookoo called repeatedly for polling on what lines might work as effective attacks on Johnson, given that tried-and-tested anti-Tory fodder was off limits. He complained that none was commissioned despite a growing consensus among Corbyn's team that Johnson would force or be forced into a general election sooner or later. No hint was too tenuous. On 5 August, Murphy shared a tip-off from the former *Tribune* editor Mark Seddon, who had forwarded Jennie Formby a message from a party member whose ex-husband's printing company had apparently been instructed to print election-ballot papers by the government, among senior management colleagues via WhatsApp.

Milne, meanwhile, had begun to think about how Labour might fight the election itself. In a memo circulated to colleagues on 18 August, he sketched out the big risks ahead. Johnson, he warned, had 'changed the game'. Labour needed to respond accordingly. The first and most important question would be when. Before 31 October, Johnson would seek 'a mandate to deliver the Brexit election: pitting Parliament and the establishment against the people'. But how to deny him? On Remain and Leave, Milne held firm: Corbyn must reject the binary. To win would mean casting Labour as 'agents of transformation and social justice and the real challenge to the establishment and the elites – while painting Boris Johnson's Tories as untrustworthy, dangerous and in the pockets of the super-rich'. They would also have to keep hold of as many as possible of the Remainers that had backed Corbyn in 2017, all the while winning over Leave seats 'at a time when both the Lib Dems and Brexit Party are still likely to be polling strongly'. He rejected explicitly any suggestion that Corbyn fight fire with fire and 'align exclusively' with Remainers, as McDonnell, Starmer, Tom Watson and others demanded. The latter two were conspicuously absent from a list of key Shadow Cabinet spokespeople. Watson was given equal billing to anti-Semitism as a potential pitfall.

It would be an uphill struggle. In analysis that just as readily applied to the atmosphere within LOTO, Milne noted: 'The Tories and the bulk of the media will seek to portray Jeremy and Labour as tired, stale, hopelessly divided, indecisive, toxic and extreme. They will try and portray Johnson as fresh, optimistic, decisive, action-oriented: setting out a new agenda of delivering Brexit, ending austerity and cutting taxes. Our response should be: Johnson and the Tories cannot be trusted to deliver, and will look after their own.' It was not 2017 any more. 'We must avoid refighting the last war ... they will not make the same mistake as Theresa May made in 2017 of attacking their core older voters and offering no sweeteners to their potential voters.'

Labour's job would be to muscle the Conservatives off the territory they had, by declaring austerity over, ordained as the 'new centre ground'. One solution would be 'to create controversies' and pick fights with vested interests. Another would be to counteract Tory promises of tax cuts. 'Hostile journalists' were to be avoided in favour of non-traditional media. Corbyn would instead be filmed on the road for social media, in a bid to counteract 'smears'. Older voters, no fans of Labour under Corbyn, would need to be wooed aggressively. As with 2017's 'For the Many, Not the Few', the campaign would need a clear, punchy brand identity.

Again and again Milne flagged Donald Trump as one of Labour's greatest assets. The US president would turn Labour's weaknesses on national security into strengths. 'The Tories are meanwhile led by a politician of proven incompetence, who is in hock to Donald Trump and in the pockets of the few, and who cannot be trusted to deliver on his promises ... Nor should we be afraid to grasp the security nettle – during a volatile period of international tension and potential flashpoints. Tory subservience to Trump offers the prospect of more war and a greater terror threat to Britain.'

None of the above would be possible, however, if the election turned into another 'proxy referendum'. Avoiding such a fate would be easier said than done. 'Although we will seek to move off Brexit on to the main domestic agenda, an October 2019 election will inevitably be a Brexit election in a way that June 2017 was not. The Liberal Democrats will also fight a more effective campaign, building on their "bollocks to Brexit" Remain/anti-establishment positioning.' The harshest judgement was on Corbyn himself. The star of 2017 was no longer an insurgent figure. 'We do not have the element of novelty and surprise we enjoyed – our policies and Leader are more familiar ... We will be subjected to even greater scrutiny as a government-in-waiting, something the media only began to take seriously towards the end of the last campaign.'

Much of Milne's analysis was unerringly prescient. His prescription, however, was in effect an instruction to defy electoral gravity. Fighting Johnson on anything but Johnson's terms, especially in a pre-Brexit election, was wishful thinking. Towards the end of August, an unwitting Labour would take the first steps towards handing him the pretence for a poll he craved.

The Conservatives were not alone in basking in a new leader's honeymoon glow. Two days before Johnson's coronation, the Liberal Democrats had elected Jo Swinson by a similarly crushing margin. A former coalition minister, the former Baby of the House was half Cable's age but harboured aspirations twice as ambitious. As her acceptance speech reached its peroration, she claimed to be standing before her party as the next prime minister.

Such was the parlous state of both main parties at the time that it sounded less like delusion and more like something approaching sincere aspiration. The ranks of her own parliamentary group had also been swollen by an influx of refugees from Change UK, with Umunna and Berger first to claim political asylum. Buoyed not only by their European election result but also victory in a by-election in the Welsh marginal of Brecon and Radnorshire, the Lib Dems could no longer be ignored. And nor could LOTO afford to if it wanted to leverage a hung parliament against Johnson to stop the no-deal Brexit he claimed to want to risk.

Swinson was among ten politicians invited by Corbyn to a cross-party meeting on 27 August to discuss just how no-deal might be stopped, with others including the Green MP Caroline Lucas and the Conservative rebels Oliver Letwin and Dominic Grieve. Journalists had spent the summer filling empty column space with what appeared to be outlandish suggestions that the opposition parties might cobble together a majority to fell Johnson's government and then form a Frankenstein coalition of their own, with the sole purpose of legislating for a referendum, or at least requesting another Article 50 delay to avert no-deal. Corbyn's own preference, revealed in a letter to other opposition parties on 15 August, was to form a government himself. To Swinson and the Conservative rebels necessary to tip a motion of no confidence against Johnson in the first place, that was anathema.

Swinson told Corbyn as much in a letter of her own on the eve of their no-deal summit. In her view there was no way that the requisite eight Conservatives would throw their weight behind a Corbyn government. 'This isn't the time for personal agendas and political games. We cannot allow party politics to stand in the way of Members from all sides of the House of Commons working together in the national interest.' She proposed as alternatives Ken Clarke, the vinegary Father of the House, and Harriet Harman, matriarch of the Corbynsceptics. LOTO did not respond directly but instead wheeled out the Shadow Cabinet minister Barry Gardiner for a media round, who in his inimitable style described Swinson as 'petulant'. Ironically, his private belief was that a unity government led by Margaret Beckett was the cleanest solution to the impasse.

LOTO's indirect reply came at the summit itself, which saw Swinson banished to the foot of the table. Nor was it a discursive encounter between equals. Corbyn, flanked by a watchful McDonnell, read his plan to muzzle Johnson off a printed script. Starmer had spent his summer holiday in Devon coordinating with Conservative rebels via phone from a field full of sheep on a plan for legislation to allow the opposition to delay Brexit without toppling Johnson's administration. In doing so, Labour would place itself at the vanguard of the Parliament that – as Milne had warned – would in the Tory telling be cast as a block on the people's will. Setting the terms of parliamentary business would allow Johnson to set the terms of an election all in LOTO knew would be a struggle, where 2017 had been a breeze.

Yet the government gave them no choice. That a no-deal Brexit could not be countenanced was about the only thing on which every Labour MP, with the exception of a handful in Leave constituencies, were able to agree. Johnson, unlike May, was more than happy to go there. Indeed, in promising to accept nothing less than a withdrawal agreement gutted of the backstop, he appeared to have guaranteed that no-deal was inevitable. Then it emerged on 28 August that Commons leader Jacob Rees-Mogg had travelled to Balmoral to seek the Queen's permission to prorogue – or suspend – Parliament for five weeks from September until 14 October, just over a fortnight before Brexit day.

Both Starmer and Johnson's adversaries on the Conservative back benches could see as much even before prorogation. Over the course of secret teleconferences with Philip Hammond and David Gauke (the highest-profile departures from government ahead of Johnson's coronation), and Oliver Letwin (the sage of the back benches), Starmer and his aide Stuart Ingham had drawn up a plan to prevent Johnson from going nuclear. The opposition would again seize control of the parliamentary agenda to pass legislation that would force the government to seek an extension to Article 50 if a deal had not been struck by 19 October.

Hilary Benn was enlisted as camouflage. His was a name cursed in Downing Street for much of 2019. Unlike his father, whose left Euroscepticism was invoked with varying degrees of sincerity by Brexiteers, by September he had become the face of the forces conspiring to thwart Boris Johnson's efforts to ram through Brexit on any terms by 31 October. 'It needed to look like a back-bench initiative rather than a Labour front-bench initiative,' said one source familiar with the discussions. 'It was just that. If it was the Starmer Act, then it wouldn't have passed.'

On 3 September, MPs – leveraging the hung parliament Johnson had inherited against him – seized control of the parliamentary agenda to table legislation in Benn's name. Its purpose was simple: to muzzle a new prime minister who was quite prepared to go rabid if it meant fulfilling the central pledge of his premiership. If a Brexit deal had not been agreed by 19 October, then the law would compel Johnson to seek the delay he had set himself repeatedly against. It even went as far as to write the request into the bill for him. The legislation would set Johnson on the sort of collision course with a Parliament apparently determined to obstruct any effort he made to enact Brexit – or so he would argue – that he had spent the summer limbering up for. Worse still for its Remainer midwives, it would ultimately provide the pretext for the election he so craved.

Pass it did, by 327 votes to 299. Conservative rebels had been radicalised by Johnson's botched prorogation the previous week. Those prepared to take radical action to prevent a no-deal began to bare their teeth. Twenty-one of them – including five members of Theresa May's last Cabinet, two former Chancellors in Hammond and Ken Clarke, and a grandson of Winston Churchill in Nicholas Soames – joined Labour and the rest of the opposition in the no lobby. Johnson removed the whip from each of them. The punishment for inflicting more of what Brexit Secretary Steve Barclay described as 'purgatory' was swift and brutal.

To LOTO it was a rude awakening. The day before the vote, Andrew Murray had undergone surgery after a heart attack. He was lying in his hospital bed self-administering morphine when his daughters came bearing news from Westminster. 'The Tories have taken the whip away from Philip Hammond and Ken Clarke, and from Winston Churchill's grandson,' they told him. It was so implausible that Murray believed he was hallucinating. The new occupants of Downing Street were willing to attack the question of Brexit with a force and clarity of purpose that Theresa May had never seemed capable of. More worryingly for Labour, it would also prove to be well beyond the powers of Corbyn and the PLP.

In intervening to block no-deal Starmer in fact encouraged Johnson to ask a question to which neither LOTO nor Labour MPs had a clear answer: were they willing to take the fight out of Parliament, where the job of frustrating, delaying or otherwise obstructing the government was relatively straightforward, to a country at best disinterested in and at worst aggrieved by the endless rounds of chicanery at Westminster? Since 2017 the call for another general election had been recited ad nauseam, like a Corbynite Lord's Prayer. The Benn Act gave Johnson the motive to call one, and with it a deadline by which to do so. Yet the question that haunted Labour MPs and divided LOTO was not whether they could recapture the spirit of the last general election – but whether they could face going to a country divided by Brexit at all.

12

The Failed Assassin

On the evening of 20 September 2019, Tom Watson and his children were halfway through dinner at the Sweet Mandarin, a Chinese restaurant in Manchester city centre, when he learned that LOTO had made an attempt to abolish him. In Brighton, 260 miles away, the NEC had gathered for its eve-of-conference meeting. At the top of the agenda was a modest proposal from Jon Lansman: the deletion of the deputy leadership from the party rulebook.

For years Watson had undermined the Project. For months he had monstered them on Brexit and anti-Semitism. His sedition had made the summer of 2019 Corbyn's most miserable yet. Corbyn and LOTO had snapped. It was time to mount a coup of their own.

*

'We need to tell the truth: that the European Union is a good thing. It's an enduring, deep, benevolent collaboration in the history of the world. It produced a lasting peace out of the ravages of war.' Voice cracking, Tom Watson spoke the language of a dove as he carried out the equivalent of a political airstrike. It was only 6.47 a.m. on 17 June 2019 and yet already he had ruined LOTO's day with a tweet. 'The core values of the EU are: Internationalism, Solidarity, Freedom. They are British Labour values. Our future doesn't need to be Brexit. We can change our future. But only if Labour makes the case for it – and we must. #proudlybritishproudlyeuropean.'

It was from the accompanying video of an anguished Watson – clad, like a hitman, entirely in black – that LOTO learned he would escalate hostilities with a speech later that morning. He would tell an audience of journalists and Europhile academics at the Centre of European

Reform that it was not only time for a second referendum, but for Labour to offer its full-throated and unequivocal endorsement of EU membership.

The intent seemed noble enough. Like much of the PLP Watson had come to the conclusion that Labour needed to crank up its pro-Europeanism to eleven if it was to stem the tide of Remain voters that had departed to the Liberal Democrats the previous month. But to say so publicly was to undercut not only party policy but Corbyn. Above all, it was an act of calculated sedition.

Seumas Milne and Karie Murphy were in Jennie Formby's office on the eighth floor of Southside when they learned of Watson's plan. They immediately recognised its explosive potential. Murphy picked up the phone to make a last-minute appeal to the ego she knew so well. It rang out to voicemail. 'Don't do this,' she said. 'Don't do it. And I'll tell you why you shouldn't do it – because the left now will have your neck in a noose.' His seat in the Shadow Cabinet was on the line. 'Until you tell me something different, you still want to do that job, Tom. Do not do it.'

She then called Alicia Kennedy, the Labour peer with whom she had worked in Watson's office, and issued the same instruction. Watson would have to back down. He neither responded to the calls nor complied. The speech was on.

Corbyn had been following negotiations from home. Informed that his deputy would not be moved, he erupted with a rage few of his inner circle believed he had the capacity for. An aide's phone was on loudspeaker but such was the raised volume of Corbyn's voice that it need not have been. It was then he gave his instruction: 'I want him out of the Shadow Cabinet, and I want to abolish the deputy role.' Then he hung up. It fell to Murphy to execute Corbyn's will – and Watson. She set to work on a plan.

Undaunted, Watson gave his speech as planned. He had taken the by then rare step of dressing in collar and tie for the occasion. The address was a mixture of high culture – ranging from Shakespeare to Erasmus to Plutarch – and low cunning. 'Our members are Remain, our values are Remain, our hearts are Remain ... we need to be loud and proud in support of Europe,' he said. 'Our future doesn't need to be Brexit.' He took a potshot at his old flatmate Len McCluskey and his pro-deal friends in the Shadow Cabinet. 'It is no "boss's club",' he proclaimed of the EU. 'It is both an engine of progress and a backstop against regressive and repressive governments.'

The intended recipients of the message were unimpressed. At 10.42 a.m., just after Watson delivered a peroration that declared Remain to be 'the patriotic choice', Ian Lavery tweeted: 'Brexit has turned this country into a toxic nation. However, ignoring the 17.4 million leave voters isn't particularly smart nor indeed particularly democratic. Is it? #simplysaying.'

After his speech, Watson sat down with Laura Kuenssberg. She asked whether the speech was the opening monologue in a drama that would see him quit Labour altogether. 'I'm never going to leave the Labour Party,' he said. 'Sometimes I wonder whether the Labour Party is leaving me.' Online Corbynites made their own preference clear by pushing the hashtag #SackTomWatson to number two in the UK's trending topics that afternoon. None of the outraged throng could know that their demand was now the policy of the leader's office itself.

As Watson spoke, Murphy was working out the practicalities of his sacking. She could not implement Corbyn's plan to abolish the post of deputy leader immediately. Not only did the enemy have his own elected mandate, but such tinkering could not be done without the acquiescence of the NEC and party conference. What they could do was sack him from a Shadow Cabinet brief in which he was deeply emotionally invested. His campaign for a fairer press would have to continue from the back benches, his time as Shadow Culture Secretary curtailed not by Rupert Murdoch, but by two women he had once employed in his parliamentary office in Murphy and Amy Jackson, who was assigned to sketch out plans for the reshuffle and a comms strategy for managing the storm that would inevitably ensue.

John McDonnell, engaged elsewhere in Southside, was then summoned to Formby's office by Murphy. Any plan of this magnitude needed his approval, but he withheld his blessing. Murphy took it as a provocation. The two were increasingly at odds on what was best for the Project. 'Well, John, here we are, yet again,' she said. 'Jeremy wants us to do something, you're saying no, you put staff in a predicament.' To dispel any suspicions of the overreach she was often suspected of, Murphy called Corbyn and allowed McDonnell to make his case against sacking Watson. But Corbyn would not give in. Defeated, McDonnell walked out.

Minutes later, Jackson's phone rang. It was McDonnell. He told her the reshuffle to which she was putting the finishing touches was off. 'Jeremy's changed his mind. Don't do it.' By then the plan was so advanced that the press officer Sophie Nazemi was about to be dispatched to inform the media of the sacking via a press release. 'We were going to press the button,' a LOTO source said. Irate, Murphy called Corbyn again. What did he want to do?

It was then that a new plan took shape. 'We're going to conference,' Corbyn said. Abortive proposals to 'democratise' the inner leadership had already been explored in Liverpool the previous year, when Watson had reacted to the prospect of a second deputy leader with enthusiasm rather than horror. Murphy suggested a similar plan of attack. She would draw up a plan to abolish Watson's post altogether, to be put to the NEC at its eve-of-conference meeting.

'OK,' Corbyn said. 'Let's do that.' Watson would be left to stew in the Shadow Cabinet until then. Murphy, having been at Watson's side during his troubled stints in Ed Miliband's top team, believed the issue would then resolve itself. She believed Watson would absent himself from the Shadow Cabinet if ousted as deputy. He had resigned when faced with difficulty in 2013. In her view he would do so again if the going got tough. Murphy suspected Watson was a quitter. Her intuition did not fail her.

*

Political successes have many parents, while the failures are quickly disclaimed as orphans. That is certainly true of the plot to dethrone Watson.

Some in LOTO credit – or blame – Jon Lansman, whose first meaningful act in Labour politics was to attempt to oust Denis Healey as deputy in favour of Tony Benn in 1981. In their Monday meetings, Corbyn's senior management team would often bemoan the Watson-shaped millstone around the Project's neck. Early in 2019, long before Watson's speech and long before conference, they had reached a tacit understanding. Said one senior LOTO source: 'If we couldn't get rid of him, he was doing so much damage, we would take him out. We had a majority on the NEC, and we would just get rid of him.'

Lansman was first to break the taboo. Senior Corbyn aides recall him asking: 'Why don't we just delete Tom Watson?' The idea of expunging the deputy leader from the rulebook altogether was originally treated as high jinks. Over time, his insubordination pushed LOTO to take it seriously.

That Lansman helped inject the plan into the LOTO bloodstream is not disputed. Whether he was the originator of the idea is another question. Radical reform to the deputy post had been on the table during Corbyn's political secretary Katy Clark's democracy review, envisioned not only as a programme for changing the party for the benefit of its swelling membership but also for the benefit of the left. Watson's survival was not only a political irritant to LOTO, it had, in the words of one senior aide, left 'two geezers' in charge of a party that prided itself on diversity. But only once Corbyn gave his signal did it leave the realm of hypothesis.

It was also a revenge mission. To LOTO and Lansman, abolishing Watson was repayment in kind. At conference in 2016 Watson had himself arrived at the eve-of-conference NEC with a package of reforms to the party's constitutional structures. It was less explosive a proposition than abolishing the deputy leadership but arguably of greater consequence.

Watson's proposals changed the complexion of the NEC by creating two extra seats, nominated by the leaders of Scottish and Welsh Labour – both of whom were at that point Corbynsceptics. The plans were voted through. As an act of procedural chicanery it was tantamount to rigging the party's ruling body against its elected leadership. It nobbled the Corbynites at the moment Owen Smith's defeat had confirmed their dominance at the grass roots. If Watson was willing to live by that sword, he would die by it too.

*

LOTO would soon learn that Watson had been working on a plan of his own. On 26 February 2019 he and Alicia Kennedy had met Sam Matthews and Louise Withers-Green, both survivors of Southside's governance and legal unit, in Parliament. Neither were friends of the leadership. Each said they had been scarred by what they had seen working at the coalface of the party's disciplinary regime. The discussion focused on how they might blow the whistle on the leadership's failure to get a grip on anti-Semitism.

Matthews had left Southside the previous June armed with a cache of emails that demonstrated the dizzying scale of anti-Semitism complaints received by the party. They appeared to show that members had been referred to the party for posting online comments such as 'Heil Hitler', 'Fuck the Jews' and 'Jews are the problem' – but not been suspended or expelled months later. At best, Southside's sluggish bureaucracy was unable to process the evidence rapidly or with sufficient understanding of the problem. In one case, Thomas Gardiner, parachuted into the governance and legal unit as Jennie Formby's fixer, advised against suspending an activist who had posted a far-right image of a parasitic creature emblazoned with the Star of David engulfing the Statue of Liberty's Face. She had written: 'The most accurate image I've seen all year!' Gardiner had also apparently declined to accelerate a probe into a member who called Margaret Hodge and Ruth Smeeth 'shit stirring cum buckets paid for by Israel'.

At worst, the files directly implicated the leadership in the handling – or mishandling – of anti-Semitism cases. Milne, Murphy and Andrew Murray had all remarked upon sensitive complaints and offered their advice to Southside on whether or how certain individuals should be sanctioned. In one instance, Glyn Secker, a radical Jewish activist and personal friend of Corbyn, was himself accused of anti-Semitism. He had contributed to Palestine Live, a Facebook group that regularly hosted anti-Semitic material, and heckled Jewish activists at party conference. One of his social media posts read 'Jew = Zionist = Israel = Jew'. When his case crossed Southside's desk, Andrew Murray emailed colleagues: 'JC interested in this one.' To Matthews, the files drove a coach and horses through the leadership's claim of non-interference in anti-Semitism complaints – and served as proof that it adopted a soft touch when it came to anti-Jewish racism. The leadership would later offer a simple defence of their involvement. In the interim phase before Formby became general secretary in 2018, Corbynsceptic officials – apparently overwhelmed by the number of complaints – had begged LOTO for administrative help. For a short period, LOTO had obliged.

Both accounts had elements of truth. Southside officials *had* apparently asked Corbyn's office for help in the summer of 2018. But Formby's staff had not covered themselves in glory or demonstrated enough awareness of anti-Semitism's precise nature subsequent to that. The claim that Formby was independent of LOTO similarly stretched credulity to those familiar with her ties to the Project.

In any case, Watson was disgusted by what he saw. The episode roused him out of the semi-retirement he had imposed upon himself in the wake of 2017, when, according to aides, he had resolved to 'get on with my own thing. My thing will be I'll be half my weight, I'll get fit, I'll do interesting things, policy-wise. I'll do my brief, to the best of my ability, and we'll see where we are.' His was a keenly felt moral objection. Yet he also had an intuitive understanding of how the issue – and the perception that LOTO had at best mishandled and at worst ignored it – might be used to destabilise the Project. Hurt by Luciana Berger's resignation from the party the previous week and alive to the prospect of further defections, Watson had already invited MPs to circumvent Southside and submit complaints of anti-Semitism and bullying to him on 25 February, so discredited were Labour's official disciplinary structures in the eyes of the PLP. Together with Matthews and Withers-Green, his next job was to expose them publicly, and tarnish them irrevocably.

At 11 p.m. on 27 February, Matthews drove from his flat to Streatham to meet Danny Adilypour, Watson's political adviser, to hand him a folder containing hundreds of documents. Matthews had spent hours printing them off in his living room. Such was their fear of being caught that they met on a pedestrian island in the middle of a deserted side street to conduct the sixty-second exchange, rather than Adilypour's home. Over the weeks that followed, Alicia Kennedy and Margaret Hodge organised legal representation for Matthews and Withers-Green from James Lisbon of Mishcon de Reya, the Magic Circle law firm. James Robinson, Watson's former spin doctor, structured the evidence so that it would be digestible to the media. Their goal was to expose LOTO as having obfuscated, delayed and interfered on the most egregious disciplinary cases to have crossed their desks. The *Observer*, *The Times* and the *Sunday Times* were selected to deliver the message.

On 28 May, eight weeks after the *Observer*'s first article had been published, the Equalities and Human Rights Commission (EHRC) confirmed that the story was not going away. Up until that point, LOTO had sought to dismiss the leaks as vexatious and peddled by disgruntled staffers. Now the EHRC said that it would begin a statutory investigation into anti-Semitism in Labour – only the second time that it had investigated a political party (the first had been the neo-fascist British National Party in 2009). Under powers granted to it by the Equality Act, the EHRC would examine whether Labour had unlawfully discriminated against Jews or failed to respond to complaints of racial discrimination in an efficient and effective manner. Ruth Smeeth, herself the victim of many of the complaints in question, declared: 'Today is a day of great shame for the Labour Party and one that could so easily have been avoided if the leadership of my once great party had acted on, rather than ignored thousands of complaints from our members.' LOTO was more equivocal, with a spokeswoman saying: 'We support the efforts of the EHRC to draw attention to the obligations all political parties have under the Equality Act.' The party, she said, would cooperate fully with the EHRC as it set about its investigation.

John Ware, the veteran investigative reporter, was not prepared to wait for the commission to reach its conclusions. His lengthy back catalogue of films for BBC's *Panorama* on jihadism and radical Islamism had invited accusations of racism. He also had form for riling the left. In September 2015, before Corbyn had even won the leadership, Ware had interviewed Labour's great and good for a documentary on the coming landslide. The conclusion most of his case studies had reached was that a Corbyn leadership spelled electoral disaster for Labour. A deluge of complaints followed.

So it was with considerable alarm that LOTO greeted the news in late June that Ware and the whistleblowers were collaborating on a documentary: *Is Labour Anti-Semitic?*.

LOTO believed that the title and the testimony of former Southside officials invited a straightforward answer: yes. Aware of the ton of bricks an hour-long disposition from Ware and Matthews was likely to unleash on the political news cycle, the full force of the Labour machine was deployed in an attempt to delay transmission.

On 5 July, Gerald Shamash, one of LOTO's favoured lawyers, served a threat of legal action to the BBC. He claimed that the whistleblowers were disgruntled former staff with axes to grind. He also accused

Matthews, who in April had been threatened with legal action by the infamous firm Carter Ruck, of unlawfully disclosing information on disciplinary cases to the media.

The following day Anjula Singh, Labour's head of communications, took LOTO's case right to the top of the corporation. In a letter to BBC director general Tony Hall, she complained that the party had not been given an adequate right of reply. 'The Labour Party has serious concerns that the programme will breach standards of accuracy and impartiality,' she wrote, additionally complaining that the *Sunday Times* and other media outlets seemed to know more about the accusations than the party did. To LOTO's leading lights the programme was a particularly egregious example of the broadcast media's willingness to play by different rules when it came to Jeremy Corbyn.

Watson certainly saw the programme as a blunt instrument with which to smash LOTO. By the time *Panorama* was broadcast on 10 July, Watson's thinking had not so much hardened as curdled. A close ally explains: 'It was just: fuck them. Were they incompetent? Yes. Did they want to protect their mates? Yes. Could they get a grip of it? No.' That was the story that he and the whistleblowers hoped Ware would tell.

That evening the whistleblowers and BBC production team watched the broadcast live at a pub in Islington ten minutes from Corbyn's home. Watson gathered his aides in his County Hall flat with Robinson and Gloria de Piero. Fortified by wine supplied by de Piero, the trio were joined by Kennedy, Sarah Coombes, Watson's spinner, and Haf Davies, another aide, who would formulate his response to what was to come.

The broadcast exceeded even Watson's expectations of the grim picture it would paint of Corbyn's inner circle. 'It was worse than we thought,' says one of those present. The headline was bleak for LOTO: of the hundreds of cases referred to Southside, only fifteen had resulted in expulsions for anti-Semitism. Milne and Formby were singled out and blamed for stymying investigations on political grounds.

Formby and Thomas Gardiner, the official airlifted in to replace John Stolliday as the head of the governance and legal unit, were accused of downgrading serious cases so as to impose a 'slap on the wrist' as punishment. Even Iain McNicol popped up to offer thanks to LOTO for his peerage by describing Formby's alleged conduct as 'just wrong'. The wisdom of Milne's blanket policy of broadly refusing to commit anything to text was proven when he was quoted as complaining of anti-Semitism cases: 'We're muddling up political disputes with racism.'

Mike Creighton, another Southside veteran, said Milne had laughed in his face when he suggested Corbyn might make a speech on Israel's right to exist, an allegation LOTO claimed was made up. Other former staffers came close to tears as they described the deterioration of their mental health. An emotional Matthews said that he had fantasised about leaping from the balcony of Formby's eighth-floor office. Ken Loach, the leftist auteur, later spoke for many on the left when he described the episode of *Panorama* as: 'Probably the most disgusting programme I've ever seen on the BBC.'

The revelations put LOTO in a bind. Many in Corbyn's office felt they could weather attack stories in the print press, which 2017 had taught them no longer wielded the influence or had the audience of old. In April the previous year, Murphy had emailed colleagues ahead of one *Sunday Times* story by declaring that the story would be 'shit', adding: 'They are attacking us for a reason, fuck them.' The problem was that they could not ignore the BBC. Nor was it as simple to dismiss the corporation as biased or unrepresentative.

Andrew Gwynne, the Shadow minister given the hospital pass of responding for Corbyn in the programme, was compensated for his troubles with a bottle of whisky. Jon Lansman had briefly considered fronting Labour's response but belatedly pulled out. Few others in the Shadow Cabinet were in the mood to defend their leader. Barry Gardiner was so upset by what he saw that he had to be talked out of resigning.

The official line issued in the name of a spokesperson for Corbyn cast the whistleblowers as politically motivated smear artists who were the authors of the very culture they criticised. 'It appears these disaffected former officials include those who have always opposed Jeremy Corbyn's leadership, worked to actively undermine it, and have both personal and political axes to grind. This throws into doubt their credibility as sources. Our records show that after these officials left and after Jennie Formby became general secretary, the rate at which anti-Semitism cases have been dealt with, increased more than fourfold.'

Private briefings to Corbyn's most vocal cheerleaders on social media were more equivocal. LOTO cautioned them against disputing the programme's premise. 'DO NOT ADVANCE ANY GENERAL CRITICISMS of *Panorama* or the show. They are correct to raise anti-Semitism. It's a very very real & serious problem in Labour that Jeremy & Jennie are tackling.' They were instead advised to 'amplify, amplify, amplify' a *Dispatches* documentary on Islamophobia in the Conservative Party. Most tellingly, they cautioned against attacks on Watson and the Labour right: 'This will only play into their hands.'

Watson was already primed with a response. The morning after the broadcast, he wrote to Formby. *Panorama*'s revelations had been 'shocking and distressing'. LOTO's attempt to discredit the whistle-blowers was 'deplorable'. Making for the moral high ground, he demanded the party's submission to the EHRC and promised to push through changes to the party's rules on anti-Semitism at conference. He did not yet know that LOTO were planning their own assault on the rulebook. Within hours, a strategy paper had been sent to LOTO aides setting out detailed steps to beef up anti-Semitism processes and finishing with three menacing words: 'Deputy leader – action'.

Watson's letter was merely the latest round in a grudge match between him and the general secretary. Their relationship was worse than appalling and their communication was limited to terse and subtext-heavy exchanges of letters. In September 2018 Watson had challenged her to resign if she hadn't stamped out anti-Semitism within a year. *Panorama*, he argued, had only proved his point.

His decision to take the fight to Formby unleashed a battery of criticism from the Corbynites. Her reply pulled no punches: 'Traducing my reputation and publicly attacking me when you know I am under-going chemotherapy and am unable to respond in the media is another example of the inappropriate way in which you choose to discuss this issue.'

Amy Jackson, whose reluctant affection for her former boss had curdled into cold contempt, was the letter's primary author. She later wrote to Watson under her own name in a text. 'Hi Tom, I don't contact you any more because you've lost all sense of fairness, however I want you to know that even now I have to bite my tongue every time you try and exploit everything you can get your hands on to damage the party. I have quietly lost respect for you. I used to defend you and tell people you had integrity – how wrong and naïve I was. I'm embarrassed to have ever worked for you.'

McDonnell, whose fealty to the LOTO line on anti-Semitism had been sorely tested in the months before *Panorama* aired, also attacked Watson. He tweeted: 'I just don't understand why the deputy leader of the Labour Party uses the media to demand information from Labour's General Secretary @JennieGenSec, which has already been offered to him. It goes beyond my understanding that he does so when he knows she's undergoing chemotherapy.' The Corbynites were briefly reunited in their belief that Watson was acting out of a desire to eradicate the Project, rather than racism.

Jackson was not the only former friend of Watson to disavow him. On 13 July, Len McCluskey chose to escalate hostilities with a bilious address to the Durham Miners Gala. 'I have a simple message for Tom Watson and his pals in the media: you should fucking well be ashamed of yourself.' For the benefit of said media, he later tweeted: 'I've said it today at the Durham Miners Gala so I'll repeat it here. Attacking a woman going through chemotherapy – @tom_watson you are a fucking disgrace. @JennieGenSec.'

Watson was in no mood for constructive engagement either. When the Shadow Cabinet met on 22 July to consider new proposals for expelling anti-Semites more speedily, LOTO aides found he was unwilling to even look at a joint statement being drafted on Andrew Fisher's laptop and left early. On his way out, he addressed Corbyn in a stage whisper: 'You can do a statement if you want. But I'm not going to negotiate with you.' The feeling was mutual.

By August, Jackson had drawn up a detailed plan to prevent Watson from darkening the door of the Shadow Cabinet Room again, which she presented to the rest of LOTO's senior management team on an awayday at an Islington community centre on 14 August. The symbolism of the venue was unfortunate. It doubled as a nursery and aides were barely able to fit their feet under the tables. The game of tit-for-tat that ensued also evoked memories of playground politics.

It was not just Watson who they planned to punish. Reshuffles of Corbyn's lacklustre Shadow Cabinet were perennially discussed in LOTO but never carried out, thanks in no small part to his hatred of the confrontation inherent in giving shadow ministers the chop. The verdict out of Monday meetings of the senior management team was always the same. 'Let's do it next week. Let's finalise it next week.' And then, one senior aide says, 'it just would not happen.'

Corbyn's top team had gone unrefreshed since June 2017, save for ad hoc appointments to fill the vacancies left in the wake of the resignation of Kate Osamor and sackings of Debbie Abrahams and Owen Smith. Talented heads in the PLP who were willing to put aside their misgivings about the leadership languished in junior roles, to the detriment of the Project. On that, everyone in LOTO was agreed. It was arguably the only subject on which there was consensus between Corbyn's team and the PLP – not that MPs were able to tell from a Shadow Cabinet that had been frozen in aspic for two long years.

Drawing inspiration from Watson's well-publicised health kick, Jackson proposed a job swap that would have diminished Watson's stature even more sharply than his diet. He could go from Shadow Culture Secretary to sugar tsar, or alternatively not be given a job at all.

Emily Thornberry, whose advocacy for Remain had seen her transformation from dependable loyalist to dependable irritant over the course of the previous year, would be shunted from the Foreign Office to fill Watson's shoes at Culture. Diane Abbott would move from Home to Foreign. Richard Burgon would have replaced Abbott, with David Lammy taking his place at Justice. Those promotions risked being taken as a provocation by Corbynsceptics.

Nick Thomas-Symonds and Anneliese Dodds, two young thrusters from the soft left, would have been promoted, though not to the heights they would later be propelled by Keir Starmer. Barbara Keeley, widely considered an abrasive presence as Shadow Minister for Mental Health, would have been demoted along with Peter Dowd, whose primary contribution to the Shadow Treasury team came in the form of daddish one-liners.

When Corbyn put the plan to Abbott, she had been reluctant. But she had come to rather like the idea of being Shadow Foreign Secretary. 'It's growing on me.'

Andrew Fisher had other ideas, as was often the case when Jackson and Murphy had settled on a plan of action. He circulated his own paper in advance of the meeting. Unusually, his judgement chimed with that of the PLP. 'Our Shadow Cabinet needs a refresh. Too few are really doing well on their briefs, driving policy development and taking the fight to the Tories. Too few are prepared to regularly go on the media, and too few perform well enough when they do ... We are facing an ideological, campaigning Cabinet. We are at risk of being stale, flat-footed and weak in several key areas.'

Fisher too suggested replacing Watson, who he suspected was 'angling to move', with Lammy – whose 534,000 Twitter followers were noted with some excitement. But the rest of his proposals were a recipe for rapprochement with the most hardened opponents of the leadership remaining in the PLP. Staring down the barrel of a Brexit election against an exuberant Boris Johnson government, the original Corbynite calculated that the Project could only survive if it sacrificed ideological coherence on the altar of presentability.

Welfare and social care were identified as the two biggest problem areas. Broadcast producers at Westminster liked to note with some amusement that Margaret Greenwood, the Shadow Work and Pensions Secretary, had never to their knowledge been put up for an interview. Her anonymity in the media was matched by the absence of any semblance of a new deal on the welfare system at all. Remarkably, Fisher proposed recruiting the keeper of the Blairite flame in Alison McGovern, chair of Progress, as a 'unifying option'.

Even more striking was his proposed replacement for Barbara Keeley, whose 'very bad' relationship with Jon Ashworth and her own staff was considered as much of an impediment as her failure 'to do much at all' on her brief. Again Fisher looked right before he looked left. In suggesting Rachel Reeves, many Corbynites would have judged him to have looked to the far right. As Ed Miliband's welfare spokeswoman she had suggested that Labour was not the party of benefit claimants in a *Guardian* interview that was still periodically dredged up as a political memento mori for the left, a cautionary reminder of the mindset Corbynism existed to expunge. In March 2020, the suggestion that Keir Starmer would recruit Reeves to be his Shadow Chancellor elicited the sort of reaction that the appointment of an actual Conservative MP might have. But to Fisher, she was 'solid on the finances ... and increasingly radical and in the same place on economic issues'.

Then there was Miliband himself, repeatedly linked with a return to the Shadow Cabinet that never quite materialised. He yearned to proselytise for an economic programme that had much in common with his own thwarted ambitions to recast British politics. But Miliband's decision to take on the unions after Falkirk had given Murphy cause to bear a grudge. Corbyn's victory, facilitated by the new leadership rules drawn up in the aftermath, had given her the opportunity to exact revenge. To her, Miliband's name was mud. As long as she reigned in LOTO there was next to no chance of his acceptance into the fold. Others accused him of approaching Corbyn with a degree of hauteur that belied the effervescent public persona he had carefully crafted since 2015.

Fisher nonetheless made a spirited argument for the defence. He witheringly suggested that Jon Trickett was 'intimidated' by Michael Gove at the Cabinet Office, and proposed Miliband in his place. 'We also need someone who is savvy, gets policy and is able to input into preparing for government.' His experience as a special adviser and Cabinet minister were cited as big ticks, as were 758,000 Twitter followers. Others in LOTO took the menu of options as confirmation that Fisher and McDonnell had given up on the Project, and were instead seeking to build their own.

Murphy exploded once she learned of the plan to redeem Miliband. In a WhatsApp message to Corbyn's core team, she wrote: 'I feel slightly exposed in saying this but as I understand it JT [Jon Trickett] isn't leaving CO [Cabinet Office] and am I expected to work with a man who in an act of political vindictiveness referred me to Police Scotland and my union too? I am leading on Prep for Government so this may be a difficult one.'

The leader, a Delphic presence at the head of the table, gave his blessing to neither reshuffle. But there was one idea he liked. Conscious that the PLP's talent pool might be stagnating, Fisher had suggested aping the Conservatives and appointing a slate of vice chairs of the party to sit outside the Shadow Cabinet but within television studios. He gave the nod to Clive Lewis, the Project's prodigal son; Louise Haigh, thorn in Abbott's side as Shadow Policing Minister; Paul Sweeney, Scottish Labour's matinee idol; and Anneliese Dodds. When the time came to cull the deputy leader, Corbyn remembered that plan.

With Watson temporarily put to the side, LOTO grappled with the growing prospect of an election. Fisher's intuition that Boris Johnson had built a Cabinet to campaign rather than govern was proven right when the Commons returned from its summer recess. Johnson needled Corbyn at PMQs on 4 September. Would Corbyn take his policy of 'dither and delay' on Brexit to the British people in an election on 15 October? Corbyn told the prime minister that he would accede to the request only once no-deal had been definitively ruled out via the Benn Bill. 'Fine,' he said. 'Get the bill through first in order to take no-deal off the table.' LOTO, anxious that Johnson might set a date after the Brexit deadline and thus force through no-deal by the back door if MPs acquiesced, resolved to vote against any motion for an early election when it came before the Commons.

Yet in private Corbyn's preference was clear. After Johnson laid down the gauntlet, he and Nick Brown met with Milne, Starmer, Fisher, McDonnell, James Schneider and Shami Chakrabarti in the Whips' Office to consider Labour's response. Milne, Murphy and Chakrabarti argued that the PLP's belief that the arithmetic of a hung parliament would ever result in a second referendum was a delusion, and that the Liberal Democrats and SNP would in time realise that too. 'The parliamentary numbers didn't work, and were never going to,' said one LOTO aide present. 'The Lib Dems needed to have an election before Brexit happened, so they would end up voting for it.' For those reasons they believed bouncing Johnson into a late October poll would weaken the Tory hand and strengthen Labour's.

Milne argued that Labour should reject Johnson's offer and table a bill calling for an early election on 24 October, so that Corbyn might argue: 'I'm not voting for your phoney election that's going to risk no-deal, but if you want polling day – here it is.' The Conservatives would be forced to campaign without a deal and, it seemed, with little chance of convincing Brussels and Dublin to offer one. Any incentive Leo Varadkar might have had to yield on his red lines on the Irish border would have evaporated. That, to proponents of an early poll, made for the 'perfect squeeze' on anxious Conservative Remainers and voters playing footsie with the resurgent Lib Dems: 'If you don't vote Labour, it's no-deal in a week.' More prosaic motivations were at play too. With nights drawing in and temperatures dropping, October would be infinitely preferable to the first December election since 1923.

Corbyn was attracted to the idea. Not since 2017 had he been able to seize the initiative in Parliament. But Brown disagreed. Where Milne saw opportunity, the chief whip – perhaps the only voice outside of Corbyn's immediate orbit to whom the leader would reliably listen – foresaw electoral apocalypse. Though usually unflappable, he began to panic. He warned Corbyn that to attempt to legislate for an election would be to risk the single biggest rebellion of his leadership, such was the scale of opposition in the PLP to going to the country with Brexit unresolved. Instead they hoped to delay an election as long as possible, preferably right into the spring. McDonnell, who LOTO feared was fraternising with the People's Vote campaign far too freely, signalled his agreement.

To LOTO's election hawks the argument was nonsensical. MPs had made similarly hostile noises in the run-up to 2017 and in the event only twelve of them had defied the whip to vote against holding an election. They calculated that even their shrillest opponents on the back benches would not be so foolish as to throw themselves under a train that had already left the station. As one LOTO aide put it: 'If an election is coming anyway, to vote against it is absurd.'

Wading in to support Brown, Starmer reverted to type. He attempted to quash the case for an October poll with the force of the law. To set the date in law as Milne and others wanted, he argued, would be to risk leaving the nation high and dry. Starmer argued that fixing the date of the election in legislation was a mistake. If terrorists or natural disaster struck on the eve of the poll, then he claimed there would be no legal recourse to change the date. In the event the election could not happen, the country would endure a no-deal Brexit.

To Milne and Chakrabarti, his line of attack was 'complete legal bullshit': they believed they could draft legislation that would allow polling day to be delayed in case of emergency. Said one attendee: 'He concluded that he didn't want one, but then produced the legal argument to then justify his prior conclusion.' Caught between both stools, Corbyn sided with the status quo.

The divisions between the two camps played out in public at a testy meeting of the PLP that evening, the first since recess. There Corbyn told MPs, to snorts of derision: 'We are ready for a general election, we are ready to take on this government, and win a general election.' In a public show of solidarity with his nervous flock, Brown disagreed. He told the room that he was instead minded to let the prime minister 'stew in his own juices' and take responsibility for a parliamentary mess of his own making.

But the effect of a prolonged delay on Labour would be similarly uncomfortable. McDonnell blamed Labour's internal divisions on Boris Johnson on the following morning's *Today* programme: 'The problem that we have got is that we cannot at the moment have any confidence in Boris Johnson abiding by any commitment or deal that we could construct ... That's the truth of it. So, we are now consulting about whether it's better to go long, therefore, rather than to go short.'

The strongest argument for abolishing Watson came not from LOTO but himself. As Corbyn pushed for an election, his deputy was pushing the limits of Labour's Brexit policy beyond the realms of political possibility. On Tuesday 10 September he briefed the contents of another speech to be delivered the following day to the Creative Industries Federation.

It was billed as a reflection on the future of Britain's creative sector. But, straying again from his brief, Watson instead attempted to determine the future of the Labour Party. He would argue that the party must not only campaign for Remain, but back a second referendum before a general election. It was a plan which would have unravelled the conference position which Keir Starmer had delicately negotiated a year before and, with it, Corbyn's ability to ride two horses at once.

LOTO's reaction followed the familiar pattern that had played out in June. Minutes before noon, when Watson was due to speak, Murphy sent a curt text to Alicia Kennedy. The pair had forged a genuine and enduring friendship while working in Watson's office and so Murphy would address her with an almost aggressive candour.

'Alicia, need to speak urgently. That speech can't go ahead. Please call me.' Kennedy ignored her. Murphy followed up with a carbon copy of a text she had sent to Watson. 'Tom, Jeremy wants your speech today pulled. Please confirm that you'll do this. Thanks, Karie.' Playing for time, Kennedy replied: 'Hi, I spoke to him and he said he was in direct contact with Jeremy.' Watson and Corbyn were engaged in negotiations on WhatsApp.

Murphy responded by phoning repeatedly, to no avail. She texted Kennedy again at 11.50 a.m. 'Jeremy has asked me to tell him. Yes there's been a WhatsApp exchange, but I've been asked to contact him. I've contacted you both. To be clear, JC wants the speech pulled.' Murphy could not understand Watson's behaviour. She had made clear to Kennedy and Watson that a reshuffle was unlikely to be forthcoming. Why, with his Shadow Cabinet brief secure, was he pursuing a scorched-earth policy now?

The speech went ahead regardless. Opening with a quote from Conrad's *Heart of Darkness*, he took a sledgehammer to Corbyn's conference position. 'Boris Johnson has already conceded that the Brexit crisis can only be solved by the British people. But the only way to break the Brexit deadlock once and for all is a public vote in a referendum.' While Watson did not explicitly say that a public vote should happen before an election, Kennedy had briefed the press beforehand to explain that that was the implication. For good measure, Watson stressed that if an election did take place, Labour's position should be unambiguous. 'There is no such thing as a good Brexit deal, which is why I believe we should advocate for Remain.'

It was only after he finished that Kennedy engaged properly with Murphy. She texted in reply: 'You first called when he was already at the lectern. Tom said the speech was his personal view about how to break the Brexit crisis and deliver a Labour government led by JC. He said that if Labour can have a clear run in the election on our popular social platform we will win. He didn't say anything negative about JC at all, and the media is twisting it.'

'He has just delivered a speech in contradiction of our policy,' Murphy shot back. Corbyn was similarly furious. He texted Watson to convey that 'nobody in the Shadow Cabinet could make a speech like that', according to one aide who was with him in the aftermath.

Kennedy composed a rant in response. She spoke not just for Watson but channelled the anxieties of much of the PLP. 'Policy is to break deadlock with general election or People's Vote. We just voted against a general election. We will not win a general election if it's a referendum on Brexit. We need to neutralise the Brexit issue. The polls are clear. The Lib Dems will squeeze us in the South and Scotland, and the Tories in the North. We will be fucked. We want the same thing – a Labour government. If the Brexit issue is done, Labour will win the election.'

Some hours passed before Kennedy heard back from Murphy, whose next message was full of foreboding. 'Can you ask Tom to take a call from Jeremy? Jeremy made it clear that he did not want this speech to be made, and now he wants to address this. The call is planned for 7 p.m. You can call back if there's an issue.' By the time the text had been sent, Murphy and Jackson had sketched out another plan for replacing Watson: with Nick Thomas-Symonds, the former *Coronation Street* actress Tracy Brabin, or David Lammy. All that was needed was for Corbyn to pick his preferred option and make the call to Watson. It would not prove to be so simple.

Suspecting plans were in train to sack him, Kennedy informed Watson. He was unavailable for crisis talks with Corbyn not on account of having gone to ground deliberately, as was his wont, but because he was sat in a marquee listening to a speech by Pakistan's High Commissioner to the UK. Watson sent a text to Corbyn accounting for his whereabouts. He suggested they speak instead at 9.30 p.m.

For all of Murphy's tough talk, Corbyn was content not to speak. In reply he told Watson not to worry and asked for his best wishes to be conveyed to the High Commissioner. It looked to Watson like classic Murphy megalomania. Yet it had not always been Corbyn's intention to end the evening so cordially.

Watson's Remainia would save rather than condemn him. As Murphy and Kennedy litigated the contents of the speech, a more significant discussion on Brexit policy was underway at Islington Town Hall. There Fisher, Corbyn, McDonnell, Starmer and Jackson had gathered to determine the Brexit policy the party would take into an election. McDonnell had kept the circle tight.

Knowing he had to make a decision, Corbyn sought McDonnell's counsel on Watson. According to one source present: 'John persuaded Jeremy not to do it. He asked John what he thought, and John persuaded him not to.' To others in the room McDonnell's logic was transparent. Though much diminished in physical and political stature, the deputy leader was still an important source of ballast for the Remainers.

Fisher chaired the meeting. That he was as unhappy as McDonnell with the party's stance was no secret. In early July the unions had finally agreed a position among themselves: Corbyn, once in government, would negotiate a new Brexit deal with Europe and then put it to a referendum. Fisher doubted their wisdom. For one, Starmer, McDonnell and others in the Shadow Cabinet had already pledged to support Remain. It would also gobble up Civil Service bandwidth in the first weeks of a Labour government that had grand designs on reconfiguring the British state and economy.

In his memo to the August awayday, Fisher had written: 'There are drawbacks to this approach: firstly, it would mean the first socialist government since 1945 spending huge time and resources renegotiating a deal with Europe, and then trying to get it approved in the Commons – and then fighting a referendum in which most of our movement would effectively campaign against.' He instead suggested turning the policy on its head by holding a referendum immediately. 'That could be framed as the uncertainty of the Tories bungled Brexit and internal war and damaged industry, so now we need clarity: are we staying or are we having a sensible Labour Brexit?' Corbyn would remain neutral, with his Cabinet and MPs enjoying a free vote.

By now the question was even more pressing. With conference looming and an election bound to follow, LOTO needed a settled position to take to party and country. That Labour's Brexit policy was so ambiguous as to be totally inscrutable was a common if lazy joke in Westminster. It turned out to be true. Fisher came to Islington Town Hall armed with polling that showed nobody – not one person – had been able to say they knew about Labour's alternative Brexit plan in focus groups. His thinking on a solution had shifted since their last meeting. His solution was not for Labour to go all out on Remain, as Watson was advocating. Instead it would negotiate its own deal. Corbyn would play Wilson: the government would take a stance once its deal was secured, but Cabinet ministers would be free to campaign either way.

Starmer, who had spent much of the discussion vigorously insisting that a Labour government could not stay neutral in a referendum, dropped the point half an hour in. He was palpably relieved to learn that he would be able to campaign in his own capacity under Fisher's policy, which eventually went before conference, and so said little more. The supreme irony was that they would have allowed Watson to make as many dewy-eyed speeches about Europe as he liked. But LOTO's other big plan for its weekend in Brighton would put a stop to that.

Murphy was in Dublin when she received what to her mind was confirmation that the plan to assassinate Watson was to go ahead. On Wednesday the 18th, Corbyn called. He had heard from an old Republican comrade that Murphy had spent the previous evening with Mary Lou McDonald, the Sinn Fein president. The daughter of a Catholic Glasgow publican, Karie's own links to Irish nationalism ran as deep as Corbyn's: McDonald was a friend. Brexit had figured in their catch-up, but Murphy explained they had kept the chat light.

Having given no indication that the plan had changed, Corbyn excused himself and hung up. Later she phoned back, to no reply. Radio silence from Corbyn had become an increasingly common feature of life in LOTO.

On the afternoon of Friday the 20th, Jackson and Murphy took separate trains to Brighton. They had been in constant communication over strategy for that evening's NEC meeting, which was more than could be said for Corbyn. Jackson, travelling ahead of Murphy, got off and waited for her train. The left bloc on the NEC were looking to both for guidance that LOTO could not offer. They had been promised the opportunity to sack their tormentor-in-chief, yet Jackson suspected Corbyn was going soft.

After a hushed conclave on Murphy's train, they resolved to head straight to his hotel room to seek clarity on his intentions. Before they paid Corbyn their visit, Murphy texted McDonnell. The left bloc on the NEC, she told him, were on board. Watson's head remained on the block. 'FYI the Left unanimous re Watson,' she wrote. McDonnell replied neither in sorrow nor in anger, his two default moods, but with almost childish glee. 'Great. Hee, hee!'

It was teatime when Murphy and Jackson arrived in Corbyn's room in the Metropole hotel. They found him in more chipper form than he had been at any point that summer. Apologising to Corbyn's wife Laura for the intrusion, Murphy told Corbyn of the plan to do in Watson. The motion to abolish the deputy leadership would go before the NEC that evening. Everything was in place.

Corbyn reached for the handbrake. 'John doesn't think we should do it.' Murphy snapped. 'What does Jeremy Corbyn think?' He spoke in maybes. 'Look, Jeremy, for fuck's sake. It's an hour before the NEC.'

Groping for an alternative course of action, Corbyn revived Fisher's plan for a team of vice chairs to boost the number of women and ethnic minorities in his leadership team. 'Just leave it. I want three assistant chairs.' Jackson asked him to tell her explicitly whether he still wanted to sack Watson. He replied 'I want you to look at the other options.'

Murphy was incredulous. She told the leader of the Labour Party that watering down the plan at the eleventh hour would not work.

At his behest she nonetheless met the leaders of the left on the NEC: Lansman and Andi Fox, the TSSA union's rep. 'Jeremy's changed his mind,' Murphy told them. They made clear that they had not. 'That's a fucking joke,' one said. 'We've waited all our lives for this.' Only three days previously, the NEC had fulfilled the ambition of many a teenage Trot by voting to disaffiliate Labour Students, one of the last redoubts of organised Blairism. They were not going to forgo the opportunity to kneecap Watson.

Murphy and Jackson returned to Corbyn's room to inform him that it was too late to turn back. 'So what's going to happen?' he asked. With the NEC still set on approving Watson's exit strategy, Corbyn needed one of his own. He could not be seen to have given the hit his blessing. Jackson repeated a set of instructions twice, like a schoolteacher teaching by rote. 'When the time comes, I'll tap you, and we'll leave. You can then say to the camera: I wasn't in the room. I don't know what happened.'

Neither Watson nor most of the Corbynsceptics on the NEC had bothered to show up to the meeting, usually a formality that they could dial in to remotely anyway. Said one: 'Frankly, the Friday night meeting would take ten minutes. Why the fuck would you travel? You could do it on the phone.'

In their absence, Jon Lansman limbered up. He opened by asking that the NEC's standing orders, the rules that governed its proceedings, be suspended to allow for discussion of what he euphemistically described as 'urgent matters'. Jennie Formby and Thomas Gardiner advised Wendy Nichols, the plain-speaking UNISON official in the chair, that they could.

Alicia Kennedy, who deputised for Watson on the NEC, was running late. Her phone buzzed. It was Martha Dalton, sister of Watson's political secretary Jo Dalton. Kennedy told her to text. 'Lansman is going to propose a motion to get rid of the deputy leader, just had a call.' She informed Watson. Kennedy assumed the leak had ultimately come from Joe Bradley, the clubbable millennial Murphyite responsible for relations between LOTO, the unions and the NEC, who she then approached. 'Is this true?' she asked. 'I honestly don't know.' It was taken as a yes. Having prevailed on Bradley to help her set up WhatsApp on her iPad, Kennedy then set about corralling the Corbynsceptics to ride to Watson's rescue.

At 7.15 p.m. the moment arrived. Corbyn absented himself. On his way out of the ballroom, he stooped to whisper in Lansman's ear. He had come to offer thanks, rather than encouragement. Lansman had agreed to appear in a video Corbyn was due to film for the upcoming Jewish holiday of Rosh Hashanah. Lansman had been unsure of whether the leader himself, rather than his enforcers in Murphy and Jackson, had agreed to the plan. He took the thanks as benediction and took the floor to propose a debate on the deletion of Tom Watson. His punishment for his seditious speeches on Brexit, Lansman argued, would be the removal of the deputy leadership and any reference to the position from the party rulebook.

Momentum's press team sent a briefing note to journalists: 'No one person is more important than beating Boris Johnson, ending austerity and tackling the climate emergency. We just can't afford to go into an election with a deputy leader set on wrecking Labour's chances.' But one NEC member had wrecked the left's.

Wendy Nichols listened to Lansman's case before dismissing it. She insisted the motion was out of order. The man who had spent a lifetime studying the party's internal democracy had failed to reckon with the fact that his proposal was not on the agenda. He pushed it to a vote. To overturn the chair's decision a two-thirds supermajority was required. Twenty-eight NEC members were in the room. Eighteen of them were of the left. Diane Abbott and Rebecca Long-Bailey both voted to let the meeting adjudicate on deleting Watson. One of the left group, Claudia Webbe, had turned up after the meeting began, as was invariably the case at NEC meetings. Under the rules, she could not vote. The left fell one vote short of the two-thirds threshold. A senior LOTO aide complained: 'Claudia Webbe was fucking late. You couldn't make it up. One of the people who was pushing hardest for it, and she was late.'

Watson's stay of execution was not intended to last. After conferring with Murphy, Lansman immediately tabled an identical motion for the following morning's NEC meeting at 10 a.m. The absent Corbynsceptics busted a gut to make it on time. Nick Forbes, the leader of Newcastle City Council, boarded a train to London at 4.15 a.m. At Victoria he bumped into James Asser, and both took their places at the very front of the train to Brighton so that they could sprint to a taxi. They made it to the Metropole with time to spare, as did Islington councillor Alice Perry, who had packed her baby into her car and left London at 6 a.m.

They need not have bothered, for by 10 a.m. Watson was already safe. The backlash from the PLP had been predictably swift. Wes Streeting branded it 'outrageous' and 'self-destructive'. Jess Phillips melodramatically suggested it was a 'desperate attempt' to eradicate independent thought from the party altogether. The ghosts of conferences past returned to pour scorn on Lansman. Tony Blair, himself no stranger to an internal fix in service of ideology, enjoyed a brief visit to the moral high ground. 'The Labour Party has always contained different views within it and the deputy leader's position has been one way of accommodating such views. Getting rid of it would be a signal that such pluralism of views was coming to an end despite being cherished throughout Labour's history.' Ed Miliband fumed: 'Those who came up with the idea for the eve of Labour conference have taken leave of their senses.'

At midnight Kennedy had emailed Gordon Brown in the hope of adding his voice to the chorus on the following morning's *Today* programme. 'Jon Lansman just tried to abolish Tom,' she wrote. At 7 a.m. Brown growled down the phone from North Queensferry. 'What's going on? I'll phone Tom.' Watson himself appeared on the airwaves to accuse LOTO of attempting 'a drive-by shooting'. Just before 10 a.m. Brown came bearing good news. 'It's not going to happen. I spoke to John McDonnell. They're changing their mind.'

Corbyn had spent the evening far from the madding crowd he left in his wake upon leaving the NEC. Rather than deal with the fallout he had gone for a private dinner at an Indian restaurant with Laura and a friend from JVL, without notifying his aides or the police who shadowed him.

When the NEC did eventually meet the following morning, the proposition had changed. Lansman, who had taken considerable heat from Momentum's own executive for not consulting them before making his move, withdrew his proposal. Corbyn instead proposed a vague review of Watson's post with a view to increasing its accountability to the membership and better reflecting the party's diversity. 'We need to make sure the deputy leader role is properly accountable to the membership while also unifying the party at conference,'

Lansman tweeted. 'In my view, this review is absolutely the best way of doing that.' The reverse ferret was complete.

In public, Corbyn did his best impression of his usual self. Pursued by a scrum of reporters along the Promenade, he chirruped: 'Tom Watson is the elected deputy leader and I enjoy working with him!' On the question of whether he had known about the plot he had set in train two months previously he was elliptical to the point of incoherence: 'The NEC agreed this morning that we are going to consult on the future of diversifying the deputy leadership position to reflect the diversity of our society. And the conference will move on to defeating austerity, to the green industrial revolution, green new deal that we are putting forward and giving the people a final say on Brexit. Our NEC left this morning in a happy and united mood.'

In private, his rage dwarfed that of all his predecessors combined. After the firing squad failed on Friday night he was bundled into a taxi to an event. He rang a close friend and laid into an unnamed woman they could only assume was Murphy. 'I don't want to fucking see her, she better stay the fuck away from me.' The next day he told another LOTO aide that he was 'furious' with his chief of staff's decision to plough on with the plot in the face of his opposition. When Murphy's and Jackson's lobbying of the unions delivered victory for LOTO's favoured Brexit policy on the Monday of conference, he could not bring himself to thank either.

Murphy sought desperately to absolve herself of blame. She called Kennedy. 'It's nothing to do with me. It was all them, and I've got texts to prove it.'

'I don't care Karie,' Kennedy said. 'It is what it is, and now it isn't what it is, so we're just moving on.' To those within the Project who harboured doubts about Murphy, the coup's spectacular collapse meant it was time for her to be moved on too. Just before John McDonnell's speech on the Monday of conference, Seb Corbyn crossed paths with Bob Kerslake, the man who had created Karie, in the lobby of the Metropole. Seb suggested that his father and McDonnell wanted to meet Kerslake. The counter-revolution had begun.

For Watson, what remained of conference became a victory lap. The belated cancellation of his speech, due to the Supreme Court's ruling on the Tuesday of conference on Boris Johnson's proroguing of Parliament, meant that he did not get his chance to defy Corbyn and LOTO in full glare of the media, although its text did make its way to the autocue manager. 'Turning in on ourselves is a gift to the Tories,' it read. 'Voltaire said that "Discord is the great ill of mankind; and tolerance is the only remedy for it." And it's as simple as that ... We mustn't let tactics triumph over strategy; nor even strategy over ethics. Let's leave that to Johnson and Cummings. We succeed when we are bigger and broader and bolder.'

The peroration would have twisted the knife: 'I've thought about this every day for three years and I've come to understand that Brexit is not a tactical question. It's a matter of principle. For me, to leave the EU is to misunderstand and misrepresent the United Kingdom. We have to be in Europe because that's a central part of what Britain is now ... We can't be a party tainted by anti-Semitism. We can't, ever, let there be any doubt. But there is doubt. Because what matters, and what people judge us by, is not what we say but what we do.'

Yet Watson had already said all he had intended to the left that weekend. On Saturday Lansman was deep in conversation with a broadcast journalist when Watson walked by, enjoying his martyrdom in life. 'Ah, the failed assassin! I'm not fucking dead!'

13

Karie on Regardless

'Are the stories true? Is Karie a bully?' It was early June 2019 and Jeremy Corbyn looked defeated. Alone in his office, he had sought the counsel of a trusted confidant on the controversial management style of his chief of staff. The fallout from the anonymous letter on her conduct and the culture of harassment and bullying in LOTO submitted the previous December had a long half-life. Not only had it toxified life and electrified the ugly factionalism in Corbyn's office, but it appeared to have slowly poisoned Corbyn too.

'I know you've had some issues with her,' Corbyn asked his aide. 'But have you been bullied by her?' He wondered aloud whether it might be time to speak to staff and take his concerns to Jennie Formby, as John McDonnell and Diane Abbott had urged him to. 'Jeremy,' they replied. 'Karie can be really tough, really difficult, and dismissive. But Karie is not a bully.'

They cautioned Corbyn against action not out of any great sympathy for Murphy, but in knowledge of what would follow if he acquiesced. His chief of staff had become a totem for both sides of a divided Project. There were those, like McDonnell and Abbott, who believed Murphy and Milne not only stood in the way of sensible policy on Brexit, but were isolating and dominating their old comrade. Others, like Ian Lavery, believed her to be the last castle of working-class dignity inside LOTO.

To countenance sacking Murphy, for all the misgivings of staff against her, would be to force Corbyn to confront a civil war that he was ill-equipped to handle. So his confidant kept quiet. Others in LOTO, however, would not prove so demure or altruistically minded.

In late July, just after Parliament rose for its summer recess, Andrew Fisher met Kerslake for a coffee in King's Cross. As they parted, Fisher made a cryptic appeal. 'Jeremy's still keen to review how his office is working.' The subtext was obvious enough. There were problems with Milne and Murphy. A review by Kerslake might resolve it, just as the first – in the eyes of critics – had created the problem. It was suggested that Kerslake get in touch with Corbyn, which he duly did. No reply was forthcoming.

Fisher's irritation with the LOTO hierarchy was all too obvious to colleagues. On one occasion that summer, it is claimed that he had confronted Corbyn with a curious grievance. Why did only Seumas enjoy his veneration? Why did he call him The Great Milne? Why did nobody else get a nickname? Corbyn offered to bestow a nickname upon Fisher too. The exchange, denied by friends of Fisher, only deepened his humiliation.

But the dissatisfaction ran deeper. Fisher had been a Corbynite before the coin was termed. The economic thinking that underpinned the Project was to a large extent his. Yet as far as the press were concerned, Milne was the only aide in LOTO worth paying attention to. He admitted his annoyance with the media's lack of interest in his exploits to Milne, who said of the coverage: 'It's all bad. Why would you want that?' Soon newspapers would be taking a closer interest in Fisher than ever before.

On 14 September, Fisher took the first step towards airing LOTO's dirty linen in public. Having already written to Formby to serve her with notice of his resignation as Corbyn's head of policy, he wrote to a seventeen-strong WhatsApp group of senior LOTO staff to inform them of the news. 'I wanted to let you know that I have today written to Jennie Formby to resign,' he said.

There followed a ten-point polemic on a day in the life of Andrew Fisher as justification for his departure. It painted a grim picture of an office riven by dysfunction. He complained of speeches and policy announcements pulled without notice, and a conference still lacking in a slogan with a week to go before its launch: 'Tens of thousands of pounds have been spent on focus groups and polling for this and there is no end-product, just a blizzard of lies and excuses.' He pointed to confidential documents intended for Corbyn alone shared around the office and left for all to see on top of a printer, and of policies leaked to hostile newspapers like the *Telegraph*, which had scooped Corbyn's conference speech by revealing a Labour government would abolish Universal Credit, and *The Times*.

The most pointed complaints appeared to have been aimed squarely at Milne. Given the unease and irritation about the patrician languor with which LOTO's most senior public schoolboy went about his work, it did not require much by way of analytical ability to decode the intended target of the assertion: 'A member of another team complained to me that there is a "class divide" in their team.' Nor the subtext of a gripe about LOTO's approach to foreign policy: 'A tweet was drafted for Jeremy in light of the recent Russian bombing of hospitals in Idlib. The tweet condemned Syrian and US bombings in Syria (I kid you not).'

Having set out his wealth of evidence, Fisher moved to the summing-up. It was delivered with cold fury: 'None of these things individually would be enough to make me leave. All of them happening three or four years ago wouldn't have been enough to make me leave. All of them happening yesterday are not why I am leaving. But they are a snapshot of the lack of professionalism, competence and human decency which I am no longer willing to put up with daily. I've tried to resolve some of these issues for a long time, but have been unable to – and yesterday just proved that I never will.'

The ultimate conclusion was bleak. So grave were the failings Fisher observed in LOTO that even he had concluded that Corbyn could no longer win an election. 'As the sole surviving staff member from Jeremy's first leadership campaign, I think I've probably put as much into this project as anyone else. I leave proud of what we have collectively achieved, but I no longer have faith that we can succeed, although I do hope I'm wrong. In fact, please prove me wrong. I remain committed to winning a socialist Labour government with Jeremy Corbyn as prime minister.'

Signing off, he pledged to uphold the Project's *omertà*. 'I also want to assure everyone that I will not be seeking a huge pay-off (or any pay-off). I do not have another job and have not applied for any. I won't be briefing the press against anyone (never have, never will). I won't be writing a book about my time working for the Labour Party. And I am not sharing this message anywhere else or with anyone else.'

Recipients of the message attest to a state of secrecy and denial in the hours after it landed. One LOTO official said: 'John Mac was arranging conference calls, and by the next day Jeremy and John were talking with Andrew as if nothing had happened.' In the days after his resignation, the senior management team convened crisis talks in an attempt to persuade him to stay. 'He wouldn't budge.' Three days later, Fisher returned to the WhatsApp group with an additional plea: 'Sorry to raise this, but out of courtesy to Jeremy and you all, I have not told my team that I have resigned. Please can you not tell your staff.' Murphy responded: 'My line on this would be it's utter bollocks.'

One of the group had already taken matters into their own hands. That same morning, they had invited Tim Shipman, the political editor of the *Sunday Times*, to a discreet rendezvous in St James's Park. Upon his arrival, Shipman was beckoned inside a branch of Costa Coffee. For a LOTO official to be seen consorting with him outside of the parliamentary estate would not only arouse suspicion but risk their career. Once safely concealed from public view, Shipman's source revealed their means and motive for leaking Fisher's resignation note. It was not to damage the quitter himself. Rather, they hoped to exact maximum damage on Milne, for whom much of Fisher's criticism had been intended. The choice of a hostile newspaper was quite deliberate. Only that way would it exact maximum damage.

By Saturday 21 September, the first night of conference proper, the Watson fiasco of the previous evening had driven most of LOTO to the dance floor of The World Transformed's conference party, a rave held beneath a strobe-lit tent in the incongruously quaint Regency surrounds of Brighton's Old Steine area. Fortified by cheap beer and soundtracked by pounding dance music, Corbyn's staff set about trying to forget the rolling embarrassment of the previous day. At 10 p.m., the ignominy would begin anew.

At 9.55 p.m., LOTO's phones began to light up. The *Sunday Times* had tweeted its front page. Even those who knew of Fisher's resignation were blindsided by the stark headline: '"Loser" Corbyn rocked as key aide walks out'. Beneath it, quoted selectively but accurately, was the note Fisher had WhatsApped to colleagues the previous week. The top line struck a body blow: 'Jeremy Corbyn's leadership of the Labour Party was plunged into fresh chaos last night as it emerged that one of his closest aides has resigned, saying Corbyn, 70, will not win the general election.'

Fisher had intended to tell the Project's junior servants that he was leaving for family reasons. The leak of the memo to the *Sunday Times* had put a bomb under that plan. The immediate reaction was one of disbelief. Initially, LOTO's senior management team did not confirm nor deny the veracity of the story. WhatsApp groups fell silent. Political advisers to the Shadow Cabinet, directly managed by Fisher, fretted. Both the story's dramatic content and the political sympathies of the outlet that had revealed it led at least some to believe it might be untrue. Even Owen Jones, the *Guardian* columnist, who knew Fisher from his days working for John McDonnell, appeared none the wiser. He asked one LOTO staffer: 'Do you know about this?'

Only a select few did. In the hours after Fisher's resignation Murphy texted LOTO staff to apologise for the manner in which they had discovered the news. She confirmed the story was true and assured them it was business as usual. But it did not have the desired effect. One member of Corbyn's staff present that evening said: 'After the Tom Watson thing, and then the Andrew Fisher thing – that's when it felt like things were unravelling.'

Only Marsha-Jane Thompson saw fit to speak to Fisher that evening. She headed to his hotel room where he sat alone, untroubled by the colleagues with whom he had now publicly cut ties. They were later joined by Owen Jones, and the trio shared a consolatory whisky. The next morning Corbyn, Milne and Fisher put on a united front. Together with Anjula Singh they travelled in full glare of photographers to the BBC's makeshift studio on the Promenade, where Corbyn underwent the customary conference grilling by Andrew Marr. The timing of the leak ensured that Fisher's future, or lack thereof, featured prominently. Corbyn suggested that Fisher had departed after tiring of his 'very stressful and full-on job'. While he would not be drawn on the grisly specifics of life in LOTO, he did – in a characteristically roundabout way – acknowledge that all was not well when pressed on Fisher's criticism of the 'blizzard of lies' that had blighted his work. 'I think he said that because he was extremely distressed at that point about whatever was going on in discussions within the office at that moment,' Corbyn said. That was certainly one way of putting it.

More distress was to come that evening, when LOTO staff gathered with Laura Alvarez, Corbyn's wife, for dinner. There the fissures between Murphy and Corbyn began to deepen.

Over the course of the dinner, wine was taken. Tense words had been exchanged between Alvarez and Marsha-Jane Thompson,

Corbyn's head of campaigns. The two knew each other well. Thompson, a former UNISON official, had been friends with Jeremy for the best part of two decades. Their association long predated his leadership: she had attended his birthday parties and summer gatherings in his garden. Two years later her voice had been decisive in convincing him to run for the leadership. Upon his victory she had become his most vocal online cheerleader. Among other things, she had invented the #JC4PM hashtag and JezWeCan slogan that studded the social media profiles of many an online Corbynite. The merchandise Corbyn's fans wore was of her design.

But in the eyes of some colleagues, Thompson had become too close – not only to LOTO's organs of decision-making, but to Murphy, into whose orbit of influence she had been drawn. That summer, Murphy had unilaterally decreed that Thompson would be welcomed into meetings of the LOTO senior management team – apparently without seeking Corbyn's approval. He would later claim to other aides that Murphy had overruled him when he objected. To those who had come to dislike or even distrust Murphy, the similarly pugnacious Thompson was a symbol of her mission creep.

Witnesses still dispute the cause of the conflagration, and the precise language Alvarez used to deliver her *coup de grâce*. One attendee recalled Alvarez 'having a pop' that Thompson, as a long-standing friend of the couple, found particularly wounding. 'Marsha finally blew and gave it right back to her.' The previous evening she herself had rowed with Corbyn, whose lax approach to timekeeping and failure to keep to diary commitments had at points threatened to derail LOTO's delicate plans for conference. That he was suffocated by his countless admirers did not help. On the night of Laura's clash with Thompson, the hotel in which they had dined shut down its bar and kitchen temporarily so 120 of its staff could have their picture taken with Corbyn. One aide likened him to a 'stroppy teenager'. When Thompson confronted Corbyn for an explanation of his behaviour, he accused her of siding with Murphy.

The row had reverberated into the following day. Alvarez had wanted Corbyn to skip the dinner and meet another associate, which Thompson and Murphy took as a further provocation. Over the course of their contretemps over dinner, she accused them of holding her husband hostage. She then uttered words whose explosive meaning would cause another altogether more significant argument. 'You don't deserve Jeremy,' witnesses recall her saying. 'He didn't even want to do this.' Thompson interpreted the words literally. To her ears, Corbyn's wife had told her that he did not want to be leader of the Labour Party – or prime minister.

Details of the exchange soon spread. Alarmed, one aide asked Corbyn whether the central claim was true. Why had Laura told his staff that he had never wanted the job? Corbyn consulted his wife, who then accused Thompson of lying. He insisted that he did want to be prime minister. According to multiple LOTO sources, Thompson was subsequently told to 'keep her distance, to minimise her engagement with Jeremy'. The Project, it seemed, was eating itself.

*

As Murphy's empire crumbled, Milne's own authority came under concerted challenge. He knew, as did his colleagues, that he had been the intended target of Fisher's ire. So too did Milne grasp that the leak was designed to precipitate his own departure. Identifying the likeliest source was not hard either. He suspected the hand of Niall Sookoo, the Irish-Caribbean former journalist whose low opinion of Milne was as immutable a feature of his character as his love of cricket. To colleagues in LOTO it was an open secret, largely because Sookoo did not care who knew.

Allies of Milne believed his briefings ran through that week's *Sunday Times* like the lettering in a stick of Brighton rock. Shipman's inside read carried anonymous briefings critical of Milne, as well as a section on the slogan Milne had devised for conference only a week before: 'People before privilege.' Sookoo had openly scoffed at the idea that an Old Wykehamist could pontificate along such lines. 'That proves irony is dead,' he told a meeting at Southside. The same form of words, attendees noted, now appeared in print. Sookoo had also moaned about the amount of time it had taken to sign off the strapline. Again, an anonymised version of the complaint had worked its way into Shipman's yarn.

Milne and friends saw the case for the prosecution as incontrovertible. It had to be Sookoo, knowingly or unknowingly. Said one LOTO aide: 'It doesn't mean that he necessarily leaked it or that he was accused of leaking it, but he was clearly involved in some way, whether directly or indirectly, whether consciously or unconsciously, because things that he said and information that he would have had got into the public domain.' James Schneider launched an investigation into the single suspect. He confronted Sookoo and 'instructed' him to provide a full account of his recent activities – and an explanation as to how his complaints had come to be reported in a newspaper that most LOTO aides would not read, let alone brief. The response was blunt. Sookoo told Schneider he could not instruct him to do anything, and certainly not to divulge details that might see a comrade lose their job.

Schneider would not let the matter lie. Several days later he emailed both Sookoo and Jennie Formby, telling the general secretary that the suspect would explain himself if she told him to. No response from either party was forthcoming. Formby, who *could* have instructed Sookoo to reveal himself, his allies or his ignorance, did not do so.

Allies of Murphy suspected another culprit. Despite his distaste for the right-wing press, John McDonnell, they thought, had been Shipman's source – or had at least directed them. After all, the leak had cast his protégé, Fisher, in a favourable light, and Milne in the worst possible. 'It smacked of a classic, Machiavellian John Mac move,' said one LOTO aide. For such an argument there is rather less evidence. But it does speak to the distrust and dislike in which the grandfather of the Project was by then held by its functionaries.

As the inquest into the leak began in earnest, Milne's Sunday morning went from bad to worse. Usually undemonstrative and unflappable in times of crisis, he became remote and irritable with colleagues. At 10.08 a.m., Corbyn had tweeted condemnation of an apparently anti-Semitic poster on prominent display at the entrance to the conference centre. Benjamin Netanyahu, piloting a warplane labelled 'THE LOBBY' and decorated with a Star of David, was caricatured firing missiles at a Palestinian-flag-adorned Corbyn. 'ANTI-SEMITE! ANTI-SEMITE! ANTI-SEMITE!' screamed the cartoon Bibi. The point, attested to by an accompanying caption, was to implore members to oppose the IHRA definition of anti-Semitism.

The tweet itself had been written and sent by Jack Bond, Corbyn's social media manager. On the face of it it seemed robust if unremarkable: 'I'm disgusted that this banner was displayed near our #Lab19 conference centre. We asked the police to remove it and I'm glad they did. This kind of anti-Semitic poison has no place whatsoever in our society.' Yet soon afterwards Bond received a call from an edgy Milne. Angered, he demanded to know why Bond had seen fit to put out such a message in Corbyn's name. To Bond, there was no debate to be had. His intention had been to show Corbyn as a decisive and disgusted leader when it came to flagrant anti-Semitism. For that reason he told Milne he had no reason to explain himself, and instead returned to nailing the running order for Corbyn's conference speech.

Milne instead took matters into his own hands. Overcoming his aversion to committing instructions to writing, he told LOTO colleagues on WhatsApp: 'From what I've been able to find out, jc did not see the cartoon this tweet was about – which has now led to a conflict with pro-Palestinian groups and Mondoweiss [an anti-Zionist news website] in the US, which originally published the cartoon. Please stick to the sign off protocol re tweets/lines about AS [anti-Semitism] and similar sensitive issues, which is that I need to see them before they go out.' Respect for his authority was in increasingly short supply.

A messy conference came to an abrupt end two days later. On the morning of Tuesday 24 September, the Supreme Court gathered to rule on the lawfulness of Boris Johnson's five-week prorogation of Parliament. A spider-shaped broach pinned to her dress, the mousy Baroness Brenda Hale, the court's president, upended the government's carefully laid plan to silence the Commons in the weeks leading up to Brexit. As she declared the suspension of Parliament 'null and void', Keir Starmer and his aides were huddled around a television in a lounge full of journalists. A collective intake of breath stilled the room. The court's ruling meant that the Commons had never been prorogued.

MPs returned to action the next day. Johnson goaded Corbyn once more into tabling a motion of no confidence and triggering an election. The bait went untaken. Together the opposition parties united to inflict a seventh straight defeat on the government the following day instead, refusing to allow Johnson a recess for Tory party conference. A week later they would meet to strategise on their next steps.

The judicial *deus ex machina* had two happy consequences for LOTO. The first was that it meant Tom Watson, due to speak the following day, would no longer be able to commit rhetorical arson from the conference stage. The second was that it shifted the media's unsympathetic eyes to Downing Street, and away from Brighton. When Corbyn took the stage to deliver his own rescheduled speech that afternoon, he stood before the political equivalent of an open goal. 'Tomorrow, Parliament will return. The government will be held to account for what it has done. Boris Johnson has been found to have misled the country. This unelected prime minister should now resign.'

In the audience were a handful of LOTO aides who, under an edict issued by Formby in advance of conference, had not been given their hotel rooms on the grounds that their services were not essential to the smooth running of conference. Later that evening, one of Murphy's assistants was assigned what was assumed to be an unoccupied room in the Metropole by LOTO aides Hannah Whitfield and Janet Thompson – the Shadow Cabinet having left in preparation for the resumption of hostilities at Westminster.

Only the occupant of the room, Jeremy Corbyn, had not left. He and Alvarez had gone for dinner with Carmel Nolan, a veteran of the 2015 leadership campaign who still served as their de facto bag carrier, ahead of their 11.45 p.m. train back to London. Nolan returned to their room to gather the couple's personal effects to find the assistant sound asleep in their bed. Incandescent, Nolan shouted: 'Who are you? How dare you be in Jeremy and Laura's bed.' The assistant snapped back. Nolan, he said, had no right to treat a junior member of staff so brutally. He told her to discuss it with Murphy if there was an issue. A passing David Prescott intervened to support him.

By the following morning, the Murphyites sharpened their knives in defence of their favoured son. Murphy prevailed on her junior to submit a formal letter of complaint to Corbyn about Nolan's conduct. One LOTO aide explained: 'An act against Karie's staff is an act against Karie. LOTO staff felt completely alienated from Jeremy due to situations like these.' Whitfield, Thompson and Prescott are said to have done the same.

Parliament returned the following morning, and with it Murphy to LOTO. Her first act was to seek a reconciliation with Corbyn, who had soured into silence in Brighton. She moved two chairs onto LOTO's veranda, overlooking the Thames, and sued for peace. Frustrated, she told Corbyn that the Watson fiasco had, at its root, been a failure of communication. If he had a problem, he should tell

her. It was her job, after all, to resolve them. Corbyn listened patiently.
He addressed her as Chuck and apologised. They embraced as friends.
Corbyn kissed Murphy on the cheek.

That evening, she left for a holiday in Spain. Corbyn had not told
her about his biggest problem. By the time she returned, her time as
his chief of staff would be over.

Two days later, on Friday 27 September, Kerslake received a text
from Seb Corbyn, following up on their brief conversation in the
lobby of the Metropole earlier that week. The next morning he travelled to Islington to meet McDonnell and Corbyn at Corbyn's constituency office. It was a secret summit, arranged entirely off diary.
Murphy's veto would have been swiftly wielded had details been
committed to text.

Upon Kerslake's arrival Corbyn offered to make him tea, which
he accepted. Apologies were extended for the use of an Arsenal mug.
Furnished with biscuits, Kerslake sat down to consider their request.
Still smarting from the Watson debacle, Corbyn and McDonnell told
him that they needed to move Murphy out of LOTO. They presented
Murphy as a rogue operator. Neither admitted to having known of
the plan. Both agreed that it would be best for Murphy to move to
Southside to take control of managing logistics for the election
campaign they all knew was coming sooner or later. The days of
her dictating Corbyn's political strategy and ignoring his will would
be over.

While the Watson episode had been the trigger, McDonnell had
long been unhappy with Murphy. He frequently told friends that she
was a negative influence on Corbyn, if not a blockage on the party
altogether when it came to Brexit. One confidant said: 'He felt they
were influencing Jeremy to unwind decisions that he had thought
were made on the issue of Europe and the referendum.'

The Great Milne's future was also on the agenda. Corbyn could
not countenance his departure. But both he and McDonnell expressed
doubts that were commonplace in LOTO and the Shadow Cabinet,
namely that the party's director of communications and strategy was
not much good at managing communications. For him they proposed
the opposite course of action. Milne would be moved closer to Corbyn
to provide the purely political counsel that Murphy would no longer
have free rein to dispense, or, indeed dispense at all.

Getting rid of Murphy remained the priority. Over the summer months it had become all too clear that to retain her in post was to risk another mutiny from staff. In July, the group of complainants whose concerns about LOTO's culture had been dismissed by Jennie Formby six months earlier had requested a private meeting with Corbyn to air their grievances about Murphy's conduct. He did not respond.

By August they had gone one further in drafting a formal collective grievance to submit to LOTO. It was to all intents and purposes a rehash of their December 2018 missive, but this time it cited specific examples of misconduct and named the culprits. Murphy was alleged to have 'repeatedly called out the dress code of young women in the office, and subjected women in the office to special meetings and pep talks'. Fisher had written and signed off the European election manifesto without even speaking to LOTO's heads of economic and international policy, both of whom were women. Milne, meanwhile, was criticised for not once acknowledging in any way the concerns of the original letter. In the complainants' telling, it all added up to an 'intimidating, hostile, degrading and humiliating environment for LOTO staff, with evidence also pointing to sex and race discrimination'.

Though the grievance was never submitted, McDonnell had been made aware of its existence. The undertow of negativity that so dogged Murphy convinced him that she needed to be gone within seven days. When he made the case for a speedy defenestration to Kerslake, Corbyn did not disagree. Together, they decided with Kerslake that they would meet Murphy the following week and serve her with notice that she would move to Southside. Then, McDonnell insisted, the truth and reconciliation commission would begin its work. With Corbyn's agreement, he asked Kerslake to carry out another of his short, sharp reviews into LOTO's internal structures. In 2016, the first had imposed Murphy to create order out of chaos. Her removal was the opening salvo of a campaign with the same objective.

It was agreed that Kerslake would attempt to interview every member of staff in the leader's office over the course of a week. His findings would inform the shape of the new regime. As they spoke, Corbyn's phone rang. Gordon Brown had called to offer his counsel on Brexit. Informed of Kerslake's presence, he was put on speakerphone and held forth as the three men listened.

Where Blair and Mandelson had worked to destroy the Project, Brown was by now reconciled to making it work – or at least mitigating its worst excesses. He had struck up something close to a friendship with McDonnell, the only man who had had the temerity to challenge his ascension to the premiership in 2007. Brown's old friends believed he had been bewitched by a politician far shrewder than he.

'Gordon went through this dalliance with McDonnell,' one New Labour grandee said. 'He didn't really have much time for Corbyn, but he played footsie with them. McDonnell is a much smoother operator. He'd have felt, on the Brexit stuff and a second referendum: "Bring these people along. Be canny about it."' The coup McDonnell was about to carry out within LOTO was an even greater feat of political cunning.

The acceptance that an election was inevitable among Corbyn's aides was matched only by the PLP's fierce resistance. On 30 September, after Jo Swinson revealed that opposition leaders had ruled out a vote of no confidence on the grounds that it could only make a no-deal Brexit more likely, Corbyn made his case for an election to MPs again. He found them united and, unusually, in a conciliatory mood. Most framed their opposition to an election as fealty to party policy. As HuffPost's Paul Waugh reported from the corridor outside Committee Room 14: 'Corbyn listened to the advice of the PLP but did not say he agreed with it. His position has been that he thinks an extension of Article 50 is a priority to stop a no-deal exit, followed quickly by a general election. Labour MPs said they strongly supported the new policy adopted at the party's annual conference, which is for a Labour government to guarantee a referendum on a credible Leave option and an option to remain in the EU.'

It gave LOTO much food for thought. In the SMT WhatsApp at 7.43 a.m. the following morning Andrew Fisher asked whether it was accurate. Both Milne and Jackson were struck by their apparent change in tone. 'Definitely something weird going on,' Jackson said. 'What was most unusual was their non conflictual/benign approach,' Milne added. With Fisher wary that the contagion might spread to the Shadow Cabinet, Jackson also warned: 'Emily [Thornberry] might raise it.' The PLP already had allies in Starmer, Brown, and increasingly McDonnell. If their view took hold around the Shadow Cabinet table, it would be rather more difficult to dismiss than if confined to the back benches.

Murphy was only three days into her Spanish break when Corbyn summoned her back to London. He told her an election was looming and that he needed her in LOTO. Nonplussed, she cut her holiday short. Upon her return to Parliament she learned from colleagues that she was to meet him for a full half-hour. For a moment, she was heartened. Finally functional communication might resume.

It was not until she sat down in Corbyn's office and John McDonnell emerged that Murphy realised why she was there. It was not a catch-up, but a summary execution. It fell to McDonnell to deliver the bad news. He told Murphy that he and Corbyn had agreed that she should go to Southside to run the looming election campaign.

'Things aren't great in here,' McDonnell said. 'The election's coming. I want you to run the election campaign.' Murphy flatly refused. 'No. I don't want to do it.' McDonnell insisted: Murphy was the only person who could make it work. They did not just want but *needed* her to do it.

'There's a reason I'm not doing it John,' Murphy said. 'The reason I'm not doing it is twofold. Firstly, you've carved out everybody who can make this election work. And secondly, the Brexit policy is going to fuck us and on that basis, I ain't taking the rap when we go down. I'm not doing it.'

Shellshocked, McDonnell paused. He reached for the button marked Kerslake. 'Well, I'll get Bob involved,' he said. 'I'll get Bob. I'll get Bob.' Those words were laced with menace. If Murphy would not agree to go, then Kerslake would impose a reorganisation upon her.

Corbyn intervened. 'Let me speak to Karie,' he told the Shadow Chancellor, who then left the room. McDonnell's argument with Murphy had taken place without the leader saying a word to his chief of staff. He had still not told her what he wanted.

With McDonnell gone, Murphy grabbed Corbyn by the hand. She pleaded with him to level with her. 'Look, comrade,' she told him. 'You know I love you. I want this Project to work. But if this isn't working for you, all you have to do is tell me. That's all you need to do – say: "I don't want you to be chief of staff." I'll find another role.'

'It's not about that,' Corbyn told her. 'I want you to speak to Bob.' She agreed to meet Kerslake the following day. As she made her way from Corbyn's office, she spied Amy Jackson at her desk. 'Stay there,' she told her. 'John Mac's doing me in.'

Murphy and Jackson both suspected the coup had nothing to do with LOTO's internal structures, but the politics of the Shadow Cabinet – especially when it came to Brexit. It was not just McDonnell who objected to Murphy's presence but Diane Abbott. Murphy, after painstaking negotiations with the unions, had thwarted both when conference voted against binding the party into campaigning for Remain in a second referendum. The SKWAWKBOX blog would later declare that the moment she had signed her own death warrant.

Abbott's grudge ran deeper. At the height of the 2017 campaign, after a disastrous radio interview in which she mistakenly argued that Labour's plan to recruit 10,000 new police officers would cost only £300,000, Murphy had been sent to Hackney by Corbyn to forcibly retire her from the election campaign and future media appearances. When asked by other LOTO aides why she had so frequently counselled Corbyn to sack Murphy in the car rides they shared home to north-east London, she is said to have said: 'Revenge.'

One Murphyite LOTO aide explained: 'Karie was the person who was trying to protect Jeremy's position, and protect him from being undermined ... I think he couldn't handle the shit any more, and John was there to swoop in and save it and say: don't worry Jeremy, I'll sort it out. But in John's mind, Karie was the biggest roadblock to getting us to adopt a public-vote position, or a more Remain position, and so John needed her out the way, and so did Diane.' That summer Corbyn's mental state appeared to be buckling under the pressure of Brexit.

Aides recall him turning up to meetings late and in states of defensive agitation. Murphyites in LOTO attributed his decline to the intense pressure being brought to bear by the Remainers in his court. 'They were putting so much pressure on him over Brexit, where would you end up if that was you in your position? Your most trusted people are trying to push you in a political direction, they're not supporting you any more, they're manipulating you.' In defenestrating Murphy he had pulled the emergency brake. It was the only way to make the pressure stop.

To Kerslake, who cast a bureaucrat's eye over the situation as well as a McDonnellite one, there was an organisational imperative at play too. As well as serving as Corbyn's chief of staff, primary political adviser and office manager, Murphy was effectively running the entire Labour Party with no heed for the well-being of her subordinates. In his eyes, she had overreached. It was time to redress the balance. He met Murphy the following morning. She insisted that she had not been responsible for the botched coup against Watson and instead blamed Lansman for refusing to budge when she attempted to call the attack off at the eleventh hour. It did not wash with a sceptical Kerslake.

As McDonnell launched his own bid for control of the Labour Party and its direction of travel on Brexit, his enemies in the Shadow Cabinet began the rearguard. As Murphy left LOTO after her meeting with Kerslake she called Ian Lavery. 'I'm being sacked,' she said. Lavery panicked. He and McDonnell did not agree on much when it came to Brexit, but on the question of Karie they were agreed: she was the only thing stopping the lurch to Remain. The outcome McDonnell wanted was the one Lavery feared.

As soon as Lavery had finished speaking to Murphy he called Jon Trickett, his 'blood brother' in the Shadow Cabinet and closest comrade in the resistance to a referendum. 'We've got to go and see Karie,' he said. Trickett had always been wary of the amount of executive power concentrated in Murphy's hands but agreed to take up arms. Together they headed to Southside, where Corbyn was ensconced in a second-floor meeting room with Milne.

They entered all guns blazing. 'This is ridiculous,' Trickett told Corbyn. 'We're just about to enter an election period. For God's sake, don't get rid of her.' It was a heated exchange but by its end Trickett and Lavery convinced themselves that they had convinced Corbyn, who left the room to speak to Murphy. Lavery turned to Trickett. 'I think it's gonna be OK,' he said. Yet there had been another characteristic failure of communication on Corbyn's part. Trickett and Lavery went on their way believing, as so many of those who engaged the leader in conversation did, that he had agreed with them. Murphy was still doomed.

That Murphy's fate was already sealed was confirmed by Corbyn's social engagements that evening. After leaving Parliament he met with Laura and Jack Bond, LOTO's social media guru, at the Lyric Theatre on Shaftesbury Avenue in the West End to watch *An Amazon Stept*

Out, a play about the life and times of another forthright woman, the eighteenth-century feminist Mary Wollstonecraft.

It was a family affair. Joining them were Bond's parents: his father Pete, a retired taxi driver, and his mother Helene Reardon-Bond, a child of a Camden council estate who had risen to the head of the government's Equalities Office. With Kerslake having turned down another offer to run LOTO, Corbyn turned to Reardon-Bond.

Those familiar with the negotiations say that her new role was not explicitly discussed that evening. But it was not long before Kerslake, on Corbyn's behalf, had visited her at home in Kentish Town to formally ask her to apply for the position. Reardon-Bond was reluctant at first. A source familiar with their discussions recalled: 'Initially she thought: "Well, why would I, having happily stepped down from full-time employment, do this?" But I think she was persuaded it would be worth a go, and the following week did agree to do it.'

On 3 October, Murphy and Kerslake met for tea in the Commons. Kerslake told her flatly that she had lost the leader's confidence. It was a moment of revelation for both parties. Murphy told Kerslake that neither Corbyn nor McDonnell had put the proposition to her so starkly. 'Be in no doubt that Jeremy wants you to move,' Kerslake said. Corbyn's aversion to confrontation had failed the Project again.

Until their bilateral Murphy's reluctance to go had posed a serious dilemma to Corbyn and his court. If she did not move of her own accord, then Kerslake and McDonnell believed that she would have to be put on gardening leave. Other trusted confidants of Corbyn were alarmed by what they saw as the unseemly abruptness of the process. One Shadow Cabinet minister said: 'I don't know what he was up to, but the idea that he should be speaking to Karie without speaking to her boss, Jennie Formby . . . and he was briefing the media, which was outrageous, really outrageous.'

By Sunday 6 October, Murphy had nonetheless surrendered. She communicated to Kerslake that she would make the move to Southside as proposed, as long as she could bring her coterie of supporters from LOTO with her. He convened a conference call with both Corbyns, Jeremy and Seb, as well as McDonnell, so they could inform Murphy of the terms of her departure together. A letter formalising the arrangement would follow. Yet the call did not happen. Murphy claimed to have left her phone in Glasgow and was thus unreachable. It fell to Jackson to suggest an unappealing alternative: ringing Murphy's close friend Len McCluskey. He and McDonnell had already rowed over the situation in a testing meeting at Unite's offices that week. The offer was politely declined. A new week began with no certainty.

Murphy sought comfort from old friends. That same Sunday, she received a text from Alicia Kennedy. Despite the bloodletting at conference, her words were warm. 'Hello. If you need anything – help or something more personal because this is shit – you can give me a call.'

Murphy replied: 'Thanks love, that's kind. I'm all ok, tell Watson to tweet something nice about me.'

'I'll give it a go,' Kennedy said. 'But I wouldn't hold out much hope.' Unsurprisingly, no show of solidarity was forthcoming.

That weekend, in an uncharacteristic show of vulnerability, Murphy also rang Corbyn. She insisted that the coup had only happened because he had allowed it to. 'I am absolutely mortified that this happened,' he told her. 'I'm so sorry.' She refused to accept his apology. Abandoned by a second Labour leader in succession, Murphy would have to stand alone.

The next day, Monday the 7th, saw the terms of the armistice agreed and announced. Corbyn and Kerslake met in LOTO at 10 a.m. before heading to Southside to meet with Murphy, McDonnell and Jennie Formby. It was then that Murphy's transfer to HQ – and that of her chosen disciples – was finally sealed. She did not take it as a demotion, rather a chance to set up a government in exile. To those in LOTO who had feared and complained about her, it would be a moment of liberation.

Formby stood four-square behind Murphy. Both were incredulous that McDonnell was attempting such a fundamental reorganisation of LOTO so close to the biggest and most important campaign the Project would ever face. 'Why make these changes now?' asked Formby. 'We're going to have an election.' One attendee said: 'Jennie was 100 per cent with Karie. She said she'd been hard done to. In the face of that, Jeremy agreed to the staff moving. I won't put it kindly: he caved in, really.' Formby offered a particularly pointed gesture of solidarity with Murphy in an email to Corbyn after their meeting. She reiterated that Murphy would retain the blue-riband title of chief of staff, and heavily implied that she would have a right of return after the election. She added: 'Jeremy and Karie will meet the LOTO staff jointly at 5 p.m. tonight to brief them to ensure that these important changes are not spun negatively in the media.'

When staff filed into LOTO's boardroom for the impromptu meeting, they found Corbyn and Murphy stood before them. It was immediately obvious to those who knew her that Murphy had been crying, a vulnerability she had revealed to few present. Corbyn, speaking with what witnesses described as a 'controlled anger', read the news from his notebook: 'Karie, very kindly, has agreed to move to Southside.' Almost everyone in the room knew the reality: she had been ousted by force. Rumours that Murphy would be sacked had been circulating for the best part of a week, since her original meetings with Corbyn and Kerslake.

That relations between the two had collapsed was obvious to all present. Murphy strained to keep up appearances. Despite the spirited resistance she had put up to moving, she attempted to spin the move as one made by mutual consent. Yet she and Corbyn spoke over one another repeatedly. One staffer said: 'He actually wasn't really letting her speak. She was actually really trying to make out like they had come to this decision together, and that they were a unified force. It was the first time I've ever seen Jeremy look quite vindictive in what he was saying.' Another LOTO aide described it as: 'The most absurd thing I think I've ever seen. It started off with a couple of sentences about Karie moving and then a few paragraphs about the new role and then a few more paragraphs about Jeremy rambling about preparing for a general election.' The palpable tension was briefly punctured when a member of Corbyn's correspondence team intervened to ask when the suspended selection for the parliamentary candidacy in Ilford South would be reopened. Corbyn sighed. 'I can't believe people are asking me questions! Fine, he's asked me a question, I'm going to answer it. Obviously the Ilford South selection process will be opening very quickly, as with all the other seats we need to select.'

Many political operatives in the room took the performance as a provocation. They had been denied clarity on Andrew Fisher's departure and even now, with their boss losing her job before their very eyes, it seemed the preference of the LOTO hierarchy was to deny it once more. Said a junior LOTO aide: 'We were very pissed off because we felt nobody was telling anyone anything. They couldn't tell us the truth.' Proceedings boiled over into open mutiny when Corbyn revealed that Kerslake would carry out a review of the office's staffing and structure.

The usually placid Joe Bradley, LOTO's head of NEC and trade union relations, rose to demand a guarantee that nobody present would lose their job. He extracted a commitment that staff would be allowed union representation in any meetings with Kerslake. That a close ally of Murphy was asking such a pointed question was not lost on others present. Another LOTO staffer said: 'It seemed like a planted question as he wasn't one to usually speak in team meetings. Jeremy was taken aback but assured everyone it wouldn't happen. The office was very awkward. The view was that Jeremy was wrong. That John was wrong. Ninety-nine per cent of the loyalty went to Karie and thus the office split.'

Kerslake had indeed reorganised LOTO, but not in the constructive manner he had intended. It soon became known that Murphy would be evacuating her closest associates to Southside, which only heightened the distrust. One LOTO aide who had been close to Murphy but did not make the cut said: 'I lost half of my colleagues, and then the ones that were left wondered: why wasn't I asked to go? Does she not think I'm good at my job? It created a really difficult atmosphere.'

News of the coup reached the public domain the next morning. At 10.31 a.m., PoliticsHome's Kevin Schofield, the best-connected journalist to the Corbynsceptic camp, tweeted news that delighted the PLP: 'Big news in Labour land. I'm told Karie Murphy has effectively been sacked as Jeremy Corbyn's chief of staff, with political secretary Amy Jackson and trade union fixer Joe Bradley also gone. Murphy will go to HQ as head of digital – a "non job", according to one source.' One MP told the *Financial Times* that they had greeted the news by singing 'Oh, What A Beautiful Morning!'

The official line briefed to the papers from the Southside press office made a valiant attempt to spin that there was nothing to see here. 'As we ramp up campaigning ahead of a general election, we are maximising the use of the resources we have to ensure we are successful. Karie will drive this crucial work from HQ, as she did during the last election.' There was no fooling the lobby, however. Reporters immediately chalked up the move as a victory not only for McDonnell and Abbott, but the Remain cause. 'She and Milne were regarded as brakes on the party's gradual shift towards advocating a second Brexit referendum,' said the *Guardian*.

To her allies, however, the struggle was not yet over. Their objective was to put the brakes on Kerslake. Two days after the media learned of Murphy's sacking, her replacement in Reardon-Bond – billed as Corbyn's head of office, rather than his chief of staff – arrived fully formed in LOTO. She was immediately met with hostility. Though Reardon-Bond had grown up on a council estate, she was derided as a well-heeled civil servant and one of Corbyn's 'North London friends'. In her first meeting with one Murphyite, she asked: 'How are you? Because I know you must be feeling like a child in a custody battle.' They retorted that Corbyn was not her father and nor was Murphy her mother. It soon became clear on whose authority she was operating. After Corbyn and Reardon-Bond convened staff in LOTO for an informal meeting, an email was circulated by Joseph Perry, the party's head of HR. 'The leader of the opposition and the Shadow Chancellor have asked that a short review take place of management structures in LOTO and that some staff would be asked to contribute through informal meetings.' Those who suspected a power grab by McDonnell had every reason to believe their intuition had not failed them.

That was certainly the case enthusiastically briefed by Murphy's supporters. On 8 October SKWAWKBOX had blamed McDonnell's lust for power for the ructions inside LOTO. Its typically punchy headline screamed: 'EXCLUSIVE: SENIOR LABOUR INSIDERS ACCUSE MCDONNELL OF TRYING TO TAKE CONTROL OF CORBYN.' An unnamed supporter of Murphy poured scorn on the Shadow Chancellor: 'Karie Murphy was Jeremy Corbyn's firewall. She absorbed key attacks on him & carried out the ugly jobs dutifully. She shovelled the s**t everyone else was either too timid and/or too self-interested to touch. There are only two potential reasons for wanting to connive to remove her. First, so they can isolate and destroy Jeremy. Second, so they can control him. We won't have long to wait to discover which of those motivations were behind this redeployment.'

By then a test of Corbyn's appeal to the electorate, with Murphy at the helm of the campaign, looked inevitable. In briefings to journalists on the same day, Downing Street suggested that it saw little prospect of an agreement with the EU. That drastic action might soon have to be taken to prevent the government forcing through a no-deal Brexit was increasingly obvious. Tony Blair weighed in to argue that it should not come in the shape of an election. To fight one before a referendum, he said, would amount to a 'vast elephant trap of great width and depth, with neon signs flashing around it saying: "Elephant trap – elephants of limited awareness please fall in." They should avoid that ... '

All the while Westminster hurtled closer and closer to the Benn Act's deadline on 19 October, and with it Johnson's ultimate reckoning on delaying Brexit. On 9 October the prime minister announced he would summon MPs to sit on deadline day, a Saturday. The following day came the breakthrough that never looked possible. After a day of talks at Thornton Manor, a luxury hotel on the Wirral, over the Mersey from Liverpool, Johnson and Varadkar announced that a 'pathway' to a deal existed. The seriousness of the occasion was underlined by the fact that perennial scruff Dominic Cummings had suited up for the proceedings. While Labour's two schools of opinion on an election had fought in the belief that Johnson would either call an election with Brexit unresolved or that Parliament would first resolve it by securing a second referendum, a terrifying third scenario – that a deal might be within the government's reach – was beginning to emerge.

As the two leaders discussed the contours of a deal, Corbyn was delivering Labour's 'alternative Queen's Speech' in Northampton, both a pre-emptive response to the real thing, due to take place four days later, and a dress rehearsal for the campaign to come. That an election was inevitable was increasingly taken as writ on Whitehall: that morning Johnson had authorised talks between Labour and the civil service on their plans for government.

As the PM and Taoiseach negotiated the basis for the deal that would finally deliver the UK's departure from the EU, Corbyn offered an unwitting echo of the Tory slogan that would define the coming months: 'The first task of a Labour government will be to finally get Brexit sorted.' Striking a utopian note, he also road-tested the tagline that would accompany Labour's own campaign: 'The future is within our grasp. Together we can build a country fit for the next generation. The future is ours to make. *It's time for real change.*' As soon as he left

Northampton he was itching to avoid Westminster, and go to the annual conference of the Party of European Socialists. That night at 11.07 p.m. Marsha-Jane Thomspon wrote to SMT colleagues on WhatsApp: 'JC said he wants to go to Brussels.'

As ever at times of crisis, Corbyn felt himself impelled to escape. The peaceable demeanour that usually governed his behaviour when the Project was under maximum pressure vanished once more. So recalled a senior LOTO aide: 'He's a very nice guy to work for, and very easy-going, and quite Zen-like in those sorts of situations ... That was less true in the autumn and the run-up to the general election and during the general election. He was under more stress. It was a very stressful situation.'

In the absence of a leader willing to do so himself, Shadow Cabinet ministers jostled to set the tone on Brexit. LOTO in response ran an active campaign to keep Remainers off the airwaves. On 11 October, Amy Jackson intervened to keep Emily Thornberry off Radio 5 Live's *Pienaar's Politics*. 'Emily T has agreed not to do pienaar,' she wrote in the SMT WhatsApp. Danielle Rowley, a leadership loyalist, was instead dispatched to hold the line on the question of whether Labour could vote for a Johnson deal.

John McDonnell was beyond silencing. The same day he enjoyed more than an hour's chummy repartee with Alastair Campbell for the benefit of readers of *GQ*. Corbyn was furious: neither the intervention nor its contents had been signed off by him or anyone in LOTO. As well as throwing red meat to Remainers by calling for his interviewer's reinstatement to Labour membership, McDonnell stated unambiguously that he and Corbyn would resign in the event they lost a forthcoming election. He then hinted that he might be willing to tear up party policy on the order in which a referendum and election would come. 'We've said up until now that we want a general election. That, of course, is what our objective is, but let's see what actually Parliament will wear in the end ... Within Parliament itself there is a large number of people who are saying we'd rather have a referendum attached to any deal.'

Not everyone had accepted that an election was inevitable. In LOTO, Karie's supporters launched an energetic bid to undermine Kerslake and save their patron, who had been at pains to stress his review was not a formal process. Murphyites had smelt a rat. They believed the process had been fixed to discredit Murphy and her followers once and for all. 'I'm sure that this was just an oversight but I'm worried about this causing unnecessary suspicion,' Joe Bradley wrote to Joseph Perry on 11 October, complaining that the review had already interviewed aides without their trade union representatives present. 'I'd be much more comfortable if the interviews could be organised through our union, do you think that's possible, to give people a little bit more confidence in the process and make sure that they are arranging times that the reps are available?'

One member of staff who did not struggle for union representation was Murphy herself. When she was interviewed by Kerslake on 15 October she came flanked by Howard Beckett, Unite's leading lawyer. For the best part of an hour, he made explicit – and furiously – the case that disgruntled staff had been hinting at: that the entire process was biased against Murphy.

As life began under the new regime, her followers reached the same conclusion. Banished to Southside and isolated from the levers of executive power in LOTO, there was little meaningful action the Murphyites could take to reclaim the initiative from McDonnell and his supporters. One noted with grim amusement that Kerslake's assistant had conducted interviews off-site at 4 Millbank wearing an EU flag bracelet, as if to teasingly confirm the worst suspicions LOTO staff had about the purpose and motivations of the review.

Murphy herself made her displeasure clear to McDonnell, who had made grateful entreaties to her after her move. He told Murphy that he had never briefed against her to the press. 'John,' Murphy replied, 'I would love to believe that. But I don't believe a fucking word out of you. But nonetheless, I'll do anything you want me to do, and I'll do it.'

Yet McDonnell appeared to be in no mood to ask Murphy and her team to do anything. Jackson, though still in possession of her title and status as Corbyn's political secretary, began to feel marginalised and undermined by Andrew Fisher, who in his final months in LOTO had finally assumed the authority he believed was his alone to claim. On 23 October she raised her grievances in a series of texts to McDonnell, which she shared with Corbyn and Reardon-Bond. Her message was met with inaction from all parties.

On Saturday 26 October, four weeks to the day since his first visit, Kerslake returned to Corbyn's constituency office in Islington. He came armed with a PowerPoint that collated the findings of his review. By then he had interviewed some 70 per cent of LOTO's staff. Its primary conclusion was that the office had been divided between those who adored Karie and those who feared her. Some staff in the latter category had to be practically coaxed into talking, such was the residual anxiety about retribution by Murphy.

Kerslake put it in buzzword-heavy euphemism. 'What is working well . . . strong and loyal support for the leader; high levels of commitment with staff prepared to go the extra mile; good examples of where the team has been able to respond quickly to an urgent issue; strengthened links between LOTO and Southside.' His 'areas for improvement' spoke to an office where power – and the keys to Corbyn's office – had been concentrated in too few hands: 'Management practices and working culture; decision-making, the communications function; political strategy and translating this into action.' Southside officials should be allowed 'more face time' with Corbyn. Junior staff should have more information. The head of Corbyn's office should 'not take on any additional party functions'. Tea-making and washing-up duties should be shared between aides. Staff should know the scope of their own roles and who exactly they answered to. Communications practices needed to be thoroughly reviewed. Clearer regulations on hiring, firing and pay were needed.

In short, it was a manifesto against Murphy the empire-builder and Milne the chillaxer. Yet Kerslake warned Corbyn that he needed time to implement it. Signing off, he echoed the anxieties of the PLP: 'If you can find a political way of not having a general election for a little while, you should do so. Because you really are not ready.'

Corbyn was already too far down that road to turn back. A Brexit deal had arrived on 17 October, when Johnson succeeded where May had so persistently failed. Months of warm words and solemn vows to the DUP evaporated, with Northern Ireland hived off into the EU's customs territory and regulatory orbit for at least four years after the end of the transition period. It was the very thing he had promised not to do. But in breaking his promises he had confounded the expectations of the Westminster commentariat and Remainers in Parliament. Most of their number had laboured under the assumption that agreement was impossible and a no-deal exit on 31 October inevitable. Johnson upended that calculus.

Michel Barnier announced the deal with an enticing promise – that it could be ratified in time to meet the prime minister's do-or-die deadline of Halloween. Donald Tusk left the door open for a further extension, but Johnson did not intend to use it. MPs formally agreed to their first Saturday sitting since the outbreak of the Falklands War. Though the DUP made their opposition clear, the government was set on its date with destiny.

It was at that moment that those set on exploiting the unique arithmetic of the 2017 parliament to ram through a second referendum knew the jig was up. Until the moment a deal was agreed, the strongest argument in their armoury had been the prospect of Johnson using an election to sneak through a no-deal Brexit by calling it so that 31 October would fall during the campaign. That had always been a check on Labour's rush towards voting for a snap poll. Most of the Conservative rebels opposed to no-deal took Johnson's return from Brussels as a return to sanity: no longer was their party leadership gambling with the likely economic catastrophe that was a no-deal Brexit. Their motivation to support a second referendum disappeared, and with it any route to a parliamentary majority.

Jo Swinson recalled: 'The pivotal moment, really, was Johnson getting the deal, because overnight – it didn't become clear for some days afterwards – the chance of getting a majority for a People's Vote just evaporated. The majority of Tory rebels then just suddenly fell back into line: you had your Greg Clarks, and your Oliver Letwins, and Ken Clarke. They always wanted there to be a deal ... I think it was enough of a cover for them.' Yet Letwin still worried about the prospect of a crash-out Brexit even after the deal had been approved and so cooked up another amendment, withholding Parliament's approval until such time that the legislation writing the new with-drawal agreement onto the statute book had been passed. In voting for it MPs would ensure Johnson missed the Benn Act's deadline and compel him to seek another extension. On the eve of the sitting, Labour and the other opposition parties gave it their support.

Come Super Saturday itself, a majority for the deal did look like it was about to materialise. Steve Baker and the 'Spartans' who held out against the deal three times finally relented. Yet a majority for Letwin was also forthcoming. The ten DUP MPs repaid Johnson in kind for his betrayal, ensuring the amendment passed by 322 votes to 306.

Johnson responded by cancelling the vote on the deal itself, and briefly played autocrat. 'We must get on, and get Brexit done on 31 October,' he boomed from the Dispatch Box. He insisted, despite the letter of the law, that he would 'not negotiate a delay with the EU, and neither does the law compel me to do so'.

By that night's 11 p.m. deadline, however, his words were shown up as bluster. Three letters were sent to Brussels, despite Johnson's claim that he would play no part in negotiating an extension: an unsigned photocopy of the request for an extension that the Benn Act obliged him to send; an accompanying letter from Tim Barrow, the UK's ambassador to the EU, explaining why Johnson did not mean it; and a signed letter from Johnson himself, clarifying that he really did not want an extension. That the EU27 would grant an extension was no foregone conclusion. Emmanuel Macron's advisers had made clear to Swinson that France, the most hawkish of the member states on a delay, would play ball only if the purpose of an extension was for a referendum or an election.

After the parliamentary action drew to a close, Jeremy Corbyn's oldest comrades made the short walk from the Commons chamber to Parliament Square to make their own preference clear. Together with Thornberry and Starmer, McDonnell and Abbott broke publicly from Corbyn and took to the stage at the packed Final Say rally for a second referendum. Their presence had the dense thicket of Remainers before them, EU flags fluttering high, singing a merciless parody of the tune that had soundtracked the 2017 campaign in its headiest days: 'Where's Jeremy Corbyn?' Alastair Campbell welcomed and choreographed the quartet from backstage. The Blairites' oldest adversaries were now their co-conspirators.

Abbott left them in no doubt as to where she was on the question of Europe. 'I'm a Remainer,' she told the crowd. Thornberry laid it on thick. 'We are internationalists, we are Europeans, and we want to stay that way ... Labour is a Remain party and later we will prove that this is a Remain country!' McDonnell, abandoning any pretence of abiding by the LOTO line, said: 'We believe that our future best lies within the European Union itself.' Starmer argued: 'When we get that vote, we need to fight for Remain.'

Away from Westminster, Shadow Cabinet ministers were greeted not as heroes for their part in staving off Brexit once more but as pariahs. On his return to his Greater Manchester constituency on Sunday, Andrew Gwynne was spat on in the street while out with his family.

On 24 October, Corbyn and Gwynne, along with Lavery, went to gee up the troops at Southside ahead of a snap poll that was now a question of when, not if. That afternoon Boris Johnson had laid down the gauntlet in a letter to Corbyn, having abandoned his pledge to deliver Brexit 'do or die' by 31 October. 'An election on 12 December will allow a new parliament and government to be in place by Christmas. If I win a majority in this election, we will then ratify the great new deal that I have negotiated, get Brexit done in January, and the country will move on.' In response, Corbyn pledged only to accede to the demand once no-deal had been ruled out. But with the EU all but certain to agree to an extension to the Article 50 period long enough to allow an election to take place, that his answer would soon be yes was inevitable.

The tone he struck at Southside was messianic: 'We are going to be in for the fight of our lives in a very short space of time. Maybe today, maybe next week, maybe even next year, I don't know exactly when that is going to happen or when it's going to happen. On our shoulders rests the hopes and the lives of millions of people that their lives will be better. And millions more people around the world.' Brexit, he insisted, did not daunt him as it did McDonnell. 'We're not a Leave party, we're not a Remain party, we're a socialist party who wants to bring people together. We are determined to push for a customs union and push for a credible relationship with Europe in the future in order to protect jobs and investment in this country and maintain that dynamic relationship on workers' rights and other rights. Our issue is to unite people around that vision of what the future of this country will be.'

He signed off with an eccentric flourish that belied the low moods that had dogged life in LOTO for months: 'I'm absolutely looking forward to this election campaign. I've been doing extra training for this election campaign, I'm eating more porridge every morning to make sure I can get through even longer days. But we're going to be out there on the road and across the whole country.'

Murphy spoke with almost unhinged optimism. She skirted around the unhappy genesis of her new role and embraced the opportunity.

'Jeremy has come across and asked me to come and run the general election with Ian Lavery, Andrew Gwynne and also with John Mac. Our campaign will be the most confident and ambitious election campaign that Labour has ever run. We'll take our message to every part of the country. There will be no no-go area or parts of the electorate. The aim of this campaign is to win that majority for a Labour government and we're in it to win it. To do that we'll be working to both consolidate what we did in 2017 but much more importantly to extend into areas and parts of the electorate that we need to win. So what's our message to the country? The message that will go out to the regions will be much broader than this, much more in-depth, but in essence today, the message we want to get out to you all as early as possible, is the future is ours to make, it's our time, it's time now, it's time for real change. The choice at this election could not be clearer.' Then came an unfortunate slip. 'We are divided to bring ... Sorry, we are determined to bring a divided country together.'

Going to the country without the deal approved was something the government was still determined to avoid. On 21 October, Jacob Rees-Mogg introduced the Withdrawal Agreement Bill to the Commons and made clear that ministers hoped to have it passed on a breakneck timetable of three days, so that they might still fulfil an exit by Halloween. Speaking in the Commons the following day, Corbyn dismissed the deal and with it the legislation as 'a charter for deregulation and a race to the bottom'. Though a clear majority of MPs voted to give the bill a third reading, the government's truncated schedule was defeated amid grumbles over insufficient time for scrutiny. Unclear as it was to some of those who trooped through the no lobby that afternoon, in playing for time they merely added another plank to Johnson's election platform. 'I must express my disappointment that the House has again voted for delay, rather than a timetable that would have guaranteed that the UK was in a position to leave the EU on 31 October with a deal,' Johnson said, with more than a hint of menace, after the timetable fell. With that he paused the legislation, effectively placing parliamentary democracy on ice.

Corbyn offered Labour's hand in cooperation: 'I make this offer to him tonight: work with us – all of us – to agree a reasonable timetable, and I suspect that this House will vote to debate, scrutinise and, I hope, amend the detail of this bill. That would be the sensible way forward, and that is the offer I make on behalf of the opposition tonight.' Yet behind the scenes the operation was not speaking with one voice. Between votes, with the uncertainty intensifying, the Shadow Cabinet held a series of impromptu meetings in its old meeting room behind the Speaker's chair. The rising stars of the left – Laura Pidcock, Richard Burgon and Dan Carden – harried their leader for an election, champing at the bit to go out and evangelise. Some suspected they had been put up to the task of 'bludgeoning' Corbyn into backing an election by Murphy. Said one Shadow Cabinet minister: 'The young Turks were insistent.'

Most of their colleagues, however, were resolutely opposed. Nick Brown, Starmer and Thornberry were among the most vocal opponents of going to the country. Sue Hayman, whose Cumbria seat of Workington would later become a totem for Tory ambitions of remaking the electoral map, described the idea as 'disastrous'. Corbyn was not yet willing to enforce a judgement one way or the other. 'This was the problem,' an aide present for the discussions said, 'we didn't make decisions.' To the sceptics of a poll it appeared that the left of the Shadow Cabinet thought the Project had reached its last-chance saloon. 'Richard Burgon and Ian Lavery talked openly about "losing our opportunity to fight an election, we might not get another one for four years",' said a Shadow Cabinet source. 'I think what they actually meant was: Jeremy won't get to fight another election.'

For a brief moment on Wednesday 23 October it appeared that they might be disappointed. That morning Corbyn, Milne and Nick Brown met Johnson, Dominic Cummings and Mark Spencer, the government chief whip, in an attempt to thrash out a new timetable for the Withdrawal Agreement Bill. 'Is this the moment Brexit got done?' asked Francis Elliott, the political editor of *The Times*, in a tweet revealing the summit. The answer was a resounding no.

Corbyn had told Johnson that Labour would agree to a 'reasonable' timetable for debating, scrutinising and amending the bill. More pertinently, however, he redoubled Labour's commitment to supporting an election as soon as the prospect of a no-deal exit was no longer live. By the next morning it became all too clear that Johnson was interested only in an early poll. His next communication with Corbyn, on Thursday 24 October, was a public demand for him to support a motion under the terms of a Fixed Term Parliaments Act – requiring a two-thirds majority – for an election on 12 December. Swinson followed hot on his heels with a plea for support on an amendment to the Queen's Speech that, if passed, would have delivered a second referendum.

All Corbyn could do in response to Johnson was repeat his mantra on no-deal. McDonnell, however, offered a firmer clue as to the direction the wind was blowing. To those who feared an election he was the last bulwark against certain annihilation. In the days before Corbyn pulled the trigger he was inundated with pleading texts from restive MPs. The man whose friends in the PLP were once so few as to number one was now its only hope. But that afternoon he told lobby reporters: 'I'm always up for an election. I've ordered a winter coat.' His comments only added to the sense of a growing and unstoppable momentum towards the polls.

Labour's support went from likelihood to certainty later that evening. At 7 p.m., the inner leadership of LOTO and the PLP piled into Corbyn's office to discuss whether they could allow an election to happen. Gathered around the leader's desk, leaning on bookshelves and squeezed onto and perched on the arms of the office sofa, were McDonnell, Abbott, Milne, Schneider, Fisher, Luke Sullivan, Helene Reardon-Bond, Dawn Butler, Anjula Singh and Seb Corbyn. Barry Gardiner, who arrived late, made the sensible judgement to remain outside. He busied himself with small talk with staff and a glass of whisky.

The overriding mood in the room was one of caution, if not outright opposition. Singh tapped frantically on her laptop, collating the views of those who spoke. Brown and McDonnell both made spirited cases against acquiescing to Johnson's demands, as did Abbott. 'The overwhelming weight in the room was not to give him a general election,' one attendee said. Another describes the consensus that an election would be fraught with potentially fatal political risk: 'They all seemed in agreement that the election was a Boris stitch-up, as it would be all about Brexit.'

But Milne and Schneider made the case for the prosecution regardless. Schneider argued: 'We've been calling for this, we've repeatedly said we want a general election, we said when no-deal was off the table is our aim – how can we sustain this position?' Milne also had cause to know that the dam of parliamentary arithmetic was about to burst. He argued not out of conviction but pragmatism. Even those who made the case for an election knew that going to the country with Brexit unresolved, even with a deal having been secured, would be immensely difficult for Corbyn.

Such were the numbers in the Commons, however, that if the SNP moved to support the government, then an election was inevitable: together the Nats and Tories had a majority of MPs which, though not enough to pass a motion for an early dissolution under the Fixed Term Parliaments Act, could make an early election happen via legislation, which only required 50 per cent of the Commons plus one. Milne had met the Westminster leadership of the SNP the previous week. 'We're not going to be able to hold this much longer,' they warned him.

For the SNP's leader Nicola Sturgeon the incentives were obvious. For one, the intensity of Brexit drama in the Commons seemed directly proportionate with the SNP's strong position in the polls. In this alone they found common cause with Johnson – fatigue with the European question, and with it the dysfunction of Westminster, spelt electoral opportunity. There was also the unsavoury matter of the looming trial in March of its former leader Alex Salmond on thirteen charges of sexual assault. That spelt negative publicity and uncomfortable questions for the SNP at best and a split in its ranks fomented by Salmond's army of hyperactive supporters at worst. No matter how inclement the weather or scant the winter light, a winter election made far more sense than any alternative.

Where the SNP went, the forces of political gravity demanded Labour follow. A senior LOTO aide said: 'If you're going to have an election anyway and you know that they can bring it about, you don't want to look like you're trying to stop the electorate having their say. If you know it's going to happen anyway you might as well embrace it.' Those present could not gauge whether Corbyn agreed. He sat stony-faced as his party argued around him. One close confidant believed they knew his true feelings: 'Jeremy did not want an election. He knew he was going to lose. I think there was only a pea-sized part of his brain which thought he could win.' Like Milne, however, he appreciated that there was no other way out.

Yet those who had argued against agreeing to an early election, having overwhelmed Milne and Schneider by force of numbers, left thinking that Corbyn's answer would be no. One said: 'A position was eventually agreed that we would say no, we're not giving you an election.' Schneider, who had been distracted by his phone for much of the meeting, tuned back in and immediately both men sensed that the line would collapse on contact with political reality. After the room cleared, Milne had Corbyn rehearse the line ahead of a BBC News interview. It was soon apparent to both that it would not wash. Milne instead furnished Corbyn with a line that more or less ignored the preceding discussion.

'Take no-deal off the table, and we absolutely support an election,' Corbyn told the BBC. Asked specifically how he would whip Labour MPs to vote if the government brought forward a motion the following Monday, he deferred to the EU. 'Tomorrow the European Union will decide whether there's going to be an extension granted or not, that extension will obviously encompass whether there's a no-deal or not.' Pressed again, he laid out the logic even more plainly: 'The principle is: EU answer tomorrow, take no-deal off the table, then we decide.'

In saying so he shook off the weight of the consensus that had taken hold just minutes earlier. In making clear that the inevitable extension met his price on no-deal, he signalled that his support for an election was a question of when, not if, and that the answer would come much sooner than most of his MPs were emotionally prepared for. The decision that for many of them amounted to a political death sentence was, for Corbyn, a release from the stifling, procedural drudgery his leadership had become. Over the weekend, the message went out from LOTO to the Whips' Office and Shadow Cabinet that Corbyn, despite his near-silence at the Thursday evening summit, had 'meant to say' that his preference was to agree to an election. 'The sense that was given,' said one Shadow Cabinet source, 'was that he'd felt pressurised to go along with the consensus against an election, when what he really wanted was to fight one'.

In public, Corbyn spoke in more confusing terms. The EU27 agreed to the principle of an extension as expected on Friday 25 October, leaving its decision on the length until the Commons voted on Johnson's election motion that Monday. Having as good as named the extension as the only condition that remained to be met the previous night, Corbyn appeared to have gone cold by the time he reached ITV's *This Morning* sofa. He was at once insistent that he would win an election and curiously reticent to say he would allow one to happen, instead demanding Johnson 'take no-deal off the table' in a statement to the Commons. Even then, however, it seemed that Corbyn would not be satisfied. To fight an election on 12 December, he complained, would be 'odd for many reasons', not least for its potential to disenfranchise his student fans if they had gone home for Christmas.

An impatient Downing Street looked to call his bluff. In a statement that morning Johnson's spokesman stressed that he would not bounce the UK into a no-deal exit in the middle of a campaign. The most pointed line vindicated Milne's argument that Labour risked joining King Canute in its approach to the forces of electoral nature: Number 10 demanded Corbyn 'man up' and vote it through.

Chuka Umunna would make the decision for him. That Thursday the Lib Dems had held their own summit on the wisdom of an election.

Private polling over the course of the summer had put them in pole position in some seventy-three seats. Its effect had been to intoxicate Swinson and her inner team. They had travelled to Bournemouth for their conference the previous month as if under the influence. Umunna had even dared suggest that his new party could win as many as 200 seats on a modest swing from Labour and the Conservatives. Defections from the Conservatives and the charred remnants of Change UK had boosted the ranks of Swinson's parliamentary party to a chunky twenty. An election promised riches untold since the days of Cleggmania.

After a detailed discussion that Thursday, Swinson dispatched Umunna to liaise with the Commons clerks on how they might word early election legislation that would come with a watertight guarantee against a no-deal exit on 31 October. His was a voice Swinson had come to value alongside the old sages of her parliamentary party. As a former Labour MP he was accorded the status of seer of LOTO by Swinson, with the former Conservative minister Sam Gyimah enjoying similar status for Number 10. Over the preceding months, Ed Davey, Swinson's priestly deputy, had chewed over the party's options with a strategy group. They had concluded that if an election was to take place before Brexit, then the most prudent timing would be for it to take place after Johnson had broken the foundational promise of his premiership. 'If you were going to do a pre-Brexit general election, it would be better that he hadn't met his do-or-die deadline,' explained one senior Liberal Democrat.

By the time Swinson reported the fruits of Umunna's discussions to a conference call of Lib Dem MPs on Friday night, the mood was positively gung-ho. In a concession to the gravity of the situation, however, they agreed to sleep on their decision ahead of an 8 a.m. conference call the following morning. Swinson then boarded the Caledonian Sleeper from Glasgow to London, accompanied by Andrew, her 5-year-old son. He had been similarly animated by events, though not by the early election: the prospect of a first trip on the Sleeper had proved so exhilarating that Swinson had to shake him awake at 6.30 the following morning. An hour and a half later, the election had effectively been called. Swinson called the man whose party would unseat her: the SNP's Ian Blackford, who quickly gave his blessing. The election, unusually, would be held on 9 December – a Monday – so as to ensure that Parliament was dissolved too soon for Johnson to pass the Withdrawal Agreement Bill.

That evening the *Observer*'s Michael Savage revealed Swinson's and Ummuna's plan and the SNP's backing for it on Twitter. 'Their plan: a bill that amends the Fixed Term Parliaments Act, fixing an election for Monday December 9,' he wrote. 'It also states that the plan is cancelled should the EU only offer a short Brexit extension, to safeguard against no-deal. Their plan would be that the bill, if adopted by Johnson, could be taken through Parliament on Tuesday, Wednesday, Thursday. Parliament dissolves next Monday. Election December 9. Happy days.' Happy days indeed, albeit not for Labour. The story was spun as a consequence of their indecision: Swinson and Blackford insisted they had been impelled to fill the vacuum left by the notional leader of the opposition.

It proved a watershed moment for Starmer and McDonnell. That the two parties who made up the bedrock of any majority for a second referendum had endorsed an election spelt the end of any rational hopes for an alternative outcome. 'Parliament just wasn't able to coalesce around anything,' said one ally of Starmer. 'He just thought an election was now inevitable.' Of McDonnell, a Shadow Cabinet source said: 'I think he saw the *Observer* story break, him and others who had been at least constructing an argument as to how you could delay a general election believed it wasn't sustainable any more.' When

the paper went to print the next morning it carried a clue as to how
that election might go, barring a repeat of 2017: a 16-point polling lead
for the Conservatives.

Corbyn's reaction to the story was almost Pavlovian: 'I would be
very happy to fight an election once all vestiges of a no-deal exit from
the EU have been taken off the table.' Swinson by then knew that a
three-month extension was coming. Clement Beaune, Macron's lead
adviser on Europe, told her that Sunday that her election bill had all
but secured a delay of sufficient length. Opinion in LOTO had hardened regardless. Milne and Murphy together encouraged Corbyn to
pull the trigger. In that crucial respect, the coup against her had failed.
She still had the leader's ear as he resolved to take the decision that
would accelerate the Project's destruction. 'Her influence never
subsided,' said a LOTO aide. 'She was ever present, and dominant.'

When Johnson made his first attempt to win parliamentary approval
for a December election, on Monday 28 October, forty Labour MPs
abstained. Downing Street, hoping to convince the Lib Dems and SNP
that they would have the pre-Brexit election they wanted, then pledged
to bin the deal as long as the 2017 parliament continued to sit.

Johnson then paid the price Corbyn had spent the previous week
demanding, and with it broke the promise that had defined his premiership. He accepted an extension until 31 January 2020, with the potential of an earlier departure on 1 December or New Year's Day in the
unlikely event that a deal was ratified by Parliament before then. To
LOTO it was almost academic: its will was settled in favour of an
election, though the public and PLP did not yet know it. That evening
the whips were informed of what was to come. 'We got told on the
Monday night that they'd agreed they were going to have a general
election,' one recalled.

At 8.17 p.m. Amy Jackson told LOTO colleagues on WhatsApp: 'I
understand that we want to amend the bill tomorrow for a GE on
December 9th, and to include votes for 16-year-olds and those
European citizens with settled status. We just really need to get all
our ducks in a row now in terms of amendments and political management.' Much more pressing was the need to herd the Shadow Cabinet
into the same place.

Before it met the following morning, Corbyn summoned the two
men who would in theory run the campaign – Gwynne and Lavery

– to an early meeting at Southside with Milne, Murphy and Jennie Formby. Having spoken to the Lib Dems and SNP the previous evening, he presented the election as a fait accomplit. 'An election was coming with or without Labour support, and Jeremy had come to the conclusion that we couldn't appear to be running from the voters,' one person present said. 'There was no dissent on that, though there was an acknowledgement that it was going to be a difficult election, and the preference was to hold out to the New Year.'

He employed the same approach when the full Shadow Cabinet met. Reading directly from his notes, as was so often the case at moments of national importance, Corbyn again presented an election as a done deal. So opaque and confusing had his public pronouncements been that even those in the Shadow Cabinet Room who had agitated to go to the country were genuinely surprised.

Emily Thornberry made a vain attempt to challenge the diktat, only to be swiftly shut down by Lavery. 'It's like having a boxer in the prime of his life and telling him he can't fight!' he clucked. He was about to take the extended metaphor to its peroration when McDonnell, for much of the year one of the room's agents of division, sought to unite the Shadow Cabinet. Like Corbyn, he insisted that the decision had been made. There was no plausible way out either. Initially, he had been so opposed to the plan that, in a fit of pique, he had threatened to resign rather than give it his imprimatur. Aides present when he laid down the gauntlet at a weekly strategy meeting had not expected him to follow through, and so it proved. Corbyn steamed ahead unencumbered. But now, wildly different though their individual journeys had been, he and Corbyn arrived at the same destination.

Richard Burgon recalls now: 'It had become inevitable. The party was therefore faced with a choice of being dragged into the ring seeming unwilling to fight or going into the ring up for the fight and up for putting the case that, after a decade of austerity, this election was about more than Brexit and trying to win on that basis.'

It was certainly not to the PLP's taste. Nick Brown left early, avoiding the cameras thronged outside, to deliver the bad news to his team. Like McDonnell, they had spent the preceding month hearing anguished pleas to stave off the reckoning with the electorate. 'We had MPs in uproar saying they wouldn't vote for it,' said one. 'We spent a lot of time trying to tell people that it was going to happen: go back to your seat if you can't vote for it, and start campaigning now. The decision has been taken. Nothing is going to stop it now.' When the Commons came to vote on the unamended bill, more than a hundred of them abstained. Eleven went as far as to vote against.

Yet Corbyn enjoyed the moment. He emerged to face the media flanked by McDonnell, Rebecca Long-Bailey and Jennie Formby. Starmer and Abbott were nowhere to be seen. 'We will now launch the most ambitious and radical campaign for real change this country has ever seen.' That was certainly one way of putting it. So began the most disastrous Labour campaign of any election since 1935.

14

It's Time for Real Change

Team Corbyn learned that Labour would lose the 2019 general election three months before a single voter had gone to the polls. On the Sunday morning of conference, John McDonnell walked with his wife Cynthia to a meeting room in the bowels of the Metropole hotel, on Brighton's promenade. Hours earlier, MPs and journalists had digested news of Andrew Fisher's resignation in the upstairs bar. What the Shadow Chancellor was about to learn would prove altogether more difficult to stomach. Over the preceding weeks, officials at Southside had fought bitterly over just which seats Labour ought to target come an election. By conference, they had their list of the ninety-six key seats without which Corbyn could not win a majority – and polling to show that it would never materialise.

In the last days of August, Niall Sookoo, Labour's director of elections, and Tim Waters, its head of data, commissioned a super-poll from YouGov that turned the optimism of Corbyn's inner circle on its head. Far from winning a hundred new seats, Labour was projected to lose far more. According to a poll of 20,000 voters, it would end a campaign with just 138 MPs – its worst result since 1917.

Sookoo had invited those who would run Labour's campaign to this private meeting to warn them of the calamity that awaited. Alongside McDonnell and his wife sat Ian Lavery, Andrew Gwynne and Carl Shoben, LOTO's director of strategy. Nursing hangovers from the first night's festivities, they convened at 9 a.m., and gathered round a television with Danish pastries purloined from a nearby breakfast event to watch the Labour leader sit down for his traditional conference interview on the BBC's *Andrew Marr Show*. McDonnell 'pissed around' with the remote control for minutes but could not get the TV to work. By the time room service had arrived to provide technical support, Corbyn's interview was over.

Waters, a veteran of Ed Miliband's field operation, took the floor. Unlike Sookoo, he was no fan of the leadership. But the paper he presented was too bleak to permit even the faintest pang of *Schadenfreude*. He explained that not only was Labour on course to lose nearly half of its MPs, it was haemorrhaging support in every direction and particularly to the Liberal Democrats, emboldened under their new leader Jo Swinson and, as of their conference the previous week, committed to cancelling Brexit altogether via the revocation of Article 50. A significant chunk of Labour voters would not turn out at all. He argued that Corbyn, who lionised Nye Bevan, would emerge from an election as living proof of his idol's old adage: that if Labour stayed in the middle of the road, it would get knocked down.

Waters stopped short of telling the room that it needed to pick a side on Brexit, apparently fearful of diverting attention away from the data or triggering a defensive response. A Shadow Cabinet minister present recalls: 'It was really depressing. The white working classes had moved away from us, and the liberal intelligentsia had moved away from us – in either direction of the Brexit result.'

Lavery was in no mood to listen, despite the fact that the polling suggested he would lose his own seat of Wansbeck, in the heart of the Northumberland coalfield, to the Conservatives. 'People in the north just won't vote Tory,' he boomed. 'It just won't happen!' Waters suggested that he had misunderstood the nature of the problem: Remainers were abandoning Labour in their droves. The Liberal Democrats would quadruple their 2017 result and win forty-four seats, overturning majorities of more than 20,000 in the process. But they would also deprive Labour of enough votes in Leave-voting seats to let the Tories in through the middle. Gwynne, who was similarly incredulous, asked: 'But aren't we losing Leave votes to the pro Brexit parties?' The answer was yes, albeit at a much smaller rate. Europhiles made up the bulk of Labour's support. For every one Leaver who abandoned Corbyn, three Remainers did the same. Waters ended his address with a conclusion that dramatically contradicted the gambit Labour had pursued since 2017 of trying to win over Leave voters in marginal seats. Now, he warned, telling Leavers that Labour would deliver Brexit risked fatal consequences, and a Conservative majority of 150. The scale of Corbyn's projected losses to the Liberal Democrats was such that London strongholds with Labour majorities in the tens of thousands, like Greenwich and Woolwich, would fall to the Liberal Democrats. Other Remain redoubts, like Vauxhall, would have their Labour vote so badly split with the Lib Dems as to fall to the Conservatives.

McDonnell listened in silence. His worst fears had been vindicated: despite his best efforts to cajole Corbyn into supporting a second referendum, Labour was repelling pro-EU voters. As Waters sat down, the Shadow Chancellor delegated the inquisition to his wife. Cynthia, like Lavery, initially struggled to believe what she had been told. She had spent much of her career at market-research companies and queried whether the research was watertight. An angry Lavery went further. YouGov, attendees recall him fuming, had been founded by card-carrying Conservatives, a charge he raised with Waters and Sookoo repeatedly. He insisted that they could not and should not trust a 'Tory firm'.

But McDonnell had already made up his mind: Labour must do everything in its power to win back pro-EU voters. It would refrain from discussing the detail of Brexit, still less delivering it, whilst extolling the virtues of giving voters the final say on the issue via a second referendum. It was a strategy which Milne had long argued against, warning that the working class could desert Labour en masse. But he was not present on the day. He was also increasingly outmuscled by Corbyn's oldest comrade, who was by then in the process of plotting his demotion. 'From that point out, our strategy was to hug the Remainers,' says an official present that morning.

In the days that followed, the only things that McDonnell and Milne did agree on were the products of political reality: within the party – and in the country. The central plank of its strategy would be to divert attention away from the issue of Brexit wherever possible. They might have differed on tone and emphasis when it came to the EU, but both knew Corbyn had to attempt to rise above it and would instead advocate policies that appealed to Remainers and the less militant Brexit backers alike. As Milne had written earlier that summer, if Brexit was still unresolved by the time of an election, Labour would instead run a campaign which would turn the issue 'into one of transformation in or out of Europe and prevent the election becoming another proxy referendum. So the crucial election choice becomes not in or out, but the many or the few.'

What no one disputed was that the strategy had to be aggressive. Despite the headwinds of national opinion, Sookoo produced a list of target seats in the wake of the meeting that included sixty-six offensive seats – constituencies which Labour believed it could capture – and thirty which it needed to protect. Many felt it was a political, rather than psephological, decision. With the knowledge it might be the Project's last shot at glory, Labour was going for all or nothing. Soon, that gambit would look like the biggest miscalculation of Corbyn's and McDonnell's four decades in politics.

Ian Lavery had embodied the combination of weariness and Panglossian optimism the previous month when he had told staff gathered at Southside: 'It will be a Brexit-type election. And we're going to get mixed results … We're trying to transform society – it's not going to be easy! You're going to feel like crying at times, not with joy! But I hope that will come at the end of the election! So please remember this is normal. It will be normal during this campaign … but we need to be united.'

Many in the room still believed. The general election of 2017 had shattered the old certainties, and Corbyn was determined to do so again. Even the doubters felt there might be a narrow path to victory, if only, as Milne had told colleagues in August, they could move the argument beyond Brexit. Earlier that month, LOTO had seen research which suggested that most of Labour's target voters cared more about what Corbyn deemed to be his meat and drink: the NHS and cost of living. On 30 October, he offered a preview of the campaign to come when he faced Johnson for the final Prime Minister's Questions before the dissolution of the 2017 parliament. 'This election is a once-in-a-generation chance to end privatisation in our NHS, give it the funding it needs,' he said. 'Our NHS is up for grabs by US corporations in a Trump trade deal. This government is preparing to sell out our NHS. Our health service is in more danger than at any time in its glorious history.' Victory would be difficult but was possible, if only Labour could hammer home this message and fight the disciplined and energetic campaign they had done two years previously.

It would also require Corbyn to summon every drop of the energy that the preceding months of Westminster drama and internal scandal had drained from him. Those closest to him suspected he was in no state to do so, but still believed he would inspire the country once more with daily policy announcements. As one aide to McDonnell recalls: 'In 2017, "For The Many, Not the Few" captured the imagination as a slogan. Now the task was for Jeremy to explain what it would look like in practice.'

Yet repeating 2017 would be no mean feat. Not only were Corbyn and his team deeply divided, Corbyn himself was no longer the politician he had once been: Brexit and anti-Semitism had sapped his confidence – and made him the most unpopular Labour leader of the last forty-five years. Paul Hilder, a data consultant to the campaign, was asked to produce a pitch for how Labour might recapture the spirit of the last campaign. Having spent 2016 trailing Bernie Sanders around the US, he emphasised that political insurgencies were once-in-a generation events – and could not be confected by strategists. His anxieties were best expressed by Marcus Roberts, a YouGov pollster who told the *Today* programme of Corbyn's chances just before the campaign began: 'The soufflé never rises twice.' Hilder's research made for bleak reading for those, like Murphy, who believed Corbyn's difficult 'second album' could ultimately win over the public. He warned – just as Labour MPs did after their weekly surgeries – that their leader had become a liability. He instead recommended that the party deploy a broader team of spokespeople to neutralise the damage a campaign that relied on Corbyn alone would do. Most striking of all, he also proposed that Labour avoid putting its politicians centre stage at all. 'Brexit meant that everyone just fucking hated politicians,' recalled one aide. It was instead the words of ordinary people which won the most positive responses in focus groups – and an authenticity which offered Labour a recipe for viral reach online. In September, one voter in Morley, West Yorkshire, had captured the mood when he was filmed telling Johnson: 'Please leave my town.' In another viral clip, one of Johnson's own constituents, an elderly woman, told Sky's Sophy Ridge of her MP: 'Don't you ever mention that name in front of me, that filthy piece of toerag.' These were the people Hilder recommended that Labour put front and centre – not Corbyn. Others felt that amplifying the concerns of *real* people about Johnson's character was the only way to puncture his popularity, rather than familiar attacks on his alleged racism and philandering. A LOTO aide recalled:

'There are lots of MPs saying you can't trust Boris Johnson. We went into focus groups saying that, but people don't trust any politicians so I don't think it was effective. It was like saying: you can't trust estate agents, but here's an estate agent you can trust.' Those around Corbyn heard their concerns but had little option but to ignore them, for by then, he was the only thing holding the Project together.

★

With unfortunate symbolism, Corbyn launched his campaign on 31 October – the day that Britain, thanks to legislation drafted by Starmer and supported by LOTO, would not be leaving the European Union as Johnson had promised. Despite the polls giving the Tories a 12-point lead, Corbyn appeared undaunted at the scale of the task to come. Taking to the stage at the Battersea Arts Centre in South London, he announced 'the most ambitious and radical campaign our country has ever seen'. Brexit, he explained, was not the real dividing line: 'Labour will put wealth and power in the hands of the many. Boris Johnson's Conservatives, who think they're born to rule, will only look after the privileged few ... Whose side are you on? The billionaire media barons like Rupert Murdoch, whose empire pumps out propaganda to support a rigged system? Or the overwhelming majority who want to live in a decent, fair, diverse and prosperous society?' On Brexit itself, the speech was a familiar exercise in riding two horses at once. 'Labour will get Brexit sorted by giving people the final say in six months.' He insisted: 'It really isn't that complicated.'

But despite Corbyn's outward display of insouciance, even the slogan behind him suggested he was already on the defensive on the central issue of the campaign. Over the summer, McDonnell had commissioned Harry Barlow, an advertising executive who had worked for Ken Livingstone at the GLC and was venerated by some as the 'Saatchi of the left', to come up with a tagline. It had to transcend Brexit and have as much impact as 'For the Many, Not the Few'. Taking inspiration from the successful campaign of Jacinda Ardern, the New Zealand prime minister who had led her own Labour Party to an unlikely victory in 2017, Barlow suggested borrowing her slogan: 'It's Time'. He envisaged it as a one-size-fits-all peg for each of Labour's policies. A source explained: 'It's time ... to transform our NHS. It's

time ... for a real Living Wage. It's time ... for investment in education.' The problem, however, was that the Tories could bastardise the
formula for their own means. Johnson had himself sought guidance
from Down Under in the form of Isaac Levido, the Australian strategist who had masterminded Scott Morrison's surprise victory over
Labour's Antipodean sister party. His mischievous digital operation,
helmed by the Kiwi twentysomethings Sean Topham and Ben Guerin,
would have made short work of 'It's Time'. A spoof 'It's time ... to
Get Brexit Done' poster was repeatedly cited by worried aides. Milne
also argued that it was unoriginal and lacked bite.

    With that ruled out, Team Corbyn looked elsewhere. Hilder had
come up with a suggestion that polled well: 'We Need to Rebuild
Britain'. It was also attractive for its lack of ideological baggage and
ability to speak to Remainers and Leavers alike. Yet LOTO vetoed it.
One of the few men the office resented more than Hilder, Tony Blair,
had used it as the title for the party's 1997 manifesto, and it was again
said to lack appeal. All that was left was another idea that had polled
adequately: 'Real Change'. The two ideas were merged, without
recourse to polling or focus groups, resulting in: 'It's time for real
change'. Arun Chaudhary, a former campaign official to President
Obama and Bernie Sanders who worked alongside Hilder, was said
to be horrified by the 'shitshow' on display. As Corbyn reached his
peroration in Battersea, he mangled the agreed strapline: 'Friends, the
future is ours together. IT IS *NOW* TIME FOR REAL CHANGE!'

    But before he could devote himself fully to the job of making the
case in the country, LOTO had one piece of unfinished business to
attend to: Tom Watson.

                                   *

Murphy had spent the days that followed LOTO's botched coup against
her former boss telling Watson that she had not been responsible: the
idea had not been hers. Neither Watson nor Alicia Kennedy believed
her, but it did not matter. The deputy leader had come to regard the
plan not with disbelief but with disinterest. His abiding emotion from
the night he learned of the plot was, he told friends, one of relief. A
process of conscious uncoupling from Westminster was already
underway. In Brighton he reached the end of the road. The Corbynites

had failed to oust him, but they had shown that he no longer had a reason to stay. His four years as deputy had not unfolded as planned: he had been an organiser, yes, but of a factional resistance, not a movement. Politics was no longer fun. It was time to go.

In the final week of October, Watson met Corbyn to hammer out the terms of his departure. Their discussion was held in secret. Arranging a time – kept off-diary – proved difficult. Corbyn had effectively been banned from meeting his deputy privately since the coup. It was only after a frank discussion that Amy Jackson acceded to Helene Reardon-Bond's request for a ten-minute meeting between Corbyn and Watson, who had assured them it would be worth their while. The two men met along with Reardon-Bond and Kennedy in the old Shadow Cabinet Room in Norman Shaw South.

Watson told Corbyn that he had concluded his career was over. The events of conference had proven that much. 'Look, Jeremy, I've been thinking about this, obviously what went on at conference has been weighing on my mind, the deputy leadership stuff, but the decision I've made is beyond that, this is much wider than politics. I think it would be easier for me and easier for you if I was to stand down, so I'm just telling you that's what I'm going to do.'

Corbyn, the man who had set the plan to assassinate Watson in train, later told aides he was not surprised. Only in the rarest circumstances would his adversary have requested a meeting. Yet in the moment he feigned surprise. Corbyn took a long pause before offering his response. 'Are you sure you want to do this?' he said. 'You don't have to do this.' Watson said that he was in a better place than he had been for years. He was not for turning. Once it became clear his mind was made up, Corbyn made no attempt to change it. To do so was not only beyond him but at odds with the Project's objectives. They haggled over the price. Corbyn would offer Watson a peerage, in keeping with the tradition that saw John Prescott, Roy Hattersley and Denis Healey elevated to the Upper Chamber. In return, Watson would allow the Project to fight the election on its own terms. They would break the news together.

Business attended to, the conversation mellowed. Corbyn asked about Watson's children. Watson brought up their shared interest in horticulture. He suggested that he might say he was resigning to spend more time with his vegetable patch. They then discussed the challenges

of growing horseradish, an invasive vegetable, at length. One person
present recalls that the discussion took up more time than the practicalities of his resignation. Later that week, Reardon-Bond visited
Watson's office bearing a peace offering: a horseradish plant.

News of the arrangement became public on 6 November, when
Labour announced the decision via press release in the middle of Boris
Johnson's campaign launch in Birmingham, the heart of Watson's
West Midlands fiefdom. His last act in Labour politics would be a
show of unity with Corbyn. 'Now is the right time for me to stand
down from the House of Commons and start a different kind of life.
The decision is personal, not political,' read Watson's letter to Corbyn.
The leader responded in idiosyncratic style: 'I've always enjoyed our
very convivial chats about many things, including cycling, exercise and
horticulture. I hope the horseradish plants I gave you thrive.'

The news, which knocked Johnson's launch off the rolling news
channels, blindsided Westminster and with it Peter Mandelson. Watson
had not forewarned his mentor. He knew that to do so would be to
allow Mandy to talk him out of it. If anybody could, it would be him.
'You don't know what it's like. I have to turn up to these meetings, I
have to go on these NEC officers' calls. I see the brutality, I see the
vindictiveness,' Watson told him. 'I see not just what they're doing to
the Labour Party – destroying it – but the sheer brutality with which
they're doing it and I can't bear it. I just feel contaminated.' He likened
life as deputy leader to swimming through a 'terrible swamp'. But it
was not just the Labour Party. Jo Swinson had offered him the Liberal
Democrat candidacy in Lewes. He had turned it down after considering
it, in the words of one friend, 'for five minutes'. Life outside of politics looked more inviting. He had found a new, apolitical partner, a
headteacher, and had made a home in his native Worcestershire. He
wanted to spend more time with his young children. The supreme
irony was that it was the Corbynites who had given it to him. The
following week, he reunited briefly with Murphy at Southside. She
came close to weeping and told her old boss of her deep and abiding
affection. Even then, Watson thought, she did not quite realise that
he was not forgiving her. He was thanking her.

Watson reflects now: 'When I was in that little Chinese restaurant
with my boy, it almost felt like they'd given me a dignified way to
exit politics ... It seems silly to say it but I felt almost gratitude that

I could find a different course in life, and I know this sounds really insane ... I'm almost grateful to Jeremy, for inadvertently allowing that to happen.'

The stakes were too high: he had carried the burden of opposition for too long. 'I knew there was about to be a volcanic explosion when the story broke. I knew it would destroy the conference, I knew the Labour Party could split. I knew that our members on the cusp of a likely election would be bewildered at the sheer hatred of it all. I knew there'd be a media scrum that I just once again did not want to be in the middle of, but I also knew that one way or another it would be over for me.

'I'd felt such a sense of duty and obligation, and I was carrying the projected anxieties of people who want to win elections for all the right reasons, different political groupings, who thought I was the only one standing up for them. The sense of obligation to them was enormous, and I knew it was almost impossible that I could fulfil their expectations.

'If I've got one little conceit, it's that by walking away, for all the right reasons in life, it meant that the responsibility for the electoral outcome was totally the responsibility of the hard-left faction on our NEC who by this point were often ignoring Jeremy. Their failure shocked party members and helped contribute to the conditions that allowed the party to elect someone like Keir, who looks like a prime-minister-in-waiting. I don't know whether it's true or not, but I'd like to think that.'

LOTO also had cause for gratitude. Milne's August memo had warned: 'We cannot expect much from the deputy leader. While it would be welcome to be proved wrong, it would be prudent to be prepared for some unhelpful intervention at some stage in any campaign.' It was not just his own life that Watson had made easier.

With Parliament dissolved and Watson on his way out, Corbyn's time on the road could begin in earnest. He travelled with John McDonnell to the Shadow Chancellor's home city of Liverpool to unveil Labour's battle bus. Flanked by the party's Merseyside candidates, Corbyn addressed reporters in front of the vehicle that, in theory, would convey him across the country. Clambering aboard, he smiled and waved for the cameras. He flashed a thumbs-up as he fired the starting gun on his month on the campaign trail: 'This message will go across the whole country!' Few knew it would be the only time that Corbyn set foot on the bus – or the problems that the red double-decker had portended.

Antagonism set in early and festered until polling day. The day before the campaign got underway, Corbyn had what one aide described as a 'tantrum' when he learned that – unlike the bus propelling Jo Swinson and the Liberal Democrats across the country – his campaign wheels were powered not by an electric battery but a diesel engine of the sort that his own manifesto would promise to outlaw by 2030. Years of media scrutiny had taught him how the scurrilous minds of the Westminster press pack operated. He could smell the tabloid charge of hypocrisy already. In his exasperation, he wrote to Murphy and other close aides from his personal Gmail account: 'I see the (diesel) bus appears which I hope does not get too many negatives. As soon as rest of grid and operation notes are available can I get them so I can know a week ahead what is being planned and other requests that may appear can be factored in.' The response, from Marsha-Jane Thompson, would do little to soothe him: 'Once we win we can mandate investment in electric buses!' She then turned to the SMT WhatsApp group: 'JC unhappy that lib dems have an electric bus'. Aides quickly agreed it would not be feasible to change tack. Murphy responded: 'Can someone let JC know this?' Thompson refused. 'Can't take any more bullets.'

Corbyn's seemingly trivial objections spoke to deeper dysfunction. His detractors at Westminster often contended that he had no idea what he was doing. For once, the jibe was accurate – though not for want of trying on Corbyn's part. Strategy for the campaign he was supposed to be leading had largely been decided – or, more accurately, disagreed on – in his absence.

Before arriving in Liverpool, Corbyn had demanded to know why he had even been asked to spend the morning in the drizzle at all – not least when the NEC was meeting at Southside. 'Hi JC,' came Thompson's reply. 'It was noticed but as Amy, Andrew and Seumas said in the meeting yesterday the advice was to have a speech to launch campaign as not appropriate for you to be at the NEC.' Corbyn shot back: 'Yes that may have been the advice but it was never given to me at any time. I am therefore stuck between not being at the NEC or upsetting the events that have been organised when I was not consulted on any of it. Can we please make sure I am fully consulted in future and have the grid at least a week ahead. I realise everyone is working very hard to deliver but I am fully entitled to be consulted before these decisions are made.'

The Watson debacle had revealed that Corbyn could barely trust his closest lieutenants even when he was in the same room. Now he would be marooned over 200 miles away as they met without him, with only two twentysomething junior aides for company, and seemingly no amount of information to placate him. The following day, he repeated his plea. 'I need to see the whole grid not just parts of it. Can you send it now?' Each day of the campaign began with a 7 a.m. conference call. McDonnell, the self-appointed chair of the campaign, led the conversation. Murphy, Milne, Fisher, Gwynne, Lavery and Sookoo would also dial in. By the end of the first week of the campaign, Corbyn was insisting on participating as well.

The idea that their party leader would interrupt his packed schedule to join this routine discussion would ordinarily be preposterous. He had not dialled in once in 2017. But for Corbyn, who had grown distressed whilst being denied access to information, it became an imperative. He began to dial in every day, regardless of his location. An aide recalled: 'He came onto the call every morning asking for his diary.' It would often take hours of back-and-forth between Corbyn and Murphy, egged on by an impatient Alvarez, before he was satisfied that he had been given a sufficiently detailed agenda. His refusal to travel on the diesel bus, meanwhile, meant that he was travelling the country on trains. It made communication near impossible. Corbyn frequently cut in and out of reception and was forced to borrow the phones of those around him. He made one Sunday morning call as he tended to the marrows on his allotment, buffeted by wind which rendered his voice inaudible. The man on whose shoulders the hopes of the left rested had been reduced to spending vital hours of the campaign bickering over his right to see his own schedule. 'It was like he'd had a breakdown,' said one aide. 'He just wouldn't drop the stuff about the diary and dialling onto the calls. It was his way of trying to regain control.'

More worrying perhaps was the nature of the calls he insisted on joining. McDonnell nominally led the discussions. Murphy would often step in. But she was wary of being made the fall guy by

McDonnell and would remind participants that she was not in charge. ('It's not my thing. Never made one strategic decision, all this, you know, this election guru – what a load of fucking bollocks,' she says now.) Whereas in 2017, Milne had signed off on all strategic decisions, now he was merely one of many voices in the room. Fisher, meanwhile, had refused to share the draft manifesto with him – or anyone he regarded as being in the Milne/Murphy Brexit axis – while Murphy responded by closely guarding the grid. Sookoo, who despised Milne, in turn refused to share his list of key seats with Milne, Murphy or Jackson. The three were forced to go behind his back during the early days of the campaign and get a copy from Lavery instead. Said one aide: 'Nine-tenths of my bloody day was spent communicating on behalf of people who wouldn't communicate directly with each other.' Amid the bitter personal divides and the political fractures created by Brexit, the group was left to listlessly discuss the day's itinerary and explain to Corbyn why he was being asked to go to particular events. 'We simply didn't have the structure to make actual decisions so it became an exercise in diary management.'

As it turned out, that first fortnight of the campaign did not unfold in the way that either party had hoped or expected. Large parts of Yorkshire and the Midlands – and with them dozens of Labour-held Conservative targets – were submerged by floods. Johnson's visits to comfort the afflicted went about as well as might have been expected. On a belated trip to Stainforth, a village in Ed Miliband's Doncaster North constituency, the prime minister was heckled. 'I'm not very happy about talking to you, so, if you don't mind, I'll just motor on with what I'm doing,' came the reply from one middle-aged woman glad-handed by Johnson. In 2017, Corbyn might have seized the opportunity to demonstrate his warmth and compassion. But events during those first two weeks had presented precisely the opposite image to the public. The soundtrack to Labour's campaign thus far had not been its own policy announcements but a drumbeat of vicious personal criticism of Corbyn himself. The former Labour MPs Ian Austin and John Woodcock, two of his most vociferous critics, had set the tone on 7 November, when they jointly announced they would vote Conservative to lock the man they believed to be an anti-Semitic extremist out of Downing Street. The Tories had wanted Austin, who had beaten them by just twenty-two votes in his Dudley North constituency in 2017, to go even further. They made a secret approach to him to run for them as a parliamentary candidate. He declined, but that did not stop broadcasters giving the intervention blanket coverage – much to the consternation of Corbyn's team. For Corbyn himself, it was yet more evidence that the media was preoccupied with what he derided as 'Westminster tittle-tattle'.

His own MPs knew that the public no longer saw it that way. Shortly after campaigning had begun, *The Times* revealed that Battersea MP Marsha De Cordova, the woman alongside whom he had launched his own campaign, had omitted the leader from her election literature and replaced him with Sadiq Khan. Sookoo shared the story on the SMT WhatsApp group, noting: 'So it has begun.' Jackson responded that De Cordova's conduct was 'outrageous given we launched in her constituency'. That loyal Shadow ministers like De Cordova had concluded that Corbyn was too toxic a liability even in London was a mark of just how low his public standing had sunk.

Given the perceived hostility of the mainstream media, which had covered the Woodcock and Austin story prominently, LOTO developed a strategy of using 'soft media' to compensate. For Milne, the BBC and ITV were no longer even adopting the pretence of impartiality. He held out particular contempt for Robert Peston, political editor of ITV News. In LOTO's view, Peston never reported on Labour when he could editorialise instead. He would not be given an interview. Aides instead put forward Muslim News; the *Weekly Desh*, a Bangladeshi diaspora newspaper; *I-D* Magazine; GRM Daily; and Arsenal Fan TV as unconventional outlets to bring Corbyn to the masses. On the morning of Saturday 9 November, Dan Carden, the 32-year-old Shadow International Development Secretary and one of Corbyn's mooted successors, found himself at the centre of a media storm. A regular on the Westminster party circuit that most of his Corbynite peers shunned, Carden had accepted free tickets to the horse racing at Cheltenham Festival from Ladbrokes the previous year. On the bus home, surrounded by Conservative MPs and journalists, onlookers claimed to BuzzFeed News that they had heard Carden replace the lyrics to 'Hey Jude' with 'Hey Jews'. It was the last thing Corbyn needed. Incandescent that his subordinate should be fraternising with Conservative MPs and lobby journalists as a guest of a bookmaker, he rang Carden, a close ally of McCluskey and Murphy, from an already delayed announcement on children's services in Leeds to tell him that he must resign if he could not disprove the story. Corbyn told Carden: 'You're going to have to resign unless you can provide evidence.' An aide recalled: 'He was so angry about that. He thought: why is he taking hospitality from a fucking betting company to go and get pissed with Tories and Guido Fawkes? He was all set to sack him.' But by the time Corbyn emerged from his engagement, Carden had defied him and publicly denied the story himself: 'I have been categorical in my denial about allegations relating to a coach trip some twenty months ago,' he said. 'This was a coach full of journalists and MPs. If anyone genuinely believed any anti-Semitic behaviour had taken place, they would've had a moral responsibility to report it immediately. Yet this allegation is only made now when a general election is imminent.' 'We had to tell Jeremy once he finished his visit,' said one of Corbyn's travelling team.

McDonnell knew that Corbyn would need to go into fifth gear in order to recover from the slow start. He attempted to recapture the agenda the following day. Corbyn, he proposed, would upstage Johnson by making a second visit to areas affected by the floods to highlight cuts to flood defences overseen by the coalition. There was one problem: Corbyn himself. He refused to go, yet again citing his diary and the fact he had not been kept in the loop. Thompson wrote: 'JC currently doesn't want to go with John's suggestion of a visit today. So would need convincing by someone.' Anjula Singh shot back: 'What's his objection?' No reply was forthcoming. Instead, LOTO was left to debate the best way of shaking Corbyn out of his sulk about the diary commitments. 'He could have them WhatsApp in advance if possible? Stops any suggestion he isn't getting them,' said Murphy. Thompson replied: 'He has them given to him in his hand and his personal email ... as he requested.'

On occasions where Labour's policy offer did cut through on the airwaves, the attention was of little help. Lynton Crosby, the Australian election guru who had masterminded Johnson's mayoral victories and David Cameron's 2015 win, often invoked the phrase 'clearing off the barnacles' at the start of a campaign to denote a ruthless focus on a single core message or policy. Risky policies or gimmicks were to be avoided. It was a strategy which Johnson adopted himself at the outset, repeating his three-word slogan 'Get Brexit Done' ad nauseam. Labour, in contrast, was announcing a major policy – or more – a day. While Johnson deferred to his Wizard of Oz, LOTO relied on the assets that they believed had delivered them 40 per cent of the vote in 2017: its policy programme. On 14 November, McDonnell told the BBC's Laura Kuenssberg that Labour would nationalise BT's Openreach infrastructure division and provide free broadband to every home and business in the country. For Corbynites at the grass roots, it was precisely the sort of ambitious policy they had hoped to see. Voters felt differently: it tanked in focus groups and was mocked by Boris Johnson, who called it a 'crazed communist scheme'. The Shadow Cabinet did not know it was coming, so were ill-equipped to defend the plan. One Corbyn loyalist recalled: 'It went down like a cup of cold sick on the doorsteps, because it really did say to people: is this really your priority over the NHS, over education, over policing?' One Shadow Cabinet minister said: 'There were far too many policy announcements, so rather than things sticking in people's minds, they'd forgotten and it was another policy, another policy, another policy, and nobody was actually considering what those policies were. They just thought: there's another one from Labour.'

In some respects, their analysis was optimistic. Many voters were taking no notice at all. By the time Prince Andrew sat down on 16 November to be interviewed by *Newsnight*'s Emily Maitlis on his links to the disgraced financier Jeffrey Epstein, Corbyn's aides knew he had failed to capture the public imagination as he had in 2017. The coverage that followed the prince's interview continued to distract for another week.

As pessimism began to take hold in LOTO, Corbyn's press team briefed friendly journalists that the drift was all part of the plan. The week of 18 November had been pencilled in as the end of the beginning for Labour's campaign – or the beginning of the end for Johnson's dominance in the polls. Internally, it became known as 'Bazooka Week': on Tuesday 19 November, Corbyn would face Johnson in a head-to-head debate, the first of its kind in British political history, on ITV at Salford Quays. On the night, Corbyn failed to land a decisive blow on either of the two subjects that Johnson believed to be Labour's greatest weaknesses, and exploited ruthlessly: its support for a second referendum on Brexit, and apparent willingness to countenance granting the SNP its own second referendum on Scottish independence. The

audience laughed as Corbyn attempted to spin Labour's plan for a
public vote as a way to 'get Brexit sorted by giving you, the people,
the final say', just as they did when he attempted to defend his policy
of a four-day working week. Host Julie Etchingham elicited another
laugh by ordering both men, clearly uncomfortable, to shake hands.
Twitter was overcome by a collective cringe – and in some cases
explicit accusations of anti-Semitism – when Corbyn mispronounced
'Epstein' as 'Ep-shteen'. A snap poll by YouGov showed a dead heat,
with 51 per cent of people declaring Johnson the winner. The Labour
leader's travelling entourage responded with cautious optimism. They
had not lost, after all. In the country, however, MPs felt differently.
One defending a marginal in the north-west of England warned
colleagues: 'This is our 1983. The public will remember "Get Brexit
Done" and any deal with the SNP. We will lose dozens of seats.'

Two days later, Corbyn travelled to Birmingham to launch the 2019
manifesto. Its ambition when it came to public services was immense.
Labour would increase the health budget by billions and introduce
universal social care. Universal Credit would be abolished and the
welfare system overhauled. As promised in 2017, it would nationalise
water, Royal Mail, and the railways, as well as going further and taking
BT's Openreach into public ownership with a view to providing every
home and business with free broadband. It promised 100,000 new
homes would be built a year. Meanwhile, Labour would seek to remove
the charitable status of private schools and raise taxes on the wealth-
iest 1 per cent. Though they appeared in the manifesto substantially
diluted from original proposals tabled by grass-roots activists at conference, the promises amounted to Corbynism on steroids in the eyes
of the media, and in any case came at much greater cost. On Brexit,
the party's position remained unchanged. In the first week of
November, when party figures and union representatives gathered for
the traditional Clause V meeting to sign off the manifesto's content,
Brexit was discussed for only a 'few minutes', with most present
resigned to the fudge of a renegotiation and a second referendum.
That Labour had not inched further towards Remain was a relief to
Milne and Murphy. Unbeknownst to most in the room, Fisher had
not shared the manifesto with Milne in full, as a supposed precaution
against the sort of leak that had occurred in 2017. He and Murphy
were left to learn of its contents in a six-hour meeting along with

everyone else. Similarly, the unions, who were usually kept in the loop, had been left in the dark by Fisher, who feared they would pass it on to Milne's people. 'It's just seen as unprofessional and it's an insult,' remarked one LOTO aide. Most significantly, Milne's exclusion meant that there was little framing or narrative to the manifesto. If the policy bonanza appeared to have been written by a policy wonk alone, that's because it had been.

Taking to a makeshift stage in the atrium of Birmingham City University on 21 November, Corbyn hailed it as a 'manifesto of hope. A manifesto that will bring real change. A manifesto full of popular policies that the political establishment has blocked for a generation.' But, unlike in 2017, the promises of nationalisations and increased spending failed to have any meaningful impact on the polls, which continued to show Johnson with a clear lead. If anything the scale and ambition of the Project's programme for government would have the opposite effect. While many of the initiatives were individually popular, together they did not, in the eyes of most voters, make for a coherent package.

Corbyn left his manifesto launch in a coach only to be diverted as an emergency precaution. Police had discovered that fifteen far-right English Defence League members were awaiting him at his next destination, Dudley, armed with fireworks.

That Sunday McDonnell deployed the first in a series of make-or-break policy pitches. At a cost of some £58 billion, the Shadow Chancellor pledged Labour would compensate every woman born between 1950 and 1955 who had been affected by changes to the state pension age – the so-called WASPI (Women Against State Pension Inequality) generation. It was an offer that cut directly against McDonnell's new image as a softly spoken champion of fiscal responsibility. Nor had it appeared anywhere in the costings for Labour's manifesto. Some speculated that the policy had been formulated in response to a hostile leak to the *Sunday Times*, who had been sent Labour's draft election timetable in its entirety the previous month, which included an announcement on the WASPI generation's plight pencilled in for Sunday 24 November. In the aftermath, a furious Corbyn vented to LOTO aides via email: 'I must say I am absolutely sick of these leaks, briefings and distortions that originate somewhere in our offices and teams. It is disgusting the degree of self-absorbed disloyalty that some person or persons have. Our members do not sweat night and day to see their party damaged by this behaviour.' Murphy promised reprisals: 'I will work to see if we can narrow some of this down to certain individuals but it's coming from many directions at the moment I fear.'

WASPI campaigners took just as keen an interest in the leak. Soon after its publication the campaigners had deluged the Shadow Cabinet with pleading emails. Such was the publicity that there could be no rowing back.

In fact, some months earlier, McDonnell, alive to the risk of alienating one of Westminster's most vocal policy lobbies, had enlisted his actuary friend Bryn Davies to draw up plans to help those affected. Davies had proposed a generous change to pension tax relief, which was vetoed by Milne. In the wake of the leak, however, Milne was forced to submit to McDonnell's £58 billion alternative. The only reason it had not appeared in the manifesto was because the Shadow Treasury team had not been able to complete the preparatory work in time. The *Sunday Times* story forced LOTO to assent to McDonnell's plan regardless. Some of the Shadow Chancellor's allies saw it both as a trump card and an important sign that he retained control over the campaign. Yet the effect was to undermine the painstaking work McDonnell had done to salvage a reputation for fiscal credibility.

Andrew Gwynne, whose patience had been nearly entirely eroded by the secrecy and obfuscations of Corbyn's inner circle, was one of Labour's many MPs who knew nothing of the WASPI compensation offer until he read the *Observer* early front page that Saturday night. He knew as much about the campaign he was notionally overseeing as the owner of his local newsagent. On his way back to Westminster from his Manchester constituency the following afternoon, he resolved to quit. Fortified by Waitrose Merlot, he confided in Lyn Brown, the veteran West Ham MP at whose East London home Gwynne dined every Sunday. Brown, who had arrived in Parliament with Gwynne in 2005 and had become his closest friend in politics, convinced her 'absolutely blotto' companion to hold fire. He would remain in post, but the damage to his relationship with LOTO was done.

Corbyn was similarly resigned. With less than three weeks to go and Labour 10 points behind the Tories in most polls, some aides had arrived at the extraordinary conclusion that he was sabotaging his own campaign. Corbyn was often late and appeared to purposely overstay at events in order to minimise his day's commitments. During a visit to Stoke, Thompson relayed the assessment of another colleague: 'JC was deliberately adding extra things and talking to people to delay and then spoke for 30 mins plus at the campaign stop once they had arrived 40 mins late.' Others feared that Laura Alvarez was encouraging her husband's worst instincts in order to protect him from the pressures of campaigning. Such was the disintegration of trust within LOTO that aides nicknamed her 'Yoko'. On the morning of his visit to Stoke, he had begun the day's activities at a canal boat serving home-made Staffordshire oatcakes. According to one source, Alvarez was 'in one of her moods where she decided Jeremy needed to be on TV with his wife'. As an ITV crew filmed Corbyn preparing an oatcake with the local parliamentary candidate, Alvarez defied protocol and marched up to Corbyn: 'Make me one.' She then sat down and said to him in Spanish: 'Make me one with honey, I want one with honey.' Two junior aides frantically intervened and attempted to remove Alvarez, who was obscuring the shot. Yet she refused, giving the staff an upbraiding in full view of the rolling camera. 'I'm trying to make him happy and you're stopping it,' she snapped. 'I'm his wife, you need to let me do this, you don't understand what's good for him.' Corbyn declined to intervene. A cameraman whispered to one aide: 'What the fuck is going on?' Another aide said: 'This is really awkward, what do we do? There are like ten cameras here, this is fucking mental.' In the end, it took a nervous call to ITV that afternoon to prevent them from using the footage. Yet the incident underscored one of LOTO's unhappiest conclusions: in his poor state and during the long days, Corbyn had come to rely on Alvarez as an emotional shield.

★

Ephraim Mirvis was a man unaccustomed to the national media spotlight. Unlike Jonathan Sacks, his worldly predecessor as Britain's chief rabbi, Mirvis had been selected as a compromise candidate for his gentle touch and aptitude as a congregational leader. Yet the possibility of a Corbyn government, however distant, now led him to invite the full intensity of that spotlight in a manner entirely out of keeping with the traditions of British Jewry – not to mention his own retiring personality. Months of touring synagogues, where he canvassed the opinions of what his aides jokingly referred to as 'the Jews in the pews', had convinced him of the moral and political imperative to take the sort of stand that few religious leaders in Britain had ever done. When in August 2018, at the height of Labour's protracted internal row over whether to adopt the IHRA definition of anti-Semitism, Sacks had used an interview with the *New Statesman* to compare Corbyn to the race-baiting Enoch Powell, Mirvis had maintained a conspicuous silence. Fifteen months later, with polling day looming, the chief rabbi sat in the living room of his grace-and-favour Finchley home planning an intervention of his own.

Fuelled by Appletiser and artisan crisps, Mirvis and a coterie of trusted friends – among them leading academics on the Holocaust and anti-Semitism – deliberated over what, if anything, he should say about the possibility of a Jeremy Corbyn premiership. That he had a duty to speak out against the Labour Party, for decades the natural political home of Britain's Jews, was in little doubt among those in the room. The question that fell to his kitchen cabinet to consider was whether he should appeal directly to the public to vote against him. It was a proposition further complicated by the law, and his official status as the leader of a charity, which in theory constrained his ability to intervene in electoral politics. Denouncing Corbyn explicitly, especially in the middle of the short campaign, was deemed so risky by Mirvis's own in-house lawyers that they had told him flatly that any public statement was 'out of the question' and 'a non-starter'. But the chief rabbi would not take no for an answer. So it was that he turned to Anthony Julius, the esteemed solicitor at Mishcon de Reya, to find a way.

Julius assured Mirvis that he could go ahead – as long as he did not instruct voters on how they should cast their ballot. The advice dovetailed with Mirvis's desire to lay out the moral questions at play, rather than issue a directive to the voting public. The opinion of the eminent British Jews gathered in his living room was near enough unanimous: something must be done. There was one dissenting voice. Michael Levy, the Labour peer and Murphy's friend, was nervous. He counselled Mirvis against speaking out. What if Labour was to form the next government? What might happen to an already vulnerable Jewish community if it had burned its bridges with an emboldened and empowered Labour Party? As a wealthy, centrist Jew, Levy embodied every demographic that Corbyn had alienated during his leadership. Yet unlike his fellow travellers, he still believed that his party leader could win – with potentially disastrous consequences for Mirvis and the British Jews he represented. His appeal fell on deaf ears. Together with his advisers, Mirvis set to work writing an article that would detonate with extraordinary force.

After a day's deliberation, Mirvis and his team settled on a form of words. In an opinion piece that they envisaged offering to a daily newspaper, he would say: 'A new poison – sanctioned from the top – has taken root in the Labour Party … It is not my place to tell any person how they should vote. I regret being in this situation at all. I simply pose the question: What will the result of this election say about the moral compass of our country? When December 12 arrives, I ask every person to vote with their conscience. Be in no doubt, the very soul of our nation is at stake.' The *Daily Mail* promised Mirvis several pages, but negotiations broke down after Geordie Greig, its editor, attempted to haggle on Saturday – when the chief rabbi and his entire team were off grid for the Sabbath. The piece was eventually placed with Henry Zeffman, *The Times*'s millennial political correspondent. It was unleashed upon an unsuspecting Corbyn on 26 November – the day, by coincidence, that Labour was to launch its race-and-faith manifesto.

The news sent Corbyn into a spiral. Even at his lowest moments on the campaign trail, his appetite for chummy small talk with his staff – or a restorative Twix or Wagon Wheel – remained undimmed. But allegations of anti-Semitism struck at the very core of his sense of self. He could not comprehend that he was accused of tolerating racism – or worse, prosecuting it himself. That morning, Corbyn texted Murphy to flag his irritation at yet another diary dispute: 'Sorry. Not happy about any of this.' As one close aide and confidant puts it: 'Those were the only times I ever saw him completely silent.' The gravity of Mirvis's intervention was such that Corbyn, who had been scheduled to speak at the launch of the manifesto for a maximum of ten minutes, if at all, was dispatched to Tottenham's Bernie Grant Centre for an extended speech. Luckily, or perhaps unluckily, it was within easy reach of Westminster and Islington by car and Tube.

Corbyn faced the indignity of travelling to a venue named in honour of his old comrade and constituency neighbour, one of the first black MPs ever elected to Parliament, to explain that he was not a racist.

A hostile crowd gathered outside while within a gospel choir serenaded the roomful of journalists. 'It was so tense up there, there could have been violence,' one of Corbyn's team recalls. 'It could have been five seconds away. I was getting abused. Staff were getting abused.' One Jewish Labour official wept. Discussions over just what Corbyn could say delayed his arrival, and with it put Shadow Equalities Minister Dawn Butler, who was fronting the launch, in the spotlight. An official present said: 'Jeremy was really, really, really, really late ... Dawn was angry, and throwing around wild threats about cancelling the event.' In a moment of outright insubordination, Butler threatened to call the event to a close after her speech, denying Corbyn the chance to respond to Mirvis. In the end, she permitted her leader to speak. But over the course of that speech, in which he railed against 'the scourge of anti-Semitism', he did not provide the apology that both his opponents and critics so desperately wanted.

Later that day, Andrew Neil would attempt to make him. Unlike Boris Johnson, Corbyn had agreed to be interviewed for thirty minutes by the BBC's most feared inquisitor at prime time. The bulk of the interview focused on the day's big news: Mirvis's article. Corbyn, who had arrived two hours late to prepare for the debate, was in no mood to be interrogated. He shared Milne's and McDonnell's view that the BBC had conned them into participating whilst knowing all along that the Tories had never agreed to put Johnson forward for the same treatment. He scoffed and sighed as Neil tried in vain four times to induce an apology. He dismissed Mirvis as wrong. 'You said in the ITV debate that anyone who has committed any anti-Semitic act in the Labour Party, they've been suspended or expelled and you've investigated, your words, "every single case",' Neil said. 'The chief rabbi has called that "a mendacious fiction". And he's right, isn't he?'

Corbyn shot back: 'No, he's not right.'

'Really?' said an incredulous Neil.

Said Corbyn: 'Because he would have to produce the evidence to say that's mendacious.' As was always the case when his anti-racist credentials were questioned or impugned, Corbyn became emotional. 'It's not the language they should use, not the language I would use,' he said of Labour members who spread Rothschild conspiracy theories. 'All I would say is that I have spent my life opposing racism in any form. I made the point that in the very place where we launched our manifesto this morning in Tottenham I've been on the streets there in the 1970s and 80s, when I lived in that area, opposing racism and that is what my life—' Neil attempted to interject. Corbyn barked the words he was wont to when his patience with a journalist had snapped. 'Andrew, can I finish, *please*?' His team watched with angst and incredulity. They knew what was to come: a series of headlines which accused Corbyn, not inaccurately, of failing to apologise to Britain's Jews. *The Times*'s splash headline read: 'Corbyn refuses to apologise'. The *Telegraph*'s: 'Corbyn refuses to apologise to Jews'. Even the studiously impartial *i*, Corbyn's favourite daily, socked it to him: 'Corbyn refuses to say sorry'. In the *Independent*, sketchwriter Tom Peck's verdict was withering: 'To wonder whether Neil/Corbyn was as bad as Frost/Nixon or Maitlis/York is to ask the wrong question, really. Because the sheer agony of it could not be contained within the parameters of the simple TV interview format.'

On the following morning's conference call, Ian Lavery's patience snapped. He had always been inclined to dismiss the worst headlines as politically motivated smears but even he conceded something now had to give. 'Why can't you just say sorry?' he barked. 'Just do it, man!' Privately, Corbynites had often consoled themselves with the knowledge that the UK's Jewish community was sufficiently small as to be of negligible importance in all but a dozen or so constituencies. Now MPs in seats well outside of the Jewish hubs of London and Manchester reported hearing the allegations repeated to them on the doorstep. Still Corbyn would not heed Lavery's appeal – and by any measure, it would be too late anyway.

Later that afternoon, Corbyn had one of the campaign's better moments when he used a hastily arranged press conference in Westminster to disclose that Labour had been leaked a document detailing trade negotiations between the UK and US. The document, he said, served as definitive proof that the NHS was 'on the table' in a post-Brexit trade deal between Britain and the Trump administration. Corbyn managed to muffle his frustration and his grief over the chief rabbi's intervention to deliver an improved performance. 'This is not only a plot against our NHS,' he told the audience. 'It is a plot against the whole country.' With the subsequent release of the 451-page document, Labour successfully pushed the chief rabbi off the news bulletins.

But it was late in the day for a surge. At 10 p.m. that evening, *The Times* published YouGov's first seat prediction of the campaign. The same model had successfully predicted a hung parliament in 2017, in spite of Westminster's received wisdom that Corbyn was on course for a defeat of historic proportions. It had turned some on the left into cargo cultists. No matter what the polls said, YouGov would bear good news. And so it did – for Johnson. The Conservatives would win 359 seats, and Labour just 211.

The bazooka had failed. As Milne had warned, it wasn't 2017 any more. Ian Lavery, who was facing exactly the sort of Conservative challenge he thought would never reach mining towns like his, issued daily instructions to officials to add seats to their target list. Shadow Cabinet ministers including Angela Rayner, Richard Burgon and Rebecca Long-Bailey were among those whose constituencies were earmarked for extra resources, lest the electorate wipe out the left entirely. One recalls: 'Ian would call in and say: "I've just spoken to so and so and they say they're in real trouble."' McDonnell's hug-a-Remainer strategy was failing badly: alienating those who had voted Brexit whilst failing to nullify support for the Liberal Democrats and the Greens.

Milne and Murphy responded by turning to a man they knew could be relied on to do their bidding. 'Seumas felt that our policy had two legs, negotiating Brexit, then hold a referendum, but by focusing almost exclusively on the referendum, we only ever stood on one fucking leg! That's why he got in Steve,' said one campaign aide. A former *Guardian* sports journalist and childhood friend of Peter Mandelson, Steve Howell had advised Labour during the 2017 campaign and written a book about his experiences, *Game Changer*, in which, some complained, he took credit for their work and sexed up his own achievements. Tim Waters, enraged by the perceived snub to his expertise, even gathered signatures for a letter trying to block Howell's appointment as a consultant to the campaign. But as the final fortnight loomed, Howell elbowed his way in.

With almost manic energy, he started tabling ideas for winning back Labour Leavers. In one meeting, he suggested that Corbyn name his

Brexit negotiating team – and commit to including the likes of Lavery, who by then had made clear he would vote to Leave in a second referendum. Howell wanted to change the narrative put forward by other Shadow Cabinet ministers, namely McDonnell, Keir Starmer and Diane Abbott, all of whom had said repeatedly that they would campaign to Remain. The unions, who had kicked off the campaign with a joint piece for the *New Statesman* in which they implicitly rebuked Starmer and McDonnell, agreed with him. Yet the Shadow Chancellor's camp blocked the plan. They claimed it would lead to 'silly' Westminster stories about who was where on Corbyn's pecking order. Howell also said Labour should produce more digital content with 'trusted Leave voices' – naming, among others, Grace Blakeley, a 26-year-old *New Statesman* journalist. That she lived in London and was 'only known on Twitter' led to another veto. Conversations such as these started to fit a predictable loop: Milne's or Murphy's camp would propose throwing red meat to Brexiteers. But McDonnell or one of his acolytes would block the idea for fear of angering Remainers.

Behind the scenes, even the party's in-house pollsters had gone rogue, commissioning contradictory studies behind each other's backs. At the outset of the campaign, Waters and Sookoo had negotiated a discount on the party's YouGov polling by eschewing an exclusivity agreement and allowing the company to sell on the data generated by their polls to others. This created a 'slush fund' of leftover cash with which they commissioned top-up research that revealed that Brexit was in fact a low priority issue for most, even Labour Leavers. 'Brexit is only ranked as number one by 7 per cent of respondents in this group, a similar proportion to those who choose climate change,' Sookoo wrote in one paper. Yet Milne and Carl Shoben, the latter using the talent for covert operations he had honed during his years as a Blairite foot soldier in Downing Street, enlisted their own firm – ICM – to track national opinion, the results of which they shared selectively with allies. Shoben routinely passed information to Howell to buttress his case that Labour needed to embrace Leave voters and explicitly address the issue of Brexit. In one November memo, Howell declared: 'In my view, the "Don't mention Brexit to Leave voters" policy was always unsustainable because voters don't live in a bubble – they watch the TV debates and they talk to friends and family who, if they're Remain supporters, may have had "final say" content [on a second referendum] from us. We need to take the argument on and win it.' In the world of the Labour Party, where officials weaponise information to advance their own ends, these tactics were not new – but the fact they were being deployed during an election campaign was extraordinary. As the penultimate week approached, Waters announced he was resigning. He would see out the campaign, but could no longer work in an environment so toxic.

At 3 p.m. on Sunday 24 November, as Boris Johnson prepared to launch his manifesto in Telford, Labour's campaign team had gathered in the Northern Room of Southside to patch over their divides and agree on a last minute new strategy for the final fortnight. Corbyn was not invited. Later in the day, he would be appearing alongside Lily Allen to launch the party's cultural manifesto – and aides were cautious not to dent his morale as he entered the home straight. In the event, McDonnell chaired the meeting, which included Andrew Murray, recovering from his triple bypass, and Jennie Formby, herself recovering from breast cancer, among others. From the outset, they were in unanimous agreement on one thing: Labour's campaign was not working. The party had edged to within 10 points of the Tories in some polls, but it was not nearly in hung-parliament territory. Even the basics, such as the slogan, were agreed to have been a disaster. It fell to Andrew Murray to propose an alternative: 'We're on your side'. Some felt that it had not been sufficiently road-tested in focus groups or polls. Yet he argued that it encapsulated Labour's offer to Leave voters – 'we're for ordinary people, while the Tories are for the rich' – and managed to get it approved. 'This is bonkers stuff,' one person present recalls thinking. 'You have to repeat one message throughout the campaign and here we are changing our slogan.'

Far more fundamental to the campaign than its slogan was Labour's targeting strategy. The party's original list of target seats, fuelled by Murphy's and Milne's optimism, included sixty-six seats they hoped to gain and thirty seats they needed to defend. Again, the room was unanimous that Labour had to rip up its plans and adopt a radically defensive approach: the party would retain its offensives but bump up the number of defensives to sixty-seven. Howell read out a list of seats which the party would now send last-minute resources to, most of which lay in the Midlands and north-east. Sookoo exploded. For weeks, he had been agitating for resources to defend seats in Labour's heartlands, only to be ignored. 'I'm pleased for Steve Howell that he hasn't been ridiculed and derided to the same extent that I was when I proposed the same seats,' he said venomously. The comments were directed at Milne, who said nothing and went red in the face.

One question lingered, however: what would Labour actually do over the next fortnight? Would it run away from or towards Brexit – and would Corbyn do anything differently himself? At this point, Steve Howell, who was dialling in from his home in Cardiff, acknowledged the elephant in the room and said that Labour had to do more to win over Leavers in the coming days by clarifying its Brexit policy. He then revealed that he and Shoben had drafted a questionnaire to see which of Labour's Brexit lines won the best reaction from the public. ICM, the polling company, was ready to press 'go'. All that was required was for the team to sign off the necessary funding. Sookoo said there was no evidence that Leavers cared about Brexit more than the NHS. 'Why are we wasting money talking to people about Brexit?' he said. 'We're meant to be talking about other stuff.' Andrew Fisher rowed in behind him, saying that Howell had failed to provide any evidence that Labour had more of a problem with Leavers than Remainers. Few spoke in Howell's favour, except Shoben, who, given his previous employer, was regarded in the room with inherent suspicion. With Howell 150 miles away, McDonnell delivered the kiss of death. Earlier in the day, the Shadow Chancellor had infuriated several present in the room by telling Sky's Sophy Ridge that he would not stay neutral in a second EU referendum. Now he spoke into the phone to Howell: 'I don't think you got enough support in the room for your proposal.'

The following morning, the BBC's Iain Watson reported that Labour had adopted a new strategy with just two weeks to go until polling day. Despite the decision not to follow Howell's proposals, Watson's report bore Howell's fingerprints to such an extent that it might as well have carried his byline. 'Insiders told the BBC that in the first half of the election campaign, a key error was that the Liberal Democrat threat had been overestimated, while the willingness of Leave voters to switch from Labour to the Conservatives had been underestimated,' Watson wrote. 'In the last two weeks of the campaign, this will change.' Though McDonnell had not assented to a formal change in plan, he had, as a concession to Howell, agreed to send Lavery on a tour of Leave areas – and to promote more Brexiteer Shadow Cabinet ministers in public. The seats most at risk were like his own in Wansbeck: deindustrialised 'Red Wall' towns in the north and Midlands that never, or only seldom, backed the Conservatives. Some had fallen to the Tories at the high-water mark of Thatcherism, only to rapidly return to Labour hands. Others had been solidly red – but fading – for decades. In 2017 Theresa May had coveted them. She and Nick Timothy, her wonkish aide, believed they were susceptible to a new, communitarian conservatism that believed in Brexit and a strong state, but hoved to the right on questions of identity, nation and culture. In only six seats had she succeeded. Ben Bradley, the MP for Mansfield, liked to call himself the first blue brick in the Red Wall. LOTO had devoted much of its time and energy to winning such towns back. But as the 2019 campaign ground on, it became painfully clear to the likes of Lavery that far more were about to fall.

Labour's 'new strategy' did not go much deeper than changing the window dressing. Labour had merely agreed to disagree, and soldier on, until the finishing line.

As the final week of the campaign began, chinks of light began to appear. With Britain's hospitals sinking into a winter crisis, Johnson endured a torrid week. On 9 December, three days before polling day, the *Daily Mirror* ran a front page that some Conservatives believed might cost them a majority. Pictured beneath the headline 'Desperate' was a sick 4-year-old boy forced to sleep on the floor of Leeds General Infirmary. When confronted with the picture live on ITV, Johnson had snatched it out of reporter Joe Pike's hand and stuffed it in his pocket, refusing to even glance at it. Here was the prime minister Labour had longed for the public to see: unempathetic, cold, heartless. The polls had narrowed too. In a vindication of McDonnell's strategy, Liberal Democrat voters were returning to Labour. In some surveys, Johnson's lead had narrowed to just 5 points. The hung parliament – and with it Corbyn's path to Number 10 – was back in sight. With two days to go, YouGov updated its seat predictions. The projected Conservative majority had fallen to twenty-eight. For those who wanted to believe, it was manna from heaven.

Others were under no illusions. Earlier in the week, according to the WhatsApp group of senior aides, an exhausted Corbyn had instructed Murphy to book a rally in Middlesbrough but 'cancel other stops'. Then, on 10 December, footage emerged of Jon Ashworth, the Shadow Health Secretary, dismissing Labour's chances in a phone call to a Tory friend who had secretly recorded him: 'I've been going round these national places, it's dire for Labour ... it's dire ... it's awful for them, and it's the combination of Corbyn and Brexit ... outside of the city seats ... it's abysmal out there ... they can't stand Corbyn and they think Labour's blocked Brexit. I think middle-class graduates – Remainy people – Labour's doing well among ... but not in big enough numbers to deny the Tories a majority.' Ashworth, who despite his unerring accuracy pretended to have been joking, immediately called Corbyn to apologise. Corbyn was immediately forgiving.

Some at the heart of Corbyn's operation still believed. As the clock ticked down to polls closing at 10 p.m. on 12 December, Helene Reardon-Bond and her team put the finishing touches to their plan for government. Corbyn had told Mark Sedwill, the Cabinet Secretary, that a Labour government would remodel Whitehall and transform Britain: a Department for Housing, a Department for Women and Equalities, a Ministry of Labour and a Ministry of Employment Rights would be set up on day one. The machinery of government would immediately set to work renationalising mail, water and the railways, and negotiating a new deal with the European Union. A list of ministers had already been prepared. Everything was in place – apart from a willing public.

The scale of the disaster that had befallen the Project became clear for LOTO just after 11.30 p.m., when Blyth Valley in Northumberland declared its result. This, in the Labour imagination at least, was coal country. So ferocious was the historical aversion to the Conservatives in this corner of the north-east that it had in the 1970s been a marginal seat contested by a Labour candidate and an Independent Labour candidate. But in 2019 its voters were willing to do what was once unthinkable. The bashful face of the Conservative candidate Ian Levy, a bespectacled mental health nurse, said it all as his victory was declared. In Downing Street, Boris Johnson leapt to his feet and punched the air. Dominic Cummings, sat nearby on a laptop, surveyed the data. The exit poll and its prediction of a Tory landslide was accurate. The Red Wall was crumbling.

A little under two hours later, Ian Lavery took to the same stage and learned he had just kept hold of Wansbeck. His majority cratered from over 10,000 to just 854. Using lines primarily authored by Milne, he cast the Project as a victim of Brexit. 'This isn't about Jeremy Corbyn – this is about Brexit,' he boomed. 'This is about the rerun of the 2016 referendum. You ignore democracy at your peril.' Across the north and Midlands the pattern was repeated. In nearby North West Durham, Laura Pidcock, the Project's heir apparent, fell too. Safe seats became marginals with majorities in the low thousands and hundreds at a stroke.

As the Project sought to justify its humiliation, would-be contenders to the throne circled. All blamed Corbyn, in name or otherwise. In Birmingham, Jess Phillips delighted in twisting the knife. Smiling, she told reporters: 'Of course somebody like me could be the leader of the Labour Party! Will I be is an entirely different question.' In Wigan, Lisa Nandy cast herself as a voice for the communities Labour had lost. 'This has been a long time coming . . . I have listened. I have heard you. I will make it my mission from this day forward to bring Labour home to you.' For other opponents of the Project, it was a moment of catharsis. Years of resentment came to the fore, bursting the dam. On ITV, the former Home Secretary Alan Johnson, who had long blamed the Corbynites for sabotaging the Labour Remain campaign he had helmed in 2016, let rip as Jon Lansman sat impassive in a Hawaiian shirt. 'The working class have always been a big disappointment to Jon and his little cult,' he fumed. 'I want them out of the party. I want Momentum gone. Go back to your student politics and your little left wing.' Corbyn, he positively spat, 'couldn't lead the working class out of a paper bag'.

The leader himself seemed to have internalised the criticism. Just after 2 a.m. Corbyn arrived at Southside. Embossed on a wall near the entrance were the words of Tony Blair's Clause IV: 'By the strength of our common endeavour we achieve more than we achieve alone.' As Blair's old seat of Sedgefield fell to the Conservatives, and the Project's reign disintegrated into another civil war, they read more like gallows humour.

He needed to apologise. Heading to Jennie Formby's office on the eighth floor, where the leaders of Britain's unions had gathered, Corbyn immediately sought out Murphy. Together they stole a moment's peace in a side room. An era collapsed around them. Murphy was weeping.

The Conservatives had asked an exhausted nation to Get Brexit Done. Another future was possible. Corbyn had stood before the British people and asked them, for the second time in two and a half years, to put their faith in the Project. In no uncertain terms they had told him no.

Corbyn had not yet apologised to his MPs or his voters. First he made peace with Murphy. He stood alone before the woman he had sacked so unceremoniously. 'I regret it, and I never should have done it,' he told her. Corbyn was speaking of the damage he had wrought on their relationship over the previous weeks, rather than his leadership. But that night even his closest comrades wondered what they had done.

15

Winning Keir

Keir Starmer's campaign for the Labour leadership began long before the 2019 election was called, let alone lost. It was in the wake of that May's local elections that Labour MPs first began to catch wind of the Shadow Brexit Secretary's ambition, or at least that nurtured by his loyal acolytes on his behalf. In the Commons tea room Jenny Chapman, the MP for Darlington, and Carolyn Harris, the plain-speaking deputy leader of Welsh Labour, would hold court with colleagues. It would not take long for their conversations to arrive at Starmer's virtues.

By then it was clear to many Labour MPs that the Project's days were numbered. Divided by Brexit, flatlining in the polls and trapped in a hung parliament which enabled neither government nor opposition to achieve anything constructive, a general election inevitable, their party's defeat was merely a question of when. That obliged them to consider the altogether more pertinent – and existential – question of *who*.

Chapman's adoration for Starmer, under whom she had served as a Shadow Brexit minister, was not news to the PLP. Gareth Snell, who like Chapman had seen his council fall to pro-Brexit parties in the wake of the locals, joked that she ought to run for leader herself. 'Then we could keep the same hashtags: JC4PM!' Chapman did not humour him but instead made an alternative suggestion. It should be Starmer. Harris, elected alongside him in 2015, had come to the same conclusion. She had urged her friend to run when the time came. By the summer of 2019, it was obvious that the time would soon come.

There was nothing inevitable about Starmer's succession, though. Labour's collapse had unfolded in what were once the party's heartlands. Immediately the essay question was set: how could Corbyn's successor reclaim these seats, surrendered to the Conservatives for the first time, not only overnight, but after decades of steady decline? And if Brexit had been the trigger, how could the answer be Starmer – the very architect of the policy that the Corbynites believed had most alienated them? And yet the Project ultimately did lose control of the party to him – a man who had served loyally, yes, but without ever truly believing.

That the Corbyn story should end with the defeat of his chosen successor – Rebecca Long-Bailey – would reveal much about a membership that had sustained the Project for four years without ever being truly understood. Unlike the seats Labour had lost, it was an overwhelmingly Europhile body of opinion. Starmer had become its champion quite accidentally. He had not entered Parliament in 2015 to agitate endlessly for EU membership. Nor had he become Shadow Brexit Secretary with a view to making the case for Remain. Again and again he had warned advocates of a second referendum in private that their cause was doomed. His mission was to deliver Brexit as painlessly as possible.

The year 2018 had changed everything. At that year's conference Starmer had pushed loyalty to its limit. He took ownership of a Brexit policy authored by a membership that largely loved Corbyn, but could not stomach leaving the EU. Inch by inch, he dragged Labour towards a policy that he himself had once dismissed, to the delight of a grateful membership. He addressed their rallies and, by the end of 2019, was giving voice around the Shadow Cabinet table and on the airwaves to their demands that Labour should back not just a second referendum but *Remain*. In Starmer a weary membership saw a man who had been just as willing to fight what they saw as a historic injustice as Corbyn. The PLP, themselves ground down by the Project, saw a saviour too. And to those who wished to consign Corbynism to history, the man who had given a human face to its division and equivocation over the most fundamental question of British politics in decades became, despite their misgivings, their only hope of winning back the membership.

Starmer's victory would not only mark the end of the Project, but would expose the breach that had opened up between Corbyn and the grass roots he had pledged to represent when he first ran, albeit reluctantly, in 2015.

*

It had been widely assumed that the Project would anoint its successor, that they would be a true believer, and that the membership, who had proved so loyal to Corbyn in his hours of need in 2015 and 2016, would duly follow. That successor was also likely to be a woman, the Conservatives having built up a 2–0 lead over Labour in gender representation at the top. On all counts, the odds seemed stacked against Starmer.

Yet in poll after poll the Labour membership said he was their first choice. On 17 July, a week before Boris Johnson entered Downing Street, YouGov revealed that 68 per cent of voters believed Starmer would make a good leader of the Labour Party – more than any other candidate, including John McDonnell, the Project's owner-architect. In the absence of a leader willing or able to take a decisive stand on the dominant issue of the parliamentary year, Starmer had owned Labour's response to Brexit. Not only that, he had been willing to respond in terms that a largely pro-Remain grass roots had liked. With the Stakhanovite work ethic that he had applied to his career at the bar, he traipsed from local party to local party, preaching his gospel to party members. To what end, he was not yet willing to say. But both his direction of travel and the eventual destination were clear.

That Starmer could expect support from some of the Project's most prominent evangelists became apparent on 29 August, the day news broke of Johnson's decision to prorogue Parliament in pursuit of Brexit. That night he took to Parliament Square to lead a rally against the decision. Europe had not only made a front-line politician out of Starmer, but to the grass roots it had also given him the air of the protestor against historic injustices – a mantle that had proved so lucrative for Corbyn. Alongside him were Diane Abbott, John McDonnell, Paul Mason and Laura Parker. Together Mason and Parker formed the vanguard of the Project's pro-EU wing. In that moment they saw the candidate who might carry their politics forward once Corbyn left the stage. 'It's not like Keir was particularly thinking: right, I'm going to launch a campaign if we lose,' said one friend. 'But there was definitely a moment of coalescence around him by activists.'

The next day, Starmer and Mason would meet again at the Rose pub, just off the Albert Embankment. Their summit would be filmed

covertly by an observer and leaked to Guido Fawkes, who duly head-
lined its video: 'Starmer plots with loopy Mason'. 'Embarrassing' was
its pithy verdict. What readers could not have known was that Starmer
had been summoned for an anointment. Out of shot was Parker. In
the frame but unidentified was Eloise Todd, the chief executive of
anti-Brexit campaign group Best for Britain. They had summoned
Starmer to tell him that he might need to take the helm of an interim
coalition government in the event that Johnson's administration fell.
He listened patiently, but was non-committal. Yet the nascent team
around him had another job in mind: leader of the Labour Party.

By the time the general election campaign had begun, so too had
Starmer's leadership bid. Early in the campaign he met Parker and
Mason again over an Indian takeaway from Westminster institution
Kennington Tandoori. Their host was Tom Kibasi, a former McKinsey
partner and the director of the Institute for Public Policy Research.
Once a laboratory for Blairite thought, the think tank had assumed a
new life under Corbyn as an engine room for bold economic thinking.
Kibasi himself, like Mason, had been much closer to John McDonnell
than Corbyn. He was of the left, but not the Project.

Kibasi, whose corporate hinterland and second-row-forward's
physique set him apart from most other Westminster wonks, played
host in his kitchen. There were three items on his agenda. The first
was how Labour's campaign was likely to go, to which all agreed
that the answer was a variation on badly. The second was just *how*
badly things were likely to go: would Labour merely lose, or would
they be annihilated? The third, and for Starmer the most important,
was where Labour might go afterwards – or, rather, where he would
take it.

On Monday mornings and Thursday afternoons during the
campaign, Starmer headed to chez Kibasi to hammer out the answers
to those questions. It was a professionalised operation from the outset,
with seven individual groups assigned to working out the practicalities
of fundraising and securing the necessary nominations from MPs and
trade unions. By the time the exit poll revealed that Corbyn had led
Labour to its worst defeat since 1935, Keir Starmer already knew how
he would win the leadership election that would follow.

Alongside them at the Thursday meetings was Morgan McSweeney.
Nobody understood Labour's membership as well as him, even if

recent history suggested otherwise: in 2015, as Corbyn cruised to victory, he had led Liz Kendall's doomed campaign to just 4.5 per cent of the vote. He had spent the years since working out how his wing of the party might recapture Labour from the Project, as he had managed to do while running the resistance to the leftist administration at Lambeth Council and in Vauxhall's fractious Constituency Labour Party. McSweeney hailed from a distinct Labour tradition. Together with Labour First's Matt Pound and Nathan Yeowell, who had become director of Progress the previous year, they had spent much of the preceding months organising to help MPs win reselection as candidates in the teeth of opposition from the left. McSweeney and his kitchen cabinet plotted in private, over restaurant meals. Theirs was a localism agenda. Though McSweeney and Yeowell were close to Peter Mandelson, they had ascended not through Oxbridge and Westminster, or the Blairite spadocracy, but through councils. They believed that New Labour had lost its way in its second and third terms. It had ceased to speak a language that could root its own politics not only in the country it sought to represent, but its own party. One of their number summed up the attitudes of the Blairite hierarchy to its party thus: 'I'm gonna fuck you hard with a broom handle, and you're going to turn around and say, "Thank you, Tony, that was great."' An autocratic culture had left Labour's modernisers estranged not only from their communities, but from their members.

Labour Together, set up in the wake of the 2017 election, had been McSweeney's answer. Unlike Labour First and Progress, it did not face outwards but inwards. Its aims were at one with the two last bastions of organised Corbynscepticism in the party, but unlike them it looked to unite members rather than divide them along factional lines, and Pound and Yeowell kept its work deliberately separate from their own operations. Between 2007 and 2009 McSweeney had worked beneath David Evans, an assistant general secretary of the Labour Party under Blair, at a little-known Croydon outfit called the Campaign Company. Its work – most successfully applied in Barking, where the Labour council spent much of the late 2000s battling with the BNP – was formulating psychological and political strategies for binding disparate groups behind a common mission. Rather than segmenting the electorate and slicing and dicing communities, how might Labour bring them together with language? Moreover, how might the Corbynsceptics use that very formula to turn the Project's internal coalition against itself?

McSweeney had spent the 2017 parliament in the background, commissioning focus groups in an attempt to get beneath the skin of a selectorate that many assumed had been lost to the Project's supporters for ever. Said one Corbynsceptic organiser: 'Morgan was at the centre of thinking of new ways of building new coalitions within the Labour Party and actually thinking about how you try to get the MPs to think critically about how they work better with each other, instead of just being a bunch of egos in a room.' Another added: 'He has a good understanding of the kind of language and stuff that members want to speak.' In Starmer he found a candidate willing to speak it.

Kibasi and McSweeney would school Starmer in what it meant to win a Labour membership that few understood. For a start, it was not composed of the ideological Corbynites of the popular imagination. Indeed, many members were not particularly political. Their devotion to the Project was not unconditional. In most cases it was barely devotion. Slides shown to Starmer at their early meetings by the strategists hammered home those points. Only a quarter of the membership were ideologues: 20 per cent of them of the left, and 5 per cent of them of the Blairite, pro-privatisation, Iraq-apologetic right. Neither camp was likely to row behind Starmer. Nor were the 10 per cent of identitarians, those for whom diversity was the lodestar of their politics.

But beyond those groups lay a winning coalition. A quarter were instrumentalists, for whom politics was a means to an end defined primarily by success or failure. They could be convinced to vote for anyone likely to help the left *win*. The remaining 40 per cent were the idealists, for whom politics was an expressive, emotional, values-led exercise: on Brexit but also on austerity. To win the idealists, as Corbyn had twice over, was to win the leadership. From his focus groups McSweeney knew how to do so. Labour members cared about two issues most: ending homelessness, and improving mental health provision. Crack those, and Starmer would win.

★

It took nearly a week after the election result for Starmer himself to go public. In the meantime Lisa Nandy, the Wigan MP and tribune of the towns Labour had lost in their dozens, had all but announced her candidacy. The thinking of Starmer's aides was that to have declared with unseemly haste in the wake of the defeat would have been lethal. Candidates thus engaged in a phoney war in the weeks before and after Christmas: first indicating that they were seriously considering standing, then confirming their candidacy, and then launching physically, so as to guarantee three bites of the news cherry.

Starmer's proxies were not so reluctant. On the morning of 13 December, Harris had texted him urging him to put himself forward and put an end to the destructive years of the Project. Three days later, Chapman – who had lost her seat in pro-Leave Darlington – appeared on the *Today* programme and cast herself as the devil on the shoulder of an otherwise reluctant Starmer.

'Labour can rebuild. But the choice we are facing now is whether we defeat the Tories in four years' time or face another decade of austerity of right-wing government. That's why I will be sitting in Keir Starmer's office until he agrees to stand,' she said. Of course, Starmer had spent the campaign sitting in Kibasi's kitchen working out *how* he would stand. By 17 December, Carolyn Harris was already in place as his de facto parliamentary private secretary and all-purpose hype-woman in the PLP. That evening Starmer soft-launched his campaign, without formally announcing his candidacy, in an interview with the *Guardian*.

His first intervention was laser-focused at the values-driven chunk of the selectorate that his team had identified as the lynchpin of any winning coalition. A Clause IV moment it was not. Starmer's first objective was to dispel suspicions that his leadership would mean a lurch to the right. He made clear from the off that the bulk of the Corbynite economic programme would remain intact. His would be a 'radical' Labour government. 'It's important not to oversteer,' he said. 'I don't think anyone would call me a Corbynista, but I'm a socialist … I don't need somebody else's name tattooed on my head to know what I think.'

In his secret sessions during the campaign, McSweeney had impressed upon Starmer the importance of not blaming Corbyn personally for defeat. Instead, he should emphasise values – specifically those Labour had abandoned, be it on austerity in 2015 and Europe in 2019. Rather than a candidate handpicked by what aides dubbed 'the clique wot lost it', he would be the man to unify the party around the sort of radical programme that Corbynites could get behind.

There was no explicit criticism of Corbyn as there was of the Blair and Brown governments' decision to 'stray' from their values. But he did, per the advice of Kat Fletcher, an aide and alumna of Corbyn's leadership campaigns, offer a glimpse of ankle on electability. 'I want trust to be restored in the Labour Party as a progressive force for good: and that means we have to win. But there's no victory without values.' He also argued that Labour had not offered a robust enough challenge to Johnson's clarion call to Get Brexit Done. 'We should have taken it down. Frankly I'd have liked the opportunity to have done it.' It was an explicit criticism of LOTO for keeping him as far from the media spotlight as possible in the preceding weeks.

The claim was not the cry of a bruised ego but was borne out by data: research by Loughborough University had found that, in three out of five weeks of the campaign, Starmer had not even been among the top twenty politicians mentioned in television and newspaper reports. In the two weeks that he had, he had languished towards the bottom of the pack.

He certainly did not want for attention now. Not all of it was positive. The Red Wall's many casualties found his complaints about airtime particularly galling. Gareth Snell, his team's old nemesis, tweeted: 'Those of us in Leave seats with small majorities in towns and small cities *begged* @Keir_Starmer to listen to us and our constituents when we told him that the party's Brexit policy was losing us votes. He wouldn't listen and we lost.' But in Starmer's early interventions the case for continuity Remain was also ostentatiously binned. Brexit was settled. They were playing a different game now.

The following morning, Starmer repeated his arguments on the *Today* programme. In the hours after Starmer's interview, the grandfather of the Project summoned its children to hear his last will and testament. By the time Corbynism's leading outriders had reached McDonnell's parliamentary office – among them LOTO's former spinner Matt Zarb-Cousin and Novara Media's Aaron Bastani, Ash Sarkar and Michael Walker – Long-Bailey had surrendered her position as the bookmakers' favourite to Starmer, whose *Guardian* piece had spooked some in the room. McDonnell was unambiguous nonetheless. Long-Bailey would be the candidate of the left. It was the duty of the outriders to get behind her.

He was not undaunted by the scale of the challenge ahead. McDonnell, according to those present, praised Starmer's opening offer to the selectorate as politically astute. His protégée, he acknowledged, would have a difficult time. Her name recognition, even among Labour members, was low, despite her turn opposite Rishi Sunak during the election debates. In the event that she won, she would head straight into an unforgiving set of local elections against the ascendant Johnson. It was an uninviting vista for the Labour left, if not a straightforwardly bleak one – and to get even a chance of surveying it, Long-Bailey would have to overcome Starmer, whom Milne also saw as the man to beat. Later that day Tony Blair told *Newsnight*'s Kirsty Wark that Labour would be 'finished' should the left retain control of the party. In private, some of the Project's most loyal adherents pondered whether the task was beyond them.

Where her rival had already assembled a team, a campaign infrastructure and a social media operation, Long-Bailey had nothing. The left had been beaten to the starting line. Zarb-Cousin offered his services, only to be told that the chosen candidate would assemble her team 'soon'. To some her willingness – still less her ability – remained a live question. In the weeks after the election she took a holiday to recuperate from the stress of the campaign. Some supporters now chalk that up as a strategic misstep. Said one supportive Shadow Cabinet minister: 'Becky wasn't really out of the traps as it were, and we were three, four weeks behind at the very beginning.' Nor was she a creature of the Westminster bubble but was settled in Salford. The campaign would be long, demanding and would take her far from home. To accept the mantle of the left was a big decision, and one she did not take lightly.

That she was expected to do so was above all a reflection of the left's generational weakness. There were plenty of MPs of Corbyn's, Abbott's and McDonnell's vintage – men and women in their 60s or 70s who had been selected and in most cases elected in the 1980s. But under Kinnock, John Smith and Blair, the left had effectively been locked out of Parliament by a hostile leadership. The 2015 and 2017 intakes had blooded relative youngsters in their 30s: the Long-Baileys and Burgons. But the Project had lost the generation in between. Stuck with a choice between has-beens and yet-to-bes, they were compelled to plump with the latter – and Long-Bailey was compelled to step up.

Neither frontrunner had yet admitted that they would definitely run by the time Emily Thornberry's fully formed bid was announced, also via the *Guardian*, on the afternoon of 18 December. It was an opening salvo met with wry smiles in LOTO. Front and centre was Thornberry's assertion, leant on heavily throughout the campaign, that she had warned the Shadow Cabinet that to back an election before a second referendum would be 'an act of catastrophic political folly'. For her prescience she would not be rewarded. Nor for her attempts to establish herself as the strongest foil to Johnson, whom, she insisted, she had already 'pummelled' from across the Dispatch Box during his ill-starred stint as Foreign Secretary.

Unlike Starmer, however, Thornberry had not been allowed to launch on her own terms. The previous weekend, a liberated Caroline Flint had taken the opportunity to pre-emptively douse Thornberry's platform with petrol in a post-defeat interview with Sky's Sophy Ridge. In answer to the question that now obsessed the pundits – how Labour might win back Red Wall seats like her old patch in Don Valley – Flint offered a clear and combustible opinion: by not electing a Remainer as its leader. In particular, it was not to elect Thornberry, who, Flint delighted in telling Ridge, had once told a fellow MP sitting for a Leave constituency: 'I'm glad my constituents aren't as stupid as yours.'

Neither woman was in the mood to surrender. Thornberry responded by threatening legal action. 'People can slag me off as long as it's true, I can take it on the chin,' she said. 'But they can't make up shit about me – and if they do, I have to take it to the courts. It's ridiculous, absolutely ridiculous. I have better things to think about than people going on television and making up shit.' It would be the most attention Thornberry's run would receive.

By the week after Christmas, Starmer had still not formally declared his bid but had assembled something close to a fully functioning campaign. Team Starmer's hard core worked out of the Camden Town home of Jenny Chapman and her husband, the Blaenau Gwent MP and whip Nick Smith – in a previous life an election agent for Starmer's predecessor as MP for Holborn and St Pancras, Frank Dobson. Having met and married as MPs with constituencies and families on opposite sides of the country, the couple were well accustomed to the hard yards of logistical planning. Their street gave the nascent campaign a code name for one of its WhatsApp channels – 'The Arlington Group' – a moniker whose significance was lost on new recruits. Before 2019 was out, adviser Kat Fletcher had drawn up a grid for the weeks to come. The road map to victory was in place.

The Project's own, meanwhile, were fighting among themselves. On 29 December, Ian Lavery – who had hitherto only flirted with a run for deputy – revealed via his spokesman he was 'seriously considering' a run of his own. Corbyn's more vocal online supporters – the likes of the SKWAWKBOX blog and Rachel Swindon, the Project's tweeter-in-chief – saw Lavery as the candidate who could rebuild the Red Wall with his bare hands: Lavery's own majority in Wansbeck, historically rock solid, had been cut to under 1,000; he blamed it squarely on Brexit. Long-Bailey, meanwhile, had yet to announce. Though Lavery had not originally intended to run, the groundswell of online support – and Long-Bailey's apparent reluctance – had piqued his interest. One SKWAWKBOX blog suggested he run on a joint ticket with Dawn Butler, adding that his 'tough image' – a barely coded reference to his miner's physique and tattoos – was just what Red Wall voters wanted. 'Neither he nor Dawn take any s***,' it added.

As if to underscore the Project's lack of coordination, Lavery's admission that he might enter the race coincided with Long-Bailey's. In a *Guardian* column she said she was considering a bid, waxed lyrical about the trade unions and made a tentative call for Labour to adopt a 'progressive patriotism'. The latter was ridiculed by the right and met with a mixture of disgust and concern on the left. In texts to Shadow Cabinet colleagues she described the piece as a 'starter for ten'. The Corbynite tastemaker and academic Alex Niven tweeted: 'Her statement seems like a cobbled-together press release of weak, half-heard ideas from the 2010s, not a radical vision for Labour revival.'

Starmer continued to press the advantage as 2020 began. On 4 January came his formal declaration via a social media video directed by Flo Wilkinson, the film-maker wife of Starmer's aide Ben Nunn (the couple had spent their Boxing Day driving across the country in pursuit of shots). Initially, the plan had been to follow a time-honoured tradition inaugurated by Neil Kinnock, whose personal life and

personality had been examined in close detail in a critically lauded
1987 election broadcast dubbed *Kinnock: The Movie*. Starmer would
introduce himself as a leadership candidate with a video about Keir
the man. But that plan was moderated in one of the campaign's first
meetings at Starmer's home. The problem was not so much with the
format but its subject. Though a clubbable and almost blokeish presence in private, Starmer's public personality was not his unique selling
point. One aide summed up the problem by describing how, on the
Eurostar home from an early trip to Brussels during her time in LOTO,
the Labour delegation had allowed themselves some rest and recu-
peration: Corbyn contented himself with a railway magazine and a
cup of tea; Thornberry kicked off her shoes and made short work of
a gin and tonic; Starmer, still immaculately clad in jacket and tie, had
delicately decanted a beer into a small plastic cup. Box office it was
not. So they decided instead to focus on Starmer's professional story
as Keir the lawyer. In that context, seriousness and earnestness were
his strongest virtues. It helped that Starmer too was much more
comfortable talking about his work than his family.

Starmer's tweet, in which he shared the film, struck a utopian note:
'I believe another future is possible – but we have to fight for it.' The
video's opening monologue, delivered by a retired miner in a thick
Yorkshire accent, offered a detailed testimony of Starmer's work
defending trade unions. His bona fides as an environmentalist were
also stressed. The Labour peer Doreen Lawrence, mother of murdered
teenager Stephen, gave a heartfelt personal endorsement. Blairism was
duly bashed: both Starmer's opposition to the Iraq War and a case in
which he had sued the New Labour government for denying welfare
to asylum seekers were given top billing. In this sentimental, selective
and well-crafted telling, Starmer was the real continuity candidate.
He had been to Blair and Brown in the courts what Corbyn had been
in the division lobbies. And crucially, he had actually managed to
achieve something in the process. In the PLP the reaction was close
to rapturous. No sooner had the video appeared than six MPs – more
than a quarter of the twenty-two required to clear the first stage of
nominations – offered public endorsements.

The Project's chosen continuity candidate was still nowhere near
ready. It was not until the same week as Starmer's official launch that
Matt Zarb-Cousin finally received a call from Jon Lansman taking him

up on the offer to head up comms for Long-Bailey's campaign he had
made more than a month earlier. Zarb-Cousin accepted the job with
alacrity. But he was nonetheless alive to the risks ahead. The Project's
succession plan had in fact been predicated on the survival of Laura
Pidcock, the outspoken star of 2017's Corbynites, in North West
Durham, who had lost her seat. In Long-Bailey they had an alternative
who had served the Project loyally but lacked Corbyn's long history
of left activism: he had emerged fully formed as a Shadow Cabinet
minister and putative successor after the Coup. Her attempt in her
launch article in *Tribune* magazine on 7 January to situate herself in
a recognisable left tradition invited ridicule. 'I don't just agree with
the policies,' she wrote, 'I've spent the last four years writing them.'
In an interview with ITV News the same day she was asked to give
a score to the outgoing leader and said: 'I thought Corbyn was one
of the most honest kind principled politicians I've ever met ... I'd give
him ten out of ten, because I respect him and I supported him all the
way through.' Starmer, asked the same question, made a protracted
song and dance of refusing to subject 'a colleague and a friend' to the
indignity of a rating out of ten.

Lansman knew instinctively that Long-Bailey would not win easily.
In leading Labour to its worst defeat in nearly a century the Project
had lost the ballast any leader needed to assemble a winning internal
coalition: the soft left. Long-Bailey not only needed to win them back,
but she needed to do so without alienating her own base, which was
smaller than most pundits realised. Said one campaign aide: 'The idea
that we were bequeathed 60 per cent of the membership is nonsense.
Jon was very astute, and he learned as well in the 1980s that the soft
left went with the right, that's how the right took control of the party,
because the left marginalised itself.' On the same evening as her formal
launch, Lavery offered his endorsement, reducing the potential number
of competitors on the left to just one, Clive Lewis, whose long-shot
bid had attracted little by way of media attention or grass-roots
support. Yet beyond the *Tribune* article and accompanying broadcast
round there was nothing: no logo, no slogan, and no plans for a formal
launch. 'Keir had millions of views on his video, and we had nothing,'
said one staffer. Two aides, Rory Macqueen and Mary Robertson, had
concluded the campaign was over before it really began. Both walked

out early as others protested at what they saw as control-freakery on Lansman's part.

Some wondered whether he himself had concluded the jig was up. From the beginning he emphasised the importance of what would come after a defeat. At times he seemed more preoccupied with the role Long-Bailey might play in Starmer's top team than her own. Lansman insisted that, in the event she lost, she should take up a seat in the Shadow Cabinet. The left could not afford to marginalise itself again, as it had done after Kinnock's victory in 1983. A colleague said: 'He wasn't just thinking about the leadership contest, he was thinking about after, and the future of the left.' To those on the inside of Long-Bailey's faltering campaign, it seemed increasingly obvious that the future would not involve her winning.

The extent to which Long-Bailey had failed to convince even Corbyn's stoutest supporters was illustrated in tragicomic fashion on 8 January, when HuffPost and *Newsnight* reported that Barry Gardiner – the Shadow International Trade Secretary known in Westminster as the Inconstant Gardiner – was considering a run. His spirited defences of the leadership, all the more incongruous for his past life as a junior minister under Blair and Brown, had won him cult-hero status among activists. Nobody, however, had considered him a serious contender or, indeed, a contender at all. The content of both reports was unremarkable but for the intriguing suggestion, briefed by a friend of Gardiner, that Len McCluskey had encouraged him to stand after concluding that Long-Bailey could not win. The story landed to a chorus of amusement and bemusement, such was Gardiner's reputation. But the notion that the power brokers of the left remained unconvinced by Long-Bailey did ring true.

Gardiner was stranded 3,500 miles away in the incongruous setting of a climate-change conference in Abu Dhabi when he received a call from McCluskey. 'Barry,' he said, 'you've got to deny this!' McCluskey issued a carefully worded denial that clarified he had not been approached by Gardiner, who nonetheless persevered for another twenty-four hours. After canvassing opinion from his Gulf hotel room he concluded that it would be 'insane' to run with no money, no campaign team and – on the basis of his phone conversations with colleagues – no support. Though Gardiner disappeared from the field as quickly as he arrived, suspicions that Long-Bailey was not even the first choice of the Project's most reliable supporters would linger.

That founding members of the Project had concluded that their own future lay with Starmer did not help either. The day before Long-Bailey's launch in *Tribune*, Kat Fletcher and her namesake Simon – both survivors of Corbyn's 2015 campaign – were publicly announced as senior members of Starmer's campaign staff. Their first step toward rebuilding a winning coalition was in persuading Starmer and Jenny Chapman to ban the use of the word Trot, until then used liberally by campaign staff to describe Project loyalists. 'I'm not a Trot, and all the majority of people who support Jeremy are not Trots,' Fletcher insisted. Chapman obliged. As one member of his team put it, Starmer's campaign had grasped that the membership didn't want to be told 'how stupid they were to have voted for Jeremy in the first place'. The two Fletchers certainly did not think that had been the case. And even if the intellectual chieftains of Starmer's campaign privately disagreed, they knew that winning the membership back from the Project required them to keep the sentiment to themselves.

Announced alongside Kat and Simon were their political opposites in McSweeney and Matt Pound, the national organiser of Labour First. McSweeney and Kat Fletcher shared an aim: to unite as much of the membership behind Starmer as possible. Preferably a majority of them, so that he won in the first round and with it became the party's undisputed master, as Corbyn had twice over. But while they were united on means, the ends differed. The ultimate aim of the Starmer campaign for McSweeney was to convince a pro-Corbyn membership to marginalise Corbynism without their realising it, a specific purpose that was directly at odds with some of its backers on the left. McSweeney's was an exclusive vision of party unity. The Starmer campaign was, in effect, subcontracted to Labour Together. As Peter Mandelson reflects of McSweeney now: 'I don't know who and how and when he was invented, but whoever was responsible ... They will find their place in heaven.'

The news that the leading lights of organised Corbynscepticism had identified Starmer as their man was fatal for Jess Phillips. She had beaten him to the punch with a glossy launch video of her own on 3 January, but her candidacy – which sought to sell the force of her divisive personality as an antidote to Johnson's own freewheeling style

– would burn short and not terribly brightly. Where Team Starmer would make a conscious effort to dissociate their man from Brexit, Phillips used her first broadcast interview with Andrew Marr to suggest that she might campaign to rejoin the EU. It ensured that her campaign's image would be one of kamikaze Corbynscepticism. Phillips would last barely three weeks in the race – and the institutional infrastructure that might have otherwise supported her was instead buttressing Starmer.

On the same day that McSweeney's appointment was confirmed, Starmer's status as front runner was cemented by the early endorsement of UNISON, the biggest of the Big Four unions. Having given his first speech of the campaign at Manchester's Mechanics' Institute, the birthplace of the TUC, on 11 January, that status was confirmed come the close of MP nominations two days later. Starmer, with eighty-eight, won more than Long-Bailey, with thirty, and Nandy, with thirty-one, combined. Phillips and Thornberry both squeaked over the line with twenty-three, one more than the requisite twenty-two.

On 14 January Paul Mason offered Starmer his public endorsement. Mason's pro-Remain stance and public attacks on LOTO – and in particular the influence of Seumas Milne, Len McCluskey and Andrew Murray – meant the decision was no surprise to close observers. His relationship with the Unite axis of LOTO had become so acrimonious that he had been barred from campaigning on the stump in Birmingham Northfield, a plum marginal lost to the Conservatives, on election day. Mason's endorsement of Starmer was the inevitable destination of a long journey. Mason had come to believe that Corbyn himself was culpable for the Project's failure. He says now: 'The blame has to lie with Jeremy Corbyn, because that's what leadership is. When people see Keir Starmer leading they'll realise what was missing – professionalism, prudential principle, resilience, communicative ability, and the ability to focus a team around a task – none of that was there, and you know, it could have been there, but for some reason those around Jeremy wanted something different.' Laura Parker's endorsement for Starmer would follow a little over a month later, despite Momentum's endorsement of Long-Bailey.

Mason was among those who had helped Starmer sketch out the contours of his own vision. Starmer loathed selling himself and the process was neither an easy or straightforward one. It had taken some time for the newcomers to his team to draw out his personal phil-osophy, which was less a fully formed ideological world view than it was a more inchoate moral compulsion. 'Sum up for us why you want to be leader,' Mason had asked at an early meeting. 'Because,' Starmer said, 'if I see something wrong in society, I can't turn my head and walk on the other side of the road. I've got to do something about it.' After some cajoling, Starmer as the Good Samaritan duly became the campaign's leitmotif. On 15 January he took to the *Guardian* to set out his case for a new 'moral socialism', writing: 'I have always been motivated by a burning desire to tackle inequality and injustice, to stand up for the powerless against the powerful. That's my socialism.' It also attempted to steal Long-Bailey's thunder with a promise to 'hard-wire' into his policy platform the Green New Deal policy she had overseen under Corbyn.

The intervention served a dual purpose. The first was to situate Starmer firmly on the left of the field. The second was to carve out an identity distinct from his advocacy for Remain, which his inner team had identified early on as his Achilles heel. 'We needed to move Keir out of the box of just Brexit, because he'd been defined by Brexit,' said one senior aide. 'Brexit is actually a boring, technocratic subject once you get into it. It's about customs unions, alignment standards and all that crap. The campaign was all about breaking Keir out and allowing Keir to be Keir.'

Whether the left was willing to let Rebecca be Rebecca was alto-gether less clear. On 17 January, a cold Friday night, Long-Bailey took to a stage before a packed room at Manchester's Museum of Science and Industry to launch her own campaign. Her speech majored on the suggestion that she might replace the House of Lords with an elected Senate, to be located in the north. It was also heavily seasoned with a self-deprecation that only exacerbated her detractors' suspicions that her candidacy was a reluctant one. Evoking the chemically enhanced partying of the Madchester years, she joked: 'If someone had told me thirty years ago when I first came here that I'd be back in 2020, stood on a podium, running to be leader of the Labour Party, I'd have thought they must have just stumbled out of the Hacienda.' But in her supporters' eyes, she had given a relaxed turn before a friendly audience. The crowd made a valiant attempt to make Long-Bailey's name fit the metre of 'Oh, Jeremy Corbyn!' 'Hey guys, you're going to have to think of a new song, you know? No pressure!' On that count the Project appeared to be failing. The same day, YouGov's latest poll suggested that Starmer would beat her comfortably in the second round by a margin of 26 per cent – nearly identical to that of Corbyn's victory over Owen Smith.

The first hustings, held the following day in Liverpool, would do nothing to change the dynamic between Starmer and Long-Bailey. The crowded stage and a stilted format – according each contender only forty seconds to speak – did neither front runner any favours. The biggest cheer of the afternoon came when Starmer pledged not to give an interview to the hated *Sun* newspaper during the campaign. For Phillips it was the end of the road. In a *Guardian* article the following day, written without the knowledge of her campaign team, she wrote, 'The hustings was awful. I was awful because I was trying to hit a million different lines and messages in forty seconds.' Within forty-eight hours, she had pulled out.

On 23 January, Starmer made a temporary exit of his own, cancelling his campaign for two days after his mother-in-law was hospitalised in a fall. He spent much of the following period agonising over the demands of a nationwide campaign and the desire to tend to his family. Said a close parliamentary confidant, 'It was a dreadful time. He took some time off, but he literally was fighting back tears on many occasions. His family is his life.' At times, a campaign that Starmer already instinctively disliked turned from a chore to an ordeal.

Long-Bailey's team were finding its own extended family difficult to manage. Despite offering red meat to the grass-roots left with a pledge to force MPs to undergo mandatory reselection – the cause célèbre that had driven her campaign chief Lansman's long career in Labour politics – other utterances had the effect of losing friends and alienating people, even among her comrades. It was a superficially anodyne comment to the *Guardian* on 3 February that saw her provoke the ire of Karie Murphy and Unite. Long-Bailey had pledged to run Labour as a meritocracy: under her leadership, promotions would be based on 'what you know, not who you know'. To listeners it was something of an aural Rorschach test. Murphy heard a nudge-nudge-wink-wink reference to her close friendship with McCluskey, and suspected her qualifications to have run LOTO were being impugned. Long-Bailey was also forced to make private phone calls to Laura

Murray and Seb Corbyn, in which she assured them that the words had not been intended to cast them as undeserving beneficiaries of nepotism.

But while the intent had not been to single out individuals, Long-Bailey's aides had been keen to signal that her election would naturally mean regime change. She would be a continuity candidate, but of *ideological* rather than *institutional* continuity. A senior campaign staffer explains: 'It was definitely an acknowledgement that things had to change, and we had to try and put some distance between Rebecca and the previous "regime", it wasn't just gonna be Rebecca just replacing Jeremy and everything carries on as it was, which I think is what a lot of people thought would happen, because she was seen as the continuity candidate. We wanted to convey that she would have her own team and do things in a different way.'

At Southside, distrust in outsiders resulted in an effective declaration of war by the leadership on its likeliest successor on 9 February, when two members of Starmer's team were reported to the Information Commissioner by the Labour Party. The specific – and to Starmer aides, spurious – charge was that they had hacked into the party's membership database. Team Starmer suspected the hand of Murphy and Formby. 'This was coming direct from Jennie and Karie,' one senior campaign aide claimed. When the BBC's John Pienaar revealed the allegations, Starmer's team dismissed the story as 'utter nonsense'. For all their public bravado, however, panic set in behind the scenes. A crisis meeting was convened and a battle plan for fighting a campaign without access to party data was hammered out. Southside demanded the sacking of Alex Barros-Curtis, the campaign's data controller, as a quid pro quo for accessing the membership's contact details. 'We agreed that we weren't doing this,' said one senior aide. Rather than throw a junior member of staff beneath a bus for the sake of political expediency, they concluded that any stitch-up could, in fact, be turned to their advantage. Simon Fletcher had first-hand experience of winning a David and Goliath electoral battle – in his case as the strategist behind Ken Livingstone's insurgent independent campaign against the New Labour machine for the London mayoralty in 2000. It was from that famous upset that they took their inspiration, as well as the failure of the leadership challenge that had come hot on the heels of the Coup. 'We wrote it into a David versus Goliath struggle: "poor Keir, look how mean and nasty the party is" – because the one thing the membership hates is unfairness ... That's why Jeremy did so well in 2016, because they thought he was being treated unfairly, so we were just gonna spin the whole narrative around that, and I have no doubt that would've boosted our own data collection massively.' In the event, Southside backed down.

While Starmer had no problem standing up for his staff – be it on stage or behind closed doors – standing up and talking about himself was something he did not relish. His first proper rally of the campaign on 16 February would see him address a near-capacity crowd at Camden's Roundhouse, a venue usually reserved for rock acts. Starmer struggled to perform with the requisite brio. Crowds were not his bag, still less the vogue for extemporising speeches as one walked up and down in front of them. In the early stages of the campaign he had insisted on a lectern, but was later denied the crutch by aides acutely aware of the need for him to confect a public image that was altogether less stiff and lawyerly than the one he had cultivated at the Dispatch Box as Shadow Brexit Secretary. The ensuing performance saw him roam the stage with a handheld microphone. Confirmation that Britain's comedians could sleep easy came in the form of a protracted monologue about a Newcastle hotel's failure to give him the correct room keys two days earlier. Clips of the mirthless silence were gleefully shared by supporters of Long-Bailey: on that evidence, the strait-laced Starmer surely lacked the charisma to put up a fight against Boris Johnson. His own aides, however, saw it as a turning point. Said one: 'People forget Blair was not Blair in 1994, it took him a while to warm up.'

LOTO was also struggling to get its biggest names to perform. On 26 February, with voting finally underway, James Schneider enlisted Corbyn to star in a Long-Bailey campaign video. Milne had joined Schneider in lobbying the leader to throw his weight behind the Project's chosen successor. Jack Bond, who oversaw Corbyn's social media output, was meanwhile deeply uneasy, as was Corbyn himself. Though Corbyn's sympathies were entirely obvious – and he had already given Richard Burgon the same treatment – he was palpably uncomfortable with the prospect of being seen to endorse his preferred successor explicitly. He wrote in a WhatsApp message to colleagues: 'I thought the idea was that we did a video of a cause like workers' rights and let the viewers draw a conclusion.' That, in the end, was what they did. When the video appeared on Twitter two days later, it showed Corbyn and Long-Bailey chatting amiably about the environment. He duly promised her his 'absolute support' in the event of her victory.

Though utterly transparent in its purpose, the video put both LOTO and its semi-detached protégée in an awkward position: leaving Corbyn vulnerable to cries of stitch-up and Long-Bailey vulnerable to the accusations of cronyism and dependence that her campaign team were doing their utmost to shake off. It was no coincidence that the day before the video landed she told the *i*: 'If I'm a continuity socialist, then fine, I will accept that title, but there is no such thing as Corbynism.'

It would not be long before the Project would have to confront that uncomfortable truth themselves.

*

As February turned into March, McCluskey, Lavery and Jon Trickett busied themselves with repeated calls for Starmer to publish his list of donors. The subtext of their demands – which in the event turned out not to be entirely misplaced – was that Starmer, for all his claims of unity, was running a Trojan Horse campaign for Blairite financiers. On 9 March, Long-Bailey herself joined the chorus. 'Donors always expect to be paid back in the end,' she told the *Evening Standard*. She went on to openly mock the Starmer campaign's decision to send a huge poster of his face to members as 'cheesy'. Altogether more pointed was the claim that he could not truly understand voters in the Red Wall. 'A couple of door-knocking sessions isn't really going to show you,' she said.

The onset of the coronavirus pandemic meant that nobody would be knocking on doors anyway. Lockdown, imposed on 23 March, effectively froze the contest in aspic with more than a fortnight to go. By then, however, that the result was unlikely to be anything but a comfortable win for Starmer was accepted by all still involved in the race. What little factional debate remained was put on hold as the virus subsumed all, including the news agenda. If a universe existed in which Long-Bailey or Nandy was likely to enjoy a late surge, it would not happen via Zoom. By the end of the long campaign, none of the candidates could do very much at all. That dynamic naturally favoured Starmer, the man who began the campaign as he ended it – with a commanding lead.

For Corbyn, the long goodbye was as much a chance to forge new friendships as to serve old ones. The most implausible alliance of his four years as leader was brokered on 9 March, when the royal family and Westminster bigwigs gathered at Westminster Abbey for the annual Commonwealth Service. There Corbyn and Laura, enduring one of their last official engagements, met a couple undergoing a withdrawal from public life of their own: Prince Harry and Meghan Markle.

Upon meeting the Sussexes, Laura slipped them a book of verse by the seventeenth-century Mexican poetess Juana Inés de la Cruz, a nun whose willingness to attack the hypocrisies of the colonial classes had made her a target for establishment hate. In Sister Juana, Alvarez hoped Meghan might find a kindred spirit. The Corbyns had privately offered sympathy for the duchess's treatment at the hands of the tabloid press, whose misdemeanours they felt similarly familiar with. The following day the Sussexes sent a personally signed note of 'great thanks' to 'Jeremy and Laura' for their support and said they looked forward 'to learning more about her life and works!' Such was Corbyn's dislike of the mainstream press that it had even convinced him to moderate his lifelong republicanism.

By 3 April, Team Starmer had privately declared victory. At 10 a.m. that Friday morning, socially distanced celebrations began via Zoom. Each staffer had been sent a bottle of champagne in expectation of a comfortable win. The following morning, that is precisely what they got. At 56 per cent in the first round, Starmer's victory was very nearly as comfortable as Corbyn's first in 2015. The heiress to the Project, Long-Bailey, could only muster 28 per cent, with Nandy in third with 16 per cent. It took Angela Rayner three rounds to win election as deputy, but there the Project's chosen son fared even worse. Richard Burgon finished third, behind the relatively inexperienced Rosena Allin-Khan.

The leadership of the left offered grudging congratulations. Said Len McCluskey: 'It is the job now of our movement to support them in this as they move forward to ensure our party plays its full part in our national political life in these unprecedented times.' Momentum named its price: 'His mandate is to build on Jeremy's transformative vision, and this means appointing a broad Shadow Cabinet who believe in the policies and will work with members to make them a reality.'

Briefings from the Starmer camp to the *Sunday Times* the previous week had already made clear that the hardest Corbynites would not be retained at the top table. In would come a Shadow Cabinet of relative unknowns from the soft left and right of the party: Anneliese Dodds, the Oxford East MP, as Shadow Chancellor; Nick Thomas-Symonds as Shadow Home Secretary. Nandy's reward for a creditable third place would be Shadow Foreign Secretary. For the Tricketts and Laverys of the PLP, however, their days on the front line were over.

Starmer's first act as leader was to do what Corbyn never could. Standing before his living-room blinds in a pre-recorded acceptance speech, Starmer said slowly and deliberately the words that had always proved beyond his predecessor: 'Anti-Semitism has been a stain on our party. I have seen the grief that it's brought to so many Jewish communities. On behalf of the Labour Party, I am sorry.'

His warm words for Corbyn were drowned under a torrent of implicit criticism. Starmer would not 'oppose for opposition's sake', even on matters of life and death. 'This is my pledge to the British people. I will do my utmost to guide us through these difficult times, to serve all of our communities and to strive for the good of our country. I will lead this great party into a new era, with confidence and with hope. So that when the time comes, we can serve our country again in government.' With that, Keir Starmer put the Project out of its misery.

Epilogue

History will record Jeremy Corbyn's tenure as leader of the Labour Party as having ended on 4 April 2020. He himself declared his reign over a week earlier, on 26 March. That day Corbyn, Laura and his closest aides interred the artefacts of his LOTO. Lockdown having been imposed three days before, it was an intimate occasion – as befitted a family in grief.

Corbyn busied himself with conference calls, meetings via Zoom and a valedictory interview with the BBC's Laura Kuenssberg, among his least favourite journalists, as his wife packed up his office. One by one she took her husband's books from his shelves and wiped them clean: Tony Benn's speeches, Joseph Stiglitz on inequality, *Fascist Europe Rising* by former Ukip leadership candidate Rodney Atkinson, the Chilcot Report into the Iraq War in its entirety.

The ornaments came down too: the prints of Picasso, the thank-you plaque from the Palestinian Paralympic Committee, the jar of Marmite bearing his name. Laura dusted each down, before packing them neatly into crates and boxes. Every trace of Corbyn would be expunged.

Corbyn did not partake in the ritual, despite having promised to do so. Some of his intimates suspected he had overloaded his agenda deliberately, so as to spare himself the pain of confronting the end. After his busy morning he returned to his private quarters to find it nearly empty of his personal effects. In that moment he was silenced. He steadied himself with a deep breath. 'Wow,' Corbyn said, quietly. 'It really is the end of an era.' The couple took a moment to themselves. Their difficult journey was at an end.

The day before, Corbyn had addressed the Commons as leader of the opposition for the final time. The chamber heard him in near-silence: not out of reverence or respect for the occasion, but having been emptied by social-distancing rules. But even Boris Johnson accorded him a respect and courtesy that Conservatives never extended, even perfunctorily. 'We may not agree about everything,' the prime minister said, 'but no one can doubt his sincerity and his desire to build a better society.'

Corbyn could not resist a final show of defiance. 'He was talking as though this was a sort of obituary. Just to let him know – my voice will not be stilled, I'll be around, I'll be campaigning, I'll be arguing, and I'll be demanding justice for the people of this country and, indeed, the rest of the world.'

In that moment, Corbyn had been his authentic self – a luxury he had not always enjoyed at the Dispatch Box as Labour leader. Under the heat of Brexit and in the unforgiving glare of the media, his sense of self had never dimmed. His political priorities remained unchanged. He believed that he was, and remained, the warrior for the oppressed, at home and abroad. From that firm principle he never wavered, even at his weakest and most unhappy as Labour leader. For the causes that the establishment ignored, he would always be a champion. Not for him the studious silence of other elder statesmen, cowed in retirement by shame and respect for their successors. He had come into politics an activist, and would remain one. Moral certitude had always been his lodestar. It had kept him on the back benches under New Labour, and catapulted him to the leadership in 2015.

Of his legacy as Labour leader, he said nothing. In December's election his voice *had* been stilled emphatically by the electorate. He *had* demanded justice for the British people, only to find that they were not interested in his vision. Despite his private contrition to close comrades, Corbyn had not apologised publicly for the result, nor to the MPs and candidates who had carried his banner and lost. Why would he? In his view he had done his best in inhospitable climes. Labour had been filleted by Brexit. The media he loathed never wanted to give him a fair hearing. His own MPs and party officials had monstered and undermined him. Men and women in his own party came to devote their whole lives to fighting him. Corbyn, so the sympathetic case goes, could only play the cards he had been dealt by circumstances rigged against a tribune of transformative change.

Yet still the Project had failed, at least on its own terms. Corbyn had never wanted to be leader of the Labour Party. But, in the wake of 2017, he had come to like the idea of being prime minister. His was a mission waged on behalf of hundreds of thousands of people who had invested their hopes in him in the vain belief that politics might change. They invested their hopes in a man of firm principle: a Bennite signpost, rather than a Blairite weathervane. What of their return?

Corbyn failed himself. That much is unquestionable. On so much of his politics he had proved willing to compromise. A woolly headed ideologue on the questions that had long animated him as a back-bencher – the monarchy, a united Ireland, unilateralism, NATO membership – he was not. Yet on no subject was he more stubborn than his own sense of identity. The painful compromises inherent in the unusual lives of holders of high office – the encroached privacy, the punishing schedules, the relentless demand for executive decision-making and swift judgement – never felt within his command. That he loathed confrontation and disappointing friends is testament to the deep well of kindness that existed within Corbyn. Unable to rewrite the rules of the game as he had promised, he preferred to ignore them. When in doubt, he sought solace from those he knew would support his judgement no matter what, be they Laura or his friends in Islington. It was understandable and human. But it was not what the Project or the Labour Party wanted or indeed needed from its leader.

It is easy to argue that Corbyn and the Project were victims of circumstance, particularly on Brexit. Yet the art of politics is about carving out and communicating new possibilities. Corbyn's indecision is chief among the reasons why the party could never define the Brexit question in its own terms or seize the initiative from the Conservatives. Nor did it seek a compromise deal when one was possible. That might have helped cauterise the PLP's conversion to Remain. By 2019, Corbyn had created a vacuum for others to fill. Keir Starmer in particular has reason to be grateful for Corbyn's squeamishness with power. The Project not only squandered its inheritance from the membership, but left its children without any meaningful bequest.

So too on anti-Semitism. Corbyn has often been cast as the prisoner of his advisers. 'The good king and the bad viziers,' is how one close aide puts it. When it came to Labour's relationship with the Jewish community, the failure was his. The empathy that defined him as a man and politician escaped him. In the face of accusations of racism, he too often empathised with himself. It might reasonably be argued that here was a leader whose preference was to split his own party, rather than apologise.

But it is true that even a fulsome mea culpa would not have been enough for many of his internal opponents. Those who split would have always found their excuse. Those who stayed, however, were guilty of even more profound political failures than any of the Project's adherents. At Southside, there was never any meaningful appetite to understand just how the left had won the leadership, or why Labour members had yearned for such a decisive breach with establishment wisdom. They were never reconciled to the Project, whose paranoia on this front appears to have been justified. That much was indisputable even before one of their number inadvertently uploaded thousands of their own abusive and openly seditious WhatsApp messages onto party servers, later collated in the leaked report whose contents inform much of this book. Were they to have cooperated, the Project might have stood a better chance of success. But to them Corbyn and Corbynism was never legitimate.

Nor is their critique of the Parliamentary Labour Party without foundation. In Parliament, Corbynism's longevity was to a large extent a consequence of the PLP's toothless internal opposition. They hated the early period of Corbyn's leadership because of its inability to appeal to the public, beyond the young voters he had energised anew, and those on the left who had been alienated by New Labour. Corbyn was loathed because he could not win, and because his world view was incompatible with that of his MPs. They paid rather less attention to their own crushing losses within the Labour Party. When he did demonstrate public appeal, in 2017, they chose to supplicate themselves, rather than continue their isolation.

Corbyn too failed to jump one way or the other. LOTO could never decide whether it wanted to legitimise itself in the eyes of the PLP by opening its front-bench ranks to repentant sinners, or whether it would continue to impose its authority by locking otherwise willing MPs out of jobs in which their talents might have found productive, rather than useful expression. This was not for want of trying among LOTO officials. Corbyn, tired and demoralised by a job whose responsibilities he did not enjoy, could not or would not choose. On so many issues of import his Labour Party was neither brutal nor conciliatory. It was nothing.

At points in the narrative, Corbyn is a felt absence. But to say he was left out is not wholly accurate. As Murphy herself says now: 'I have never done anything that Jeremy Corbyn did not want done. Never. I've never instigated something he didn't want done. I've never signed off anything that contradicted anything that he wanted to the extent that I've had to hold my tongue when people have sat right there and told me, Jeremy said that's not what happened. I've had to look at that person and say, well, I'm sorry, OK, you know, maybe it's my misunderstanding, whatever. I have never ever betrayed Jeremy's trust in that regard. And he has been led to believe, at times, that I did. I can look in the mirror, I've never done it.'

The Project's weaknesses and its internal divisions, be they the distrust of Murphy's combative style, the deep resentment that festered among junior staff in LOTO, or John McDonnell's freelance excursions on Brexit, all flowed directly from Corbyn's own. Power was not something he pursued. At times it felt like he was a man living in anticipation of another happy accident.

The Shadow Chancellor, without whom the Project would have never existed, was the opposite. For four years he worked himself ragged in the pursuit of power. He set aside his sectarianism and moderated and mellowed, or at least had the good sense to pretend to. Again and again McDonnell did what Corbyn could not: the contrition on anti-Semitism, the hawkishness on foreign affairs, the building of alliances with those with whom he disagreed, within and without the Labour Party, the gymnastic approach to the question of Europe. His singular talent as a politician had kept the Labour left alive in its darkest hours. In McDonnell's eyes, say LOTO aides, it was a joint premiership.

But that justified self-belief was eventually the Project's undoing. Without Corbyn, the only member of the Campaign Group willing to put himself forward in 2015, McDonnell would never have had his final shot at power. In pursuing it so obsessively over the heads of those appointed to execute the will of the man his wife described as his only friend in politics, he sowed a corrosive distrust. By 2019, the Project – pulled apart by the centrifugal forces of Brexit and personality clashes – was barely a coherent entity. So says Murphy: 'John may have felt he couldn't influence JC as much as he would like to, whilst myself and Seumas were so close and loyally defending him. He moved against both of us … This should never have happened. Ultimately it fucked our project. He wasn't alone in acting like this at times but the fracture became a divide.'

In the wake of the election, Corbyn did claim one victory. Labour, he said, had won the argument. On that much the Project deserves credit. The Project never did win power but it did precipitate lasting political change. The Conservative Party disavowed austerity and elected a born-again statist of its own in Boris Johnson. Labour's own centre of gravity has been dragged conclusively and irrevocably to the left. The 2019 intake of MPs was further to the left than ever. Never again will the Labour left be hobbled by the lost generation that saw Corbyn followed as the left's standard-bearer by an inexperienced and unready Long-Bailey. Keir Starmer won power by embracing Corbynism, rather than repudiating it. The Project's legacy is a parliamentary left that can no longer be ignored.

A once moribund grass roots has flourished anew. Keir Starmer leads the biggest political party in western Europe. Centrism in British politics, at least as it was recognisable at the beginning of the 2010s, is dead. In unlocking something long repressed on the British left and opposing the status quo in a clear, unambiguous voice, Corbyn did precipitate lasting change to the political and economic settlement he and his comrades had spent a lifetime railing against. Yet it is a mark of their failures that the process has hitherto ended with the Conservatives as the ultimate beneficiaries.

On 30 March, McDonnell and Corbyn reunited in the leader's suite for one last time. The Project had exerted strains on their friendship that they could never have foreseen. Colleagues of both men doubt that their relationship will ever be the same. But as they posed for photographs on the balcony of Norman Shaw South, overlooking the Thames, one truth remained: they would always be comrades.

They smiled and embraced. Together they had gone further than any of their forebears. Perhaps none would ever go as far again. As night fell on Westminster, McDonnell stood alone on the balcony and gazed at County Hall, where he had last wielded power. He and Corbyn had missed their last chance to do so again. Without power, the Project was nothing.

Acknowledgements

A year ago, neither of us envisaged spending 2020 chronicling the past three years in the life of the Labour Party. To do so as first-time authors locked away some 200 miles apart as a pandemic raged felt at times like an insurmountable challenge. That we managed to do so is largely down to the belief and generosity of other people, not all of whom, sadly, can or should be named here.

When we first approached Victoria Hobbs of A.M. Heath in January, she took a chance on a pair of literary novices who, while aware of the scale of the peak they had volunteered to climb, had little idea of how gruelling it was to be.

Victoria was the locomotive of this project at its outset. Her belief and vision affirmed our desire to do it. Martin Redfern of Northbank had patiently heard many of Patrick Maguire's terrible ideas for books and without his support and wise counsel the first good one could not have materialised.

At The Bodley Head, Will Hammond was the best Sherpa for the ascent we could have hoped for – even though our relationship quickly became a virtual one. Without him as editor the task of turning around some 130,000 words in four months would have been a chore rather than the pleasure it turned out to be, mostly thanks to his preternatural calm and bottomless well of patience.

Will's greatest service to the reader was his gentle and good-humoured consignment of our worst excesses to the cutting-room floor. The great David Milner's copy-editing spared our blushes too. We are also grateful to Joe Pickering and Stuart Williams, who heard our initial pitch. Without them this book would not be in your hands. The legal guidance of Tim Bainbridge and Martin Soames helped us chart a safe course to completion.

We are grateful to one man above all: Tim Shipman. Throughout 2019 he encouraged both of us to commit this story to text. When last Christmas he did so publicly on Twitter, we knew we had to do it. Without his belief that we were the people for the job, and without his advocacy for our double-act behind the scenes, you would not be reading this book. Most readers will be aware of Tim's unrivalled record as a journalist and author. But as mentors go there could be none more generous. *Left Out* went from half-formed thought to serious idea over a chilli con carne at his home. It would not be half the book that it is, and nor would Gabriel be half the journalist, were it not for his guidance.

Stephen Bush was similarly encouraging from the off. Lesser managers would have baulked at the prospect of losing one of their reporters to a project that very quickly demanded more time and energy than most days allow. Yet his first instinct was instead to insist that we could and should take Tim's advice. That is not only his measure as a mentor of young talent, but as a friend. This project, and Patrick Maguire in particular, owe much to his generosity but also his peerless work on Corbynism, and the space Jason Cowley, Helen Lewis and Tom Gatti gave over to the *New Statesman*'s reporting on politics in Westminster and beyond.

We are indebted to many more fine colleagues. Ben Preston and Becky Barrow are endlessly supportive news editors at the *Sunday Times*. They have made the newspaper the ultimate place for any young reporter. Sarah Baxter, Clare Conway, Tom Harper, Ria Higgins, Martin Ivens, Mark Edmonds, Richard Kerbaj, Eleanor Mills, Tim Rayment and Caroline Wheeler are among *Sunday Times* colleagues past and present to whom Gabriel is especially grateful.

The staff of the *New Statesman* were the best comrades a journalist could ask for, ditto *The Times* parliamentary team. Francis Elliott and Matt Chorley are bosses one always wishes to have in their corner. Adam Macqueen, Ian Hislop and the Anthony Howard Award gave the best breaks a young hack could have hoped for. Henry Zeffman has our enduring gratitude for the time he took to provide shrewd and judicious feedback on the draft manuscript. Hugo Gye and Ben Judah also offered sage advice.

Turning many hundreds of hours of recordings and thousands of pages of primary source material into coherent prose was a job we could not have done alone. For that, our thanks go to Ethan Croft, Ben van der Merwe, Kyle Fitzgerald, Noah Vickers and Henry Dyer for all they did, and without Gabe Milne's industry and dedication we would never have met our deadline.

A hundred or so people shared their testimonies and much else besides with us. Nobody in the Labour Party asked us to write this book and many, we are sure, would rather we had not. It is unauthorised but from the outset our one goal was to write an account that was as fair and comprehensive as possible. Without the many hours our sources spent talking through often difficult and distressing memories there would be no story to speak of, and for their time we will forever be grateful. Their service was not just to the authors but to history. We hope ours holds water as a first draft.

It would be invidious to single out sources for special thanks; indeed, many asked us not to. Those whose information features in the narrative will know how helpful they have been and have our gratitude. Any words quoted were spoken by, or to, those who were in the room.

Some of those who experienced this tumultuous period at first hand were kind enough to allow us to quote their recollections on the record. For this we thank Tom Baldwin, Tony Blair, Richard Burgon, Michael Chessum, Margaret Hodge, Ken Livingstone, Peter Mandelson, Paul Mason, Peter Mason, Karie Murphy, Andrew Murray, Alison McGovern, Gavin Shuker, Anna Turley and Tom Watson.

Names which do not feature in these pages heard far too much about them as they were written. Of these, Gabriel would like to thank Adam Dayan, Ben Goldstein, Laura Janner-Klausner, Louis Patterson, Sam Peterson, Lawrence Langley, Sky Kang, Emily Wolfson and Joe Grabiner. Patrick will spare friends and fellow travellers in London, Birmingham, Belfast, Richhill, Kansas City and Southport the embarrassment. They know who they are and effusive thanks will always be available on request. Helen Bouton, John McCarthy, Shelagh Crosbie, Sarah Heath and Julia Clayton are the teachers he long ago resolved to thank if he ever wrote a book.

Gabriel's loving family were fierce advocates of this project long before it started: his parents, Melanie and David, his brothers, Matthew and Adam, his sisters, Ellie and Phoebe, and his grandma, Leah. A special thank you must also go to Beatrice Kelly, who was not a political obsessive when they first met. She now displays the zeal of a convert. Her love, wit and devotion made this book possible.

From Des and Jenny Maguire has come unconditional love and support in all Patrick has done. He could not have done this or anything else without them or his grandparents Thomas, Phyllis, Ken and especially Pat, on whose shelves this book ought to have found a happy home. Tom, Michael, Billy and Lily were welcome company at home during the locked-down writing process, as was Kate, even if that sentiment was not always communicated in more than one syllable or, indeed, at all. Sam and Jo Cleary are always there when it matters. And of all the immeasurable debts incurred throughout this project, the one owed to Paula is greater than any other.

When the authors first met to cover a university debate by George Galloway in January 2014, they could not have predicted that they would end up here. A source's analysis of Jeremy Corbyn's relationship with John McDonnell springs to mind when we reflect on the past six months. Whenever our friendship was challenged, our comradeship kicked in – and whenever our comradeship was challenged, our friendship kicked in. Here's to many more.

Gabriel Pogrund and Patrick Maguire
London and Southport, July 2020

Index